Bite wounds, as seen on this reticulated python (*Python reticulatus*), occur when two or more reptiles are fed within the same enclosure. Photo courtesy of Carl L. Ponder.

REPTILE KEEPER'S HANDBOOK

Susan M. Barnard

Department of Herpetology

Zoo Atlanta

Keiko Y. YONETANI

KRIEGER PUBLISHING COMPANY

MALABAR, FLORIDA

1996

Original Edition 1996

Printed and Published by
KRIEGER PUBLISHING COMPANY
KRIEGER DRIVE
MALABAR, FLORIDA 32950

FROM A DECLARATION OF PRINCIPLES JOINTLY ADOPTED
BY A COMMITTEE OF THE AMERICAN BAR ASSOCIATION
AND COMMITTEE OF PUBLISHERS:

This Publication is designed to provide accurate and authoritative
information in regard to the subject matter covered. It is sold with the
understanding that the publisher is not engaged in rendering legal,
accounting, or other professional service. If legal advice or other expert
assistance is required, the services of a competent professional person
should be sought.

Library of Congress Cataloging-in-Publication Data

Barnard, Susan M.
    Reptile keeper's handbook / Susan M. Barnard. — Original ed.
        p.   cm.
    Includes bibliographical references (p.   ) and index.
    ISBN 0-89464-933-7
    1. Captive reptiles—Handbooks, manuals, etc.   2. Reptiles as
pets—Handbooks, manuals, etc.   I. Title.
SF515.B37   1996
639.3′9—dc20   95-4075
                                                      CIP

10   9   8   7   6   5   4   3   2

To my granddaughter Sarah,
in the hope that she will share
my passion for wildlife.

Contents

Acknowledgments

My deep appreciation to Debra Melton for contributing the book cover photograph and to Yosi Yonetani for the title page illustration. I am indebted to Dennis W. Herman for his contribution to Chapter 1, John S. Dobbs for contributing to Selecting in Chapter 2, and to Rita McManamon for contributing to Limited Necropsy Procedures for the Herpetoculturist in Chapter 5.

I thank those who graciously gave their time to review selected portions, or all, of the book manuscript; Chris B. Banks, Lawrence Bayer, Johnathan A. Campbell, David G. Cook, Bela Demeter, Laurie G. Doyle, Oscar Flores-Villela, Richard C. Goris, R. Howard Hunt, John B. Iverson, Donald W. Jackson, Lyn Kirkland, Jeffrey W. Lang, Howard E. Lawler, Rick McCarthy, John McCormack, Rita McManamon, the late John M. Merhtens, Richard A. Ross, C. Dietrich Schaaf, Francisco Soberon, and Romulus Whitaker.

I am indebted to the editors of journals, publishers, staff at various institutions, and individuals who generously shared information, allowed me to redraw and reprint previously published works, and to those who spent their valuable time photographing and illustrating needed material for this book; American Association of Zoo Keepers, American Association of Zoo Veterinarians, American Museum of Natural History Library, BROMOfoto, Charles J. Cole, Commonwealth Serum Laboratories, William E. Duellman, Clarence Dunning, Jr., Richard W. Etzel, Howard E. Evans, Kenneth C. Fletcher, Murray E. Fowler, W. H. Freeman and Company Publishers, Fredric L. Frye, Fuhrman Diversified, Inc., Gregory A. George, Ronald R. Goellner, Gregory C. Greer, Elliott R. Jacobson, Krieger Publishing Company, Ellen Beattie Nicol, Rick E. Perry, Carl L. Ponder, Richard A. Ross, Manny V. Rubio, W. B. Saunders Company, Robert George Sprackland, S. K. Sutherland, Cathy A. Taibbi, Bern W. Tryon, University of Auburn (College of Veterinary Medicine, Small Animal Clinic), Veterinary Learning Systems, Veterinary Medicine Publishing Company, and Joel D. Wallach.

My appreciation to Fred H. Alvey and Tamara A. Romaine for assisting with the literature search, and Jeffrey R. Muenster for typing the initial drafts of the book manuscript.

This acknowledgment would not be complete without thanking Constance Waterstradt Haynes who, 15 years ago, encouraged me to write this book.

Introduction

When one considers that reptiles are beautiful with their varied colors and striking patterns, that they are clean, hypoallergenic and quiet, that they can be maintained in reasonably small areas, that most are still relatively inexpensive to purchase, and a great source of curiosity to many, it is no wonder that tremendous numbers are held in captivity by private collectors, zoological parks, research laboratories, educational institutions, and in the pet trade. The increasing popularity of reptiles as pets in urban areas also may be a consequence of landlords denying apartment dwellers permission to house cats and dogs.

Unfortunately, the fascination that many people have for reptiles far exceeds their knowledge about them. Because reptiles require less time to care for than furred or feathered animals, they tend to be neglected by their "keepers." Also, reptiles are not as demanding as talking birds, meowing cats and demonstrative dogs, and cannot express pain or discomfort, or call upon their owner to be fed. Reptiles do not interact in a seemingly affectionate manner as do many homeothermic pets, also contributing to their neglect.

In addition to the overcollection of reptiles to supply the international pet trade, reptiles are also over-collected to supply high school and college biology laboratories, to satisfy the gourmet food industry, as well as meeting the needs for local consumption by inhabitants of Third World countries. In such countries, some reptilian species are also consumed because it is believed that they possess medicinal properties. In particular, these animals are consumed for the treatment of impotence.

Fitch, et al. (1982) reported that agricultural workers in the neotropics hunt iguanas for outdoor recreation. In many parts of the world, small reptiles may be used as bait to catch large species, such as crocodiles, to meet the demand for hides in the leather industry. Third World nations rarely enforce their wildlife laws, and hides from many reptiles, especially snakes and lizards, are stripped from the animals while they are alive. Turtles are slaughtered for tortoiseshell products, and endangered sea turtles are trapped in shrimp nets.

In combination with the issues discussed above, rapid habitat destruction, the accumulation of chemicals in the environment and the general public's ignorance, fear and subsequent killing of reptiles, are contributing to the increasing rarity of nearly all species in the wild. In fact, even populations of reptiles traditionally kept as "common" pets are in serious decline. Consequently, reptiles that are maintained in captive breeding populations assume enhanced significance for their potential role in species conservation, and the responsibility for their overall care becomes essential. In other words, as our wildlife rapidly diminishes, those who take captive the animals that are left must understand their habits and needs, and must be responsible and caring. Toward these ends, the literature contributed by experts on the husbandry, biology, and medical aspects of reptiles has become increasingly available over the last decade, and many veterinary practitioners are now accepting them as patients.

There is, unfortunately, a downside to the recent proliferation of published material concerning the captive care of reptiles. Errors have been repeated so often over the years that they are now being accepted by most readers as "facts." One example is the well-published theory that the green iguana (*Iguana iguana*) requires animal protein in its diet for proper growth. It is my opinion, based on years of experience in the care of these lizards, that this theory is not valid. Field studies by Van Devender (1982) showed that green iguanas in Guanacaste Province, Costa Rica, did not consume animal protein, not even as juveniles. In fact, hatchlings with yolk still left in their intestines fed on vegetable matter. At Zoo Atlanta, adult iguanas have thrived for 10 or more years in solaria used to exhibit crocodiles. The lizards fed exclusively on the tropical plants used to decorate the enclosure. The point of this discussion is to emphasize that it often takes long-term, personal experience in the care of a wide variety of reptiles, and under a wide variety of circumstances, to determine which information has merit and which should be questioned.

1

This book is presented from the point of view of the professional zoo keeper. It provides the reader with a practical, hands-on approach to the captive care of reptiles. Topics are presented concisely and in a manner that enables the reader to obtain information quickly. Although this book is written with the zoo keeper in mind, all reptile enthusiasts, amateur and professional alike, should find portions useful.

I invite comments where errors occur, or where information has been omitted inadvertently. For the reader's convenience, products mentioned in the text have been summarized in Appendix XIII. However, the mention of such products or institutions does not necessarily imply my endorsement.

Chapter 1

Brief Notes on Nomenclature, Taxonomy, Anatomy, and Physiology

Since the beginning of time, man has been preoccupied with classifying, naming and pigeonholing animate and inanimate objects. The field of herpetology utilizes this in the form of systematics (classification of related animals), taxonomy (assigning names to animal groups), and scientific nomenclature (the Latinized, technical or "scientific" names of animals).

A series of categories comprises the present system of classification: kingdoms are divided into phyla, phyla are divided into classes, classes into orders, orders into families, families into genera (singular = genus), and genera into species. These are the accepted standard categories, but some organisms may be further separated. For example, the scarlet kingsnake (*Lampropeltis triangulum elapsoides*) would be classified in the following manner:

Kingdom	Animal
Phylum	Chordata
Class	Reptilia
Order	Squamata
Suborder	Serpentes
Family	Colubridae
Genus	*Lampropeltis*
species	*triangulum*
subspecies	*elapsoides*

Scientific names are necessary to avoid confusion. For example, the northern copperhead is locally known throughout its range as a highland moccasin, chunkhead, poplar leaf or rattlesnake pilot. This same copperhead has one scientific name, *Agkistrodon contortrix mokasen,* which is recognized worldwide. Furthermore, scientific names are useful in describing an animal's physical characteristic, coloration, pattern, habitat, locality, or a person that it may be named after. Some examples follow:

1. Characteristic	ophis:	snake
	pellis:	skin
	phagus:	one who eats, a glutton
	scutum:	scale
	stomus:	mouth
	venter:	belly
2. Color	albus, leucus:	white
	ater, niger:	black
	aureus:	golden
	cinereus:	ashy
	flavus:	light yellow
	roseus:	rosy
	ruber:	red
	viridus:	green
3. Pattern	annulatus:	ringed
	cinctus:	girdled
	fasciatus:	banded
	lineatus:	lined
	maculatus:	spotted
	punctatus:	dotted
4. Habitat	aquaticus:	living in water
	delticola:	living in a delta
	deserticola:	living in the desert
	terrestris:	living on land
5. Locality	carolinensis:	of Carolina
	floridana:	of Florida
	mojavensis:	of the Mojave Desert
	oreganus:	of Oregon
	utahensis:	of Utah
6. Name	blanchardi:	F. N. Blanchard
	conanti:	R. Conant
	dunni:	E. R. Dunn
	klauberi:	L. M. Klauber
	rossalleni:	E. R. Allen
	schmidti:	K. P. Schmidt

When a scientific name or binomial is written, the genus is always capitalized and the trivial or species name is in lower case. In some cases, the trivial name is repeated and the scientific name becomes a trinomial, such as with the eastern milksnake, *Lampropeltis triangulum triangulum*. This indicates that there are other subspecies within the species. If a scientific name has only two parts, then no subspecies are known or recognized.

Basic knowledge of reptile nomenclature, taxonomy, anatomy, and physiology may promote a better understanding of an animal's habits and natural environment, aiding reptile enthusiasts in providing the best possible care for their charges.

Reptiles belong to the class Reptilia. There are approximately 6,000 species and all are ectothermic, air-breathing vertebrates, covered by scales or plates. In most species, sexual dimorphism is not readily apparent. Females may deliver their young by laying eggs (oviparous), or by delivering live offspring (viviparous). Fertilization is internal.

Reptiles possess no sweat glands, and their excretory products may be ammonia, urea or uric acid, depending on the animal's natural environment. For example, alligators excrete primarily ammonia and tortoises excrete primarily uric acid. Chelonians and some lizards possess a urinary bladder; however, this structure is absent in other lizards, snakes, and crocodilians. Reptiles have a three-chambered heart (or an imperfect four-chambered heart), metanephric kidneys and their red blood cells are nucleated.

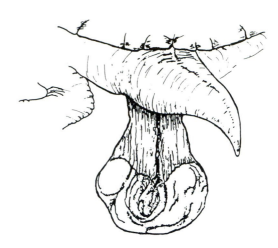

Fig. 2 Chelonians have well-developed copulatory organs. Sperm is guided down the dorsal groove to the glans. After Evans, 1978.

ORDER TESTUDINES

Over 250 species of turtles comprise this order. Chelonians have a sharp-edged, toothless beak called the tomium (Fig. 1), and lack external ears. The Jacobson's organ is small and is not as well developed as it is in snakes and lizards. Female chelonians are oviparous, and males possess a well-developed copulatory organ (Fig. 2; also see Fig. 101, Chapter 6). Sexual dimorphism is pronounced in many species.

Turtles (several families)

Turtles may be terrestrial, semiaquatic or aquatic. Their shells vary from having bony plates (Fig. 3) to being soft and leathery (Fig. 4). Turtles also vary in their eating habits, being herbivorous, carnivorous, or omnivorous.

"Tortoises" (one family)

Tortoises are also turtles. They are terrestrial, have bony shells, elephantine limbs (Fig. 5), and are herbivorous. Interestingly, in Australia all turtles are called tortoises.

ORDER CROCODILIA

There are 25 species of crocodilians. These animals are semiaquatic and possess scaled skin with osteoderms. Females of this order are oviparous, and both sexes have strong parental instincts. Males possess a well-developed copulatory organ.

Crocodilians have sharp conical teeth without roots, have well-developed eyelids and nictitating membranes, lack a Jacobson's organ and are carnivorous.

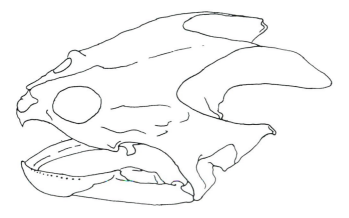

Fig. 1 Chelonians are toothless. Their beak has a sharp cutting edge called the tomium. In life, the beak is covered by a horny sheath. Some turtle beaks have serrations that act as teeth. After Evans, 1978.

Fig. 3 Yellow-bellied turtle (*Pseudemys scripta*). Its shell is hard and is composed of bony plates. Photo courtesy of BROMOfoto.

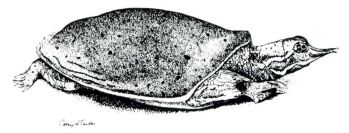

Fig. 4 Spiny soft-shelled turtle (*Trionyx spiniferus aspersus*). Its shell is soft and leathery as its name implies. Illustration by Cathy A. Taibbi.

Fig. 5 Note the bony shell and elephantine limbs of this margined tortoise (*Testudo marginata*). Because of these features, tortoises are well-adapted for terrestrial life. Photo courtesy of BROMOfoto.

Alligators and Caimans

These animals are distinguished from the crocodiles by their fourth lower tooth, which fits into a socket of the upper jaw, and is not visible when the animal's mouth is closed (Fig. 6). Alligators and caimans are generally more tractable than crocodiles.

Crocodiles

The fourth lower tooth of these animals fits into a groove in the upper jaw, and is still visible when the mouth is closed (Fig. 7).

With some exceptions, crocodiles are more aggressive and unpredictable than alligators.

Gavials (Gharials)

There are two species of gavials, *Gavialis gangeticus* and *Tomistoma schlegelii*. These reptiles have a long, slender snout (Fig. 8) that is an adaptation for a piscivorous way of life.

ORDER RHYNCHOCEPHALIA

Only two species of *Sphenodon* (Fig. 9), exist today. They have a limited range on small offshore islands of New Zealand.

Male tuataras lack a copulatory organ, and females are oviparous. These animals possess a prominent parietal eye (Fig. 10) and functional nictitating membranes. The tuatara is strictly carnivorous, and it prefers lower optimum ambient temperatures (6.8–16.5°C; 44.2–61.8°F) than most other reptiles (Dawbin and Batham, 1969).

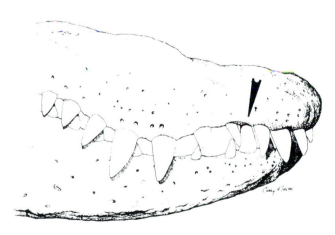

Fig. 6 Alligator dentition. The fourth lower tooth (arrow) fits into a socket of the upper jaw and is not visible when the mouth is closed. Illustration by Cathy A. Taibbi; after Frye, 1981a.

ORDER SQUAMATA

Members of this order comprise approximately 5,500 species. They are extremely diverse in structure, habitat preference, dietary requirements and behavior.

Fig. 7 Crocodile dentition. The fourth lower tooth (arrow) fits into a groove in the upper jaw and is visible when the mouth is closed. Illustration by Cathy A. Taibbi; after Frye, 1981a.

Fig. 9 Tuatara (*Sphenodon punctatus*). Appearing lizardlike, the tuatara is the only living member of the ancient order Rhynchocephalia. Photo courtesy of Ronald Goellner.

The Jacobson's organ (Fig. 11) of many squamates is more highly developed than in chelonians. This structure is absent in crocodilians. Female snakes and lizards deliver their young either by laying eggs (oviparous) or by delivering living young (viviparous), depending on the species, and males have a paired copulatory organ (Fig. 12).

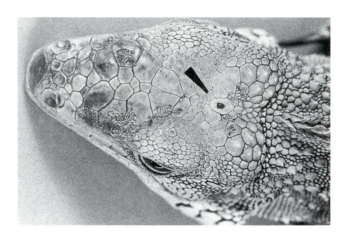

Fig. 10 Parietal eye (arrow) of the green iguana (*Iguana iguana*). This third eye, present in the tuatara and many lizards, may function for photoreception, but its exact function is not known. Photo courtesy of BROMOfoto.

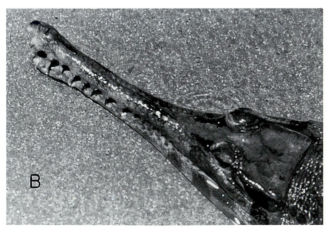

Fig. 8 A) gavial (*Gavialis gangeticus*). Note the long, slender snout. (Photo by Rick E. Perry, Atlanta, GA.); B) the gavial is sometimes mistaken for the false gavial, *Tomistoma schlegeli*. Photo courtesy of BROMOfoto.

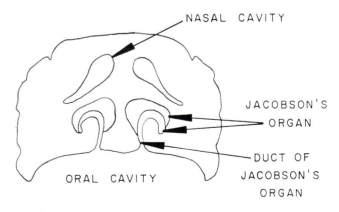

Fig. 11 Cross-section through the head of a lizard showing a highly developed Jacobson's organ. The forked tongue of snakes and some lizards are flicked to pick up scent-bearing particles from the air or substrate. The particles are then transferred into the pockets of the chemoreceptor organ where they are analyzed to give the reptile information about its environment. Reprinted with permission from *Introduction to Herpetology* by C. J. Goin, O. B. Goin and G. R. Zug. W. H. Freeman and Company © 1978.

Fig. 14 The glass lizard (*Ophisaurus*) lacks external limb, giving a snakelike appearance. Unlike snakes, however, this lizard has movable eyelids and external ear openings. Photo by Raymond L. Ditmars, neg. #16587; courtesy of the American Museum of Natural History, New York.

Fig. 12 Engorged hemipenes of a male snake. Lizards and snakes have these paired copulatory organs. During copulation only one hemipenis is actively engaged. Reprinted with permission from Fowler, 1986.

Lizards

Of the nearly 3,000 species of lizards, only two comprising the genus *Heloderma* (Fig. 13), are venomous. All lizards possess internal pelvic girdles, and most

have legs, although some lizards have vestigial limbs and others lack external rudiments altogether (Fig. 14).

With the exception of most geckos, lizards have movable eyelids. Most diurnal lizards have a well-developed parietal eye that may serve as a "light meter" to assist these animals in regulating their body temperatures. Unlike snakes, lizards possess external ear openings (Fig. 15).

The dietary habits of lizards vary greatly; they may be herbivorous, carnivorous, or omnivorous.

Fig. 13 Lizards in the genus *Heloderma* are the only known venomous lizards. Above, the Mexican beaded lizard (*H. horridum*); below, the Gila monster (*H. suspectum*). Photo courtesy of BROMOfoto.

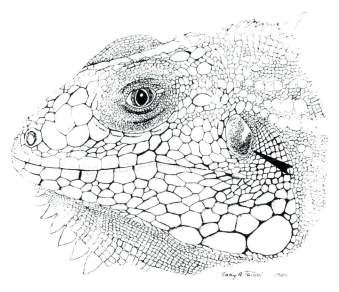

Fig. 15 Arrow shows location of external ear opening of this common green iguana (*Iguana iguana*). Illustration by Cathy A. Taibbi.

Snakes

There are approximately 2,500 species of snakes. Although no snakes have legs, some boids do possess vestigial limb elements (Fig. 16). Also, snakes do not have movable eyelids or external ear openings. Diurnal snakes usually have round pupils and nocturnal species possess vertical or horizontal, elliptical pupils. Some snakes, including the pit vipers and many boids, have thermoreceptor pits (Figs. 17, 18) that enable these animals to hunt at night. Snakes vary in their dentition (Fig. 19), but all are carnivorous. Approximately one-third of all snakes worldwide are venomous.

Amphisbaenians (Worm Lizards)

There are 23 genera of amphisbaenians (Fig. 20), comprising about 130 species. These reptiles inhabit Florida, Mexico, South America, the West Indies, southern Europe, southern Africa and southwestern Asia. With the exception of the genus *Bipes*, which has short forelegs, amphisbaenians possess no external limbs. Amphisbaenians are burrowers, and they have the ability to move underground equally as easy forward or backward. Their family name, Amphisbaenidae, means "go both ways" in Greek. Their teeth are large, few in number, and are absent on the plate. These animals have one functional lung that is located on their left side. Most amphisbaenians are egg-layers; however, at least one African genus (*Trogonophis*) gives birth to living young.

Fig. 17 Heat-sensing pit (arrow) of an albino western diamondback rattlesnake (*Crotalus atrox*). The pits are located on each side of the head between the nostrils and eyes. Photo courtesy of Richard W. Etzel.

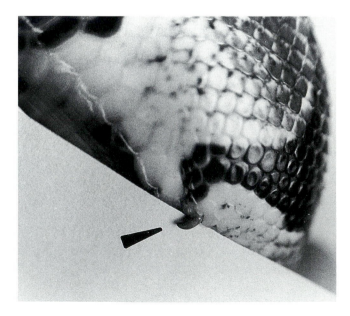

Fig. 16 Note the vestigial leg element or "spur" (arrow) of this ball python (*Python regius*). Photo courtesy of BROMOfoto.

Fig. 18 Ball python (*Python regius*). Pythons and most boas have labial heat-sensing pits (arrows). Photo courtesy of BROMOfoto.

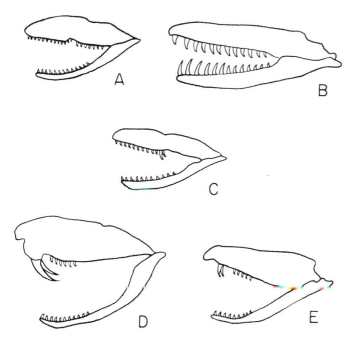

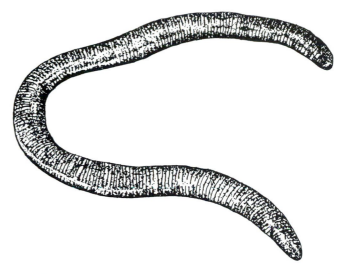

Fig. 19 Dentition of different groups of snakes: A) nonvenomous colubrids have solid teeth without fangs; B) large boids have recurved, solid teeth without fangs; C) rear-fanged colubrids range from mildly venomous forms with slightly enlarged, grooved or ungrooved teeth, to the dangerous boomslang (*Dispholidus typus*) with deeply grooved, fang-like teeth; D) vipers have two frontal, hollow fangs that fold back and lie horizontally along the upper jaw when not in a striking position; E) elapids have short, fixed frontal, hollow fangs.

Fig. 20 Amphisbaenian, also known as the "worm lizard." In Florida they are referred to as "graveyard snakes" by grave diggers who frequently unearth them while digging graves. Amphisbaenians feed on worms and small insects, especially ants and termites. Redrawn with permission from *Introduction to Herpetology* by C. J. Goin, O. B. Goin and G. R. Zug. W. H. Freeman and Company © 1978.

Chapter 2

Selecting, Handling, and Transporting

SELECTING

Deciding on the right reptile to buy often requires considerable thought. If the potential buyer is a novice, he or she must consider why a reptile is being chosen over another type of pet such as a bird, cat, or dog. Family members must be considered; the reptile in question should be compatible with others who must live with it. There is also the moral obligation of any animal keeper to research thoroughly the requirements of the intended acquisition so that it will receive the proper care. Novices should purchase a reptile that is docile, and one that does not have special or complex dietary requirements. Also, the food for the reptile should be available throughout the year. Unfortunately, many novices may purchase an innocuous pet such as a turtle, without researching its dietary and environmental requirements. The result is usually the unnecessary death of the animal from nutritional and/or medical disorders. Where the laws allow, animals that are indigenous to the pet owner's geographical area are preferable because their release may one day be necessary.

Some snakes adapt quite nicely to captivity, and suffer fewer nutritional disorders than do other reptiles. For instance, the beginner may wish to consider one of the rat snakes (*Elaphe*) or garter snakes (*Thamnophis*) as a first reptilian pet. This is not to say that these animals do not require good care, but their care is less complex than with herbivorous or insectivorous reptiles, or with many of the exotic species. Although box turtles (*Terrapene*) make gentle pets, their nutritional and environmental requirements are complex compared to snakes. Many box turtles have been picked up crossing highways as a humane gesture, and in some cases the person saving a box turtle unintentionally killed it at home through ignorance of the animal's environmental and nutritional needs. Too often these "humanely" rescued turtles are fed a diet of lettuce and ground beef, while being maintained in a cardboard box in the corner of a room. Many rescued box turtles, exhibiting signs of illness such as swollen eyes and limbs, malformed shells, and with bubbles oozing from their nostrils, have been deposited at zoos because their owners were unable to understand why the animals looked and acted differently from when originally found on the road.

Following is a checklist of basic considerations one should observe when buying or keeping reptiles that have been captured locally.

1. Observe federal, state, and local animal welfare laws. Be certain reptiles are obtained legally. Many reptiles are protected, and permits are required for collecting and/or keeping them.

2. Purchase from a bona fide animal dealer. For example, check the seller's address for permanency. Obtain a printed price list and expect a reasonable guarantee.

3. If possible, view the animal(s) before purchasing and check for overall health, considering the following:
   - Weight.
   - Vigor versus listlessness.
   - State of hydration/dehydration.
   - Lacerations.
   - Lumps.
   - Missing appendages.
   - Broken bones.
   - Firmness of shell. All turtles have firm shells except softshell turtles in the genera *Amyda*, *Apalone*, *Aspideretes*, *Chitra*, *Cyclanorbis*, *Cycloderma*, *Dogania*, *Lissemys*, *Nilssonia*, *Pelochelys*, *Pelodiscus*, *Rafetus* and *Trionyx*.
   - Missing organs (check for incision scars from their removal).
   - Retained sheds on animal.

- Gaping (may signify mouth rot and/or respiratory disorder).

- Eyes (retained spectacle on snakes and swelling of eyes if turtles).

- Number and kinds of cage mates and *their* condition.

- Housing conditions.

- Presence of fecal material. No feces should be observed in display enclosure; however, if stools are present, check consistency.

- Presence of regurgitated prey.

- Ectoparasites (ticks, mites, leeches).

- Presence of water bowl (if provided, check for cleanliness of water and presence of drowned mites).

4. If in doubt about the animal's health, have it examined by either a veterinarian experienced in reptile care or by a professional herpetologist.

5. Request background information on the prospective reptile to be purchased. It is unwise to rely entirely on information offered by the seller: exercise good judgment!

6. Venomous acquisitions should be avoided by the novice! Only sophisticated, mature collectors or professionals possess the expertise necessary to work venomous reptiles. Professional handlers also maintain safely designed housing and handling instruments. They are familiar with snakebite first aid, and they have ready access to antivenin and extensive medical aid.

HANDLING

Most reptiles will bite. Large, nonvenomous specimens can produce severe wounds that may require medical treatment. Furthermore, the recurved teeth of snakes may break off in the handler's flesh and should be removed to prevent the wound from becoming infected. The following procedures are suggested for the proper handling of reptiles:

1. Prior to handling any reptile, thoroughly wash hands to insure no scents from previously handled prey are

Fig. 21 A) depicts the correct method for handling snakes; B) depicts an incorrect method. Photo courtesy of BROMOfoto.

present. Also some chemical odors may irritate a reptile, thereby provoking it to bite.

2. Grasp a reptile firmly, rapidly and confidently. Hesitation to grasp the animal may provoke a bite. Large and/or aggressive reptiles should be held behind their heads with one hand while using the other hand to support their bodies (Figs. 21, 22). If an animal is too large for one person to comfortably support, employ an assistant (Fig. 23). When holding a reptile behind the head, care must be taken not to dislocate or fracture cervical vertebrae; a reptile's skull is connected to the spine by only one occipital condyle, and disarticulation of the head is relatively easy. Muzzle the jaws of crocodilians, preferably with tape (Fig. 24). Turtles that tend to bite can be held by the base of the carapace and/or plastron, but never by the tail. The proper methods for handling chelonians are shown in Figure 25. Many lizards have fragile tails and should not be grasped by these appendages. One method of proper restraint is illustrated in Figure 26. While leather gloves may prevent scratches and bites, they are bulky and can

Fig. 23 Giant boids become too dangerous for one person to handle when they reach about six to eight feet of body length. As these animals increase in size, more and more people are required to handle them. Photo courtesy of BROMOfoto.

prevent a firm grasp on the reptile, which could injure itself or squirm free and escape.

3. When manipulating venomous snakes, always employ a snake hook of appropriate size and length (Fig. 27), and never handle venomous or large reptiles when alone. Employ two hooks for excessively long, heavy, or squirming venomous and nonvenomous snakes (Fig. 28). A transparent, plastic tube can be used for handling venomous snakes for close examination and other procedures (Fig. 29). Holes can be cut or melted in the tube's side to allow access to a snake's body.

4. Never hang snakes around the neck. Even small snakes can inflict an injury to the face and neck when frightened, and possible odors from the handler's nose and mouth may provoke a snake to bite.

TRANSPORTING

Animal relocations should be avoided unless absolutely necessary. When a reptile must be moved, transporting

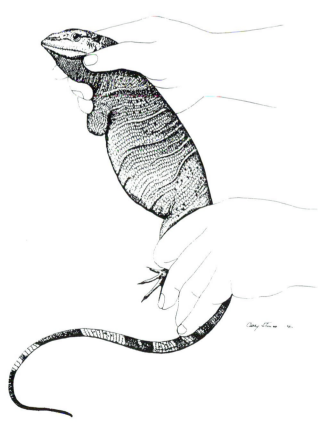

Fig. 22 To prevent bites and scratches, always grasp a large lizard behind the head and control its legs with the other hand. Illustration by Cathy A. Taibbi.

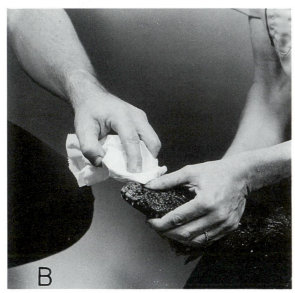

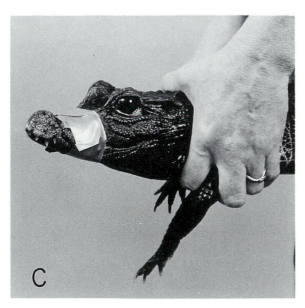

Fig. 24 A thru C) small crocodilians should be handled in the same manner as large lizards. When preparing them for transport or examination, their mouths should be taped, a task that requires two people. Photo courtesy of BROMOfoto.

should be done in such a way that stress, and the possibility of physical injury, are minimized. Too often a debilitated animal is hauled on the owner's neck, in a pocket, in a paper bag, or by some other undesirable method. Listed next are the proper procedures for transporting small- to medium-sized reptiles.

1. Place a reptile in an appropriately sized cloth sack such as a laundry bag, a laundered flour sack or pillow case. Be sure to run a finger along the seams to check for holes. To relieve pressure of the sack on small and/or fragile reptiles, include space-filling material such as crumpled newspaper.

2. Secure the bag's opening: tape or tie.

3. Regardless of a reptile's size, always place the sacked animal in a protective container. Styrofoam containers are preferable to others because they help insulate reptiles from extreme temperatures (Fig. 30).

4. Secure the container's top; tape and label contents (Fig. 31).

5. Other considerations
   • Never leave animals and/or their containers in direct sunlight.
   • Avoid overcrowding reptiles within containers.
   • Avoid mixing animals of disparate sizes; large specimens may kill or eat the smaller ones or crush them with their greater weight.
   • Launder bags frequently, preferably after each use.
   • Transport one chelonian per bag to prevent shell damage.
   • Transport under reasonable ambient temperatures to prevent chilling during winter or overheating during summer (see Table 1, Chapter 3).
   • Never leave animals in a stationary vehicle; transport at once. During the summer months, stationary vehicles overheat quickly and can cause the death of a reptile. Also, when transporting in a vehicle, do not place the containerized reptile directly beside the heater/airconditioner blower.
   • Use two bags (double bag) when transporting venomous reptiles.

6. Shipping

   Proper packing and scheduling is required in order to avoid delays. NOTE: it is illegal to ship snakes through the United States Postal Service. Call the United States Department of Interior's (USDI) Fish and Wildlife Service for information about animal regulations; call the airlines for scheduling, and contact the International Air Transport Association (IATA) for international flights, labeling specifications and required shipping container.

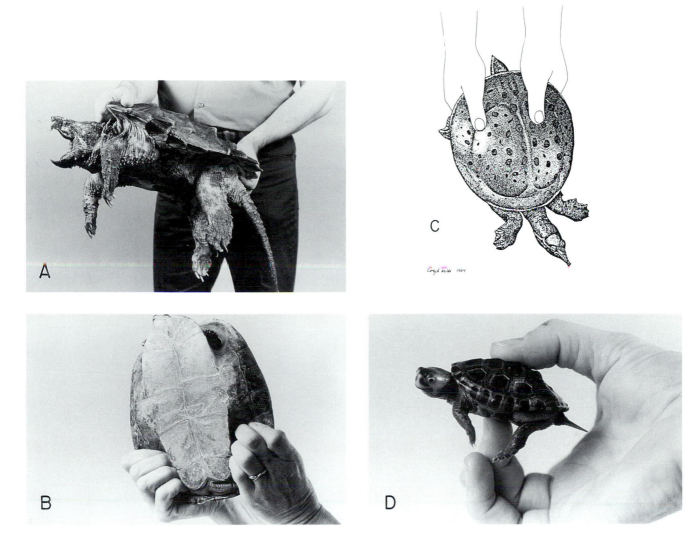

Fig. 25 A) the proper method for handling a large turtle such as an alligator snapping turtle (*Macroclemys temminckii*); B and C) the appropriate method for handling turtles that may bite or scratch when they are picked up, or when they are too small to handle in the same way one would a large snapping turtle; (D) turtles can run off the palm of one's hand very easily; therefore, always support their bodies in the manner shown here. Photos courtesy of BROMOfoto; illustration by Cathy A. Taibbi.

Fig. 26 The proper method for restraining lizards that lose their tails easily. Photo courtesy of BROMOfoto.

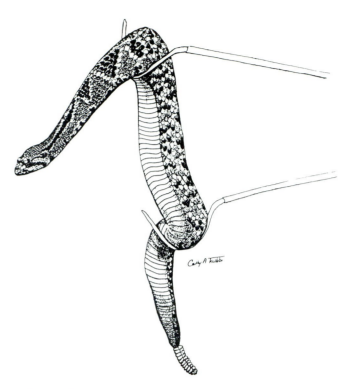

Fig. 27 ALWAYS use a snake hook when manipulating venomous snakes. Photo courtesy of BROMOfoto.

Fig. 28 Large snakes, whether venomous or not, should be handled on two hooks to prevent injury to them. Illustration by Cathy A. Taibbi.

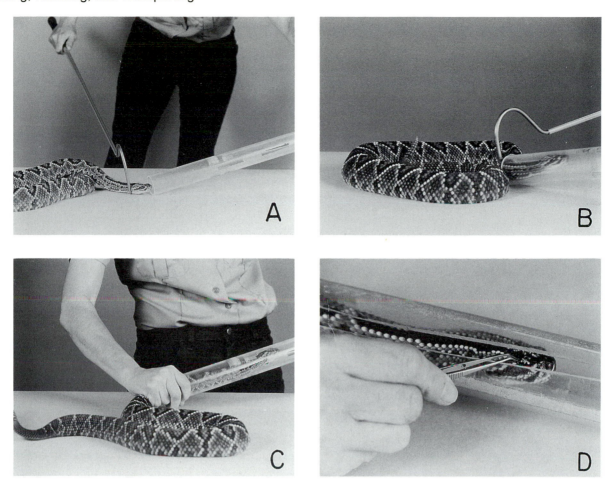

Fig. 29 A thru C) the sequence for maneuvering a venomous snake into a plastic tube; D) note the hole cut into the tube through which one can safely remove an adhered shed or eye caps, give injections, or perform other necessary manipulations. Photo courtesy of BROMOfoto.

Fig. 30 Note that the reptile is contained securely within a cloth sack before it is placed within a styrofoam transporting box. Photo courtesy of BROMOfoto.

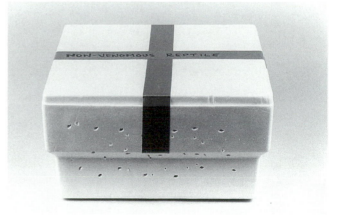

Fig. 31 A styrofoam transporting box protects a reptile from extreme temperatures that could overheat the animal or cause respiratory problems. Note that the box is secured with tape and labeled. Photo courtesy of BROMOfoto.

Chapter 3

The Captive Environment

HOUSING

When purchasing or constructing reptile enclosures, consider the safety of the reptile as well as the handler. Herpetoculturists must protect themselves against accidental injury from reptiles while also preventing animal escapes, especially when constructing cages for large lizards and boids, and venomous snakes. To prevent animal injuries, construction materials such as nails and wire should be rounded to a smooth surface. Also, be sure that there are no splinters.

Cages should be designed for easy cleaning. For example, cage corners are easier to clean if they are rounded or caulked. Surfaces can be washed more easily when cleanable materials such as high gloss paints or vinyl coverings are applied.

When designing and constructing cages, plan for future acquisitions, the growth of an animal, and for special projects such as breeding reptiles. Giant snakes and some lizards may be relatively small when they are first acquired, but may soon outgrow their enclosure. Additionally, one must consider the lifestyle of a reptile. For example, the animal in question may be arboreal, scansorial, terrestrial, fossorial, semiaquatic or aquatic (see Appendix I).

Venomous reptiles should ALWAYS be housed in cages equipped with a lock. All cages designed for

Fig. 33 All outdoor facilities used to house reptiles should be constructed in such a way that heat from the sun's rays does not overheat occupants. For most arboreal and scansorial reptiles, an appropriately sized wire-mesh cage is preferred over other construction materials. The cage is constructed with two doors to prevent animal escapes. Photo courtesy of Gregory C. Greer.

venomous snakes should be constructed with a shift-box (Fig. 32).

When housing reptiles outdoors, construct cages with wire mesh (Fig. 33). To prevent animal escapes, cages should have two doors (Fig. 33).

Basic Housing Considerations

Arboreal and Scansorial Reptiles

Climbing reptiles require several basking areas for thermoregulatory behavior (Fig. 34). Basking areas can

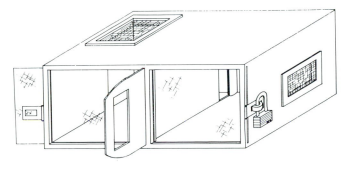

Fig. 32 Suggested cage design for housing venomous snakes. Note the shift-box which provides safety to the keeper during cage cleaning. Each side of the cage can be locked. Illustration by Rick E. Perry.

19

Fig. 35 Hatchling box turtles (*Terrapene*) may be housed in small containers such as the plastic rat pan shown here. Note that half of the enclosure contains moist sphagnum moss and the other half contains pea gravel. Without the moist moss, infant box turtles would dehydrate rapidly. Photo courtesy of BROMOfoto.

Fig. 34 Suggested cage design for housing arboreal and scansorial reptiles. The height of the cage is important to allow these animals the opportunity to seek a variety of temperatures. Perches should have many branches for thermoregulatory behavior, and should be made of non-resinous hardwood. All perches should be secured to prevent injury to the animal and cage damage. This safety feature becomes increasingly important as the size of the reptile increases. Photo courtesy of BROMOfoto.

be provided by placing clean, nonresinous hardwood branches into their cages. However, be sure that branches placed in cages are large enough to support the animal's weight, and that they are firmly anchored, thereby preventing an animal injury or cage damage.

Terrestrial Turtles

Terrestrial chelonians require relatively larger enclosures than semiaquatic ones. During warm weather these animals can be placed outdoors. A movable wire enclosure (see Frye, 1991a, Fig. 2–9) works well to allow land chelonians fresh grazing areas, and to avoid the accumulation of feces and the production of pathogens. Always make shade available to any animal when placing it outdoors. Because terrestrial chelonians have been known to climb over and dig under

fencing, and have been attacked by neighborhood pets, consider these potential risks to their safety.

Small chelonian species and hatchlings may be housed indoors in appropriately sized boxes, stock tanks or plastic containers (Fig. 35).

Terrestrial Lizards

There is no standard cage design for these animals. Enclosures may be constructed of wood with screen or glass fronts. Commercially available aquaria are suitable (Fig. 36), but the risk of escape (with some exceptions) is increased unless aquarium covers are properly secured. For example, heavy objects such as bricks can be used to anchor aquarium covers. Hardware cloth or polyethylene mesh cages usually work well for both indoor and outdoor enclosures. When using glass enclosures such as aquaria, they must be kept indoors to prevent the occupants from overheating. Restrict enclosure design to hardware cloth (Fig. 33) or polyethylene mesh when placing terrestrial lizards outdoors. Basking lizards, like all animals, must have an opportunity to cool; therefore, provide shaded areas. Regardless of the material used to construct cages for terrestrial lizards, the enclosures must be appropriately sized for the particular species.

Terrestrial and Semiaquatic Snakes

Semiaquatic snakes should be housed in the same way as the terrestrial ones (Fig. 37). When semiaquatic snakes are allowed access to a large container of water, they tend to soak excessively and can develop serious skin problems such as blister disease (see Health, Medical, and Necropsy Considerations, Chapter 5).

Fig. 36 Terrestrial lizards can be housed in a variety of enclosures, depending on the species. Many live long and healthy lives in captivity when provided with basic needs such as a hot-spot at one end of the enclosure and a place to bask and hide. Note this simplistic design allows for thermoregulatory behavior and a retreat. The newspaper substrate is easy to change, and prevents the accumulation of feces. Photo courtesy of BROMOfoto.

Allow semiaquatic snakes large water bowls ONLY when feeding.

Fossorial Reptiles

Aquaria are suitable enclosures for fossorial reptiles. Avoid heated substrates because these animals burrow to cool themselves.

Fig. 37 A typical design for housing terrestrial and semiaquatic snakes. Attached to the left of the cage is a lamp that provides the snake with warmth. A rock offers the reptile an abrasive object against which to shed, and a cardboard box offers the animal seclusion. The *size* of the hiding box is important. Snakes tend to be less nervous if they feel their coils against the sides of the box. Photo courtesy of BROMOfoto.

Semiaquatic and Aquatic Reptiles

Large, cattle stock tanks (Fig. 38) provide excellent enclosures for large species of semiaquatic and aquatic reptiles, and glass aquaria (Fig. 39) are suitable for small animals (with the exception of semiaquatic snakes). Mehrtens (1984) suggested that metal stock tanks be wiped thoroughly with vinegar, rinsed and dried, then painted with a rubberized swimming pool paint. He reported that this procedure would prevent leeching of any soluble chemical(s) present in the galvanizing.

Nevertheless, at Zoo Atlanta this procedure is not followed, and no animals have suffered chemical poisoning, although the tanks do rust.

Some reptiles including pelagic sea snakes, the elephant's trunk snake (*Acrochordus*) and some turtles, are entirely aquatic. When housing these reptiles, do not use underwater substrate material in tanks or aquaria unless filters are employed. Materials such as gravel and sand make cleaning difficult, thereby providing a breeding ground for pathogens from feces or uneaten food.

Provide several basking areas for semiaquatic turtles and crocodilians so they can regulate their body temperature. Some aquatic animals also will bask, although this behavior is rarely seen. Pritchard (1979) reported that some turtles such as the alligator snapping turtle (*Macroclemys temminckii*), some kinosternids (mud and musk turtles) and trionychids (soft-shelled turtles) do not require a basking platform. However, I have personally observed captive softshell turtles basking. Floating cork bark is excellent for this purpose and at the same time offers reptiles a hiding place. Young reptiles are particularly susceptible to stress if no hiding area is made available to them. If land areas are to be constructed for basking, provide a ramp similar to the one depicted in Fig. 40, or maintain water levels sufficiently high to allow an animal easy access to the land area. This design is useful during the breeding season, but otherwise it is not desirable because enclosures are difficult to clean, and turtles tend to uproot and eat aquatic plants. Tilting aquaria and stock tanks (Figs. 38, 39a) is preferable because tilting provides a gradation of water levels. The depth of the water should be about one-quarter or more of the length of the animal. Change the water at least two times a week, and clean all enclosure contents. Do not use detergents because they are difficult to rinse away and may cause eye, skin, and respiratory irritations (Frye, 1981a). The use of table salt, applied to a damp sponge, will clean away most unwanted deposits such as fish oils and algae.

Marine or pelagic reptiles require sea water. Commercially prepared salts are convenient to use and relatively inexpensive.

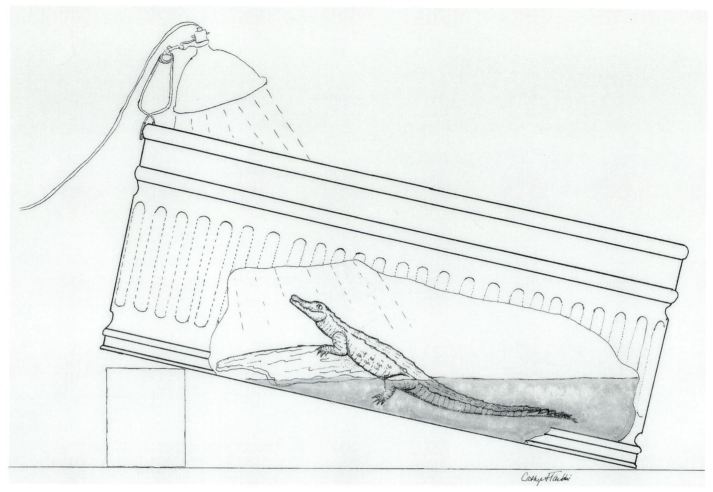

Fig. 38 Tilted stock tanks and aquaria provide suitable housing for semiaquatic and aquatic reptiles. Tilting the tank provides inhabitants with a gradation of water levels as well as a basking area. Heating devices should be placed OUTSIDE and OVER the enclosure to prevent injury to the basking animal, and to prevent the water from becoming too warm. Illustration by Cathy A. Taibbi.

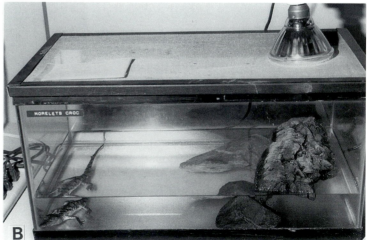

Fig. 39 An aquarium is a suitable enclosure for small, semiaquatic and aquatic reptiles; A) aquarium tilted (Photo courtesy of Rick E. Perry), B) aquarium flat (Photo courtesy of Gregory C. Greer).

Fig. 40 Generally, semiaquatic and aquatic reptiles should be placed in substrate-free enclosures. However, when breeding these animals, the females require a place in which to lay their eggs. Photo courtesy of Gregory C. Greer.

When housing freshwater turtles, water pH should be about 6.0 (Ross and Marzec, 1984). Water that is too alkaline may cause shell-rot in these animals.

Use care when placing lights over aquatic enclosures because water is a good conductor of heat and more thermostable than air. Overhead lighting, as a heat source, is more desirable than underwater heating devices because lights simulate the natural heating of an environment. Also, after semiaquatic animals have finished basking, they enter the water to cool themselves, although there are exceptions. Water temperatures should be warmed only during periods when ambient temperatures fall below an animal's thermal preference (see Table 1).

Giant Snakes and Large Lizards

Because of their great size, these animals often tip their water bowls. In addition, huge reptiles urinate large quantities of fluids. To prevent excessive humidity, unpleasant odors and serious skin problems, it is best to house these animals in open-bottom cages (Fig. 41). A collecting tray can be built in or placed under the cage. Newspaper placed over a wire mesh floor may act as a substrate, and if additional material such as mulch or gravel is desired, it can be placed on top of the newspaper. The newspaper will prevent most of the substrate from falling through the mesh flooring.

If tree limbs are to be provided for a constrictor, be sure they are strong enough to support the animal's weight. Built-in shelves provide excellent climbing and basking areas for giant snakes and they are safer than tree limbs.

Enclosure Dimensions

Reptiles require relatively less living space than mammals and birds. Nevertheless, adequate space still must be provided for their basic physiological and behavioral requirements. Consider the following suggestions for enclosure dimensions for housing ONE animal. For additional animals, add approximately one-half of these

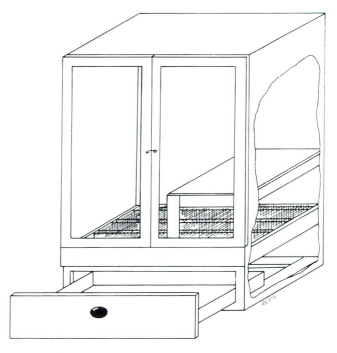

Fig. 41 Open-bottom cages, rather than solidly constructed flooring, are preferable for giant reptiles. Wire flooring prevents the accumulation of moisture. A collecting tray can be built in or placed under the cage. Newspaper placed over the wire flooring may serve as the substrate, or additional material (nonaromatic mulch or gravel) can be placed on top of the newspaper. Reprinted with permission from Barnard, 1984.

dimensions to the enclosure. Even more space will be required if territorial disputes occur.

Note: dimensions do not necessarily allow for cage props or substrates. Add extra space for such inclusions. See Appendix I for approximate adult sizes of reptiles.

1. Chelonians
   a. Terrestrial — Length: 5 × animal's length.
      Width: 5 × animal's length.
      Height: enough to be escape-proof, or cover top of enclosure.
   b. Semiaquatic and Aquatic — Length: 5 × animal's length.
      Width: 3 × animal's length.
      Height: high enough to be escape-proof, plus 1–2 ft. extra for depth of water.

2. Crocodilians
   Length: 5 × animal's length.
   Width: 2 × animal's length.
   Height: enough to be escape-proof, or cover top of enclosure.

3. Lizards
   a. Terrestrial — Length: 3 × animal's length.
      Width: 2 × animal's length.
      Height: enough to be escape-proof, or cover top of enclosure.
   b. Arboreal — Length: 3 × animal's length.
      Width: 2 × animal's length.
      Height: minimum 1 ft.; maximum 6–8 ft., or approximately 2–3 × animal's length.
   c. Semiaquatic — Length: 3 × animal's length.
      Width: 2 × animal's length.
      Height: enough to be escape-proof, plus 1–2 ft. for depth of water.
   d. Fossorial — Length: 3 × animal's length.
      Width: 2 × animal's length.
      Height: 1–2 × animal's length.

4. Snakes
   a. Terrestrial and Semiaquatic — Length: 3/4 animal's length.
      Width: 1/3 animal's length.
      Height: 1/2 animal's length (minimum height 1 ft.; maximum 8 ft.).
   b. Arboreal and Scansorial — Length: 3/4 animal's length.
      Width: 1/3 animal's length.
      Height: animal's length.
   c. Fossorial — Length: 3/4 animal's length.
      Width: 1/3 animal's length.
      Height: 1/2 animal's length plus 6 in. to 1 ft. for depth of substrate.

Enclosure Substrates

There is no single material that is absolutely acceptable. Some materials do not provide good absorption, and others are so absorbent that dehydration, shedding problems, and serious skin disorders may occur. Some substrates are easily ingested by the animal and may cause gastrointestinal impaction or suffocation, and others are excellent media for pathogens. The pros and cons of commonly used substrates are discussed below.

Newspaper

Newspaper is the most hygienic substrate that is used in reptile enclosures. It is excellent material for most terrestrial and arboreal reptiles, and permits easy cage cleaning.

Peat and Sphagnum Mosses

These substrates should be limited in their use. Exceptions include fossorial and arboreal animals, and some terrestrial lizards such as non-desert-dwelling geckos and skinks. If it appears that this material is creating health problems, however, discontinue using and switch to gravel or newspaper. When using mosses as a substrate, stir the material daily to allow moisture that has drained to the cage floor to dry. Fresh material should be used about every three months to prevent unpleasant odors and the production of pathogens.

When housing fossorial reptiles on mosses, the substrate should be at a depth of about one-quarter or more of the length of the animal.

Gravel

Large grades of gravel are suitable as a substrate for all terrestrial and arboreal reptiles. The advantage of using gravel is that it can be washed, disinfected (e.g., 1% household bleach solution), sun-dried, and reused. Clean or replace gravel about every 3 months.

Ground Corn Cob

Avoid the use of this material. Reptiles may ingest it, causing intestinal impaction. Also, ground corn cob may irritate a reptile's mouth, resulting in mouth rot or suffocation.

Sand

With few exceptions, avoid its use! These exceptions may be some desert-dwelling lizards and snakes, reptiles that live in sand dunes (see Appendix I), and aquatic turtles (esp. family Trionychidae). Most reptiles can develop cloacitis (see Health, Medical and Necropsy Considerations, Chapter 5) if sand is trapped in their cloacae when they are everted during defecation. Moreover, reptiles may develop skin or eye infections when fine particles of sand become trapped under their scales.

Synthetic Turf

This is an acceptable substrate for terrestrial and arboreal reptiles because it can be washed easily, dried and reused. On the other hand, it is not very absorbant and must be removed as soon as possible after becoming soiled.

Other Substrates

NEVER use kitty litter as a substrate. This material is extremely dehydrating and will cause skin problems. Snakes are not able to shed properly when living in this medium.

Do not use most wood by-products (e.g., cedar shavings) because many are aromatic, resulting in reptiles developing chemical pneumonia (see Health, Medical, and Necropsy Considerations, Chapter 5). Chemical pneumonia is fatal if not diagnosed and treated quickly.

When possible, do not use natural vegetation and soil unless these potential substrates are first sterilized. These materials can expose animals to parasites and toxins.

Other Housing Considerations

Hiding Areas

These can include a variety of items such as cardboard boxes for land-dwelling reptiles and cork bark for semiaquatic and aquatic animals. Some other commonly used materials are appropriately sized flower-pots and crumpled newspaper. Radcliffe and Chiszar (1983) showed that the size of a hiding area may be equally as important to snakes as the darkness it provides. These investigators demonstrated that Mozambique (red) spitting cobras (*Naja mossambica pallida*) reduced their nervous behavior when offered clear, appropriately sized hiding boxes. Their study demonstrated that hiding box size is more important than its color because snakes feel more secure if their coils touch the sides of their hiding box.

Wagner (1980) suggested attaching pieces of bark to cage walls to provide hiding areas for wall geckos.

Basking areas

Tree limbs are essential for arboreal and scansorial animals. Be sure these materials are nonresinous, strong enough to support an animal's weight, and properly secured to prevent animal injuries or cage damage. For aquatic and semiaquatic animals, provide cork bark, rocks, or tilt their enclosures (Figs. 38, 39a) to provide easy access to dry areas and a gradual increase in water depth.

Shedding/Sloughing Requirements

A small rock is an excellent object for ground-dwelling snakes and lizards to rub against when shedding their old skins. Also, aquatic snakes require a rock against which to shed. Tree limbs that provide basking areas for arboreal and scansorial reptiles also provide these animals an appropriate shedding surface. It is necessary, however, that such limbs have a rough surface.

Wagner (1980) suggested using an enclosed box, with a small opening, filled with moist peatmoss and sand to aid ground-dwelling geckos in shedding skin from their toes. If these animals are not able to remove unshed skin from their toes, it will dry and harden, cut off the circulation of blood, and cause them to lose their toes.

Cage Mates

When designing and constructing an enclosure, consider how many animals may share the facility. Avoid overcrowding! Also consider social interaction or species-specific behavioral patterns. Certain lizards alter their behavior according to the size of their enclosure. For example, Greenberg (1978) and Mayhew (1963) reported that subdominant males of the Australian agamid lizard (*Amphibolorus pictus*), the common agamid lizard (*Agama agama*), and the desert iguana (*Dipsosaurus dorsalis*) avoided aggressive behavior when housed in a small cage with dominant males of their species. Conversely, when the cage size was increased, they exhibited aggressive behavior that provoked the dominant males to abuse them. In relatively small cages, the subdominant males are apparently repressed by the continual sight of the colors and posturing of the dominant animals. However, when subdominant males have enough flight space and hiding areas, they develop aggressive behavior.

In many cases, young animals should be housed separately from adults. Some species, however, are social and may require social interaction.

Generally, it is best to avoid mixing aggressive animals with those that are timid because aggressive reptiles feed first, possibly leaving the more timid animals to starve. When feeding land chelonians, two or more feeding areas should be provided to insure adequate food intake by all.

With some exceptions, avoid feeding more than one animal in the same enclosure. A cage mate may devour its partner accidently in situations where both are attempting to eat the same food.

Generally, it is best not to mix reptiles of different taxa within the same enclosure. Also, avoid mixing animals of the same taxa that differ in their geographical origins. Microbes that seem harmless to one animal may cause serious illness to another from a different region.

TEMPERATURE

Reptiles are ectothermic animals, and depend upon such physical and biological principles as radiation, conduction, convection, evaporation, coloration, and posture to regulate their body temperatures. Most snakes, chelonians, and nocturnal lizards select temperatures of 25–32°C (77–89°F), and crocodilians and diurnal lizards select temperatures of 32–37°C (89–99°F) (Marcus, 1981). Snakes usually tend to maintain lower body temperatures than do lizards from the same geographical area, and tropical reptiles generally have less tolerance for low temperatures than those from temperate regions (Marcus, 1981). Some reptiles, especially tropical forest-dwellers, may not display heat-avoidance behavior (Frye, 1981a). Do not, therefore, expose these reptiles to basking spots where temperatures would rise above their selected body temperature (Table 1). Keep all heating devices on the cage exterior to prevent accidental burns. I do not favor heating devices that require animals to make contact for warmth. Such devices do not increase the surrounding temperature, but provide dangerously localized heat on an animal. Reptiles can suffer burns before they become aware that they have been injured when thermostats are set too high or when they fail altogether. Conversely, thermostats that fail may produce no heat at all, and tropical forest dwellers may develop respiratory problems when temperatures drop below the temperature range that is best for them. Greer (pers. comm.) noted that thermostats may fail to cut off at desired settings. If it is absolutely necessary to use heating devices requiring thermostats, this problem can be overcome by installing a limit-switch in line with the thermostat.

Selected Body Temperature or Thermal Preference (Table 1)

Selected body temperature is the temperature that a reptile voluntarily establishes when a range of tempera-

tures are available, and it must always be given voluntary access to its thermal preference. The selected body temperature is sometimes close to the critical thermal maximum (Table 1); therefore, provide cool retreats.

Unlike endothermic animals, reptiles require daily ambient warmth at their selected body temperature long enough for such physiological processes as digestion, defecation, reproduction, and according to Evans and Cowles (1959), perhaps antibody production. Failure to provide thermal preferences can result in reduced feeding and limited growth. If a reptile accepts food at low temperatures, it is likely to decompose in its alimentary tract because of insufficient enzymatic activity. In addition, reptiles may fail to reproduce if not provided thermal preferences daily (also see Reproduction and Egg Incubation, Chapter 6).

Exposure times for selected body temperatures should correspond to the species' natural photoperiods. The keeper should always research an animal's specific requirements. Limit the duration of the selected body temperature to the daylight hours and allow animals to cool during the dark cycle. The exception to this rule is for totally aquatic, nocturnal and fossorial animals. They should be maintained within their thermal preference temperature range, and extreme temperature fluctuations should be avoided.

Reptiles maintained at the high end of their selected body temperatures for prolonged periods may suffer from hyperthyroidism. For example, this occurred when Wilhoft (1958) maintained spiny lizards (Sceloperus occidentalis) at their selected body temperature for 13 weeks.

Thermal Gradient (Table 1)

The thermal gradient is the temperature range in which reptiles remain active. Providing a daily thermal gradient may induce breeding in many reptiles and stimulate the immune system to fight infections (see Health, Medical, and Necropsy Considerations, Chapter 5).

Nocturnal heat sources help to maintain reptiles within their thermal gradient, allowing the animals to become cooler in the evenings but preventing temperatures from dropping below the range in which they are active. Some reptiles are timid and will not venture from their hiding places to bask. A nighttime heat source may permit these animals to warm themselves during the evening when human activity has ceased. Either one or more 25 W red bulbs (e.g., Colortone®) or a 250 W red, infrared bulb are appropriate for nighttime heat sources. Wattage is determined by the size of the cage being heated and the temperature desired. General purpose, clamp-on utility lamps

TABLE 1 General Guidelines for Typical Environmental Temperature Ranges of Captive Reptiles (1)

Reptile	"Native" Thermal Regimes (2)	Critical Thermal Minimum (3)	Thermal Gradient	Selected Body Temperatures or Thermal Preferences (4)	Critical Thermal Maximum
Chelonians (5)	Te.	7.0– (45–)	15.5–35.0 (60–95)	22.0–27.0 (72–80)	35.0 + (95 +)
	S.Tr.	13.0– (55–)	18.0–35.0 (65–95)	25.5–29.5 (78–85)	40.0 + (100 +)
	Tr.	15.5– (60–)	21.0–35.0 (70–95)	28.0–30.5 (82–87)	40.5 + (105 +)
Lizards (Nocturnal)	Te.	10.0– (50–)	20.0–35.0 (68–95)	27.0–29.5 (80–85)	36.0 + (97 +)
	S.Tr.	13.0– (55–)	22.0–35.0 (72–95)	28.0–30.5 (83–87)	38.0 + (100 +)
	Tr.	15.5– (60–)	24.0–35.0 (75–95)	29.5–32.0 (85–90)	40.5 + (105 +)
(Diurnal) (6)	Te.	13.0– (55–)	21.0–35.0 (70–95)	28.0–32.0 (82–90)	38.0 + (100 +)
	S.Tr.	15.5– (60–)	22.0–35.0 (72–95)	29.5–33.0 (85–92)	40.5 + (105 +)
	Tr.	18.0– (65–)	28.0–38.0 (80–100)	30.5–35.0 (87–95)	43.0 + (110 +)
Snakes	Te.	7.0– (45–)	17.0–35.0 (62–95)	24.0–29.5 (72–85)	35.0 + (95 +)
	S.Tr.	13.0 (55–)	21.0–35.0 (70–95)	27.0–29.5 (80–85)	38.0 + (100 +)
	Tr.	15.5– (60–)	24.0–35.0 (72–95)	28.0–30.5 (82–87)	40.5 + (105 +)
Crocodilians (5)	Te.	10.0– (50–)	18.0–35.0 (65–95)	28.0–33.0 (82–91.5)	38.0 + (100 +)
	S.Tr.	13.0– (55–)	24.0–35.0 (72–95)	29.5–35.0 (85–95)	38.0 + (100 +)
	Tr.	18.0– (65–)	27.0–37.0 (80–98.6)	31.0–37.0 (87.8–98.6)	40.5 + (105 +)
Amphisbaenians	Te.	13.0– (55–)	20.0–35.0 (68–95)	27.0–29.5 (80–85)	35.0 + (95 +)
	S.Tr.	15.5– (60–)	22.0–35.0 (72–95)	28.0–30.5 (82–87)	38.0 + (100 +)
	Tr.	18.0– (65–)	24.0–35.0 (75–95)	29.5–32.0 (85–90)	40.5 + (105 +)
Rhynchocephalians (Tuatara)	Te.	4.5– (40–)	13.0–21.0 (55–70)	15.5–18.0 (60–65)	30.0 + (86 +)

(1) Temperatures C (F)

(2) Thermal regimes are based on latitude and elevation.

    Te. = Temperate

    S.Tr. = Subtropical

    Tr. = Tropical

(3) Also see Hibernation this chapter.

(4) Selected body temperatures are based on generalized observations of captive reptiles in controlled environments and are not derived from field data. The reader should research the literature for specific temperature requirements of particular species.

(5) Aquatic and semiaquatic species require water temperatures 3 to 5°C below the selected body temperatures listed here to provide them with a place in which to thermoregulate, and an adequate source of heat is required to accommodate heat-seeking behavior.

(6) Diurnal lizards with special thermal requirements:

    1. *Enyalius* (Brazilian Tree Lizards) prefer a nighttime temperature of 15°C (59°F). The daytime temperatures should not exceed 30°C (86°F).

    2. *Gallotia* (Canary Island Lizards) require a basking spot at a temperature of 40°C (104°F), dropping to 20°C (68°F) at night.

    3. *Tropidurus* (Lava Lizards) are active at 36°C (96.8°F).

    4. *Uromastyx* (Spiny-tailed Lizards) prefer daytime temperatures between 30 and 35°C (86 and 95°F) with a basking spot at 42°C (107°F). The nighttime temperature should be dropped to 20°C (68°F).

Fig. 42 General-purpose, clamp-on utility lamp. Illustration by Cathy A. Taibbi.

(Fig. 42) are relatively inexpensive and offer flexibility of placement.

Critical Thermal Minimum and Maximum (Table 1)

The critical thermal minimum and maximum are the temperatures that are at or near an animal's low and high lethal temperatures (also see Hibernation below).

LIGHTING

Many reptilian problems can be avoided or overcome if an animal's photoperiod (Table 2) is coordinated with its thermal gradient (Table 1). Proper light/dark cycles, along with the proper thermal gradient, are necessary for satisfactory physiological and behavioral activities. Switak (1984) reported that some species will quickly die if not exposed to adequate lighting.

Artificial photoperiods may not be observed by reptiles that can see outdoors. They may follow the natural photoperiod instead. This may be a problem for the serious reptile breeder, and windows may have to be covered when using light to stimulate breeding.

Light/dark cycles can be controlled manually or with timers. Timers are preferable because they are more accurate in turning lamps on and off at appropriate times than can be done by relying on memory. Also, nature can be mimicked more closely by creating a period of dusk or dawn with a dimmer switch or rheostat.

Unlike fluorescent tubes, incandescent bulbs provide heat. For daytime heating, incandescent bulbs should be used in combination with fluorescent lights in order to mimic natural sunlight as closely as possible. By experimenting with wattages and distances, an animal's selected body temperature can be met easily. General purpose, clamp-on utility lamps (Fig. 42) are practical for this purpose. AVOID A CONSTANTLY LIGHTED ENVIRONMENT as this is stressful and animals may refuse to eat, regurgitate if they eat, or fail to breed (pers. obs.).

It is thought that ultraviolet light (UV) is necessary for vitamin D production in most reptiles. UV can be provided artificially indoors with full-spectrum, fluorescent lights (several brands available). It is important to obtain bulbs that are full-spectrum, rather than wide- or broad-spectrum because only full-spectrum bulbs offer the spectrum of natural light.

Ultraviolet rays are filtered by glass and many types of transparent plastic. Therefore, an animal can receive natural sunlight only by placing it outdoors. Because the vitamin D-producing wavelength is short (290–315 nm), when exposing reptiles to natural sunlight, it is best if the sun is directly overhead or not angled more than 35° off a particular latitude (also see Feeding and Nutritional Disorders, Chapter 4).

When placing lizards and chelonians outdoors, house them in hardware cloth or polyethylene mesh cages. Glass cages will overheat in almost all circumstances, regardless of the season.

Reptiles must have access to shade. Animals exposed to direct sunlight for prolonged periods may die from hyperthermia or suffer from dehydration.

HUMIDITY

Generally, reptiles tolerate relative humidities between 35–70% (Marcus, 1981), depending on their region of

TABLE 2 Photoperiods of Temperate and Tropical Reptiles*

| | Light | | Dark | |
Range	min.	max.	min.	max.
Temperate Zones	14 hrs.	16 hrs.	8 hrs.	10 hrs.
Tropical Zones	10 hrs.	12 hrs.	12 hrs.	14 hrs.

* Gradually increase light cycle (from min. to max.) in spring; gradually decrease light cycle (from max. to min.) in fall.

origin. For example, desert dwellers require lower humidities than do those reptiles living in tropical forests.

Many skin problems in captive reptiles can be associated with central air conditioning and heating. These problems are often overcome by slightly increasing humidity with larger water bowls, daily misting, the placement of a damp substrate in one area of the cage, or by using a humidifier (preferably an ultrasonic or a fine mist). However, excessive water or humidity can also cause skin problems.

Relative humidity may have to be increased during ecdysis. Many reptiles often soak when preparing to shed. Provide them with water bowls for this need. If this is impractical, it may be necessary to mist the reptile daily using tepid water to prevent chilling. No reptile should be excessively wetted or allowed to soak for more than an hour or two daily.

When preparing to shed, an animal's skin will become opaque and appear blue for approximately 5–10 days. In snakes this opacity is more evident in their eye caps than with their other scales. Just prior to ecdysis, the opacity clears. It is important to inspect sloughed skins, and the animal, to insure that eye caps have been removed and that no sloughed skin has remained on the body. Handling is not recommended until shedding is completed.

Nesting animals require higher relative humidity than they would normally require during the rest of the year. See Reproduction and Egg Incubation, Chapter 6, for nesting requirements.

Most newborn reptiles are particularly susceptible to dehydration and must always have access to water.

HIBERNATION

Although subtropical and temperate-zone reptiles instinctively become torpid in response to cooling temperatures and/or shortened days, there are conflicting ideas about hibernating reptiles artificially. Hirth (1966) observed that hibernation causes significant mortality in nature, and it is reasonable to expect losses in captivity. Tryon (1985) reported that when attempting to propagate reptiles, hibernation appears to be as important for these animals in captivity as it is in nature. Gavaud (1983) reported that vitellogenesis may be stimulated in some lizards that are allowed to hibernate. This factor may also apply to reproduction in other reptiles. Many herpetologists agree that hibernation stimulates viable reproduction in most temperate-zone reptiles. Tryon (1985) suggested that hibernation may extend a reptile's life expectancy, although there is no evidence to that effect. Mehrtens (1984) reported

that reptiles do not necessarily have to hibernate to live healthy lives. However, it is known that many individuals may refuse to feed during winter months even when kept at warm temperatures. In some cases animals may die of starvation because energy expenditures are not replaced through food intake.

Prior to hibernating a captive reptile, it should be in a proper state of nutrition, free of diseases and parasites, and allowed to excrete the last food consumed. A hibernaculum can be prepared by using an appropriate container with adequate ventilation. If an entire room is to be cooled for this purpose, then the animal's own cage is appropriate as a hibernaculum. Be sure to place the hibernaculum away from all disturbances. If animals are being hibernated in areas where wild rodents or household pets may injure or kill them, be sure proper measures are taken to avoid this problem. With few exceptions, it is important to keep hibernating reptiles on dry substrates.

Costanzo (1985) reported that snakes have a better opportunity for survival when hibernated alone and when offered freedom of movement. Snakes hibernated in large groups may suffer high mortality (Goris, 1971; Vagvolgyi and Halpern, 1983). However, Meek (1978) reported that small groups of snakes can be hibernated successfully if there is adequate space for them to move around.

Animals being hibernated in refrigerators may dehydrate quickly. This hazardous practice should be avoided if possible. All hibernating animals should be checked once a week; more often if maintained in a refrigerator. Provide hibernating reptiles with fresh water ad libitum. Lawler (pers. comm.) reported that most temperate/montane reptiles will drink during hibernation.

Hibernating temperatures should be adequately low to reduce an animal's rate of metabolism. For example, temperate and subtropical species should be maintained at temperatures just above their critical thermal minimum (Table 1). Lawler (pers. comm.) reported having a survival rate of 98% and over when hibernating temperate species at between 8 and 12°C (approx. 46 and 54°F). Tropical species that naturally do not hibernate should be kept relatively warm and active year round (also see Reproduction and Egg Incubation, Chapter 6).

Collins (1980) recommended that terrestrial turtles not be hibernated outdoors. With few exceptions, this concept applies to most captive reptiles because periods of warming temperatures may induce a hibernating animal to surface and become active. If temperatures decline rapidly, they may be subjected to chilling or frostbite. For additional information on the pros and cons of outdoor hibernation, the reader may wish to consult Gillingham and Carpenter (1978), Goris (1971), Gregory (1987), Herman and George (1986) and Naulleau (1975).

The use of unsterilized soils as a substrate for hibernating turtles may cause pitted or denuded scutes on their shells. In such cases, cleanse the area(s) and, depending on severity, apply an antibiotic ointment. To avoid this problem, hibernate turtles on sterile substrates.

Reptiles awakening from hibernation may be dehydrated and should be allowed to drink before food is offered to them. However, animals that are hibernated in their cages with their water bowls (and this is the preferred technique), can be fed a small meal when they reach their selected body temperature (Table 1).

Newly born or hatched reptiles should not be hibernated until after one or two winters have passed. A delay in hibernation will allow them time to grow strong.

Clearly, most serious breeders of reptiles concur that a period of cooling enhances reproductive activity in species that naturally become torpid in winter. Hibernation reduces energy expenditure and in finicky feeders, may prevent starvation when they refuse food repeatedly during winter. This concept also can be applied to neonates if they refuse to feed repeatedly. Lastly, for those housing large numbers of reptiles, a savings in food bills and maintenance can be achieved by hibernating appropriate species.

Chapter 4
Feeding and Nutritional Disorders

FEEDING

Although it is impossible to duplicate completely the natural diet of reptiles in captivity, it is known, for example, that snakes are carnivorous and feed on a variety of whole animals. These reptiles, therefore, receive a comparable diet, even though it is not precisely that which is eaten in nature. For this reason snakes do not suffer the numerous nutritional disorders seen in herbivorous and insectivorous reptiles.

Little is known about the nutritional requirements of reptiles, and especially of those with relatively complex feeding habits. It is possible, however, to reduce the incidence of nutritional disorders in reptiles by utilizing information that is available about the nutritional requirements of other captive species such as mammals and birds, and by providing reptiles with a wide variety of foods. This concept has enabled herpetologists to maintain and reproduce reptiles in captivity with relative success.

General Feeding Considerations

Feeding Frequencies

Feeding activity of reptiles is less frequent in older animals, during the winter months, breeding season, when an animal is preparing to shed, and during other stressful times. The type of reptile being fed (e.g., snake, lizard, chelonian, or crocodilian) are other factors that determine feeding activities. For example, among the four types of reptiles, their metabolic rates differ greatly. This difference will determine feeding frequencies. Many giant boids and large crotalids have slower metabolic rates than most colubrids and elapids. Therefore, it is reasonable to expect that reptiles in the former families would be fed less frequently and, as a rule of thumb, they should be fed about one-half the number of times of those in the latter group. Also consider that some of these animals are primarily inhabitants of temperate regions (e.g., crotalids), while others are tropical (e.g., boids). The keeper may allow crotalids to

hibernate during the winter months, and they will not receive food during this period of time. On the other hand, boids would be offered food year-round, but even boids may voluntarily reduce their food intake during the cooler months. Within the various groups of reptiles there may be animals differing in ages, and the young animals should be fed more frequently than the older ones. Young animals require proportionately more food to grow, while the older animals become overweight if fed at the same rate.

Although the snakes discussed above were used as examples, these factors apply to all reptiles. Generally, chelonians, crocodilians, and insectivorous and herbivorous lizards should be fed from one to three times a week, although herbivorous chelonians and lizards should be allowed to graze on grasses or hays between feedings. Snakes should be fed once a week or every other week. Old and obese animals may be fed once a month to every 6 weeks.

Killing Food

A prey animal, such as a rodent, can become lethally aggressive when placed into a reptile's cage. Killing food animals (see Euthanasia, Chapter 5) before feeding them to reptiles will prevent potential injuries to the feeding animals (this procedure also applies to venomous snakes). Few reptiles will refuse to eat dead prey. Killing food animals also is advantageous because they can be stockpiled in a freezer and used when food is unavailable. Animals whose diets are only available "in season" may starve if a supply of food is not stored. Contrary to popular belief, freezing prey does not compromise their nutritional value. However, unless prey such as insects, small lizards, and snakes are not frozen in water, they will dehydrate. Young reptiles require small prey. Baby rodents (pinkies) can be frozen for this purpose. For humane reasons, kill pinkies before freezing them. This can be done by pinching their heads between the index finger and thumb. When killing rodents, chickens or rabbits, do so by humane methods such as cervical dislocation. Never use anesthetics or other reagents for euthanizing prey because drugs of this nature may adversely affect the feeding reptile, or the odor may discourage their acceptance by the reptile (Morris, 1986). It is preferable not to kill innocuous food sources such as mealworms and crickets.

Depending on a reptile's ability to catch prey, one may have to slow insects down by placing them into a refrigerator for about 15 minutes. In some cases, the jumping legs of crickets can be removed to allow a timid reptile or a hatchling an opportunity to catch them more easily. When feeding defrosted insects to reptiles, it may be necessary to wiggle the thawed animal on the end of forceps to encourage feeding. Do not place more insects into an enclosure than a reptile is capable of eating at one time. Offer two or three at a time and if a reptile shows interest in a few more, then also feed them one or two at a time. When feeding more than one animal at the same time in one enclosure, place the prey in several places within the cage to allow less aggressive feeders the opportunity to eat. It also is helpful to provide visual barriers in such situations to prevent fighting.

Thoroughly thaw prey before feeding it to reptiles. If the core of a food item is still frozen, the reptile may suffer gastroenteritis (Kauffeld, 1953). To simulate freshly killed birds or mammals, slightly warm the thawed animal under a lamp or in the oven at approximately 180F°.

Artificial Snake Diet (Sausage)

The sense of smell is the most acute sense a snake has for hunting and feeding. Although snakes, like many reptiles, also rely on vision for hunting, smell is without a doubt the dominant factor. For this reason, scent transfer is used to entice a snake to eat food it would otherwise reject. To complicate matters, the artificial diet, in the form of a sausage, does not have a head, fur, feathers, or scales. Because snakes instinctively eat their prey head-first, the sausage probably places a certain amount of stress on the feeding animal. All nutrients comprising a reptile's diet are not known, and therefore the artificial diet may lack essential nutrients; conversely, it may contain an excess of others.

Proponents of artificial diets would have one believe that it is safer for the feeding reptile than natural prey because natural prey may transmit parasites and other pathogens. Freezing food animals, however, kills most transmissible pathogens.

Vitamin and Mineral Supplements

Dietary supplementation is necessary when muscle meat or animal parts are substituted for whole animals.

Whenever possible, do not feed parts of prey or strips of meat to reptiles.

Marine or brackish-water inhabitants require salt (sodium chloride) either in their diet or water environment. Artificial sea water can be purchased at pet supply stores. At Zoo Atlanta, however, brackish water for diamondback terrapins (*Malaclemys terrapin*) is made with ordinary table salt.

Mealworms and Other Insects

Mealworms may cause intestinal impaction from the accumulation of chitin in the animal's gut. Also, mealworms may burrow into a reptile's cloaca, and they may feed upon small or debilitated reptiles. Corn grubs and wax worms are excellent substitutes for these highly chitinous insects. Mealworms should be fed in combination with crickets, wax worms and/or insects gathered in net sweepings. For information on culturing selected insects, see Appendix II.

Hydroponic Grasses and Vegetables

Many institutions housing herbivorous reptiles are growing hydroponic grasses and vegetables. Although Zoo Atlanta currently purchases its produce from the State Farmer's Market, the reader may wish to investigate whether or not hydroponic-grown food is financially advantageous. Murphy and Collins (1983) reported, however, that turtles and tortoises suffering iodine deficiency may have this condition aggravated by feeding them hydroponic produce.

Goitrogenic Vegetables

Iodine-poor vegetables include cabbage, kale, Brussels sprouts, broccoli, soybean sprouts, lettuce and spinach. Feeding excessive amounts of these vegetables to reptiles over a prolonged period of time can cause them iodine deficiency (see Nutritional Disorders). Furthermore, iodine deficiency may occur more readily in reptiles fed hydroponically grown produce (Murphy and Collins, 1983).

General Dietary Requirements

Nutritive values of foods commonly fed to reptiles are listed in Appendixes III–VII.

Water

Water serves to transport injested food through the gastrointestinal tract. It also serves as a transport for solutes in blood, tissue fluids and the body's cells. It provides fluids for kidney excretions, and also serves as a carrier for vitamins B and C.

Reptiles consume water in a variety of ways, and their needs are based on their drinking habits. For reptiles that consume water by lapping or licking (e.g., anoles, chameleons, geckos, most other lizards), mist cage walls and contents (Fig. 43) two times daily. Additionally, provide a water bowl containing a piece of slanted slate or pea gravel (Fig. 44). Some lizard species will learn to lap water in this manner. For reptiles that consume water by sucking or sipping (e.g., snakes, monitor lizards, iguanas, chelonians), provide fresh water in an appropriately sized bowl. Do not provide large water bowls for semiaquatic snakes, except when feeding. These animals may soak excessively, thereby, causing serious skin problems. Nevertheless, there are reptiles that obtain water through soaking or by contact with a moistened substrate (e.g., infant animals such as the common box turtle, *Terrapene*). Be sure to provide these animals with a container of water in which to soak, and be sure the container is shallow enough to prevent their drowning.

Adult terrestrial turtles such as box turtles and giant tortoises soak frequently. They should be provided with an appropriately sized water receptacle for this behavior. Measure the container so it is at least two times the animal's body size and reasonably low for easy entry. Most tortoises require water only after each meal (about three times per week). The Cape tortoises (*Homopus*) and the South African starred tortoises (*Psammobates*) require hot, dry living conditions. Do not provide them with water ad libitum (Pritchard, 1979).

Some reptiles, such as desert dwellers, obtain most of their water from their food. However, a safe rule of thumb is to supply water ad libitum regardless of an animal's mode of acquiring its water. Change the water

Fig. 43 In nature, many lizards lap dew from leaves of bushes and trees. Although some will learn to lap from a bowl that contains pea gravel (Fig. 44a) or tilted slate (Fig. 44b) most require misting twice a day. Illustration by Cathy A. Taibbi.

A   B

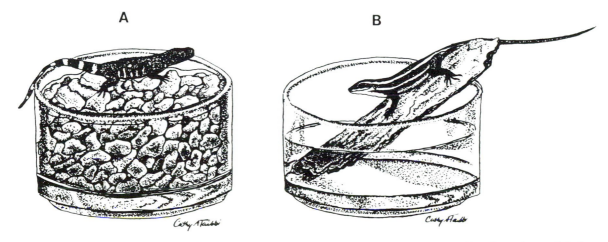

Fig. 44 A) pea gravel or, B) tilted slate should be placed into water bowls to prevent some lizard species and their prey from drowning. Illustrations by Cathy A. Taibbi.

daily. Many reptiles are attracted to fresh water which stimulates them into drinking (Ashley and Burchfield, 1966). Because large lizards and many snakes tend to tip their water bowls, use heavy containers.

Proteins

Proteins function as components of cell membranes, muscle tissue, scales, and claws. Both plants and animals are a source of dietary protein.

Lipids

Fats and oils function to supply energy for the body. They provide the body with essential fatty acids, and serve as carriers for the fat-soluble vitamins A, D, E, and K.

Carbohydrates

Starches and sugars function primarily as a source of energy. The principal sources of dietary carbohydrates fed to reptiles are fruits and vegetables.

Roughage

Roughage, or fiber, is resistant to digestion. It includes cellulose, hemicellulose, pectin, and lignin. Fiber holds water and in the diet adds softness and bulk to feces, thereby stimulating intestinal peristalsis. The consequence is a stool that is more easily passed, and one that is produced more frequently.

Minerals

Minerals are necessary in regulatory and building functions of the body. Those that are required in the body in relatively large amounts are called macrominerals, and those that are required in relatively minute amounts are called trace elements.

Calcium (Ca)

Calcium is a component of bones and teeth, and is present in the body in greater amounts than any other mineral. This mineral also is required for normal blood coagulation, serves in controlling excitability of peripheral nerves and muscles, muscle contractility, myocardial function, plus other functions. Efficient calcium absorption is dependent upon vitamin D (also see Nutritional Disorders). Some foods fed to reptiles, that provide calcium, are leafy vegetables, legumes, and small animals in which the bones are eaten.

Iron (Fe)

Iron is a trace element and is required by the body for normal oxygen transport to tissues. Iron serves in the metabolic functions of folic acid, pyridoxine and some other vitamins. It is a constituent of myoglobin, hemoglobin and a number of enzymes. Sources of iron-containing foods commonly fed to reptiles are animals, egg yolk, green leafy vegetables, and fish.

Phosphorus (P)

This mineral is in nearly all food sources, and is present in the body in almost equal amounts with calcium. In fact, most foods fed to reptiles contain greater quantities of phosphorus than they do calcium. Phosphorus is present in blood, other cells, lipids, proteins, carbohydrates, and energy transfer enzymes. Many B-vitamins require phosphorus for their effectiveness. In combination with calcium, phosphorus contributes to supportive structures of the body.

Potassium (K)

Potassium is a component of the skeleton and virtually all body cells, and it is the principal cation of intracellular fluid. Potassium also functions in energy usage. Some potassium-rich food sources are seaweeds, many green leafy vegetables such as parsley, garden cress, and beet greens, garden vegetables such as lima beans, potatoes, and yams, and fruits such as avocados, dehydrated dates, prunes, and bananas.

Sodium (Na) and Chloride (Cl)

Sodium is the principal cation of extracellular fluid and is required by the body for the maintenance of osmotic equilibrium and body-fluid volume. The most controllable source of sodium and chloride is in table salt. However, sodium is naturally in a wide variety of foods.

Chloride is the principal anion in the maintenance of fluid and electrolyte balance. It is required to form hydrochloric acid in gastric juice.

Magnesium (Mg)

This mineral is required for normal skeletal development and is necessary in maintaining electrical potential in nerves and muscle membranes. Corn, lima beans, and beat greens provide a good source of magnesium.

Iodine (I)

Iodine is a trace element and is required as a constituent of thyroxin and other thyroid-active compounds. Fish is a good source of dietary iodine for reptiles. Iodized salt also is commonly used where iodine is needed in the diet of tortoises. Eggs are a source of iodine if iodine is contained in the food fed to chickens.

Copper (Cu)

This mineral is required by the body as a constituent of proteins and enzymes and is widely distributed in nature. Sources of copper in foods commonly fed to reptiles are shellfish, raisins, dried legumes, and organs of animals.

Cobalt (Co)

Cobalt is a constituent of Vitamin B-12. The body's requirements for cobalt can be met by eating foods that contain vitamin B-12 (see cyanocobalamin).

Trace Elements

Most trace elements are bound to organic compounds to serve them in transport, storage, and function. A few include zinc, manganese, molybdenum, selenium, chromium, bromide, fluoride, and some of the elements already discussed. The requirements for reptiles is unknown. Trace elements, however, naturally occur in adequate amounts in their foods. They include green leafy vegetables, seafood, and other animals.

Vitamins

Vitamins are necessary to transform foods into energy and for body maintenance.

Vitamin A (Retinol)

Vitamin A is necessary for maintaining the normal condition of mucous membranes. Food sources of vitamin A eaten by reptiles are eggs and the livers of prey. Many plant foods contain carotenes which are the precursors for vitamin A synthesis in the body. These plants include dark green leafy vegetables (e.g., broccoli), sweet potatoes, pumpkin, papaya, and negligible amounts in yellow corn. Vitamin A is a fat-soluble vitamin that is stored in the liver, and excessive amounts are toxic (see Nutritional Disorders).

The B Vitamins

The B vitamins are chemically unrelated even though they usually occur together in certain foods. These water soluble vitamins are involved in the metabolism of fats, carbohydrates, and proteins. In humans, a deficiency may result in disorders such as stomatitis, gastritis, neurological, and hemotological problems. Althausen (1949) showed that the B vitamins are involved in the body's absorption of glucose.

- Biotin
  Biotin is essential in fatty acid synthesis as well as several other metabolic reactions including the metabolism of proteins and carbohydrates. This vitamin is widely distributed in nature.

- Choline
  Choline is required for the synthesis of components responsible for the transport of fat-soluble substances, cell membrane components and components responsible for the transmission of nerve impulses. One precursor for choline synthesis is methionine.

Choline and methionine are widely distributed in nature.

- Cyanocobalamin (Vitamin B-12)
  This vitamin is essential for the normal function of all cells of the body. It is especially necessary for the function of the cells of bone marrow, red blood cells, intestinal tract, and central nervous system. Dietary sources of B-12 are whole-bodied animals. Vegetables contain negligible amounts. Microbial synthesis occurs in food, soil, water, the intestines, sewage, and the rumen of hoofed-stock. Vitamin B-12 is absorbed by the body from the small intestine. Reptiles suffering bacterial enteritis may need increased amounts of vitamin B-12 in their diet.

- Folacin (Folic Acid)
  Folacin functions in single carbon transfers in the body's metabolic pathways and in combination with cyanocobalamin, in nucleic acid synthesis. Alperin et al. (1966) reported that pregnant women require increased amounts of folic acid, and Streiff and Little (1967) ascribed human fetal damage to folic acid deficiency. Foods commonly fed to reptiles that contain folacin are dark green leafy vegetables, asparagus, lima beans, lentils, whole grains, and animal tissues.

- Niacin (Nicotinic Acid)
  Niacin is a component of two coenzymes important in tissue respiration and fat metabolism. It is one of the most stable of the vitamins. Some foods fed to reptiles containing niacin are most vegetables, whole grains, fruits, eggs, and animal tissues.

- Pantothenic Acid
  This vitamin is involved in energy release from carbohydrates, fats and proteins, in the synthesis of fatty acids and sterols, plus many other reactions of the body. Pantothenic acid is widely distributed in foods normally fed to reptiles, particularly whole-bodied animals, broccoli, most fruits, and legumes.

- Pyridoxine (Vitamin B-6)
  Vitamin B-6 is necessary primarily for amino acid metabolism. This vitamin also functions in unsaturated fatty acid and cholesterol metabolism, in antibody production (Axelrod, 1971) and in the maintenance of nerve tissue. Of the foods fed to reptiles, only vegetables are good sources of vitamin B-6.

- Riboflavin (Vitamin B-2)
  Riboflavin is necessary for protein and carbohydrate metabolism. Good sources of riboflavin in foods commonly fed to reptiles are green vegetables, whole grains, legumes, animal tissues, fish, and eggs. Riboflavin can be lost when foods are exposed to sunlight.

• Thiamine (Vitamin B-1)
This vitamin functions in carbohydrate metabolism and is required for normal digestion, growth, fertility, and the functioning of nerve tissue. Foods commonly fed to reptiles containing thiamine are animal tissues, green leafy vegetables, fruits, fish, eggs, and, seeds of legumes.

Vitamin C (Ascorbic Acid)

Some foods rich in vitamin C are black European currants, common guavas, cantaloupes, citrus fruits (but may be too acidic as a food source for reptiles), berries, collard greens, parsley, broccoli, and Brussels sprouts. Vitamin C promotes growth and tissue repair. The primary importance of vitamin C is in the formation of collagen, ground substance, osteoid, dentine, and intercellular cement substance (Vitale, 1976). It also functions in the metabolism of phenylalanine, tyrosine, hydroxyphenylalanine (dopa), absorption of dietary iron plus other functions. When added to foods, vitamin C acts as a food preservative. Because vitamin C is a water-soluble vitamin, it is not readily thought of as having toxic effects. Nevertheless, vitamin C metabolizes to oxalate, and it can cause renal oxalosis if provided in excessive amounts.

Although freezing does not reduce nutritional benefits derived from vitamin C, losses are considerable if foods containing vitamin C are exposed to the air or heat for prolonged periods. Oxidation of vitamin C is rapid, and it is the least stable of all the vitamins. This nutrient can be lost by washing food.

Vitamin D

Vitamin D is acquired in the diet or synthesized by the body under the influence of sunlight. It is needed for normal calcium and phosphorous uptake from the gut, and is necessary for the formation of sound teeth and bones. Fish liver oils are rich in vitamin D, and bird eggs also contain it. Because excessive vitamin D is toxic, reptilian diets should not be supplemented with this vitamin when animals are receiving adequate sunshine.

The vitamin D-producing wavelength of sunlight is short (290–315 nm), and the sun must be directly over, or not more than 35° off a particular latitude for it to be effective (also see The Captive Environment, Chapter 3). Sun (1985) reported the following latitudes with respect to vitamin D supplementation. These coordinates apply to nonhibernating lizards and turtles that are maintained indoors during the winter. If your latitude is:

15 deg.,	Nov. 22; stop	Jan. 20
20	begin supplementing Nov. 3;	Feb. 8
25		Oct. 19;	Feb. 22
30	Oct. 6;	Mar. 7
35	Sept. 23;	Mar. 23
40	Sept. 8;	Apr. 3
45	Aug. 25;	Apr. 16
50	Aug. 9;	May 4
55	July 20;	May 25

58 deg., 30′ N or closer to the North Pole, supplement all year.

It should be noted that vitamin D dietary supplements should be used with extreme caution when housing reptiles indoors under full-spectrum lighting. These bulbs may promote adequate vitamin D synthesis.

Vitamin E

Vitamin E is primarily an antioxidant. This vitamin protects other vitamins from destruction by oxygen. It is present in fresh greens such as spinach, kale, and cabbage leaves. Vitamin E also is found in cauliflower, peas, and seed oils such as corn, cottonseed, peanut, soybean, and wheatgerm.

Vitamin K

Vitamin K is important in the clotting of the blood. There are three forms of this vitamin which include phylloquinone (K-1) found in green plants (esp. green leafy vegetables), menaquinone (K-2) found in animal tissues, and metabolic products of intestinal bacteria and menadione (K-3), a synthetic form used clinically.

Diets

Appendix VIII lists foods preferred by captive reptiles.

Herbivores

Diets should include well-cleaned fresh fruits, along with garden and green leafy vegetables cut to appropriate size, and offered two to three times weekly (or more often to juveniles). Choices should be varied to ensure a balanced diet (see Appendixes III–VII). At least two to three types of fruits and garden vegetables should be offered, and at least one type of green leafy vegetable. Do not feed excessive amounts of bananas because this fruit has been reported to cause constipation in chelonians (Jackson, 1982).

Tortoises require a relatively high percent of dietary roughage from fiber. Therefore, provide these animals with hay ad libitum when they are not grazing outdoors. Hays that are high in Vitamin C, and relatively low in phosphorus are alfalfa, clover, cowpea, kudzu, lespedeza, mint, peanut, saltbush, soybean, timothy, and vetch. Tortoises deprived of roughage may pass watery stools.

Marine algae, kelp and other seaweeds are exclusive foods for the marine iguana (*Amblyrhynchus cristatus*) and green sea turtles (*Chelonia*) (see Appendixes VI and VIII).

Other food suggestions for herbivorous reptiles are flowers and leaves of clover and dandelions, other nontoxic flower petals, fruit and pods of prickly pear cacti, commercially grown fresh mushrooms, and other fungi. Although most herbivorous reptiles probably can eat many plants reported to be toxic, it is best to feed foodstuffs that have proved safe. Appendix IX lists toxic plants, and Appendix X lists those plants that can cause mechanical injury when eaten.

Avoid feeding herbivorous reptiles animal protein as it may result in gout (Wallach and Hoessle, 1967) or abnormally shaped shells in turtles (Burchfield, 1982; Jackson, 1982). Unfortunately, the literature is filled with advice on feeding green iguanas (*Iquana iguana*) animal protein, and in all sorts of creative forms. There is no evidence to support the theory that juveniles, or any age group for that matter, are carnivorous (see Barbour, 1932; Iverson, 1980, 1982; Rand et al., 1990; Troyer, 1982, 1984a,b; Van Devender, 1982).

Vitamin and mineral supplements should be used sparingly.

Carnivores (also included here are insect and fish eaters)

Carnivorous reptiles include the tuatara, crocodilians, snakes (except the egg-eating snakes *Dasypeltis* and *Elachistodon*), most turtles, and lizards.

Bird and Ho (1976) calculated the nutritive values of rodents and chickens (Appendix VII). Their results agree with a study by Allen (1984), who summarized the gross chemical composition of live prey. Vertebrates contain approximately 60–70% water, 15–20% protein, 8–20% fat, and 3–4% minerals. Neonates generally contain slightly more water and less fat than adults. Vertebrate neonates, like invertebrates, are low in calcium. Offer carnivores a variety of food animals to ensure a balanced diet.

To prevent injuries to feeding reptiles, offer dead food only. Food items include appropriately sized rodents, chickens and rabbits. Skinned mammals may be fed occasionally to fish eaters (see Appendix VIII) to vary their diet. Skinning mammalian prey prevents fur impaction of the gastrointestinal tract. To avoid thiamine deficiency in piscivores, feed live fish (also see Nutritional Disorders).

To ensure that insect-eating reptiles receive proper nutrition, vary the insect types offered to them. These can include crickets, mealworms, termites, ants and

their eggs, corn grubs, wax worms, and many wild-caught insects where pesticides have not been used. However, invertebrates are low in calcium. When possible, allow the insects to eat calcium powder for an hour or two prior to feeding them to reptiles. This method of supplementation is more natural than the traditional method of shaking the insects in the powder.

Depending on the species, other food items fed to carnivorous reptiles, are other reptiles, amphibians, crustaceans, snails, slugs, and earthworms. All wild-caught animals and road kills should be frozen to prevent transmission of pathogens. Be sure to defrost prey THOROUGHLY before feeding to a reptile.

Omnivores

Some turtles and lizards require both plants and animals for proper nutrition. They include selected turtle species in the families Chelidae, Cheloniidae, Dermatemydidae, Dermochelyidae, Emydidae, and Pelomedusidae (see Appendix VIII for their preferred foods). With some exceptions, omnivorous lizards include those in the families Agamidae, Iquanidae, and Scincidae (see Appendix VIII for their preferred foods). When preparing the omnivore diet, small rodents should be killed humanely (see Euthanasia, Chapter 5) and skinned (Fig. 45). Chop them into small pieces and toss the pieces in a salad. When small rodents are not available, canned dog food may be substituted. However, there may either be essential nutrients missing in canned dog food or an excess of others present. Whenever possible, do not substitute commercially prepared foods for whole-bodied prey.

Reluctant Feeders

Be sure full-spectrum lighting is over an animal that has stopped eating (see The Captive Environment, Chapter 3), and always offer it food at its selected body temperature (Table 1, Chapter 3). Make available readily accessible hiding places because reptiles frighten easily and may refuse to feed if they cannot find seclusion. Once a reluctant feeder resumes eating, do not overload its stomach in an effort to make up for lost time. Gradually increase the amount of food being offered over several feedings, until normal intake is achieved.

Some possible causes for a reptile refusing to feed are:

- It is newly captured.

- It was recently transported.

- It is being handled excessively.

- It is newly hatched or born.

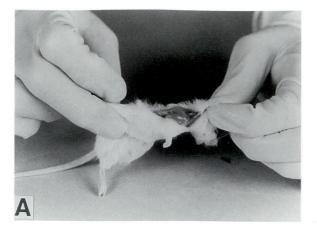
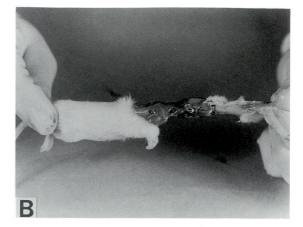

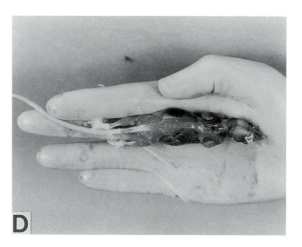

Fig. 45 A–D) on occasion, piscivorous reptiles may be fed skinned rodents to vary their diet. Skinning is important to prevent fur impaction of the gastrointestinal tract. Photo courtesy of BROMOfoto.

- It is a pregnant female or has just recently laid eggs or delivered young.

- It has a newly constructed cage.

- Its cage is too small (animal cramped) or too large (animal insecure).

- A hiding place has not been provided, or it is too large (animal insecure).

- It is incompatible with cage mates.

- Its ambient or water temperature is too low or too high.

- For a semiaquatic or aquatic reptile, its water level may be too shallow or too deep, or the water container may be too large or too small.

- Thermoregulatory provisions have been overlooked. The entire cage is at one temperature or it has been kept at one temperature for too long (days, weeks, months).

- It has been exposed to a sudden change in temperature.

- It has an improper light source or photoperiod (also, artificial photoperiod may be conflicting with natural one).

- It has been exposed to a continually lighted environment; the lamp is being left on for 24 hours a day.

- It has no exposure to sunlight (lizards and chelonians reluctant to feed may resume if exposed to sunlight; see The Captive Environment, Chapter 3).

- Its living area is too noisy (too much human traffic, loud music, etc.).

- It is being fed during the wrong time of the day (diurnal, crepuscular or nocturnal animal).

- It is being fed during the wrong time of the year (may discontinue feeding from about October through April in temperate regions).

- It just fed.

- It is being fed too much food at each meal.

- It is being fed too often.

- It is being offered the wrong food animal (vary diet).

- Its prey is too large or too small.

- Its food is being presented improperly (not being offered head-first; being offered from over animal's head; wiggled too rapidly or not rapidly enough; food too cold; not placed in water if housing semiaquatic or aquatic species; no social rivalry provided in some species).

- It is threatened by live prey (feed dead prey).

- If a venomous snake, it is not permitted to strike at or envenomate the dead prey.

- It is preparing to shed.

- It is parasitized or has another medical problem.

The following methods are commonly used to stimulate a reluctant feeder to resume eating:

- Enclose the reptile in a small container with its food.

- If the reluctant feeder is a lizard or chelonian, allow it access to sunlight (also be sure the animal is provided with shade).

- Feed live, baby prey until the reptile resumes feeding normal-sized dead prey.

- Snip off the end of the nose or peel the skin off the nose of a dead mouse to induce bleeding.

- Change its diet; change to foods with different colors if the reluctant feeder is a herbivorous chelonian or lizard. Red and yellow may be more attractive than green, or vice versa.

- Slightly warm thawed rodents, chickens or rabbits under a lamp or in an oven (approx. 180°F). Some reptiles (e.g., rattlesnakes) require warm prey as a stimulus to strike because of their heat-sensing pits.

- Consider an animal's natural behavior. Some reptiles perch and wait for prey to pass by them rather than actively foraging for food. Some perching reptiles include iguanids, agamids and chameleons. Such animals also may be stimulated into feeding by the sight of other feeding reptiles of the same species (Greenberg, 1976). Furthermore, these animals may be encouraged to feed on new prey during "food-stealing" activities. This behavior is more frequent in juveniles than in older animals where a peck order has been established (Greenberg, 1978).

- Use the scent-transfer technique. Place the available food source with one that the reluctant feeder prefers. For example, at Zoo Atlanta rabbits are not fed to reptiles because of adverse public opinion, and reptiles that have shown a preference for rabbits have been fed rats scented with a rabbit. This is an accept-able practice because both food sources are similar, and fulfill dietary needs equally well.

- Allow prey to become slightly putrid. Kauffeld (1953) reported that a group of captive prairie rattlesnakes (*Crotalus viridis viridis*) preferred decomposed food items to those that were freshly killed.

- Freshly gathered dried leaves (in autumn) may be placed into snake cages. Do not place dried leaves in herbivorous reptile cages unless it is certain that they are nontoxic. In summer, newly mowed grass can be used providing the grass has not been sprayed with toxic chemicals.

- If the reluctant feeder is a snake, place a dead rodent in its coils.

- It may be necessary to harass certain reluctant feeders. This method should not be used on a snake that is tongue flicking. Tongue flicking means the animal is smelling the prey and may eat if left alone. Some snakes, however, will flee even from dead prey. In these cases, gentle tapping on the snout may cause the reptile to strike at the prey in "self-defense." If the prey can be inserted into the snake's mouth during a strike, it may resume eating. Harassment is followed by what is called "shotgunning." Present another small food animal immediately after the first one has entered the snake's anterior esophagus because it is now reasonable to expect that the snake has been incited into a feeding reaction. Continue shotgunning until an appropriate number of prey items have been consumed by the reptile.

Force-Feeding

This is a dangerous and traumatic practice that can cause injury or even the death of an animal. For example, the inexperienced handler may puncture the esophagus, cause mouth rot by damaging delicate oral tissue or by tearing out teeth. When tube feeding a reptile, the novice may allow food to be aspirated into the lungs.

It requires patience to identify the underlying cause for an animal to discontinue eating. On some occasions, fasting may be a natural occurrence (e.g., in winter, during the breeding season or when a reptile is preparing to shed). Nevertheless, there are times when even the most experienced herpetologist cannot pinpoint a reason for a fast. If a fasting animal is kept hydrated and is in good flesh, closely monitor the animal's overall health. If there is the slightest appearance of health deterioration or the fast has gone beyond a reasonable length of time, force-feeding may become necessary at least one time. Unfortunately, it is not always possible to determine what a reasonable length of time may be. For example, most snakes can fast safely at their thermal gradient (Table 1, Chapter 3) for several months, and pythons and giant tortoises can fast safely for well over a year without ill effects. Lizards store fat in their tails and unless their fat reserves are depleted, there is little to be concerned about. However, never allow a lizard to become emaciated.

When force-feeding is inevitable, and regardless of the species involved, there are two basic methods, force-feeding by tube and force-feeding whole-bodied animals.

Tube Feeding

This is the least traumatic of the two methods, and it is the only "relatively" safe method when force-feeding venomous snakes. However, reptiles have literally drowned when food was improperly delivered. An appropriately sized flexible feeding catheter attached to an appropriately sized hypodermic syringe, is an inexpensive and excellent instrument for delivering a homogenized diet to a reluctant feeder (Fig. 46). Feed the diet discussed under Protein Deficiency below, or homogenized whole prey from a blender. Fur, feathers or scales will have to be removed to prevent the catheter from clogging. Also, bone bits may have to be sieved.

It requires two people to properly force-feed most reptiles. One person supports the animal's body while the other performs the feeding technique. The person delivering the food should hold the reptile gently behind the head, while using the other hand to insert the tip of the catheter through the hole in the rostral plate. Sometimes this provokes the reptile into opening its mouth. The catheter must be placed far enough down the esophagus to avoid filling the mouth with the contents of the syringe. Be sure the catheter is not placed into the trachea accidentally. Animals fed by this method should be held with their heads in an upward position to prevent the food from refluxing into the mouth. However, do not hold an animal in an upright position for long periods because a verticle position will prevent venous blood from returning to the heart.

Whole Food Sources

When force-feeding adult carnivorous reptiles, never use pieces of prey or strips of meat. Reluctant feeders should not have their health further compromised by being force-fed a nutritionally deficient diet. Also, when one considers the danger and trauma of force-feeding, nourishment being offered should be of the highest quality. Therefore, force-feed with the same type of prey that the reptile would normally eat, but be sure that it is considerably smaller.

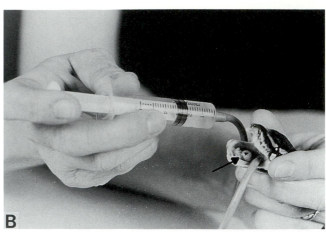

Fig. 46 A) the author inserting a feeding catheter into the mouth of a ball python (*Python regius*); B) to prevent delivering liquids into the lungs of reptiles, avoid inserting the catheter into the glottis (arrow). Photo courtesy of BROMOfoto.

Prey should be well lubricated. Appropriate lubricants include raw egg white, vegetable oil, cod-liver or wheat-germ oils, or even tepid tap water. When force-feeding piscivorous reptiles with a substitute for fish, such as a mouse, be sure to skin it (Fig. 45). These animals are more prone to intestinal impaction than those that naturally eat mammals and birds.

As with tube feeding, this method also requires at least two people. While one person supports the reptile's body, the other grips the reptile gently behind the head with one hand. With the other hand, open the mouth. To do this, use a soft object such as a rubber spatula (Fig. 47) or the snout of the prey (Fig. 48). Aggressive animals may respond to this prodding by attempting to bite. When the mouth opens, quickly but gently, place the rubber spatula into the mouth and across the mandibular teeth. If the jaws relax, they will not be able to close fully. With a pair of 10-inch forceps held along the longitudinal axis of the prey's body,

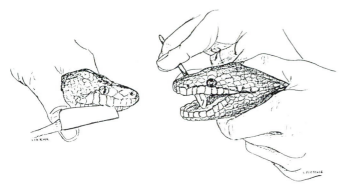

Fig. 47 To prevent injury to a reptile, a soft, but sturdy object should always be used when attempting to force open its mouth. Reprinted with permission from Fletcher, 1979.

Fig. 48 One method for gently opening a reptile's mouth during force-feeding is to use the snout of the prey. Photo courtesy of BROMOfoto.

carefully insert the prey into the reptile's mouth (Fig. 49). Once the prey is in place sufficiently to keep the reptile's mouth open, gently remove the spatula. Push the food into the anterior part of the esophagus, or at least far enough down the esophagus so that the reptile's mouth can be closed comfortably. To assist the animal in swallowing, massage the bolus gently so that it moves toward the reptile's stomach, or allow the animal (if a snake) to glide forward, whereby natural peristalsis should take over. Once the bolus is well into the animal's esophagus, massaging can be discontinued.

Some reptiles may be too large or too difficult to force-feed while they are awake. For example, such a reluctant feeder may be a newly transported crocodilian from another facility. When left to adjust in a quiet atmosphere, however, these animals usually resume feeding. Rarely is a reptile so traumatized by a change in institution or even caging that it actually starves to

death. If this appears to be the case, a large specimen can be fed after it has been anesthetized (and injected with an antiemetic) (York, 1974).

Within a clutch of reptiles there are usually one or two young that may refuse to feed. When force-feeding infant reptiles, the prey does not have to be placed into the anterior esophagus. Instead, dismember a dead, baby prey animal and place the dismembered parts (one at a time) into the reptile's mouth. After each part has been swallowed, repeat the procedure until all parts have been fed.

Force-fed reptiles regurgitate easily. To avoid this problem, be sure to hold the animal's head in an upward position while returning it to its cage. Also, reduce as many other stress-inducing factors as possible. Do not repeat either force-feeding technique until the reluctant feeder has been given an opportunity to feed normally.

Feeding Neonate or Hatchling Reptiles

The suggestions offered below are suitable for many species of reptiles. There are, however, numerous species and individuals that will need special or entirely different care. For example, it is not possible to induce a reptile such as the sail-tailed lizard (*Hydrosaurus amboinensis*) into feeding by methods presented here. In addition to the following suggestions, the reader is urged to research the literature for specific feeding care of an animal in question.

Within a clutch of reptiles, there exist young animals that are curious, timid, or aggressive, and they vary in size. Consequently, their feeding habits will vary according to their behavior and/or size. Newly born reptiles, therefore, may have to be separated, or paired according to size, to prevent them from having to compete for food or eating each other. With rare exceptions, infant reptiles in nature begin dispersing shortly after birth. In this way all have an opportunity to find food. The same principle applies when feeding captive-born reptiles. Aggressive animals naturally feed first, often intimidating their siblings and/or depriving them of their share. Additionally, some reptiles in nature may begin eating soon after their yolk has been absorbed, while others may starve or be eaten by predators. Under captive conditions, and when a neonate's yolk has absorbed (about 10 days after birth), make every attempt to encourage all members of a clutch to begin feeding.

Chelonians

Semiaquatic

Semiaquatic hatchling turtles may begin feeding if placed in small, substrate-free containers either sepa-

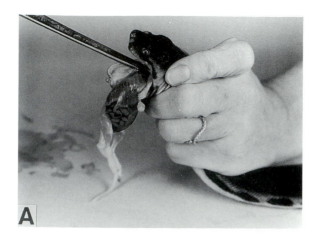

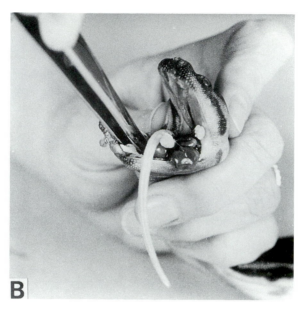

Fig. 49   A, B) once a reptile's mouth has been opened, gently insert the prey into its esophagus. The snake shown here is a fish-eater, the elephant's trunk snake (*Acrochordus javanicus*). The mouse being forced into the snake's mouth has been skinned to prevent fur from impacting in the intestinal tract. Photo courtesy of BROMOfoto.

rately, or in compatibly sized pairs. Containers should be large enough to provide a water level sufficiently high to permit swimming and diving. Place a rock, floating cork bark, or a small branch into the container so hatchlings can bask and rest.

Most hatchlings will attack eagerly small insects when they wiggle on the water's surface. Pinhead crickets (Appendix II, Fig. 119) are excellent food items for this purpose. Once a hatchling accepts food on a regular basis, place it in its permanent enclosure and be sure to start varying its diet (see Appendix VIII).

When setting up multiple hatchlings in a permanent enclosure, be sure they are not overcrowded (see The Captive Environment, Chapter 3). Keep hatchlings at their selected body temperature (Table 1, Chapter 3)

during the day and allow them to cool slightly in the evening.

Box Turtles

Hatchling box turtles (*Terrapene*) feed upon both animal and plant material. Place appropriately sized chopped leafy greens, garden vegetables, and fruits into a small, dry, substrate-free container. Place the hatchlings in the container with the salad (Fig. 50) either separately, or in compatibly sized pairs. As with semiaquatic hatchling turtles, box turtles will also attack pinhead crickets as they jump around them. As the turtles snap at the crickets, they often miss and get a mouth full of salad. Once hatchling box turtles begin to eat routinely, salads can be presented to them in their regular living quarters.

Fig. 50 To encourage hatchling terrestrial chelonians to begin feeding, it may be necessary to place them in small, substrate-free containers with their food. Photo courtesy of BROMOfoto.

Maintain hatchlings at the appropriate ambient temperatures (Table 1, Chapter 3).

Tortoises

Hatchling tortoises should be maintained in appropriately sized containers. Tortoises are grazing animals, and by placing the hatchlings on a substrate of hay, such as alfalfa and/or timothy, they have the opportunity to receive roughage and nourishment ad libitum. Avoid the use of inorganic substrates because ingested particles may cause intestinal impaction. Offer hatchling tortoises green leafy vegetables (Appendix V) every day, or every other day. About two or three times weekly, offer hatchlings chopped fruits and vegetables with the leafy greens (see Appendixes III–V). Yellow and red food items attract tortoises more readily than other colors, and the bright colors of some flowers, fruits and garden vegetables may help alert them to their food. Add a pinch of multivitamin-multimineral powder to the mash, but do NOT over supplement.

Hatchling tortoises do not require water ad libitum. Approximately four times weekly, place them in a shallow container of tepid water for about 15 minutes, either before or after every meal.

Tortoises are herbivores and do not require animal protein in their diets. Such protein can cause misshapen shells when excessive amounts are consumed (Burchfield, 1982; Jackson, 1982; author's pers. obs.).

Natural sun or full-spectrum light should be provided for these animals. When placing them outdoors, be sure they always have access to a shaded area, and that they are safe from household pets or wild predators.

Always feed hatchling tortoises at their selected body temperature (Table 1, Chapter 3), and allow them to cool slightly during the dark period of their photocycle. However, hatchling tortoises should not be housed below 25°C (77°F).

Crocodilians

Hatchling crocodilians rarely refuse to eat, but it may take them two or three feedings to learn how to grab prey efficiently. The more aggressive hatchlings usually begin feeding on their first attempt. A 150-gal. stock tank, tilted and filled half-way (Fig. 38, Chapter 3), is suitable for housing about a dozen hatchling crocodilians. When housing small numbers, it is usually not necessary to separate them for feeding; however, occasionally runts may have to be removed and fed separately to give them a head start. When given such special attention, they soon grow to the size of their siblings.

Begin feeding hatchling crocodilians with small minnows, adult crickets and freshly killed pinky mice (pinkies are humanely killed by pinching their heads between one's index finger and thumb). The amount of food placed in the tank is determined by the number of hatchlings. Each animal should receive two to four food items. Once a strong feeding reaction develops, begin feeding skinned, chopped rodents, chicks and live fish to ensure they receive enough calcium and a balanced diet. It is important not to overfeed hatchling crocodilians because they may develop gout (Joanen and McNease, 1979).

Whether using an aquarium or stock tank to house hatchling crocodilians, do not use a substrate. A piece of cork bark, placed within the tank, is suitable for hatchlings to have a place to hide and bask. A lamp should be placed at one end of the tank over the cork bark, to allow them to thermoregulate.

Hatchling crocodilians grow quickly. As they increase in size, house them in additional stock tanks.

Lizards

Depending on the species, individual animals may have to be separated at mealtime. When this is necessary, place each in a small, substrate-free container in the same manner as infant snakes (Fig. 51). To encourage carnivorous infant lizards to begin feeding, offer them pinhead crickets with their jumping legs removed, or waxworms. These food items do not provide enough calcium for proper bone growth; therefore, when feeding waxworms, sprinkle calcium powder on the floor of their container. The powder will either be licked or ingested with the insects. Crickets can be fed

Fig. 51 Infant snakes (and lizards) soon learn to feed when placed in small, substrate-free containers with their prey. Photo courtesy of BROMOfoto.

for an hour or two prior to offering them to the hatchlings.

Herbivorous infant lizards can be fed in the same manner as hatchling tortoises. Be sure infant lizards are fed at their selected body temperatures, and house them under full-spectrum lighting (see The Captive Environment, Chapter 3).

Snakes

Infant snakes usually begin feeding after their first shed (about 10 days). For best results, confine each infant to a small, substrate-free container with appropriately sized prey (Fig. 51). It is best to offer young snakes food in the evening and, if necessary, their prey should be left with them overnight. Sometimes clipping the nose of a dead pinky mouse will help them to begin eating. If this does not work, offer the infant snake a live pinky mouse. Depending on the species, food items include pinkies, *Anolis* lizards, crickets with their jumping legs removed, other infant snakes, fish, or frogs (see Appendix VIII).

Once a newly born snake begins feeding, slowly increase the size of its prey to allow it to grow normally. Too often, infant snakes are kept on prey that is too small for normal growth.

Begin to condition snakes early in life to eat dead food.

NUTRITIONAL DISORDERS

Although there may be underlying physiological problems preventing normal absorption of nutrients from the gastrointestinal tract, there is rarely an unexplainable reason for a captive reptile to suffer nutritional disorders. In most cases of malnutrition, the problem is an improper diet supplied by a novice handler, lacking knowledge about proper feeds and feeding. Additionally, many beginning reptile keepers are unable to determine that a nutritional disorder exists until advanced irreversible signs are recognized. For example, chelonians can naturally fast for long periods, and may survive minor nutritional inadequacies for many years. Due to shell coverage of vital structures, minor changes associated with improper nutrition may go unnoticed (Adkins, 1983). Nevertheless, even experienced herpetologists may overlook a deficiency if there are no obvious clinical signs. In some cases only subtle changes in behavior are clinically exhibited. For example, in domestic fowl deficient in sodium and calcium, hyperactivity may be the only indication that a problem exists (Hughs and Wood-Gush, 1973).

Most nutritional problems arise from an imbalanced diet; however, feeding reptiles at below their selected body temperatures, or failing to provide them with proper photoperiods also will cause gastrointestinal problems. Additionally, these suboptimal environmental conditions may cause infections which increase metabolic losses of nitrogen and a number of vitamins and minerals. Intestinal parasites may also reduce available nutrients. The following information is an overview of common nutritional disorders in reptiles:

Vitamin A Deficiency

This deficiency is commonly observed in selected reptiles when they are deprived of whole-bodied animals and/or plant material in their diets. Jackson and Cooper (1981) reported vitamin A deficiency in chelonians that were predominantly fed unsupplemented greens (e.g., lettuce), muscle meat, ants' eggs, or turtle diets sold in pet stores. Clinical signs are lethargy, excessive hiding, anorexia, palpebral edema (Fig. 52), abnormal skeletal development (Fig. 53), respiratory infections, or reproductive problems. Progressive bilateral palpebral swelling renders the animal blind; consequently it does not feed. In severe cases, treatment consists of parenteral vitamin A (Appendix XI). Supplemental dietary vitamin A in combination with a balanced diet of fruits and vegetables should reverse the symptoms of early deficiencies.

Vitamin A Toxicity

Long-term ingestion of immoderate levels of vitamin A, or an acute overdose during therapy may cause this toxicity, especially in tortoises. Tortoise diets routinely contain foods rich in carotenoids. Frye (1991a,b)

Fig. 52 Hypovitaminosis A in a red-eared turtle (*Trachemys scripta elegans*). Note palpebral edema. Reprinted with permission from Fowler, 1986.

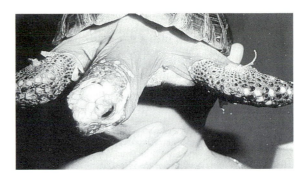

Fig. 54 An example of vitamin A toxicity in a South American yellow-footed tortoise, *Geochelone denticulata*. Note the severe loss of skin from the neck and limbs. Photo credit: Dr. Alex Rubel. Reprinted with permission from Frye, 1991a.

Thiamine (Vitamin B-1) Deficiency

Monotypic diets such as fish, muscle meat and greens can produce thiamine deficiency (Wallach, 1978). Clinical signs are emaciation, anorexia, incoordination, paralysis, and thiamine deficient animals often develop secondary infections (Marcus, 1981). These animals may also exhibit muscular tremors or twitching of the extremities. Parenteral thiamine treatment is indicated in severe cases (Appendix XI).

Mattison (1982) reported that thiaminase activity is destroyed in fish by warming them at 26.7°C (80°F) for five minutes prior to feeding to reptiles. This problem, however, is easily avoided by feeding whole animals to meat-eating reptiles, and a wide variety of plant matter to the herbivorous ones. When feeding piscivorous reptiles thawed frozen fish, supplement their diet with thiamine by inserting a thiamine HCl tablet into the dead animal before feeding it. It is best, however, to offer these animals live fish low in thiaminase activity. Jackson and Cooper (1981) lists thiaminase activity of various fish commonly fed to reptiles. On occasion, fish eaters can also be offered killed, skinned rodents. Skinning is important to prevent gastrointestinal impaction.

described clinical signs of toxicity in these animals. Dry or flaky skin develops, followed by a few days of redness, inflammation, and severe loss of skin (Fig. 54) from the neck and limbs.

Foods rich in vitamin A should be avoided until clinical symptoms abate and the animal returns to normal. Since vitamin A is fat-soluble, and repeated doses may accumulate in adipose tissues, toxicity may take a long time to reverse.

Biotin Deficiency

Lizards in the genera *Varanus*, *Heloderma* and *Tupinambis* are often fed a raw egg diet in captivity. Reptiles fed large quantities of raw eggs may exhibit muscular weakness. Raw egg white contains avidin which bonds with biotin in the gastrointestinal tract, making biotin unavailable for absorption. The problem is easily avoided by substituting cooked eggs, small mammals (rodents), and birds (poultry) as a food source, and by offering raw eggs as an occasional treat. Admittedly, in nature these animals eat eggs; however, wild eggs contain embryos, and the embryonic tissues

Fig. 53 Malnutrition in a baby eastern box turtle (*Terrapene carolinensis*). Note malformed shell. This turtle lived on a diet of lettuce and ground beef until it was donated to Zoo Atlanta at approximately one year of age. Photo courtesy of Rick E. Perry.

contain biotin. With few exceptions, eggs are only a portion of the diets of egg-eating reptiles.

Vitamin C (Ascorbic Acid) Deficiency

A deficiency of vitamin C may cause weight loss, edema and diarrhea. Wallach (1969) reported that hypovitaminosis-C may be associated with ulcerative stomatitis (mouth rot), and Frye (1981a, 1991a,b) reported acute skin rupture and gingival bleeding. In either case, the underlying causes may be due to reduced collagen synthesis or tissue strength.

Several investigators reported that some reptiles are capable of synthesizing ascorbic acid (Chatterjee, 1967, 1970, 1973; Vosburgh et al., 1982). Ross and Marzec (1984) were unable to identify any evidence of vitamin C deficiency in snakes, or determine that these animals even require it. Yet it should not be overlooked that prey allowed to void their intestinal contents prior to being fed to reptiles may be deficient in vitamin C. Consequently, the continuous feeding with such prey may result in vitamin C deficiency. Reptiles that naturally produce vitamin C in the kidneys, colon and caecum, may become deficient under prolonged antibiotic therapy because such therapy can kill normal intestinal microflora (Jackson and Cooper, 1981).

To avoid the potential for vitamin C deficiency in reptiles, feed carnivorous species well-nourished prey, and offer vegetable matter rich in vitamin C to herbivorous reptiles (see Appendixes III–VI). In cases where animals exhibit symptoms of vitamin C deficiency, or are subjected to prolonged antibiotic therapy, treatment with parenteral vitamin C may be indicated (Appendix XI).

Vitamin D and Calcium Deficiencies

Vitamin D, calcium and phosphorous are essential in the formation of bone through a highly complex set of interrelationships. Simplified, a condition called metabolic bone disease results when one, a reptile is deficient in vitamin D either dietarily or from the lack of ultraviolet radiation; two, when calcium is deficient in the diet; or three, when the diet contains an imbalanced ratio of calcium to phosphorus. Ideally, a diet should contain a calcium to phosphorus ratio of 1:1 to 2:1. Monotypic diets such as skeletal muscle meat, visceral organs, many vegetables, mealworms and crickets are low in calcium and high in phosphorus, and if these food items are not properly supplemented, metabolic bone disease will occur. For this reason, metabolic bone disease is more apt to be observed in herbivorous and insectivorous reptiles than those that consume whole vertebrates. Other factors affecting a reptile's requirement for calcium are its age and sex.

Growing and gravid reptiles require more calcium in their diets than males or older animals.

Symptoms of metabolic bone disease include painful joints, anorexia, retarded growth, loosening or loss of teeth, bone deformities and fractures, and misshapen (Fig. 53), soft and pliable shells in chelonians. Calcium may be supplied by feeding bone meal, crushed egg shells or calcium carbonate powder. For aquatic species, cuttlebone or plaster of Paris blocks may be placed in the water. When exposing animals to natural sunlight for vitamin D synthesis, provide shaded areas for cooling. For an in-depth discussion of metabolic bone disease, the reader is directed to Fowler (1986).

Vitamin D Toxicity

The highest incidence of vitamin D toxicity was reported in the green iguana, *Iguana iguana* (Wallach, 1966). In fact, Wallach reported that long-term supplementation of vitamins and minerals containing vitamin D, calcium and phosphorus are deleterious to green iguanas. Clinically, anorexia and lameness may be observed. Radiographically, there may be abnormal depositions of calcium in soft tissues and medial calcification of large blood vessels (Marcus, 1981). Prevention requires the avoidance of excessive supplementation of dietary vitamin D.

Vitamin E Deficiency (Steatitis)

Originally described in crocodilians by Wallach and Hoessle (1968), this condition is not always clinically apparent, and therefore is usually not diagnosed until necropsy. Crocodilians fed exclusively oil-laden fish such as smelt, mackerel or herring may develop steatitis. It also has been reported by Frye (1981a) in aquatic chelonians, and in snakes fed obese laboratory rodents (Frye 1981a, 1986). Langham et al. (1971) reported steatitis in a captive Marcy garter snake, *Thamnophis marcianus,* and Frye (1981a), Rost and Young (1984), and Farnsworth et al. (1986) diagnosed the disorder in lizards as "white muscle disease."

Frye (1981a, 1986, 1991a,b) described deficient reptiles as having "grossly abnormal adipose tissues, often appearing to be abnormally firm and unyeilding on palpation." He also mentioned that the overlying skin may bear a yellow or orange hue.

In severe cases, parenteral vitamin E should be administered (Appendix XI), while in less severe cases, supplemental vitamin E can be provided orally. Reptiles consistently fed obese rodents should also be supplemented with dietary vitamin E. Furthermore, crocodilians can be fed dead, skinned mammals or chickens instead of fish. Chickens also are an excellent addition to rodent diets for snakes.

Vitamin K Deficiency

Frye (1981a, 1986; 1991a,b) reported vitamin K deficiency in long-term captive crocodilians. Prolonged bleeding of the gums occurred as the animal's shed their deciduous teeth. Vitamin K deficiency is usually a result of prolonged antibiotic therapy whereby the vitamin-producing intestinal microflora are killed. However, Frye described the deficiency in well-fed crocodilians as being spontaneous and without clear causal factors. Prevention is by occasional supplementation with synthetic vitamin K. When gingival bleeding is apparent, parenteral vitamin K may be administered (Appendix XI). Vitamin K is fat-soluble, and repeated doses may accumulate in adipose tissues.

Copper Deficiency

Excessive zinc or molybdenum in the diet will cause copper deficiency. Murphy and Collins (1983) reported that chelonians suffering from this deficiency will exhibit slow growth and hypochromic anemia. It can be prevented in aquatic turtles by placing copper tubing or coins in their water environment. However, Ritchie (pers. comm.) warns that leaching properties of tubing varies; for example, softer coppers could rapidly reach toxic levels. Salads fed to herbivorous chelonians should always be supplemented with a good vitamin-mineral powder.

Iodine Deficiency

Iodine deficiency can be manifested as goiter (Fig. 55) and hypothyroidism (Wallach, 1969). Symptoms include severe generalized edema, anorexia and lethargy. Primarily, this condition afflicts herbivorous lizards and chelonians, especially the Aldabra tortoise (*Geochelone gigantea*) and the Galapagos tortoise (*G. elephantopus*). The natural diet of these animals may be rich in iodine (Frye and Dutra 1974; Frye, 1981a, 1986, 1991a,b), whereas their typical captive diet does not provide proper quantities. In addition to a natural requirement for iodine, Wallach (1969) reported that captive animals fed monotypically goitrogenic vegetables (e.g., those in the cabbage and kale families) will show clinical signs of this disorder. Representative foods include cabbage, kale, Brussels sprouts, broccoli, soybean sprouts, lettuce, and spinach. Hypothyroidism can be prevented by giving dietary iodine supplement in the form of iodized salt at a ratio of 0.5% of the total diet (Marcus, 1981), and Frye (1991a,b) suggested sprinkling ground kelp tablets on food. He advised a maintenance amount for an adult box turtle of 1–2 mg weekly, and the dosage scaled up or down for larger or smaller reptiles. It is also necessary to vary the types of green leafy vegetables provided. In severe cases,

Fig. 55 Galapagos tortoise (*Geochelone elephantopus*) with goiter. Reprinted with permission from Fowler, 1986.

sodium iodide can be administered orally or parenterally (Appendix XI).

Protein Deficiency

Chronically anorectic reptiles, or those fed an imbalanced diet, may exhibit symptoms of protein deficiency. Animals suffering from protein deficiency may become lame. Also, they are compromised immunologically and may develop secondary bacterial infections. Clinical signs are steady loss of weight and depletion of fat stores. Protein-deficient reptiles may suffer osteomalacia and exhibit skeletal protuberances, especially of the spine, ribs, and pelvis. In addition to allowing the affected reptile to attain its selected body temperature (Table 1, Chapter 3), treatment should begin by balancing the animal's electrolytes and ensuring adequate hydration. This is accomplished by administering (SC, IP or IV) 5% dextrose with 0.3% potassium at 4% of the animal's body weight for 4 days (Jackson and Cooper, 1981). This regime is followed with the feeding of easily absorbable proteins, amino acids, and dextrose for 2 to 4 weeks (Jackson and Cooper, 1981). The reptile should then be physiologically capable of digesting a rich diet designed for debilitated animals (see below) for 2 to 4 more weeks of therapy. It can reasonably be expected that the reluctant feeder will return to a normal dietary program after 6 to 8 weeks. The following diet for debilitated and anorectic reptiles is modified from Frye (1981a):

Ingredients:

    1 chopped, skinned mouse

    1 part beaten raw egg (including shell)

    1 part water

    1 part Nutrical®

Mix ingredients thoroughly, and administer via stomach tube (Fig. 46). Note: do not overfeed this rich, unnatural diet; it may cause enteric bacterial proliferation.

Constipation, Gastrointestinal Blockages, Diarrhea

Reptiles vary in their frequency of defecation. When fed regularly, some boids and crotalids may defecate after every third or fourth feeding, while water snakes may pass stools every other day. In addition to differences in metabolic rates, the quantity and type of food determines stool consistency and frequency of voiding. Large prey with denser hides, larger bones, and greater ratio of volume to surface area, require more time for digestion than small prey. If a food source is temporarily limited, and an animal is fed a reduced quantity of food, stools may be passed less often. Sudden changes in diet may cause loose stools as well as large quantities of lettuce, or citrus fruits that may be too acidic for reptiles. When changing an animal's diet, do so slowly.

When feeding large reptiles, the animal may be given a single large food item (e.g., a 250-g rat) or numerous small items such as a total of 250 g of mice. Under such circumstances, better digestion is achieved by feeding the single, large food item. Referring to surface/volume ratios, a 250-g rat has less surface area than 250 g of mice, thereby providing less fur and more nutrition.

Reptiles require their selected body temperature (Table 1, Chapter 3) to properly digest their food. If the animal is not allowed to reach its temperature preference, digestion is prolonged, resulting in decomposition of food in its stomach. Additionally, stools will be passed more slowly than is normally expected.

To stimulate peristalsis, a certain amount of roughage is required in all diets. However, too much roughage, especially in the form of fur or feathers may cause constipation, leading to an intestinal blockage. As the bolus of fur or feathers sits in the colon, fluids are continually absorbed. Eventually, the bolus becomes dry and adheres to the intestinal mucosa.

Some substrates such as sand, small aquarium gravel or ground corn cob are easily ingested and may cause gastrointestinal impaction (Fig. 56). Naturally, stools may not be passed in such cases. Additionally, the chitinous exoskeletons of some insects (e.g., mealworms) may block the intestines when fed in large quantities to small reptiles.

Many reptiles readily defecate in their water bowls; a good example is the box turtle (*Terrapene*). Tortoises that are not passing stools at a normal frequency may

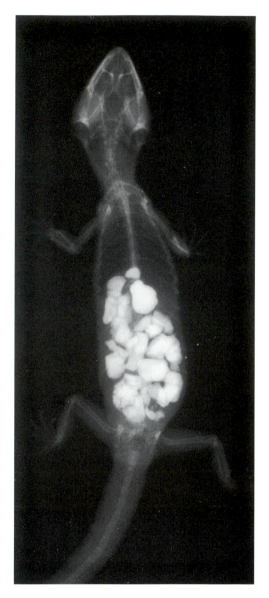

Fig. 56 Leopard gecko (*Eublepharis macularius*) with ingested pea gravel. Radiograph courtesy of Cindy Thorstad.

do so if placed in a shallow, tepid water bath after each meal. When constipation or intestinal impaction occurs, and the animal does not respond to tepid water baths (snakes included), the bolus can often be massaged out of an animal after a mineral oil enema; but occasionally, the obstruction must be removed surgically. The novice reptile keeper should not attempt to give a reptile an enema. Colonic tissue and oviducts are easily ruptured by this procedure. If simple husbandry techniques are not effective, one should seek the assistance of a veterinary clinician.

Although loose stools can be dietary in nature, one should always suspect parasitism and/or bacterial enteritis. If a fecal parasite examination and stool culture do not verify the presence of pathogens, and the animal otherwise appears healthy, it may be helpful to administer an appropriate dosage of Kaopectate®. Dosages must be scaled to the body weight of the individual. If diarrhea persists, animals must be hydrated with appropriate dosages of an electrolyte solution.

Gout

The presence of pathologic accumulations of urates in the viscera or joints has been reported in all reptilian orders (Appleby and Siller, 1960, Wallach and Hoessle, 1967). Clinical signs are seldom apparent when urates accumulate in the viscera. Urate accumulation often causes major organ malfunctions, and symptoms which do become apparent are nonspecific, being similar to many other diseases. Symptoms may include lethargy, dehydration, dysecdysis, palpebral and generalized edema. On the other hand, the arthritic form of gout may be recognized by swollen and painful joints. Reported etiological factors include severe dehydration, endogenous protein metabolism in anorectic animals (Cowan, 1968), high amounts of exogenous protein (Cowan, 1968) and aminoglycoside antibiotic therapy (Bush et al., 1978). Signs may be reversed at least partially by rehydration and nutritionally restoring nitrogen balance. However, arthritic gout is extremely difficult to cure because irreversible joint changes have usually occurred by the time clinical signs are detected. Generally, nephrotoxic products such as aminoglycosides should not be used as antibiotic therapy unless no other drugs are indicated from sensitivity testing. When possible, a nonaminoglycoside should be administered until test results arrive. In the interim, if the therapy is obviously not achieving positive results, one should immediately change to an aminoglycoside. Unfortunately, many or most diseases of reptiles are caused by Gram-negative bacteria where the only effective treatment is an aminoglycoside.

Obesity

Besides balancing a reptile's diet, the keeper must determine the amount of food a reptile should eat. To judge the proper weight of a captive reptile, it is helpful to observe many healthy individuals of the same species, preferably those in the wild. Because captive reptiles expend very little energy to obtain food, they become overweight (Fig. 57) if fed too often. Novice reptile owners tend to overfeed their animals because they feel it is cruel not to do so. Familiarity with their reptilian pet's natural feeding habits, and concern for a long-lived and healthy animal should eliminate this misguided tendency. The reader may wish to review the discussion on Feeding Frequencies at the beginning of this chapter.

Fig. 57 Obesity in an African savanna monitor (*Varanus exanthematicus*); ventral aspect. This animal was fed a diet almost entirely of scrambled eggs. Photo courtesy of Rick E. Perry.

Overgrown Horny Beaks of Chelonians

This condition is primarily a problem in chelonians fed predominantly soft foods. It may be prevented in terrestrial turtles and tortoises by allowing them to graze periodically on naturally tough grasses within a movable pen (see Frye 1991a, Fig. 2–9). Be sure that the grazing area has not been sprayed with weed killers, and that no toxic plants are present (Appendix IX). Aquatic and semiaquatic turtles can maintain normal mouthparts if their diets are supplemented with Frog Brittle® and crustaceans. When an overgrowth (Fig. 58) is first observed, a veterinarian should trim the horny tissue. This can be achieved with a rotary saw held in the chuck of a small power tool such as the Dremel Moto Tool (Frye, 1981a), then filed or sanded smooth. If fractures or chipping occur, repairs can be made with epoxy resin (Frye, 1981a). This condition should not be allowed to progress, or the affected animal may cease feeding altogether. A more in-depth discussion on this subject is covered in Frye (1991a) under Conditions Affecting the Keratinous Mouth Parts of Chelonians.

Fig. 58 Example of overgrowth of a turtle's horny beak. Reprinted with permission from Frye, 1991a.

Vomiting

Although vomiting is not necessarily directly related to improper nutrition, this disorder is associated with feeding. Common causes for regurgitation in reptiles are as follows:

- Being handled just after being fed (especially snakes and carnivorous lizards).

- Food too large (snakes and carnivorous lizards). This problem can be avoided by puncturing the prey's intestines prior to feeding it to a reptile.

- Temperature too low. Reptiles require their selected body temperatures (Table 1, Chapter 3) for proper digestion. When reptiles are subjected to subminimal temperatures, food may decompose in their stomachs causing them to regurgitate.

- Obstructions in gastrointestinal tract. Obstructions may be caused by an abcess, tumor, foreign objects, or fur and feather masses from the prey.

- Parasitism (other diseases).

- Overcrowding.

- Continually lighted environment. Reptiles require a photoperiod (Table 2, Chapter 3) and should not be maintained under continual light. If a nighttime heat source is needed, use a red light bulb of appropriate wattage.

Chapter 5

Health, Medical, and Necropsy Considerations

ANIMAL HYGIENE AND HUMAN HEALTH

When one considers the atrocities of capture, it is amazing that any reptiles survive. Most of these animals are noosed, netted, wrestled, trapped, or snared, and then bagged, boxed, and transported via a variety of methods to other countries. Those reptiles that survive the capture are usually maintained in overcrowded, filthy conditions with contaminated water or no water at all. Ambient temperatures are usually too high or too low, and photoperiods are improper. Pathogens are allowed to spread from animal to animal, with the potential for compromising human health. On arrival at animal wholesalers or pet stores, some reptiles may further endure similar inappropriate conditions. At its final destination, each reptile may harbor so many infectious diseases that it has the potential to decimate an entire established collection, or to pass pathogens on to its new owner, and his or her family and friends. In situations where venomous snakes have been purchased, there is always the possibility of a life-threatening bite (discussion follows).

Quarantine

All new arrivals and sick animals should be isolated from an established reptile collection for a period of one to three months. Even animals housed previously in accredited facilities could be incubating a contagious disease or have parasites that were not diagnosed for one reason or another. During the quarantine period, conduct a thorough physical examination (details follow). Fecal examinations should also be performed on all quarantined reptiles, and repeated every six months thereafter (see Parasites).

Enclosure Maintenance

To prevent the production of bacteria, fungi and/or parasites, promptly remove all fecal material, uneaten food and shed skins from caging.

Avoid contaminating food with excreta.

Periodically replace substrate. For example, mosses, mulch, soil and gravel, should be changed every three to four months, or sooner if unpleasant odors develop. When using newspapers as a substrate, change when soiled.

To prevent eutrophication change daily the water in bowls, tanks and other receptacles.

To prevent the spread of infectious diseases, avoid transfer of cage contents, uneaten food, etc., from one cage to another, and clean cages with sick animals last.

Avoid overcrowding. Proper cage maintenance becomes difficult and animals are stressed unnecessarily under crowded conditions.

Tools

To prevent the spread of infectious diseases, all tools (Fig. 59) used to manipulate animals or to remove uneaten food or feces from cages should be dipped in a strong disinfectant such as household bleach. Dip tools in the disinfectant immediately after attending each cage, then thoroughly rinse them before using them in another cage.

Cleansing and Disinfecting

Disinfect cages immediately following the death or illness of a reptile. The longer a disinfectant is applied, the more effective it is. Ross and Marzec (1984) reported a number of factors to consider when selecting a cleansing and disinfecting agent. They categorized these agents into three groups: soaps, detergents and disinfectants, and reported that soaps and detergents are poor disinfectants. Two of the most common types of disinfectants are quaternary ammonium and phenolic compounds. However, benzalkonium chloride is a common ingredient in quaternary

Fig. 59 At Zoo Atlanta, reptile keepers use carts to store and move products around work areas. Scoop spoons are dipped in household bleach after servicing each cage. Before removing food or feces from stock tanks, the spoon is thoroughly rinsed to prevent eye or skin irritation to animals in aquatic environments. Photo courtesy of Rick E. Perry.

ammonium compounds, and therefore such compounds are ineffective against *Pseudomonas*. Additionally, Harvey (1975) reported that quarternary ammonium compounds are inactivated by organic materials. Ross and Marzec (1984) reported that soaps also neutralize the effectiveness of quaternary ammonium compounds (e.g., Roccal®-D), but do not affect the phenolics. To disinfect cages properly, remove organic materials. Always rinse cages with water after disinfecting them.

Phenolic Compounds

Marcus (1981) reported that phenolic compounds are toxic to reptiles, but Ross and Marzec (1984) disagreed. They reported using a powerful phenolic compound for 10 years without difficulties. Such disinfectants are excellent against *Pseudomonas,* a major cause of reptilian bacterial diseases.

Detergents

As cleansers, detergents can be used in combination with quaternary and phenolic compounds. Detergents are difficult to rinse away (Almandarz, 1978), and for this reason they should not be used in water tanks.

Other Cleansers and Disinfectants

Povidone iodine and household bleach are commonly used, safe disinfectants for reptiles. In common with detergents, however, bleach is difficult to rinse away and can cause eye and skin irritation. Scalding hot water helps reduce the number of pathogens, after which cages or aquaria should be placed in direct sunlight for several hours. If one wishes to avoid the use of detergents, table salt is especially beneficial in cleaning water tanks. Salt will efficiently remove fish oils and algae (Almandarz, 1978).

Personal Hygiene

Reptile-associated salmonellosis, especially in turtles, has long been known. Over 40 references have appeared in the literature. Recently, Grier et al. (1993) gave an excellent account of salmonellosis in snakes. They reported that snake parts, including shed skins, may be contaminated with various strains of salmonellae, and their study also showed that freezing the bacteria did not kill them.

Salmonella spp. transmission is not a major health risk in healthy humans and animals. Such problems occur primarily when an individual's immune system is compromised. In reptiles, stress is a major factor and, in humans, transmission should be of concern in children, the elderly, and those with HIV/AIDS.

People maintaining reptile collections must keep in mind that they can transport pathogens to other people and reptiles. It is important to keep this in mind when attending local herpetological meetings. It is also important to be aware that pathogens may be transmitted to people when giving public education/conservation programs, or when merely displaying a pet reptile to a friend.

Because personal hygiene is essential to the continuing good health of a reptile and its keeper, one's hands should be washed after handling animals or cage contents. Other personal hygienic practices include not drinking or eating around reptiles, and not placing tools, cages or their contents in animal or human food preparation areas. Furthermore, never empty aquaria or water bowls in a kitchen sink that is used to wash the family's dishes.

Snakebite

Within the United States, conflicting ideas and controversy over the "proper" first aid technique for venomous snakebite are never-ending. The most publicized techniques proposed have included either one or a combination of the following: cutting, suction, tourniquets, ice water, and/or electroshock. The most recent recommendation is no first aid at all. Rather, the victim is encouraged to remain calm and go to a hospital as quickly as possible. In contrast, many authorities in Australia advocate a uniform policy for snakebite. It is called the pressure/immobilization technique (Figs. 60, 61). This procedure delays the movement of the venom from the bite site for several hours.

Venomous snakes in Australia belong to the family Elapidae (e.g., cobras, kraits, coral snakes, etc.), and their venoms are primarily neurotoxic. In other parts of the world, however, the snake fauna often consists of vipers and pit vipers as well as elapids. The cytotoxic venom of vipers and pit vipers is not only life-threatening, but can be terribly disfiguring. It is for this reason that snakebite authorities in the United States currently argue that any first aid technique that restricts the flow of venom from the bite site should be avoided.

Sutherland and Coulter (1981) disagree. These authors have recommended the pressure/immobilization technique for all snakebites. This recommendation was based on their investigations with monkeys (*Macaca fascicularis*) that were injected with eastern diamondback rattlesnake (*Crotalus adamanteus*) venom. They clearly demonstrated that pressure/immobilization retards the movement of venom from the bite site into the general circulation. This is a distinct advantage in the treatment of bites where neurotoxins are prevalent. Rosenberg (1989), however, raised a few concerns over the use of this technique on bites from snakes with primarily cytotoxic venom. He questioned the lack of follow-up publications by Sutherland and Coulter since their work in 1981. He also raised the point that few people would carry an ace bandage and splint around with them just in case they were bitten. Even if they did, he said, it is unlikely the bandage would be used properly anyway (e.g., it would probably be used more like a tourniquet instead of a pressure bandage). Although Sutherland (1988) reported that bandages could be applied for several hours, no mention was made of a specific length of time such application would be safe in retarding the flow of cytotoxic venoms.

It is hoped by those of us who make their living caring for reptiles, including the venomous ones, that the medical profession will continue research in this area so that, in the future, it may be possible to rely on

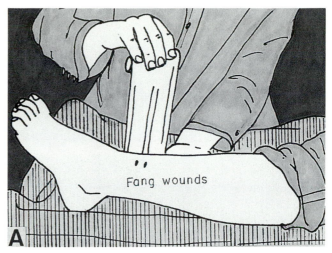

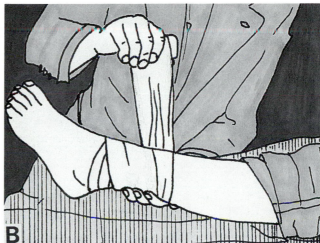

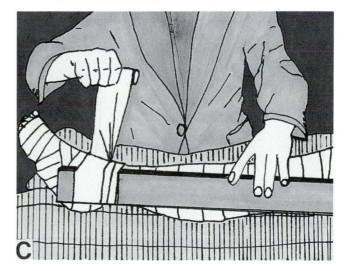

Fig. 60 Australian first aid procedure for snakebite of the lower limb. A) apply the ace bandage(s) as tightly as one would on a sprained ankle; B) extend the bandage as high on the leg as possible; C) place a splint on the leg and bind it firmly to as much of the leg as possible. Reprinted with permission from Barnard, 1990.

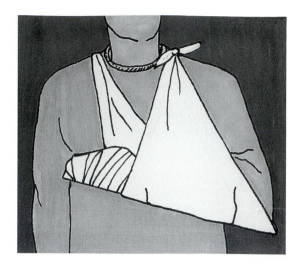

Fig. 61 Australian first aid procedure for snakebite of the hand or forearm. The elbow should be bound with ace bandages. Apply a splint and place the arm in a sling. Reprinted with permission from Barnard, 1990.

ONE safe and effective first aid treatment for ALL snakebites.

As one can see from the previous discussion, snakebite procedures vary from one country to another. The same is true of facilities within the same country. The simple snakebite procedures used at Zoo Atlanta have saved the lives of staff that were bitten by an albino western diamondback rattlesnake (*Crotalus atrox*) and black mamba (*Dendroaspis polylepis*). They include the following:

1. If possible, secure the snake.

2. Announce the bite (e.g., sound the snakebite alarm).

3. Remain calm and apply suction (e.g., mechanical suction and *NOT* by mouth).

4. Call 911.

5. Retrieve the appropriate antivenin from the refrigerator along with the list of snakebite consultants.

Note: The Arizona Regional Drug and Poison Control Center (602-626-6016) can provide data on locations where antivenin can be obtained, or one can purchase a copy of the *Antivenom Index* from the American Zoo and Aquarium Association, Oglebay Park, Wheeling, WV 26003-1698.

VETERINARY CONSIDERATIONS

A review of the herpetological literature indicates that bacterial diseases of reptiles are almost always opportunistic Gram-negative organisms that include *Pseu-* *domonas*, *Aeromonas*, *Citrobacter*, *Klebsiella* and *Serratia*. On occasion, other Gram-negative bacteria such as *Salmonella*, *Proteus*, *Flavobacter*, *Acinetobacter* and *Enterobacter* also infect reptiles. These bacteria are part of the normal body flora, and when animals are deprived of proper nutrition, hygiene and environmental conditions, or suffer trauma, they become susceptible to infection by one or more of these opportunists.

Microbiological culture and sensitivity testing can be extremely valuable in identifying pathogens, and in indicating which drugs are most likely to provide effective treatment. Test results, however, cannot be interpreted properly or applied without a basic understanding of the bacteria affecting reptiles and the drugs used. Ross and Marzec (1984) offer an excellent discussion about the proper handling of bacterial isolates and the interpretation of sensitivity tests.

It is not within the scope of this book to discuss detailed diagnosis and treatment of reptilian diseases. Nevertheless, those keeping reptiles can care for their animals more responsibly by learning how to recognize common reptilian disorders and by gaining a basic understanding about therapeutics. In this way, sick reptiles have the best chance possible for early medical assistance. Also, the reptile handler may be asked by his or her veterinarian to perform certain follow-up nursing practices such as giving injections (Fig. 62) and changing dressings. The ability of a keeper to administer follow-up care also reduces stress to an animal by eliminating unnecessary visits to a veterinary clinic.

Anyone attempting to cure a sick reptile should not base treatment entirely upon the overview presented in this book. For in-depth aspects of reptilian disorders, their diagnosis and treatment, the reader may find texts by Cooper and Jackson (1981), Frye (1991a), Marcus (1981) and Ross and Marzec (1984) useful. The reader is strongly urged to research these and other texts, and to consult a veterinarian knowlegeable about reptile care.

Case History and Record Keeping

Early detection of a health problem and accurate record keeping can make the difference between successful medical treatment of a reptile or its death. It is unreasonable to expect a veterinary practitioner to treat an animal from information that is being offered from a client's memory. When attempting to cure a reptile, a veterinarian may wish to know the following:

• Common and scientific name.

• Sex.

• Age.

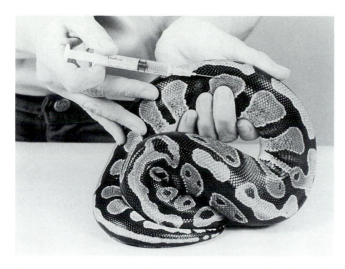

Fig. 62 Proper method for injecting a snake. Note the needle is inserted parallel to the animal's spine to avoid a spinal injury, and anterior to the kidneys to prevent drug elimination through the renal-portal system. Photo courtesy of BROMOfoto.

- When last shed and condition of shed (e.g., moist and in one piece; dried and torn).

- Were eye caps also shed.

- When last passed urates and feces.

- When last fed.

- Type of food offered.

- Amount of food offered.

- How food was stored.

- Where food was obtained.

- Was food refused, and for how long.

- Temperature and relative humidity of environment.

- If housing outdoors, amount of rainfall.

- Was animal allowed to hibernate and if so, when and for how long, temperature of hibernaculum and weight of animal prior to and after hibernation.

- Was breeding observed and if so, the date.

- If reptile in question is female, were eggs laid or live young born.

- Type of disinfectants used to clean cage.

- Type of pesticides, if any, used in environment.

- Number and sex ratios of cage mates.

- Previous disorder(s) and type of treatment received; involvement with other animals.

- Animal's current behavior.

These questions are easily answered if records are maintained on each animal. For example, one may wish to use a card similar to the sample depicted in Fig. 63.

Handling

The proper procedures for handling reptiles are discussed in Chapter 2. Before beginning a physical examination, allow the reptile to move unrestrained until its coordination can be evaluated.

Physical Examination

Reptiles should be examined on a regular basis to ensure their continuing good health. Discussed next are some basic diagnostic considerations.

Locomotion

Abnormal locomotion in a reptile may be caused by a single disease, or by a combination of problems including congenital deformity, gout, metabolic bone disease, or trauma.

Coordination

Reptiles may exhibit abnormal coordination when suffering from excessive heat or cold, injury, metabolic disease, or a disease of the central nervous system. Antibiotics such as streptomycin (Rothman and Rothman, 1960) and aminoglycosides (Ross pers. comm.) can cause incoordination in snakes.

Eyes

Sunken eyes may indicate starvation, dehydration and/or disease.

Tearing is a normal cleansing action in tortoises and crocodilians (Frye, 1981a). However, crocodilians exposed to chilling temperatures also may form tears (Vogel, 1964). When a discharge from the eyes is purulent one should consider bacterial conjunctivitis. Tortoises may receive eye injuries when brushing past certain vegetation (see Plant Injuries below). This can also result in inflammation and a purulent discharge.

Swelling of the eyelids (Fig. 52, Chapter 4) is usually observed in chelonians suffering vitamin A deficiency. However, this symptom also may be exhibited when these animals are oversupplemented with vitamin A. Conjunctivitis should be another consideration.

Retained spectacles can be a chronic problem in snakes and are directly associated with improper shedding. Some lizards also may retain their spectacles (e.g., certain gecko species).

HUSBANDRY RECORD

Given, Common and Scientific Names: *"Hissy" Burmese Python*

Python molurus bivittatus   Sex: ♂

Origin of Specimen: *Bill Chase, Miami, Fl.*

Date, Age, Weight, Length at Acquisition: *9/71; age, unknown;*

was not weighed; 3 ft.

Preferred Diet: *Large rodents, chickens, waterfowl, rabbits*

Date	Food Type Amount Weight	Accepted (A) Rejected (R)	Animal's weight, length	Shed/ Condition	Passed Urates (U) feces (F)	General Comments
7/14/82						*Placed in newly constructed cage. Varnish not "cured". Developed chemical pneumonia. Rx Re-cover® 3 ml IM 7/15 - 7/16. Installed exhaust fan 7/16. Fully recovered 7/18.*
2/9/83						*Introduced ♀. ♂ showed no interest in breeding. Separated 2/16.*
6/20/85	*(1) 15 lb. rabbit*	A				*Defecated 24+ hrs.*
7/9/85				Poor	(U)(F)	*Shed adhered. Placed warm, wet towels on those areas; manually removed.*
7/11/85			172 lbs. 16'2"			

Disposition of Specimen: _____

Date of Disposition: _____

Necropsy Finding: _____

Fig. 63 Sample record card for maintaining pertinent information about a reptile. Record keeping is essential to provide a veterinarian with a history about an animal that may become sick.

Scarring of the cornea (keratitis) can result from trauma or exposure to noxious chemicals.

Cataracts are common in aged animals. However, young monitor lizards have been known to have cataracts (Frye, 1981a, 1991a).

Stargazing and dilation of pupils has been observed in hypoglycemic crocodilians (Fig. 64), and in snakes with encephalitis and paramyxovirus.

Nares

Nasal discharge, blockage, audible and labored breathing are symptoms of respiratory disease in reptiles.

Serous discharge may be exhibited in tortoises that have been exposed to chilling temperatures (Vogel, 1964).

Mouth

Gaping may indicate respiratory disease, oral trematodiasis, retained shed, or a foreign object within the mouth. Crocodilians, however, gape as part of their normal thermoregulatory behavior.

When a reptile exhibits an oral discharge, consider respiratory disease, ulcerative stomatitis, oropharyngeal

Fig. 64 A) dilation of the pupil in an American alligator (*Alligator mississippiensis*); B) an example of stargazing in the same animal. Both are classical symptoms of hypoglycemia in crocodilians. Reprinted with permission from Fowler, 1986.

cellulitis, or mechanical injury from certain plants during feeding (e.g., in tortoises).

Ulceration of the oral mucosa indicates ulcerative stomatitis (mouth rot) (Fig. 65) or mechanical injury from certain plants during feeding.

Loosening or loss of teeth in snakes, lizards and crocodilians is normal. These reptiles shed and replace their teeth on a regular basis. Improper handling and examination of the mouth can also cause trauma to the dental arcade.

Skin

Cutaneous and/or subcutaneous swellings or nodules may be caused by abscesses, blister disease in snakes (Fig. 66), bacterial infection from *Dermatophilus*

Fig. 66 Blister disease (arrow) in a common water snake (*Nerodia* sp.). Reprinted with permission from Jacobson, 1981.

congolensis in lizards (Marcus, 1981), filarial worms, yeast infection from *Geotrichum candidum* (Marcus, 1981), fungal or mycobacterial infection, invasion of tissues by larval ectoparasites or tapeworms, tumors, or mechanical injury from abrasive or toxic plants.

Bite wounds are a direct consequence of feeding live prey to reptiles. If possible, all prey fed to reptiles should be killed. Bite wounds (Fig. 75) also occur between cage mates when two or more reptiles are housed in the same enclosure. Aggressive cage mates should be removed during feeding.

Blotches of redness and petechial hemorrhages on soft tissues are often observed in septicemic reptiles.

The skin of dehydrated reptiles may lack resilience. Also, longitudinal tenting of the skin in snakes and

Fig. 65 An example of mouthrot. Photo courtesy of Manny V. Rubio.

lizards may be observed (Marcus, 1981). Conversely, healthy reptiles often have an iridescent quality to their integument (except during normal ecdysis).

Not all shedding problems are environmental. The frequency and/or degree of difficulty an animal has in shedding can indicate its state of health.

Shell deformities in chelonians (Fig. 53, Chapter 4) may indicate malnutrition (which ultimately leads to soft shells) or a congenital anomaly. Shell fractures are caused by trauma. Shell necrosis may result in captive turtles when certain algal organisms accumulate (Frye, 1981a).

Ulceration of the shells of chelonians can be attributed to ulcerative shell disease (SCUD). Mycobacterial dermatitis will ulcerate a reptile's integument. In snakes, ulceration of scutes is known as "scale rot."

Skeleton

Skeletal deformities may be congenital or acquired (often due to malnutrition).

When observing soft or fractured bones consider malnutrition (most common cause), osteomyelitis or trauma.

Limping or swollen joints may indicate gout.

Gastrointestinal Tract

Dysfunction of the gastrointestinal tract may be caused by improper temperatures and/or diet, excessive handling, tumors, parasitism, poisoning, or septicemia.

Diarrhea and melena are consequences of parasitism, bacterial gastroenteritis, or poisoning.

Amebiasis may cause diarrhea, or constipation in reptiles other than snakes.

Causes of intestinal obstruction include parasitism, tumors, mycobacterial granuloma, dehydration, impacted fur or feathers, chitin, or plant hairs.

Cloaca

Swelling or ulceration of the cloaca may indicate trauma from calculi (Cooper, 1981), improper use of sexing probes, or loose substrate materials (e.g., sand).

Inanition, Weight Loss

Problems to consider are parasitism, maladaptation syndrome (Cowan, 1980), nutritional goiter (Fig. 55, Chapter 4), tumors, ingestion of toxic plants, and a host of infectious diseases (also see Reluctant Feeders in Chapter 4).

Retarded Growth

This is a condition which is usually produced environmentally. The causes include inadequate enclosure space, improper diet, and/or temperatures chronically below an animal's thermal preference.

Claws

With the exception of adult male turtles in the genera *Pseudemys* (includes *Trachemys*), *Chrysemys* and *Graptemys* (see Reproduction and Egg Incubation, Chapter 6), claws of chelonians and lizards may require trimming. Often, animals maintained under captive conditions cannot wear down their claws.

Beak

See Feeding and Nutritional Disorders, Chapter 4.

Commonly Encountered Disorders

Abscesses

Marcus (1981) described abscesses in reptiles as being discrete, round, and encapsulated by fibrous connective tissue, and they can be mistaken easily for other types of subcutaneous nodules caused by parasitic and mycotic infections or neoplasms. Nevertheless, one can differentiate most subcutaneous abscesses from the other disorders by the presence of a solid exudate. Frye (1991a) listed the following genera of organisms as being commonly isolated from abscesses: *Actinobacillus, Aeromonas, Arizona, Bacteriodes, Citrobacter, Clostridium, Corynebacterium, Edwardsiella, Enterobacter, Escherichia, Gemella, Klebsiella, Leptospira, Mycobacterium, Pasturella, Peptostreptococcus, Proteus, Providentia, Pseudomonas, Salmonella, Serratia, Staphylococcus* and *Streptococcus*.

Treatment includes surgically removing the purulent mass, irrigating the affected area with an antiseptic, packing it with a proteolytic enzyme such as Granulex® or Dermaaid™ (Appendix XII), and administering parenteral antibiotics. Depending on the species, the affected reptile should be maintained at temperatures between 29.4 and 35°C (85 and 95°F), or within its selected body temperatures (Table 1, Chapter 3). Lesions are not usually sutured, and the animal should be housed on clean paper towels until cured.

Skin punctures, ectoparasites, animal bites and similar trauma may cause abscesses. Pathogens invade and infect the traumatized area. Excessive humidity and tan bark bedding were also reported by Marcus (1981) to cause abscesses. In some cases, abscesses are difficult to differentiate from tumors. Recurring "lumps" should be submitted for laboratory analysis.

Blister Disease (in snakes) (Fig. 66)

If left untreated, this problem can be fatal. Lesions may become infected with Gram-negative organisms or fungi (Frye, 1991a). Blisters under an animal's scales are caused by a constantly damp environment. Living quarters should be warm (i.e., at the affected animal's selected body temperature). Giant boids void large amounts of fluids, that may result in excessively wet, unhygienic conditions. This problem is avoided by housing them in open-bottom cages (Fig. 41, Chapter 3).

Abscesses should be treated by draining the vesicles and applying antiseptic solution. Ross (pers. comm.) suggested liberally coating the affected area(s) with Polysporin® ointment (Appendix XII), and administering parenteral antibiotic therapy based on bacterial culture results. To hasten shedding, Zwart (1972) suggested the administration of parenteral vitamin A (also see Vitamin A Toxicity, Chapter 4).

Affected animals should be isolated, maintained on clean paper and in a dry environment. Water should be provided ad libitum in a small, heavy bowl and parenteral fluids should be administered if the animal has become dehydrated.

Bacterial Enteritis

Ross and Marzec (1984) reported that the causative organisms are *Salmonella* and *Arizona*. As discussed under Personal Hygiene above, *Salmonella* has been transmitted to humans via reptiles, and is becoming an increasing problem (Evans, 1994) as these animals gain popularity as pets. Marcus (1981) reported that 25 to 50% of turtles in pet shops have harbored *Salmonella* and *Arizona* without ill effects. *Salmonella* and *Arizona* are normal gut flora of chelonians; however, these bacteria may cause reptiles to become sick if they are stressed sufficiently by adverse environmental conditions or other diseases.

Clinical signs of bacterial enteritis include anorexia, lethargy, weight loss, and diarrhea. In some cases, stools may be mixed with blood and/or green-gray mucus. Ross and Marzec (1984) also reported that some animals display exaggerated peristaltic-like movements. When any one or more of these symptoms are observed, a fecal culture should be performed. A negative fecal culture does not necessarily mean an animal is free of infection because the bacterium is shed at varying rates. Marcus (1981) recommended that reptiles treated with antibiotics require sequential fecal

cultures for several weeks after the treatment has been discontinued. The administration of antibiotics may cause cessation of bacterial shedding in feces for up to eight weeks (Siebeling et al., 1975) even though the reptile will continue to harbor the bacteria.

Weber (1973) treated tortoises for *Salmonella* infection with 50 mg of oxytetracycline orally for six days. Because of the infectious nature and the zoonotic hazards of Salmonellosis, affected reptiles should be isolated. Until a cure can be affected, handlers should use extreme caution during the treatment period. To prevent the disease from spreading to other animals and humans, feces, urine, and infected reptile eggs should be considered a biological hazard and disposed of accordingly.

One differential diagnosis for bacterial enteritis is parasitism. Therefore, in addition to fecal cultures, one should also have stools examined for amebae and gastrointestinal helminths. If amebae are present, begin treatment immediately (Appendix XII). Another differential diagnosis is an infection of *Aeromonas hydrophila* (Marcus, 1981). According to Ross and Marzec (1984), treatments include one of the following: ampicillin, amoxicillin, tetracycline, chloramphenicol, or trimethoprim-sulfa. Antibiotic therapy should be administered orally, via stomach tube, for optimum effectiveness.

Cloacal Prolapses (Fig. 67)

Reptiles may suffer prolapsed cloacae during egg laying, when constipated, or because of pressure from an abnormal mass. A remedy used over many years is

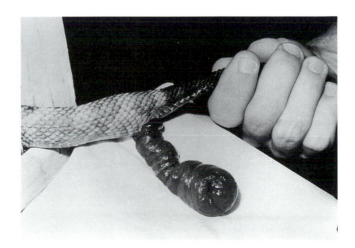

Fig. 67 Cloacal prolapse in a tropical rattlesnake (*Crotalus durissus*). Photo courtesy of the College of Veterinary Medicine, Small Animal Clinic, University of Auburn.

the application of sugar directly on the prolapsed tissue. Murphy and Collins (1983) also reported the use of ice baths. Another method is the application of an electrolyte powder (Appendix XII) (Cruickshank, pers. comm.). Once the swelling is sufficiently reduced, the prolapsed tissue is coated with an antibiotic ointment and the vent held open while the everted tissue is replaced. A compress or purse-string suture is used to hold the vent closed for several days to reduce the chance of another prolapse. In some cases, sedation may be required to prevent the animal from straining further. In all cases, the underlying problem must be identified and treated.

Cloacitis

Causes of this problem may include improper use of sexing probes, irritation from the presence of a uric acid calculus (Cooper, 1981), or substrate material such as sand particles becoming lodged in the cloaca. Depending on the severity of the problem, clinical signs include tissue swelling, ulceration, and in some cases, bleeding of the cloacal tissues and associated structures. Treatment consists of determining the cause of infection and applying the appropriate topical antibiotic ointment. In severe cases, parenteral antibiotics should be administered. Ross and Marzec (1984) do not consider cloacitis as a distinct disease, but a nonspecific disease where opportunistic Gram-negative bacteria become invasive. Reptiles being treated for cloacitis must be maintained on clean paper towels to prevent contamination of the affected area.

Dysecdysis (Retained Shed)

Shedding problems may be due to the following:

- Ambient temperature too high.

- Humidity too low.

- Stresses including excessive handling, loud noises, vibrations or overcrowding.

- No shedding implement provided (e.g., log, rock, etc.).

- Malnutrition.

- Skin problems such as trauma or dermatitis.

- Systemic disorders.

- Hyperthyroidism.

- Hypothyroidism.

Depending on the severity of the retained shed (Fig. 68), it can be removed by soaking the affected animal in a shallow, tepid water bath (Fig. 69) or saturated sphagnum moss (Fig. 70) for 1 to 8 hours (overnight in

Fig. 68 Adhered shed on a reticulated python (*Python reticulatus*). Reprinted with permission from Jacobson, 1977.

some cases). As an alternative to lengthy soaking, hydrogen peroxide can be added to the water bath in a ratio of 1:1 (Barnard, 1985b). This will aid in separating the retained shed, or retained eye caps, from the animal's body. Before adding hydrogen peroxide to the water bath, allow the reptile time to consume clean water. When using hydrogen peroxide to treat dysecdysis, it should not be necessary to soak an animal for more than 30 to 60 minutes. If equal parts of hydrogen peroxide and water do not cause a foaming reaction, add more hydrogen peroxide until the desired effect is achieved. Be sure the hydrogen peroxide has not expired.

As a cautionary note, I have observed rare instances in which a retained shed could not be removed by

Fig. 69 Soaking a snake in shallow, tepid water is a common method for removing adhered sheds. Be sure the container is securely covered to prevent an escape. Photo courtesy of BROMOfoto.

Fig. 70 When attempting to remove an adhered shed from a snake, it may become necessary to place the animal in a container with saturated sphagnum moss. Photo courtesy of BROMOfoto.

peroxide/water soaking. In three cases the sheds became even more adhered and had a flaked appearance. Unfortunately, the underlying cause of the problem was not identified.

Hyperthermia, Hypothermia

Hyperthermia is often caused by faulty thermostats, improperly placed lamps, or excessive exposure to the sun's heat (also see The Captive Environment, Chapter 3). This condition is usually fatal and the animal is found dead in its cage with its mouth open (Frye, 1981b, 1991a). Rosskopf (1977–78) described overheating in tortoises, and warned that tortoises will literally bake in their shells if shade is not provided.

Another situation occurs during combat between male tortoises (see Reproduction and Egg Incubation, Chapter 6). One male may cause the other to be knocked over. If the animal cannot right itself, it will die from stress and overheating. When found, it may be hot to the touch, foaming at the mouth, or vomiting. When a reptile has been overheated but is still alive, it should be placed in a cool water bath to drop its body temperature. In addition, the administration of physiological saline subcutaneously may be indicated (Frye, 1981b, 1991a). In some cases, a

hyperthermic reptile suffers burns. If burns are present, treat as outlined under Trauma. Any reptile that has been overheated should be monitored carefully for several days.

Hypothermia may occur when heat lamps are not employed or placed improperly. Symptoms of hypothermia may include serous nasal discharge in tortoises (Frye, 1981b, 1991a), and Vogel (1964) reported tearing in crocodilians that had been chilled. Chronic low temperatures prevent digestion of food because insufficient digestive enzymes are produced in the animal's stomach, and function is impaired. Consequently, food may ferment in the gastrointestinal tract, resulting in tympanitic colic (Wallach, 1971), vomiting, or passage in an undigested state. Ultimately, an animal starves to death or dies from infection.

Temperatures that drop to or below freezing will cause frostbite. Symptoms are loss of skin coloration, tissue necrosis and dry gangrene (Frye, 1981b, 1991a). Symptoms may not be apparent for several days or weeks. Treatment consists of increasing the environmental temperature to the species' appropriate selected body temperature (Table 1, Chapter 3) over two or three hours. Those areas that become infected should be gently, but thoroughly, cleansed and treated with an antibiotic ointment. Animals recovering from hypothermia, and those that were burned when they overheated, should be housed on clean paper towels.

Hypoglycemia in Crocodilians

Clinical signs are upward gazing and dilation of pupils (Fig. 64), swimming in circles, tremors and loss of the righting reflex. This condition has been described by Wallach et al. (1967), and is likely to occur in winter, and in spring when blood glucose of crocodilians may be at the lowest level. Such stressful conditions as low temperatures, overcrowding, excessive vibrations and handling may bring on a hypoglycemic attack. It is essential to eliminate the stressful factors, provide the animal with its selected body temperature and administer parenteral or oral glucose when necessary.

Increased Shedding Frequencies

This condition is normal when an animal has suffered a traumatic injury to its skin. Increased shedding frequencies is a function of healing. Frye (1981b) reported that this condition was also associated with hyperthyroidism. Dermatitis is still another pathological cause of abnormal shedding.

Mycotic Dermatitis in Aquatic Turtles (White Spot Disease)

Multiple white and gray foci and shell pitting are the recognizable symptoms of this disease that is caused by a variety of fungi. Turtles exhibiting white spot disease should be removed from their water environment and placed in a dry cage at their selected body temperature (Table 1, Chapter 3). Infected animals should only be returned to water for about an hour each day for feeding, drinking and excretory functions (be sure to change water daily). The affected area(s) should be debrided until the tissue appears healthy. The healthy tissue should then be swabbed one or two times daily with povidone iodine solution, followed by a liberal application of an antifungal cream. At Zoo Atlanta, miconazole antifungal cream has been effective in treating turtles with mycotic dermatitis. Before reapplying fresh medication, remove creams that were applied previously. Containers used during the daily "dry treatment" should be disinfected and rinsed thoroughly between uses.

Necrotizing Dermatitis (Scale Rot)

Excessively humid conditions, suboptimal temperatures, malnutrition, poor hygienic practices, ectoparasites, and other trauma are conditions under which scale rot occurs. Symptoms of this disorder include retained sheds and/or focal lesions. These lesions may involve large areas. In severe cases, scale erosion and ulceration occur. If the infection is untreated, it may invade the abdomen, resulting in peritonitis.

It is important to remove retained sheds (see Dysecdysis), followed by the application of the appropriate topical antibiotic ointment or antifungal cream to the affected area(s).

Ross and Marzec (1984) considered necrotizing dermatitis to be a Gram-negative bacterial problem and suggested applying Polysporin® ointment (Appendix XII) on the affected areas in mild cases. In severe cases, administer parenteral aminoglycoside therapy. Chloramphenicol also may be effective in less severe cases.

When lizards exhibit clinical signs of necrotizing dermatitis, daily exposure to natural sunlight, in addition to the treatment just described, is often effective. Care should be taken not to expose a lizard to its thermal maximum (Table 1, Chapter 3). All animals suffering scale rot must be maintained at their selected body temperature until a cure is effected.

As discussed under Housing in Chapter 3, semiaquatic snakes should be maintained in the same manner as the terrestrial ones (see Fig. 37, Chapter 3), and giant boids should be housed in open-bottom cages (see Fig. 41, Chapter 3) to allow voided fluids to drain from the enclosures.

Oropharyngeal Cellulitis

Frye (1991a) reported that this disease was most often a consequence of, and extension of, ulcerative stomatitis in snakes. Ross and Marzec (1984) distinguished this disease from ulcerative stomatitis by the absence of necrotic or caseous tissue; however, there may be a loose caseous exudate. These authors reported that oropharyngeal cellulitis produces pronounced edema and inflammation of the deep tissues of the oropharynx, and may produce soft-tissue swelling around the head and neck.

Causes may include any abrasive object or material that contact and damage the oropharynx. For example, careless insertion of a feeding catheter, or ingestion of abrasive substrates, may cause oropharyngitis.

Treatment is the same as for mouth rot (discussed below under Ulcerative Stomatitis). When the soft tissues of the head and neck are involved, those areas should not be injected locally. Maintain affected reptiles within their selected body temperatures. Also, see information on thermotherapy which is discussed under Respiratory Disease.

Panophthalmitis (Ophthalnologic Disease)

All reptiles are susceptible to eye infections. Cooper (1981) and Ross and Marzec (1984) reported that ocular infections range from mild conjunctivitis in crocodilians, chelonians and lizards, to more serious subspectacular infections in snakes. Cooper (1981) reported that the etiology of panophthalmitis to be blood-borne infections from the oropharynx. Marcus (1981) suggested that the exudate produced from ulcerative stomatitis may block the duct of the Harderian gland. Ross and Marzec (1984) noted that ophthalnologic disease may be found as an isolated condition as well, since reptiles with this disorder may not have any other infections.

Clinical signs of infection are first observed as cloudiness of the affected eye which may be mistaken for "normal bluing" (Fig. 71) during ecdysis. However, normal opacity of spectacles occurs in both eyes. In some cases the observer may merely see a slight enlargement of one eye (Fig. 72). As the infection progresses the eye will be swollen and filled with a thick yellow-white material.

Cooper (1981) suggested treating milder forms of this disease with tetracycline or chloramphenicol. Ross and

Fig. 71 Normal "bluing" of contact lenses in a snake preparing to shed. Immediately prior to shedding, this effect disappears. Photo courtesy of Rick E. Perry.

Marzec (1984) treat the milder forms with daily irrigation of the oropharynx, followed by an oral application of Polysporin® ointment. In addition to topical therapy, these authors also administer a parenteral aminoglycoside or chloramphenicol. If the infection becomes so advanced that parenteral antibiotic therapy is of no value, enucleation is necessary to prevent subsequent osteomyelitis or septicemia.

Fig. 72 Panophthalmitis is characterized by swelling of the eye. Photo courtesy of Richard A. Ross.

Poisoning (Plant and Chemical)

Accidental poisoning of reptiles can occur when pesticides and disinfectants are used indiscriminantly, or possibly when herbivorous reptiles are allowed to graze on toxic plants outdoors. Pesticides may also affect developing embryos and cause birth defects (Bellairs, 1981). When it is known that a herbivorous reptile has ingested toxic material, administer a warm water gastric lavage to remove stomach contents. Also, consult a veterinarian immediately for supportive therapy such as the administration of activated charcoal, calcium gluconate, atropine sulfate, diuretics and fluids (Appendix XII).

Appendix IX is a list of poisonous plants that are known to be toxic to humans and many animals when ingested. Tortoises and the green iguana (*Iguana iguana*), however, may be able to eat many of those plants with no ill effects. Generally, the likelihood of toxicity depends on the amounts ingested. It is difficult to say just how much concern plant poisoning is in reptiles because very few cases have been published.

Rosskopf (1977–78) reported plant poisoning in reptiles from oleander (*Nerium oleander*), rhubarb (*Rheum rhaponticum*) leaves, and marijuana (*Cannabis sativa*). Frye (1991a) reported that the feeding of excessive amounts of fresh spinach can induce the formation of calcium oxalate crystals in urine and tissues. Animals may be poisoned by ingesting plants overhanging or growing into enclosures from nearby trees, shrubs, vines, or from flower pots. Besides tossing popcorn and cotton candy to zoo inhabitants, the public also may feed leaves of poisonous plants to these animals. It is also very likely that anyone keeping reptiles, who is eager to provide a natural diet for herbivorous turtles and lizards, may include some poisonous varieties in their salads. It is important that keepers of reptiles be able to identify all such plants accurately.

Respiratory Disease (Pneumonia)

Respiratory disease is a general diagnosis, and there can be a variety of causes including parasites, fungi, bacteria, viruses, and chemical inhalation. Marcus (1981) reported that if untreated, bacterial pneumonia is usually fatal within 2 to 3 weeks from its onset.

The symptoms vary with severity, and include nasal and oral discharge (pneumonia can be confused with early stages of mouth rot), gaping, audible and labored breathing, depression, anorexia, and emaciation. Chelonians will often list to one side when swimming.

Sudden or prolonged low temperatures, and other types of stress are major contributing factors of pneumonia in reptiles. It is essential, therefore, that the affected animal's selected body temperature be met for about 12 to 16 hours per day, and nighttime temperatures should not drop below 29.5°C (85°F) during the treatment period (Ross, pers. comm.).

Ross and Marzec (1984) described the effective use of thermotherapy for the treatment of respiratory disease in infant D'albert's water pythons (*Liasis albertisii*). These animals were too small to administer an accurate dosage of aminoglycoside. The specimens were maintained at constant temperatures of 35–36.1°C (95–97°F) for 3 weeks. These authors also treated a Macklot's python (*Liasis mackloti*) successfully for 10 days, and two ball pythons (*Python regius*) for 2 weeks at 33.3°C (92°F). Thermotherapy temperatures are based on the high end of an animal's selected body temperature (Table 1, Chapter 3). Ross and Marzec (1984) published the following thermotherapy temperatures:

Genus	Day Temp. C°(F)	Night Temp. C°(F)
Python	31.1–33.3 (88–92)	26.6 (80)
Colubrid snakes (temperate zones)	29.4–31.1 (85–88)	23.9 (75)
Desert-dwelling snakes	32.2–35.0 (90–95)	26.6–29.4 (80–85)

Ectothermic animals naturally seek warmth (behavioral fever) in response to infection. Kluger (1978) demonstrated that infected desert iguanas (*Dipsosaurus dorsalis*) offered higher than normal temperatures survived over those lizards not offered such temperatures. Lang (1987) experimented with the American alligator (*Alligator mississippiensis*). After infecting the crocodilians with *Aeromonas hydrophila*, he offered them a range of temperatures from 30.0 to 35.1°C (86.0 to 95.2°F). The mean temperature selected by the infected reptiles was 33.0°C (91.4°F). Some were held constantly at 35°C (95°F) which resulted in their deaths. Cooper et al. (1985) reported that optimum temperatures are required for proper immune response, and immune responses are depressed at too high or low temperatures. Investigations by these authors suggest that reptiles have a better opportunity for successful recovery from pneumonia and other diseases if offered a range of temperatures within their thermal preference (Table 1, Chapter 3), rather than inducing immune response by a predetermined or constantly high temperature.

Ross and Marzec (1984) described two types of pneumonia, Type I and Type II. Type I can be differentiated from Type II by the kind of nasal discharge produced and degree of wheezing. Type I produces a thin clear mucus and Type II produces thick and/or yellowish opaque mucus. Antibiotic treatment for Type I includes chloramphenicol, tetracycline, ampicillin or tylosin. Chloramphenicol is the drug of choice. However, these authors reported that Type II pneumonia requires the administration of an aminoglycoside. Without sensitivity testing to determine the causative microorganism, one cannot be sure which antibiotic is appropriate. If the disease has been detected early, one may wish to begin treatment with a nonaminoglycoside. If a cure is not effected, or if improvement is not obvious within a week, one should begin aminoglycoside therapy. Verminous pneumonias should be treated with parasiticides (Appendix XII).

Chemical pneumonia can occur when fumes from aromatic products are inhaled by reptiles. A few of these products include oil-base finishes, formaldehyde in pressed board, disinfectants, and pine and cedar woodchips. Affected reptiles can be treated with an antihistamine such as tripelennamine hydrochloride injection at a dosage of 0.25 ml per 10 lb of body weight.

Septicemia

Heywood (1968) implicated the snake mite, *Ophionyssus natricis*, in transmitting *Aeromonas hydrophila* because he had observed that young septicemic snakes were often infested with these ectoparasites. Septicemia is more likely to occur when open wounds make contact with contaminated soil or water, although localized infections such as ulcerative stomatitis and pneumonia may become systemic if allowed to progress untreated.

Septicemia is a life-threatening disease process. Symptoms in reptiles include petechiae on mucosal surfaces, and in the terminal stages of infection, animals convulse or become comatose (Marcus, 1981). Rapid dehydration (within 24–48 hours) can lead to renal failure, resulting in the reptile's death. In the early stages, however, septicemic animals may be lethargic, weak, and anorectic. Since these symptoms also may be demonstrated in the presence of localized infections, septicemia is difficult to diagnose early.

Gram-negative organisms are the primary cause of septicemia, and the drugs of choice are aminoglycosides. If treatment is in progress for a localized infection and the infection has progressed to septicemia, use of a different aminoglycoside may be necessary. Sensitivity testing is advisable due to the critical nature of the disease process. Prevention of this problem, like so many others, depends on good hygiene and optimal environmental conditions.

Septicemic Cutaneous Ulcerative Disease (SCUD)

Primarily found in soft-shelled turtles (family Trionychidae), the causative organism of this disorder was reported to be *Citrobacter freundii* (Doyle and Moreland, 1968; Kaplan, 1957). Ross and Marzec (1984) also cultured *Pseudomonas, Klebsiella* and *Serratia*. Many Gram-negative bacteria are found in soil, water, and in the intestinal tracts of various animals, and can cause disease when animals come in contact with abrasive substrates and contaminated water. In the early stages of SCUD, the affected area(s) on an animal's plastron may appear reddish; softening of the shell follows. As the disease progresses, the lesions may turn light gray or yellowish. Often the turtle's legs are also affected.

Symptoms include anorexia, cutaneous ulceration and hemorrhage, lethargy, loss of digits and paralysis (Frye, 1981a; Marcus, 1981). Death may occur if lesions are not discovered in time for treatment. Marcus (1981) recommended chloramphenicol, IM or IP at an initial dose of 8 mg/100g of body weight followed by 4 mg/100g of body weight twice daily for 7 days. No mention was made by the author if there should be a reduction for the weight of the animal's shell. Supportive therapy with parenteral vitamin A, B and C was suggested by Frye (1981a, 1991a). Ross and Marzec (1984) reported using aminoglycoside therapy at a dosage published by Bush et al. (1980). The recommended dosage for turtles is 10 mg/kg every 48 hours with no reduction for the weight of the animal's shell. The affected area(s) should be debrided daily with a gentle abrasive such as a soft bristle toothbrush, followed by the application of Polysporin® ointment. Ross and Marzec (1984) also suggested maintaining the pH of the water at 6.0 with sodium biphosphate (Appendix XII) because most Gram-negative bacteria involved in reptilian diseases are inhibited by acidity.

As with many diseases of semiaquatic animals, affected reptiles should be removed from their water environment, and maintained at their selected body temperature (Table 1, Chapter 3) in a dry cage. However, allow these animals access to water for feeding, drinking and excretory functions for at least one hour daily until a cure is effected.

Stress

Stress is a term used widely among herpetologists and may be the most common factor in the disease process in captive reptiles. Newly captured animals feel these effects much more intensely than captive-born reptiles. Stress experiments have shown that some rattlesnakes possess the ability to recognize predators through olfaction (Cowles and Phelan, 1958). With the use of electrocardiographs, these authors showed that kingsnakes (*Lampropeltis*) and humans elicited fear in certain rattlesnakes. They also showed that even low intensity vibrations seriously affected the more nervous species. Clarke and Marx (1960) demonstrated that merely entering a room in which red rattlesnakes (*Crotalus ruber*) were housed, increased the heart rate of these animals. Therefore, in addition to providing proper nutrition and optimal hygiene, stress-inducing factors must be corrected. The cleanest cages and finest meals cannot prevent disease when an animal is stressed; more realistically, animals will refuse to feed when stressed.

Causes of stress also include prolonged low temperatures, inappropriate photoperiods, no provision for hiding, loud noises, excessive vibrations, excessive handling, and incompatible cage mates. There are situations in which a reptile is housed under apparently ideal conditions, yet animals fail to thrive. Cowan (1968) referred to this dilemma as "Maladaptation Syndrome."

Trauma

Veterinarians are faced with frequent requests to repair shell fractures in wild chelonians that have been hit by automobiles or chewed by dogs. Hoof and dental repair materials are just some of the common materials used for shell repair. Although euthanasia may be the only solution for some injuries, many animals can be saved. Frye (1981a, 1991a) discussed surgical techniques for the repair of many injuries.

As a direct consequence of captivity, reptiles suffer a variety of traumatic injuries. The following are common causes of accidental injuries and deaths in captive reptiles:

Animal Escapes

Reptiles commonly escape when they are housed in poorly constructed cages, when they are removed from their cages for exercising, or when they are transported improperly. Small reptiles may find their way to the outdoors and are never retrieved. Many escapees have been mangled in automobile seats, bedsprings and in one instance, a California kingsnake (*Lampropeltis getulus californiae*) was found dead in a mousetrap.

Actually, no reptile has to be removed from caging for exercising, "show and tell," (Fig. 73) or "socializing." These animals prefer not to be handled. Although all reptiles require a certain amount of exercise, this can be achieved with appropriately sized and safely constructed enclosures. Those individuals who own reptiles

Fig. 73 Many snake owners enjoy showing off their pets to friends. Have you ever seen this "scenario"? Handling reptiles is stressful to them and should be avoided unless absolutely necessary. When it does become necessary to pick one up, it should not be draped around one's neck. Even a snake of this size is capable of killing its owner, and the risk of an accident to either the snake or its owner is much greater when the owner is intoxicated. Photo courtesy of BROMOfoto.

must not expect their charges to interact with them in the same manner as do pet mammals and birds.

Burns

Faulty thermostats on heating devices and inappropriately placed lamps are major causes of burns in captive reptiles. All lamps should be located on the cage exterior. When lamps are mounted inside the cage, reptiles attempt to lie against them. A gradient of temperatures within the cage is essential. Reptiles may become burned severely when "hot spots" reach excessive temperatures (Fig. 74). Sick or subdominant animals are often unable to move to more favorable temperatures.

Burns should be cleansed gently, followed by an application of an antibiotic ointment. Ross (pers. comm.) emphasized that ointments used in such cases are meant to be dressings in the prevention of infection, and are not effective in the treatment of infected burns.

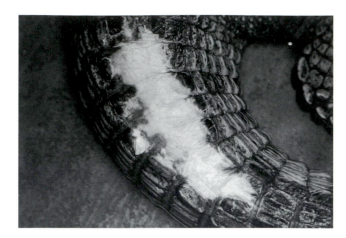

Fig. 74 Scarring on a gavial (*Gavialis gangenticus*) from improper placement of heat lamps. Photo courtesy of Clarence Dunning, Jr.

Also apply a moist, sterile cover to burns to help prevent the loss of body fluids. Fluid therapy is necessary when burns are severe. Loose substrates adhere to moist surfaces, therefore house burned reptiles on clean paper towels or newspaper.

Bites, Cannibalism

Bite wounds (Fig. 75) inflicted by cage mates occur when two or more reptiles are fed within the same enclosure. It is advisable, therefore, to separate cage mates far enough from each other when feeding them. Each animal should be offered food individually, or the more aggressive feeder(s) should be removed from the cage. Reptiles may sometimes be discouraged from stealing each other's food by misting the aggressors with cold water. Exceptions to these suggestions in-

Fig. 75 Bite wounds, as seen on this reticulated python (*Python reticulatus*), occur when two or more reptiles are fed within the same enclosure. Photo courtesy of Carl L. Ponder.

clude some perching reptiles (e.g., certain lizards). These animals may need to be stimulated into feeding through interaction with hungry conspecifics.

Another cause of bite wounds occurs when a reptile is offered live prey. The prey often bites in self-defense. There is rarely a good reason to feed live prey to reptiles. Even venomous snakes readily consume dead prey.

When bite wounds involve skin or muscle, they should be cleansed and sutured if the prey has not chewed away so much skin that closure is impossible. If this occurs, treat the injury as an "open" wound (Frye 1981b). For example, it must be kept clean and allowed to heal through granulation. Reptiles with such wounds should be kept on clean paper towels to prevent contaminated substrate particles from adhering to the exposed areas. Treatment for bite wounds include topical and parenteral antibiotics (Appendix XII).

Reptiles suffering bites from cage mates or prey tend to increase their shedding frequencies. As discussed previously, this is normal, but supportive therapy may be indicated. When the injured animal sheds, wounds may reopen. A topical antibiotic ointment should be applied to the freshly exposed area.

When possible, avoid housing cannibalistic reptiles together. The incidence of cannibalism can be reduced if animals such as kingsnakes (*Lampropeltis*), racers (*Coluber*), indigos (*Drymarcon*) and king cobras (*Ophiophagus hannah*) are housed separately. If it becomes necessary to put such reptiles together for breeding, then choose animals of equal size and do not leave them unattended.

Crushing

Falling cage props account for most crushing injuries. These injuries require medical equipment and expertise beyond that of the keeper. If crushing is suspected, seek veterinary care immediately for the injured animal.

Drowning

Reptiles, especially tortoises allowed to graze outdoors, may fall accidently into drainage ditches, ponds, or swimming pools. Hatchlings may drown in water bowls within their cages. These animals become exhausted when struggling to remain at the water's surface and they eventually drown.

Tortoises are capable of surviving relatively long periods of oxygen deprivation and hypoxia (Cooper, 1984; Frye, 1981b, 1991a). Occasionally these animals may actually be alive even though they appear dead. Therefore, it is sometimes possible to save the life of a chelonian after it has been found at the bottom of a body of water. It should be taken to a veterinary

practitioner who has the facility to administer oxygen and measure plasma electrolytes, etc. As in any drowning, first aid should be started. With light suction, aspirate the water from the tortoise's mouth and nares while holding it with its head in a downward position. As quickly as possible, oxygen should be administered. Those finding themselves in such a situation are urged to give a chelonian that "outside" chance for survival.

Nose Rubbing (Fig. 76)

This is a common condition observed in poorly adapted or "nervous" reptiles. With few exceptions, the best prevention of nose rubbing is to avoid the use of wire mesh in caging. Many reptiles, however, will still rub against glass-fronted enclosures. In such cases, the cage glass can be covered on the outside with opaque materials such as paint, newspaper or black plastic. A small observation area can be provided, allowing the keeper to monitor the progress of the animal.

When nose rubbing causes loss of tissue, exposing the bone of the rostral area, treat with an antibiotic ointment and house the injured animal on clean paper towels until it has fully healed.

Owner-induced Trauma

Common causes include improper removal of eye caps, or improper force-feeding and restraint techniques.

Plant Injuries

In nature, tortoises are probably more prone to injuries from plants than most other reptiles. In the United States, captive tortoises that are tethered to a stake or allowed to roam in the backyard may encounter such

Fig. 76 An example of nose rubbing. Note the missing scales on the end of the snake's snout. Photo courtesy of BROMOfoto.

injurious plants as are listed in Appendix X. Symptoms of mechanical injury vary depending on the part of the body in which a plant fragment is lodged. Consider the following examples:

Eyes	Lacrimation, purulent discharge, ulceration, blindness
Mouth	Excessive salivation, tissue swelling, ulcers
Skin	Lesions, abscesses
Gastrointestinal tract	Impaction (from plant hairs, or phytobezoars)
Limbs	Lameness (from plant fragments)

Treatment includes the removal of any plant fragment that can be reached. Lesions should be cleaned and infections treated with an appropriate antibiotic.

Ulcerative Shell Disease

Also known as "shell rot" or "spot disease," this contagious and chronic problem affects freshwater turtles and is reportedly caused by *Benecka chitinovora,* a Gram-negative bacillus (Marcus, 1981; Wallach, 1976). Fungi also contribute to this disease (Frye, 1981a, 1991a). Transmission is possible from one turtle to another. Also, transmission may occur when other animals such as crayfish, lobsters, and crabs are introduced into the enclosure. This condition is characterized by the loosening and shedding of shell plates. Frye (1981a) described small accumulations of brick-red to orange exudate which may fill pitted areas.

Treatment includes local curettage (Wallach, 1977), parenteral chloramphenicol, and topical antiseptics (Marcus, 1981). Frye (1981a, 1991a) suggested painting debrided areas daily with povidone iodine, Malachite green, or potassium permanganate solutions until healing has been achieved.

Ulcerative Stomatitis (Mouth Rot; Canker) (Fig. 65)

Mouth rot is a disease of the oral mucosa and can occur in any reptile, although less commonly in chelonians. Gray et al. (1966) and Page (1966) reported *Aeromonas* and *Pseudomonas* to be among the causative organisms of this condition. Symptoms include salivation, and in more advanced cases, caseous exudate. Still other symptoms include edema and inflammation of the oral mucosa, gingival petechiae, granulomatous gingivitis, and ulceration. Many animals with mouth rot are anorectic and may starve because the act of feeding is painful. Mouth rot can lead to aspiration pneumonia,

septicemia, oropharyngitis, and osteomyelitis. Some causes of mouth rot are improper hygiene, malnutrition, trauma, exposure to a prolonged low temperature, and systemic diseases.

Treatment is dependent on the "type" of canker present. Ross and Marzec (1984) described two distinct types of canker, Type I and Type II. These authors stated that Type I canker is associated with the less resistant or less invasive strains of *Pseudomonas* or other Gram-negative pathogens. It is distinguished from Type II by the easy removal of necrotic tissue from the underlying mucous membranes. It is treated by frequent removal of necrotic tissue and daily applications of Polysporin® ointment. Ross and Marzec (1984) also reported that daily debriding and flushing (Fig. 77) of the oral mucosa with ordinary tap water could effect a cure in the milder cases of Type I mouth rot. However, most professionals prefer to irrigate with povidone iodine, followed by a dressing with an antiseptic ointment. The treatment regime for Type I canker will not effect a cure for Type II, which requires

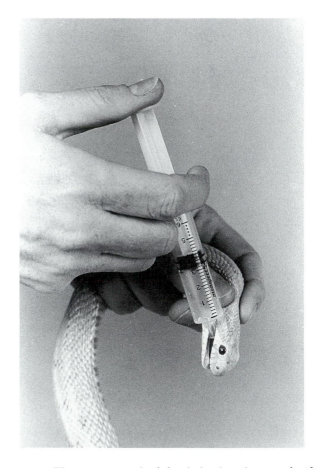

Fig. 77 The proper method for irrigating the mouth of a snake. The animal should always be held in a downward position to prevent it from aspirating the contents of the syringe. Photo courtesy of BROMOfoto.

treatment with an aminoglycoside antibiotic. Daily debridement is also necessary and, unlike Type I, the affected tissue adheres tightly to the underlying mucous membranes.

Burke et al. (1978) emphasized the need to culture recurrent or resistant cases of ulcerative stomatitis, rather than merely switching drugs if a cure is not effected. For example, he reported a case in which he treated ulcerative stomatitis with gentamicin. The problem reoccurred, and parenteral kanamycin was then used. The culture showed a yeast infection which followed the antibiotic therapy. After the animal was treated with 20,000 units of nystatin suspension, twice daily (atomized into the oral cavity) for 15 days, the infection cleared.

PARASITES

Several factors precipitate outbreaks of parasitic infections in captive reptiles. These may include immunologic capacity, age, marked changes in diet and temperature, overcrowding and general health of the host (Cowan, 1980; Keymer, 1981; Marcus, 1981; Soifer, 1978; Telford, 1971). Additional factors include the species and number of parasites, their migratory pathway, metabolic activity in the host and mode of feeding (Flynn, 1973; Frank, 1981a; Frye, 1991a; Reichenbach-Klinke and Elkan, 1965; Soulsby, 1968). Outbreaks also occur when infected prey, which serve as intermediate hosts, are inadvertently fed to captive reptiles.

Endoparasites

If a stool is unavailable, a tepid, saline enema can be administered. Depending on the type of parasite, diagnosis is made by the presence of the mature organism, cysts, larvae and/or eggs in the feces. I obtain the best diagnostic results by direct fecal smears and sedimentations. Many structures are destroyed upon flotation, and some structures, such as parasitic larvae, may be missed altogether.

For diagnostic information, the reader should consult Barnard (1983, 1986a,b) and Barnard and Upton (1994), as well as the references listed in the parasite discussions below.

Protozoa

Many protozoa form cysts or spores to protect themselves against adverse conditions, which also may serve to aid in transmission of the parasite from one host to another. Major taxonomic groups of protozoa are defined, in part, on locomotive anatomical structures (e.g., cilia, flagella, pseudopodia).

Amebae

Hosts include all reptiles. Amebae are characterized by the presence of pseudopodia. They may also possess flagella that are generally restricted to temporary, developmental reproductive or dispersal stages. Although most amebae are enteric, some may be found in the brain, respiratory tract, stomach, liver, spleen, and kidneys.

The life cycles of all amebae are direct, and transmission is by ingestion of infective cysts. The pathogenicity depends on the host. For example, amebic infections may have few or no deleterious effects in chelonians and crocodilians. Lizards and snakes, on the other hand, may exhibit one or more of the following: anorexia, weight loss, blood and/or mucus in stools, and vomiting.

Diagnosis is made by microscopic examination of feces or sputum. Treatment for pathogenic amebae (see Appendix XII) is usually unsuccessful. Meerovitch (1961), however, demonstrated that the severity of amebiasis is lowered when snakes are maintained at 35°C (95°F) as opposed to 25°C (75°F). Because reptiles can dehydrate quickly at high temperatures, they must be monitored carefully.

As one can see, preventing amebic infections is essential. It is best to avoid housing lizards or snakes with turtles or crocodilians. Furthermore, house animals by geographic region (e.g., do not mix boas and pythons).

Flagellates

Hosts include all reptiles. Although most flagellates are enteric, some species may be found on the dermis or in the circulatory system.

Depending on the parasite species, life cycles are either direct or indirect. Transmission is usually by ingestion of the trophozoites or, if present, cysts. However, those flagellates inhabiting the circulatory system are transmitted by the bite of an invertebrate intermediate host. Pathogenicity of flagellates varies according to species, age, and general health of the reptile, as well as the type of flagellate present. Symptoms of infection include enteritis, lethargy, anorexia, and weight loss.

Diagnosis of enteric species is by microscopic demonstration of motile organisms in FRESH feces using the direct smear technique. The reader should refer to Appendix XII for treatment.

Opalinids

Reported hosts included monitor lizards (Lavier, 1927; Reichenbach-Klinke and Elkan, 1965), the false yarara, *Xenodon meremmii*, and a South American ground snake, *Liophis jaegeri* (Frank, 1984). Opalinids are covered with cilia/flagella, and inhabit either the host's colon or cloaca.

The life cycle of *Opalina* spp. in reptiles is unknown; however, it is thought to be direct. Transmission is probably by ingestion of infective cysts. There is no evidence of pathogenicity.

Diagnosis is by microscopic demonstration of trophozoites or cysts in fresh feces using the direct smear technique. No treatment has been reported in reptiles.

Ciliates

Primarily parasites of tortoises, ciliates also infect lizards and snakes. Generally, reptilian ciliates are enteric, but some species may be found on the outer body surface of aquatic reptiles.

Ciliates have a direct life cycle. Trophozoites of body-surface ciliates attach to the host's skin and form colonies. Transmission of intestinal ciliates is by ingestion of infective cysts. Both forms can be detected by microscopic examination. I prefer the sedimentation technique for examining enteric species. It should be noted that cysts of *Nyctotherus* spp. are routinely misdiagnosed as digenetic trematode eggs. To avoid this problem, see Barnard and Upton (1994). These authors show typical *Nyctotherus* structures.

Balantidium spp. may be pathogenic when present in large numbers, or in association with other parasites or pathogenic bacteria (Flynn, 1973; Keymer, 1981). *Nyctotherus* spp., however, are thought to assist the host in the digestion of complex carbohydrates (Frye, 1991a). Unless a ciliate is causing apparent harm to its host (such as symptoms of colitis or enteritis), no treatment is indicated. In the event a reptile needs medicating, refer to Appendix XII.

Coccidia

Hosts include all reptilian groups. Depending on the coccidian species and developmental stage, these parasites may be found in many areas of the reptilian host's body; for example, the intestinal epithelium, gallbladder, kidneys, and red blood cells.

The mode of transmission varies. In species with homoxenous life cycles, infections are transmitted by the ingestion of sporulated oocysts in feces; those with heteroxenous life cycles require an intermediate host such as rodents. Blood-borne coccidia are transmitted via the bite of an arthropod vector.

In nature, coccidian infections are self-limiting. Under captive conditions, however, coccidiosis may cause illness and, in young animals, death. Adverse effects of intestinal coccidiosis may include restlessness, anorexia, weight loss, enteritis, and regurgitation. *Cryptosporidium* spp. may cause mid-body swelling, gastritis and bronchopneumonia (Brownstein et al., 1977; Dillehay et al., 1986; Frye, 1991a; Godshalk et al., 1986; Heuschele et al., 1986; Marcus, 1981; Upton, 1990; Upton and Barnard, 1987). Heavy infections of blood-borne coccidia may result in anemia and inanition (Fantham and Porter, 1954; Fiennes, 1959).

Diagnosis of enteric coccidia is by microscopic demonstration of oocysts in feces by either the sedimentation or flotation techniques. However, positive identification of a species usually requires sporulation of oocysts (see Barnard and Upton, 1994). *Cryptosporidium* spp. are best demonstrated in stained fecal smears because they are easily missed in flotations or direct smears (Brownstein et al., 1977). Blood-borne coccidia can be diagnosed by microscopic demonstration of intraerythrocytic gamonts or meronts in stained blood smears. *Klossiella* spp. are diagnosed by microscopic demonstration of sporocyts in the urine. Currently, no effective treatment has been reported for blood-borne coccidiosis; see Appendix XII for treatments for enteric species.

Myxozoa

Two genera, *Myxidium* and *Henneguya* have been reported in freshwater turtles (Hoffman, 1967; Johnson, 1969; Mitchell, 1977; Reichenbach-Klinke, 1977; Reichenbach-Klinke and Elkan, 1965; Will, 1975). They inhabit the host's intestine, kidneys, gallbladder, urinary bladder and various other organs and tissues. Although important pathogens of fish, little is known about myxozoans in reptiles. No treatment in reptiles has been reported.

Microspora

Microspora have been found in snakes, turtles, lizards, and the tuatara (*Sphenodon* sp.). These parasites inhabit muscle and other tissues, and probably involve opportunistic infection of an abnormal host following immunosuppression. Symptoms of infection in reptiles include lethargy, anorexia, and weight loss, possibly resulting in death. No treatment in reptiles has been reported. For additional information, the reader may wish to review Canning (1981), Canning and Landau (1971), Frank (1984), Gardiner et al. (1988), Liu and King (1971), Reichenbach-Klinke (1977), and Reichenbach-Klinke and Elkan (1965).

Trematodes (Flukes)

Trematodes may range in size from a "speck" to several inches. Many of these parasites attach themselves to various parts of the host, but others penetrate into the body and invade one of the host's internal organs.

Those attempting to diagnose reptilian trematodes may find the following literature helpful: Dawes (1946), Schell (1970), Schmidt and Roberts (1985), and Yamaguti (1958, 1963).

Monogenea

These trematodes affect only ectotherms, occurring mainly on fish. Few ever exceed 3 mm in length, and about 20 species have been described from reptiles (primarily freshwater chelonians). Although most species in reptiles are ectoparasites, some occur in the urinary bladder, nose, mouth, esophagus, and lungs.

With few exceptions, monogenetic trematodes have a direct life cycle involving a single host. Transmission occurs when a free-swimming, ciliated oncomiracidium hatches from the egg and actively seeks a suitable host. Pathogenesis results both from mechanical damage to the mucosa, and the resulting secondary bacterial infection.

Diagnosis is by visual demonstration of adults in the host's mouth, or by microscopic demonstration of eggs or hatched oncomiracidia in feces. No chemotherapy has been reported.

Aspidogastrea

These trematodes inhabit the stomach and small intestine of their chelonian hosts. Transmission is by ingestion of freshwater snails (and other mollusks). No clinical symptoms or pathology has been reported.

Digenea

Digenetic trematodes are endoparasitic, and collectively inhabit nearly every organ of a host. The life cycle of these parasites is complex, involving one or more hosts including copepods, amphipods, mollusks, snails, insects, and vertebrates. Reptiles may occasionally serve as second intermediate hosts for trematode species of other reptiles, birds, or mammals. Reptiles, as well as mammals, birds, and amphibians, serve as the final hosts of digenetic trematodes. Captive-reared reptiles become infected when fed food contaminated with metacercarial cysts, or when exposed to infected wild animals.

Pathogenicity is prevalent. Infections of digenetic flukes may cause wounding of the tissues, mechanical obstruction of ducts, hyperplasia of certain tissues, nutritional deprivation, and toxic effects (Frye, 1981a; Nigrelli and Maraventano, 1944; Noble and Noble

1964; Reichenbach-Klinke and Elkan, 1965). Depending on the species, diagnosis is by demonstration of the following: adult flukes in the host's mouth; operculated eggs in feces, urine or saliva by sedimentation; at necropsy, flukes in areas of the body such as the gastrointestinal tract, lung, liver, blood vessels, heart, urinary bladder, kidneys, and/or free within the coelomic cavity (Flynn, 1973; Frank, 1981a; Frye, 1981a; Kiel, 1975; Marcus, 1981; Reichenbach-Klinke and Elkan, 1965).

To prevent captive reptiles from becoming infected with digenetic flukes, avoid feeding potential intermediate hosts unless they have been frozen first. Treatments are listed in Appendix XII.

Cestodes (Tapeworms)

Cestodes typically consist of three major parts, the scolex, neck, and strobila. They may be either unsegmented (subclass Cestodaria) or segmented (subclass Eucestoda). Among the unsegmented tapeworms, only one species has been reported to parasitize a reptile. The strobila of segmented tapeworms is generally segmented into proglottids, and these are the worms that typically parasitize reptiles.

Those attempting to diagnose reptilian tapeworms may wish to refer to keys in Schmidt (1970), Schmidt and Roberts (1985), Skrjabin and Spasskii (1951), Wardle et al. (1974), Wardle and McLeod (1952), or Yamaguti (1959).

Proteocephalidea

The order Proteocephalidea represents more than half of all the tapeworms found in reptiles. Mature worms inhabit the small intestine of the reptilian host.

With few exceptions, the life cycles of proteocephalids involve at least two obligatory hosts; an invertebrate or vertebrate host in which the larval stage develops, and a vertebrate host in which the adult cestode develops. Transmission to reptiles is by ingestion of an intermediate host such as copepods, fish, frogs, tadpoles or other reptiles (Frank, 1981a; Frye, 1981a; Reichenbach-Klinke and Elkan, 1965). Heavy infections may cause anorexia, enteritis, and sometimes intestinal impaction (Marcus, 1981; Toft and Schmidt, 1975).

Diagnosis is by microscopic demonstration of the irregularly shaped, gelatinous eggs either by sedimentation or flotation techniques. The eggs contain a thin-walled embryophore containing a completely formed oncosphere. Because proteocephalid proglottids break off the adult worm easily, these elongated structures also may be observed during fecal examination.

Under captive conditions, infections can be prevented by not feeding wild-caught, potential intermediate hosts (e.g., frogs) to reptiles unless they have been frozen first. See Appendix XII for treatments.

Pseudophyllidea

These tapeworms have been found mainly in boids and varanid lizards (Frank, 1981a; Reichenbach-Klinke and Elkan, 1965; Yamaguti, 1959). They are moderately sized, 8–10 cm long by 8 mm wide. The numerous proglottids are broader than they are long. Larvae, or spargana, are often found in the subcutaneous tissues, intercostal muscles, coelomic cavity, or the serous membranes of reptiles. Adult worms may cause emaciation and enteritis, and larval forms may result in the death of a host when they inhabit internal organs (Kiel, 1975).

Diagnosis of adult forms is by microscopic demonstration of operculated eggs (measuring 60–70 um long by 40–50 um wide) in feces by either sedimentation or flotation techniques. However, because the eggs possess an operculum they resemble eggs of trematodes, making diagnosis difficult.

Under captive conditions, infections can be avoided by not feeding wild-caught frogs and mammals to captive reptiles unless they have been frozen first. See Appendix XII for treatments.

Cyclophyllidea

Reptilian hosts include lizards, snakes and chelonians (Cheng, 1973; Dupouy and Kechemir, 1973; Frank, 1981a; Harwood, 1932; Kiel, 1975; Meggitt, 1933; Reichenbach-Klinke and Elkan, 1965; Schmidt, 1970; Widmer, 1966; Yamaguti, 1959). Adult worms vary in length from 1 mm to 3 m.

Relatively little is known about the development of cyclophyllidean tapeworms in reptiles. Where life cycles are known, arthropods serve as first intermediate hosts. Lizards may ingest the first intermediate host when feeding, and snakes may become infected when they ingest mite-infected rodents.

Diagnosis is by microscopic demonstration of eggs in feces by either sedimentation or flotation techniques. *Oochoristica* spp. eggs are irregular to triangular, and a hexacanth embryo may or may not be present. Eggs measure 40–70 um, with oncospheres measuring 15–30 um. *Ophiovalipora* spp. eggs contain hooked oncospheres, are covered in a gelatinous capsule, and may be clustered at deposition.

Trypanorhyncha

Primarily a parasite of sharks and rays, trypanorhynchans also parasitize sea snakes and crocodilians (Reichenbach-Klinke and Elkan, 1965).

These parasites are small to medium, ranging in length from 2–100 mm. Proglottids are separate, although not apparent. No pathology or treatment in reptiles has been reported.

Nematodes (Roundworms)

Nematodes comprise the largest group of helminth parasites of reptiles. Nematodes affecting reptiles usually inhabit the alimentary tract or lungs, but some occur in the abdominal and thoracic cavities, liver, muscle, heart, blood vessels and eyes (Walton, 1964). Most nematodes infecting reptiles have a direct life cycle, involving a single host. However, a few such as spirurids and some members in the order Ascaridida require an intermediate host. Reptiles may also serve as definitive or intermediate hosts.

The host-parasite relationship is usually in balance, and most nematodes rarely cause harm. When pathology occurs, it is usually in young animals, or reptiles infected with unusually high numbers of worms.

The taxonomy presented below follows Baker (1987). Those attempting to diagnose reptilian nematodes may find the following literature helpful: Anderson (1978), Anderson and Bain (1976), Chabaud (1974, 1975a,b, 1978), Lichtenfels (1980a,b), Petter and Quentin (1976), Schmidt and Roberts (1985), and Yamaguti (1961).

Enoplida

Capillaria spp. are medium to large worms and are the most common parasites of this order to infect reptiles. Although snakes are the primary hosts, lizards, turtles and crocodilians may also be infected. Generally, capillarids are intestinal nematodes, but they may be found in other organs.

The life cycle of capillarids is direct, but some species use paratenic hosts. Transmission is probably by direct contact with the organism and, to date, no symptoms have been reported.

Diagnosis is by microscopic demonstration of the doubly operculated eggs in feces by either sedimentation or flotation techniques. Eggs range in size from 45–70 um long by 25–31 um wide.

Chemotherapy may be ineffective. If the worms are encysted in the host's liver, they may be isolated from contact with orally administered anthelmintics (Stuart, 1978). Treatments used against capillarid infections are listed in Appendix XII.

Ascaridida

Reptilian ascaridid nematodes inhabit the host's esophagus, stomach, and small intestine. The life cycles of these parasites may be direct or indirect, depending on the species. Where indirect, rodents often serve as intermediate hosts. Because of their large size, heavy ascaridid infections can occlude the digestive tract, and if not treated, may result in death of the host.

Diagnosis is by microscopic demonstration of the thick-walled, round to ellipsoid eggs in feces by either the sedimentation or flotation techniques. Many members of this order, however, are viviparous, allowing an infection to go unnoticed. Anthelmintics used against ascaridids are listed in Appendix XII.

Oxyurida

Oxyurid nematodes parasitize primarily lizards and tortoises. Members of this family inhabit the host's colon.

The life cycles of oxyurids are direct. In most species, transmission is by ingestion of infective eggs.

In captivity, large populations of these parasites may build up and cause intestinal blockage when reptiles are untreated. Frank (1981a) reported anorexia in heavily parasitized tortoises awakening from hibernation. In nature, however, these parasites may serve a commensal role, in that they may prevent constipation by breaking up fecal masses in the host's intestine (Telford, 1971).

Diagnosis is by microscopic demonstration of the eggs in feces by either sedimentation or flotation techniques. Eggs range in appearance from thin-walled, ellipsoid and asymmetrically flattened, to thick-walled with surface markings. In some species, eggs are operculated, and still others are pointed at both ends. Oxyurids respond to the same chemotherapy used in the treatment of ascaridid infections (see Appendix XII). Because fenbendazole is ovicidal, I prefer it over other anthelmintics.

Rhabditida

Rhabditid nematodes parasitize primarily lizards and snakes. Two of the most commonly occurring and highly pathogenic genera are *Strongyloides* and *Rhabdias*. They are microscopic and inhabit the host's lungs and gastrointestinal tracts.

Members of this order can exist under free-living conditions for several generations. The life cycle is direct. Transmission for both genera is by ingestion of embryonated eggs or infective third-stage larvae.

Reptiles infected with *Rhabdias* spp. exhibit respiratory distress (Frank, 1981a; Frye, 1991a; Kiel, 1975). Although *Strongyloides* spp. may also migrate through the host's lungs, resulting in respiratory disease (Frank, 1981a), members of the genus primarily inhabit the esophagus, and small intestine, sometimes causing diarrhea (Holt et al., 1978). Reptiles infected with rhabditids also exhibit anorexia and weight loss.

Diagnosis is by microscopic demonstration of the thin-walled, embryonated eggs or first-stage larvae in feces. Because larvae do not tend to float, fecal sedimentation is the preferred diagnostic technique. The eggs of *Rhabdias* spp. and *Strongyloides* spp. cannot be differentiated solely on microscopic examination of feces. A *Rhabdias* infection may best be diagnosed if eggs can be demonstrated in wet mounts from bronchial washings (Jacobson, 1978). See Appendix XII for treatments.

Spirurida

Most spirurids live in the mouth and gastrointestinal tract of their hosts, but they are also found in other parts of the body such as the coelomic cavity, serous membranes, subcutis, and major blood vessels. Spirurids have an indirect life cycle, with arthropods serving as first intermediate host. Reptiles may serve as second intermediate hosts for birds and mammals, or paratenic hosts. Aquatic reptiles become infected when feeding on copepods, amphibians or fishes. Arthropods serve as a source of infection for terrestrial reptiles.

Diagnosis for oviparous species is by microscopic demonstration of eggs in feces. Frye (1991a) cautioned that bird-eating reptiles may pass avian spirurids, such as *Tetrameres americana*, which may be mistaken for a primary reptilian infection. Filarial spirurids are diagnosed by microscopic demonstration of adult filariae and microfilariae in fresh blood mounts (Obst et al., 1988). Skin biopsies of subcutaneous nodules may reveal either the adult filariae or microfilariae (Kiel, 1975; Marcus, 1981).

Treatment for spirurid infections varies. Telford (1971) reported killing adult filariae by maintaining the affected reptile at a constant temperature of 35–37°C for 24–48 hours. To prevent filarial infections, practice good mite and tick control, screen windows and doors against mosquitoes, and maintain a leech-free environment for aquatic reptiles. Also see Appendix XII for chemotherapy against both oviparous and filarial spirurid parasites.

Strongylida

The genus *Kalicephalus* is one of the most commonly occurring hookworms of reptiles, and it is found worldwide (Reichenbach-Klinke and Elkan, 1965; Walton, 1964; Yamaguti, 1961). Depending on the species, strongylids inhabit the host's esophagus, stomach and intestines.

Kalicephalus spp. have a direct life cycle (Cheng, 1964; York and Maplestone, 1926), and transmission is by ingestion of the ova or infective third-stage larvae. Frye (1981a) reported that strongylid species inhabiting the esophagus may produce discomfort for the reptilian host causing it to gape, and Frank (1981a) reported that the parasites may be expelled from the mouth with mucus. Heavy infections of intestinal strongylids (e.g., *Oswaldocruzia* spp.) may cause obstruction and peritonitis (Frank, 1981a; Reichenbach-Klinke and Elkan, 1965). Cooper (1971) reported hemorrhagic ulcers and anemia in reptiles infected with *Kalicephalus* spp.

Strongylids inhabiting the esophagus may be diagnosed by taking oral swabs, and examining the mucus microscopically. However, diagnosis of all species is best by microscopic demonstration of the transparent, oval eggs in feces by either sedimentation or flotation techniques. In reptiles that defecate infrequently, eggs may contain embryos or first-stage larvae. For anthelmintics used in the treatment of strongylid infections, see Appendix XII.

Acanthocephalans (Thorny-headed, Spiny-headed Worms)

Acanthocephalans primarily infect aquatic turtles and snakes; however, Kiel and Schmidt (1984) reported an infection in a king cobra, *Ophiophagus hannah*. Adult acanthocephalans range in size from a few millimeters in length to 12 cm or more (Frank, 1981a).

The life cycle of acanthocephalans involves an invertebrate intermediate host and one or two vertebrate hosts (Hyman, 1951; Van Cleave, 1948; Yamaguti, 1963). Reptiles serve as definitive, intermediate, or transport hosts (Walton, 1964). Because cockroaches and soil-dwelling insects or crustaceans are often involved as intermediate hosts, adequate sanitation and pest control will prevent the completion of the life cycle in well-maintained captive collections.

Acanthocephalans may cause intestinal occlusion (Elkan, 1974), and Frye (1981a) reported that reptiles affected with these parasites may exhibit blood and/or mucus in their feces, anemia and weight loss.

Diagnosis is by microscopic demonstration of the embryonated eggs in feces. Frye (1981a) recommended direct smear or sedimentation techniques over flotation methods for preparing samples for examination. Those attempting to diagnose acanthocephalans may find Yamaguti (1963) helpful. See Appendix XII for drugs and dosages used in the treatment of acanthocephalan infections.

Pentastomes (Linguatulids, Tongue Worms)

Pentastomes infect snakes, lizards, chelonians, and crocodilians. Adults are large, ranging in size from a few millimeters to approximately 14 cm. They are aerobic endoparasites, which accounts for their attachment site within the host's mouth and/or respiratory tract.

With the exception of members of the genus *Raillietiella*, life cycles of pentastomes are indirect; however, *Raillietiella* spp. can also complete their cycles via an intermediate host. Cosgrove et al. (1984), Deakins (1973), Frye (1991a), Hazen et al. (1978), and Zwart (1963) have described the pathology of pentastome infections. Major damage is caused at the site of attachment in the lung. Clinical symptoms of infection may include lethargy, anorexia, and dyspnea. Frank (1981a) reported audible breathing and the production of viscous oral mucus in reptiles with heavy pentastome infections.

To prevent transmission of pentastomes to captive reptiles, avoid feeding them wild prey unless these have been frozen first. Maintain reptiles, and rodents intended for food, in cockroach-free environments. Pentastomid larvae and nymphs are not highly host-specific, and humans can serve as intermediate hosts of reptilian pentastomes (Fain, 1966; Self and Kuntz, 1967).

Diagnosis is by microscopic demonstration of embryonated eggs in feces or sputum. Eggs measure approximately 130×140 um. Those attempting to diagnose pentastomes may find Reichenbach-Klinke and Elkan (1965) and Schmidt and Roberts (1985) helpful. For chemotherapy, see Appendix XII.

Ectoparasites

Arthropods

Arthropods comprise the largest phylum in the animal kingdom. There are between 740,000 and 800,000 species. Although most arthropods are free living, those that are parasitic may be found on or within a host. Furthermore, they often serve as intermediate hosts in parasitic life cycles, and some also serve as vectors of disease.

Mites

Hosts include turtles, snakes, and lizards. In addition to the body surface, mites also inhabit other parts of the body such as the cloaca and lungs. The most common mite infesting captive reptiles is the snake mite, *Ophionyssus natricis*. Adults measure 0.6 mm to 1.3 mm in length. Unfed females are yellow-brown and, engorged females, dark red or black. These mites are prevalent in facilities housing reptiles. They are also found on wild reptiles in Africa (Fain, 1962; Yunker, 1956).

The life cycle of *Ophionyssus natricis* is direct and can be completed on a single host. Transmission is by contact with one infested individual to another, or by contact with infested materials that have previously been in contact with an infested host.

Symptoms of mite infestation are rubbing and twisting. Infested reptiles soak excessively, and they may shed more frequently than usual. Heavy infestations can cause anemia, and even death.

Ophionyssus natricis may migrate up to fifteen feet per day (Lawrence, 1983), therefore it is best to treat the entire area (room) with dichlorvos-impregnated pest strips. To provide immediate relief to a mite-infested reptile, soak the animal in tepid water to drown as many mites as possible. Those mites which climb to the animal's head can be wiped off with a moistened piece of gauze. Soaking reptiles in water, however, does not eliminate mites altogether.

Cloacal mites can be diagnosed by gently inserting a lubricated swab into the host's cloaca and microscopically examining the material collected. Lung mites are usually diagnosed at necropsy. No treatment has been reported for either cloacal or lung mites.

Ticks

All ticks are blood-sucking parasites. They infest primarily terrestrial chelonians, snakes, and lizards native to tropical and subtropical regions. Most ticks measure approximately 4 mm in length; however, Frye (1991a) reported that some may reach 2 cm or more on East African leopard tortoises.

Because ticks serve as vectors for diseases, they should be removed when observed on a reptile. Usually, they attach themselves under scales and around body folds of their reptilian hosts. To facilitate removal, first relax the ticks with an application of alcohol. Use sharp, rather than blunt, forceps to achieve proximity to the skin, and decrease the chance of breaking off mouthparts (Barnard, 1986a). When mouthparts do break, secondary bacterial infection may be prevented by applying a topical antibiotic to the affected area.

Flies

The most significant flies in veterinary medicine are blow flies, flesh flies, horse and deer flies, biting midges, mosquitoes, sand flies, and tsetse flies. Blow flies are large, and their bodies are metallic green or blue (sometimes copper or violet). Depending on the species, larvae (called maggots) develop on carcasses, excreta, and in wounds causing myiasis. Transmission is by direct contact with larvae, or by eggs being deposited directly on the animal. Symptoms are not always apparent. Cyst-like subcutaneous lesions occur,

and death is imminent if not diagnosed. Diagnosis is by egg deposition on the animal. The affected area(s) should be debrided and flushed with povidone iodine. Some caretakers pack the wound with a proteolytic enzyme (e.g., Granulex® or Dermaaid™) and an antibiotic ointment (e.g., Polysporin®). Also see Appendix XII.

Flesh flies are gray or silvery in color. Like blow flies, flesh flies are also parasitic in the larval stages and cause myiasis. Graham-Jones (1961) reported that flesh flies lay their eggs around the cloaca of chelonians. Frank (1981b) reported these flies penetrating healthy skin of lizards, feeding on their tissues, and ultimately killing them. As with blow flies, symptoms are not always apparent, and they also cause cyst-like subcutaneous lesions, resulting in death if not diagnosed. Diagnosis and treatment is the same as for blow flies.

Horse flies and deer flies feed on reptiles, but only the female is hematophagous. Stone (1930) reported blood intake of up to 0.20 cc. Thus, many flies feeding on an animal can consume a significant amount of blood. Generally, these flies have large and stout bodies, measuring from 7 mm to 30 mm in length that are often brown, black, orange, or metallic green.

Biting midges, also called no-see-ums, have small bodies ranging from 0.6 mm to 5.0 mm in length. Because no-see-ums can pass through normal screening, animal areas must be treated with appropriate pesticides such as dichlorvos-impregnated pest strips.

Mosquitoes breed in moist soil or standing water, not only outdoors, but inside. Of the parasitic species, only females suck blood. Heavy infestations can cause anemia, and prevention is by screening all windows and doors. When necessary, place dichlorvos-impregnated pest strips (Appendix XII) in animal areas. Also, eliminate standing water, and regularly change water in reptile enclosures (e.g., stock tanks and pools).

Sand flies have hairy, mothlike bodies, and measure 4 mm in length. Only females are parasitic, feeding on the host's blood. As with mosquitoes, prevent infestations by screening all windows and doors. When necessary, place dichlorvos-impregnated pest strips in animal areas (also see Appendix XII).

Although tsetse flies are only a problem on the African continent, south of the Tropic of Cancer, reptiles imported from that area could harbor trypanosome and other protozoan infections.

True Bugs

Only members in the family Reduviidae parasitize reptiles (Frank, 1981b). They are also called assassin bugs because they prey primarily on other insects.

Reduviid bugs are large, measuring 1.5 to 2 cm. No pathology or treatment has been reported in reptiles.

Leeches

Although leeches parasitize primarily freshwater and marine reptiles, they are also known to feed on a few terrestrial species. Captive reptiles become infected from contact with contaminated water plants. When parasitizing a reptile, they attach to the host's skin, buccal cavity, and on the animal's eyelids.

Leeches have been implicated in the transmission of the herpesvirus of grey-patch disease in sea turtles (Frank, 1981b), and they have also been postulated to cause fibropapiloma tumors in sea turtles (Nigrelli and Smith, 1943). Heavy infestations have been known to cause anemia.

When freshwater leeches are observed on captive reptiles, the reptiles should be removed from the water and the leeches dusted with table salt, or swabbed with alcohol, vinegar, or hypertonic saline solution. It may take several hours for the leech to dry out and drop off. Choy et al. (1989) treated marine leeches by soaking infested turtles in fresh water. The treatment must be repeated several times to eliminate leeches newly emerged from egg cases.

Pseudoparasites

Anyone responsible for fecal diagnostics should also become familiar with the variety of spurious structures frequently found (see Barnard, 1983, 1986b; Flynn, 1973). Host-specific prey parasites and undigested plant and animal parts can be mistaken for reptilian parasites, leading to unnecessary and potentially dangerous treatment. Misdiagnoses can be avoided by sequential screening of reptilian feces and routine fecal examinations of prey such as chickens, rodents, rabbits, amphibians, and other reptiles. For photomicrographs of parasitic ova common in food animals routinely fed to reptiles, see Barnard (1983) and Habermann and Williams (1958).

EUTHANASIA

The taking of an animal's life, for any reason, is unpleasant. Anyone not able to sacrifice the life of one animal to feed another, should seriously reconsider having a reptile as a pet because wounds inflicted on a reptile by its prey are also unpleasant and, moreover, avoidable.

Euthanasia, a combination of two Greek words meaning "good death," is the procedure of killing rapidly and painlessly. Euthanasia techniques, there-fore, should result in rapid loss of brain function, or more specifically, central nervous system (CNS) depression and insensitivity to pain.

The euthanasia method used depends on several factors including the animal species, number being killed, purpose for death, and effects on the person performing the act. The euthanasia techniques discussed in this book will encompass the humane killing of reptiles and their food using acceptable methods published by the American Veterinary Medical Association's 1993 panel on Euthanasia.

Reptiles

Inhalants

Reptiles, being poikilotherms, can stop or reduce their air intake for prolonged periods. This must be kept in mind when using inhalants such as gaseous anesthetics and carbon dioxide (CO_2) gas as a means of killing. When euthanizing with CO_2, it is best to use compressed gas from a cylinder, rather than other sources such as dry ice or CO_2 from a fire extinguisher, because the rate of flow to the euthanasia chamber can be regulated: the flow rate should displace at least 20% of the chamber volume per minute.

Preferred gaseous anesthetics include halothane, enflurane, isoflurane, and methoxyflurane. When feeding reptiles other reptiles, however, it is best not to euthanize with gaseous anesthetics (discussed under Food Animals).

Noninhalant Pharmaceuticals

All barbituric acid derivatives used for anesthesia are appropriate drugs for euthanizing reptiles. Unacceptable injectable agents include strychnine, nicotine, caffeine, magnesium sulfate, potassium chloride, and all neuromuscular blocking agents. Depending on the size of a reptile and the ease/difficulty of handling it, injectable agents can be administered intravenously (IV) or intraperitoneally (IP). NEVER use noninhalant pharmaceuticals when euthanizing reptiles as food for other reptiles (discussed under Food Animals).

Physical Methods

The type of physical method used to euthanize a reptile depends on its size. Large crocodilians may be killed with a properly placed captive bolt or bullet. Cooper et al. (1989) published line drawings of the various reptilian heads and recommendations for placement of projectiles.

Small reptiles can be euthanized by cranial concussion. If it is impossible to destroy the head with a single blow, then immediately decapitate the animal. However, decapitation alone is unacceptable because reptiles are tolerant to hypoxic and hypotensive conditions (Cooper et al., 1989). Prior to delivering a blow to a reptile's head, it may be necessary to immobilize it first under refrigeration. Do not freeze reptiles following cooling as ice crystals may form on the skin and in the tissues of the animal causing it pain and distress (Cooper et al., 1989).

Cranial concussion is also an acceptable method for killing reptiles intended as food for other reptiles.

Food Animals

Under captive conditions, prey may cause serious harm to a feeding reptile. Killing them first will avoid the problem. Potentially harmful prey includes all rodents, rabbits, and fowl. The methods used for euthanizing animals intended for reptile consumption should have no residual effects on the reptile (discussed next).

Inhalants

Of the acceptable inhalants generally used for euthanasia, only carbon dioxide gas should be used for killing reptilian prey. I have attempted to feed prey to reptiles that had been euthanized with gaseous anesthetics, but in every instance the feeding reptiles refused the food. The same types of food, however, had been accepted when killed by physical methods or CO_2 gas. It is thought that the gaseous anesthetics may contain odors that are offensive to reptiles.

Noninhalant Pharmaceuticals

Injectable agents should NEVER be used to euthanize reptilian food. Such chemicals are not metabolized and thus not eliminated from the body. The lethal dosages of chemicals injected into the prey are ingested by the feeding reptile, and may cause its death as well.

Physical Methods

In zoos, cranial concussion is by far the most widely used method for killing rodents (adults, "hoppers," and "pinkies"). Anyone who is uncertain as to the step-by-step procedure for killing rodents should contact the reptile department at the nearest zoo. Universities housing rodent colonies may also offer assistance.

Birds are routinely killed by cervical separation, a method that requires practice if it is to be done properly.

Medium and large rabbits are difficult to kill by physical methods as they are strong and can inflict painful wounds with their hind feet. If no carbon dioxide gas is available, rabbits should be euthanized by cranial concussion.

LIMITED NECROPSY PROCEDURES FOR THE HERPETOCULTURIST

The concepts of acceptable husbandry practices do not end with the death of a reptile, especially if the owner possesses more than one animal. Some disorders are highly contagious and to prevent the spread of pathogens to others, it is essential to seek out the cause of death for any animal. This begins with the necropsy. Any reptile that dies should be necropsied by a veterinarian who is knowledgeable about these animals. This is generally a relatively inexpensive procedure that could prevent the unnecessary death of other reptiles in a collection.

When an animal dies and absolutely cannot be taken to a veterinarian, it is helpful if the reptile owner understands the basics necessary to prepare tissue for histopathology and parasitology. This does not mean that one has to become proficient in necropsy procedures, as that is the job of the veterinary practitioner, but he or she should be willing to increase his or her competence and knowledge in this aspect of reptile husbandry. This can be achieved by learning how to recognize pathological processes even though an in-depth postmortem examination cannot be performed. The amateur prosector should not become frustrated if results are inconclusive. Often this annoying situation also plagues the veterinarian because many diseases do not alter the tissues enough to provide a definitive diagnosis.

It is essential that the lay person provide the professional examiner with a detailed case history of the dead animal (see Case History and Record Keeping) as well as a description of what was observed during dissection. By asking the right questions, the veterinarian may be able to piece together helpful postmortem information even if the dead reptile was not personally examined.

Although some postmortem analysis such as toxicology requires frozen tissue, no carcass should be frozen unless otherwise instructed by the veterinarian. Freezing causes the body's cells to rupture, and vital histological information will be lost in the process. The postmortem examination should be performed immediately after the death of a reptile to minimize autolysis. Unless a reptile has completely decomposed, every effort should be made to salvage tissues. When immediate necropsy assistance by a veterinarian is not available, either store the dead reptile temporarily in a plastic bag under refrigeration, or prepare to perform a limited necropsy. Special precautions should be taken during the dissection because some diseases affecting reptiles may be transmitted to the handler. A bathroom may be suitable for a make-shift necropsy room. When the procedure is completed, the temporary work area should be disinfected thoroughly and proper disposal procedures followed (discussed later). This is especially critical if other household members use the selected room.

Materials

Anyone keeping reptiles should have basic necropsy materials readily available (Fig. 78). The following is a list of essentials:

• Rubber gloves.

• Disposable masks.

• Dissecting scissors.

• Tissue forceps.

• Scalpel or single-edge razor blade.

• Straight pins.

• Teasing needle or large safety-pin that has been straightened.

• Waxed paper (preferably) or newspaper.

• 8-oz. (250-ml) to 32-oz. (1-L) jar with lid, depending on the number of sections taken.

• 10% formalin (mix 1 part 37% formaldehyde with 9 parts of water).

• Hacksaw.

• Pencil, paper and masking tape.

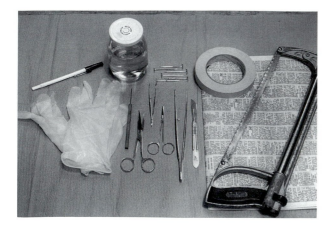

Fig. 78 Basic items necessary to perform a necropsy. Photo courtesy of Gregory C. Greer.

• Cleanable cutting board (e.g., hard plastic).

• Camera (optional) to record lesions.

Postmortem Examination and Dissection

It is of help to the pathologist if one attempts to describe and record any noticeable anatomical changes. Information of this nature may enable the pathologist to visualize such alterations without having attended the necropsy. The description should include the specific site(s) of the diseased tissue(s), and the pattern(s) and size(s) of the abnormal area(s). Be as specific as possible. For example, depending on one's understanding of anatomy, try to record a lesion as being present in the duodenum, rather than in the "small intestine." When describing details, attempt to use such terms as medial (in the middle), lateral (on the side), dorsal (toward the back), ventral (toward the belly), cranial (toward the head) and caudal (toward the tail). Other helpful terms are focal (limited to one area regardless of size), mutifocal (many discrete locations, which should be counted), patchy (irregular/poorly delineated spot or area) and diffuse (spread throughout). Also important is to note size, color, shape and consistency of organs, as well as any lesions located on the surface or distributed throughout an organ. It is important to *describe* what is being observed, rather than making interpretations. For example, a good description would be . . . "two inches round, creamy-white mass with thick capsule," rather than . . . "abscess filled with pus."

When performing a necropsy, record the following information:

• Owner's name, address and telephone number.

• Reptile's given name, species, age and sex.

• Number of reptiles in same cage, how many affected and/or lost.

• Reptile's feeding record.

• Date and time of death if known, or date and time reptile was found dead in cage.

• Ambient temperature.

• Date and time of necropsy.

• Treatment and response if applicable.

• Tests requested should routinely be histopathology and/or parasitology.

• Description of anatomical observations.

• List the number of sections taken from each organ, and write this information on the label (masking tape) of the jar of fixative.

An appropriately sized jar should contain 10% formalin so tissue sectioned from the reptilian carcass can be placed into the fixative immediately. Never place sectioned tissues aside; they may be misplaced, and they will continue to deteriorate until placed in the fixative.

Initial Examination

The skin should be inspected for superficial wounds (Fig. 75) that may have resulted from aggression by cage mates, injuries from prey or burns (Fig. 74) from improperly placed lamps. Also look for swelling that may occur from fungal and/or bacterial infections, abcesses, tumors and/or parasites. When examining a chelonian, note any unusual shell disorders. If nothing extraordinary is observed on the skin (or shell) note that the integument and/or shell was "unremarkable."

Extremely small reptiles such as an *Anolis* lizard may be incised along the ventral midline from the cloaca to the mandibular symphysis and placed intact in a jar containing 10% formalin (Fig. 79). For all other animals, use the following procedures:

Dissection

First prepare an area for the dissection that will be free of other activities and people, and that can be cleaned properly afterwards. Put on gloves and a mask, and begin the dissection (except with venomous reptiles; cut off their heads and store safely BEFORE starting). If the animal is not a chelonian, place it on its back. On waxed paper or newspaper, incise along the ventral midline from the cloaca to the mandibular symphysis. Be sure to reflect the skin away from the midline to expose the animal's internal organs (Fig. 80). If necessary, pin the reflected skin to the newspaper.

When opening a chelonian, use a hacksaw to separate the carapace (dorsal shell) from the plastron (ventral shell) at the bridges joining the animal's fore and hind legs (Fig. 81). Bluntly dissect the plastron away from the carcass (Fig. 82) with a pair of dissecting scissors or sharp blade.

Now that the carcass is opened, look in a general manner for major alterations and abnormalities. Note whether organs have been displaced from their normal anatomical locations, or whether the tissues are discolored. Also note if blood, fluids, or other abnormal exudates are present in the body cavity. The source of such abnormal fluids should be identified before removing or changing the location of the organs.

In addition to seeking the cause of death, a careful dissection is also a valuable way in which to learn anatomy. It is important that the prosector proceed in a consistent, orderly fashion to collect ALL representative tissues. Do not become distracted by one or two "dramatic" abnormalities.

Each prosector has his or her own method for dissection. The method described here is my personal preference. Begin by inspecting the heart and major blood vessels. After removing the heart (Fig. 83), dissect out and fix any areas that appear diseased. In relatively small- to medium-sized reptiles, such as the Palestine viper, *Vipera xanthina palestinae*, depicted throughout this chapter, place the entire heart in the fixative after cutting it in half (Fig. 84). With large reptiles, such as adult crocodilians or large pythons, cut the heart vertically and again horizontally, making four smaller pieces to be placed in the fixative. When placing any tissues in fixative, maintain a ratio of 1 part tissue to 10 parts fixative at all times. Tissues intended for microscopic examination should be no more than 1/2 in. (1 cm) in thickness.

The liver, gallbladder (and ducts), pancreas, and gastrointestinal tract are parts of the digestive system. The normal liver (Fig. 85) is relatively large compared to the size of the other organs and should be deep red-brown. Often the liver contains pathologic changes, causing tremendous variation in color and texture. Be sure to take several small sections of liver (Fig. 86) from different sites. When performing a necropsy on female specimens, remove the reproductive organs (Fig. 87) to facilitate access to other tissues such as the gallbladder.

The gallbladder (Figs. 88, 89a) is green, making it easy to locate. It is connected both to the liver and

Fig. 79 To fix tissues properly, place 1 part specimen to 10 parts fixative. Photo courtesy of Gregory C. Greer.

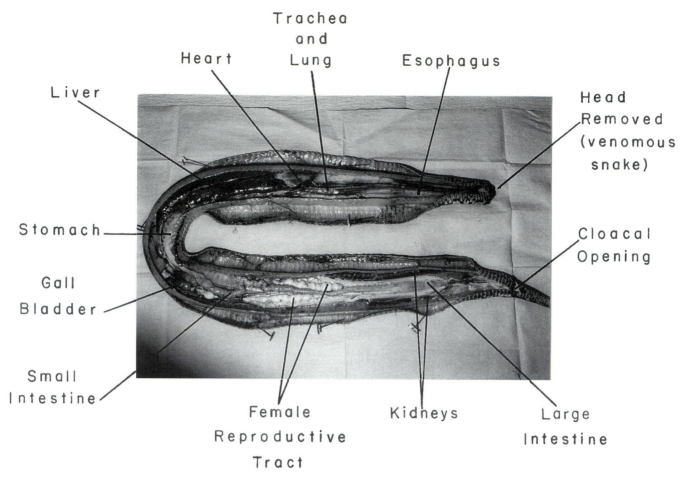

Liver

Heart

Trachea
and
Lung

Esophagus

Head
Removed
(venomous
snake)

Stomach

Gall
Bladder

Cloacal
Opening

Small
Intestine

Female
Reproductive
Tract

Kidneys

Large
Intestine

Fig. 80   Exposed organs of a female Palestine viper (*Vipera xanthina palestinae*). Photo courtesy of Gregory C. Greer.

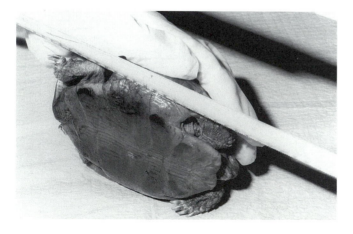

Fig. 81   To perform a necropsy on a chelonian, it is necessary to separate the carapace from the plastron. This can be achieved with the use of a hacksaw. Photo courtesy of Gregory C. Greer.

Fig. 82   The plastron is dissected away from the carcass to expose the animal's organs. Photo courtesy of Gregory C. Greer.

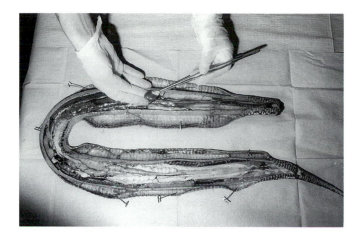

Fig. 83 There are numerous ways in which to begin dissection. Here, the heart is the first organ to be removed. Photo courtesy of Gregory C. Greer.

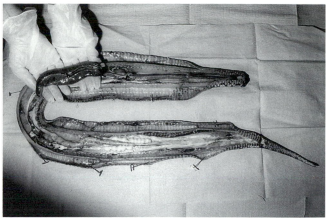

Fig. 85 Liver. Photo courtesy of Gregory C. Greer.

duodenum by ducts. Incise these ducts to check for the presence of parasites or calculi.

The spleen is usually dark pink to reddish purple. It is located in the region of the stomach or pancreas.

In some lizards and snakes the pancreas may be located near the duodenum and gallbladder. In most reptiles, however, it is situated near the spleen and is usually pale orange. Cut a small section of pancreas for fixation, or if the entire organ is no larger than 1/2 in. (1 cm), take it in its entirety (Fig. 89b).

Inspect the respiratory system (Fig. 90), including the animal's nares and oral cavity. Do NOT, however, inspect the oral cavity of a venomous reptile. When examining the respiratory system, look for lesions, excessive mucus and parasites. With a sharp blade, remove one to three small pieces of lung (approximately 1/2 sq. in. or 3 sq. cm.; Fig. 91). In many snakes, only the right lung will be present. If parasites are visible, collect as many as possible and preserve them with the reptile's tissues.

The normal lung is pink and tissue should be collected from those areas that appear diseased. In some reptiles, such as chelonians and some lizards, pigmented areas are normal. Nevertheless, when in doubt take several sections.

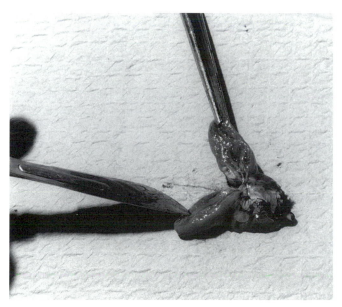

Fig. 84 Heart cut in half. Photo courtesy of Gregory C. Greer.

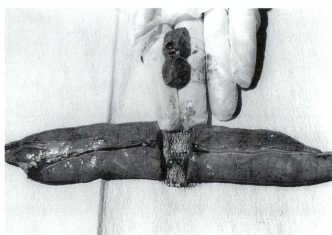

Fig. 86 When sectioning organs, be sure to use a sharp blade to prevent tissue damage. Photo courtesy of Gregory C. Greer.

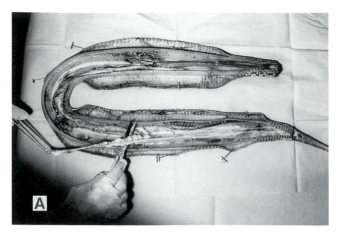

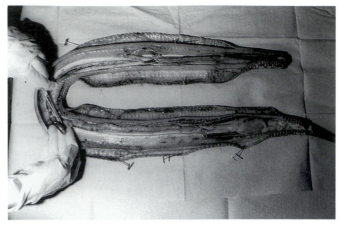

Fig. 88 Dissection of the gallbladder. Photo courtesy of Gregory C. Greer.

Fig. 87 A) dissection of the female reproductive tract; B) note developing eggs. Photo courtesy of Gregory C. Greer.

may contain lesions. Be sure that sections taken are small as described above for the lung.

Remove feces that may be present in the intestines (Fig. 95). Place a small sample of feces into a plastic slide-film canister containing 10% formalin (Fig. 96) and submit with the jar containing the animal's tissues (see Submission of Samples). Once the feces have been removed, check the intestines for parasites. Not all parasites, however, are visible grossly. Attempt to distinguish the difference between the small and large intestines. The small intestine (Fig. 94c) has many

With the removal of the lung(s), continue dissection on the digestive system. Begin by making an incision across the esophagus cranially. With forceps, hold the tissue while dissecting it away from the body (Fig. 92). Continue this procedure until the esophagus, stomach and intestines have been freed from the body cavity. Then separate the gastrointestinal tract into their respective sections (Fig. 93). To open these sections, cut each longitudinally and lay them flat on the necropsy table (Fig. 94). Check for changes in color, texture or morphology as well as for parasites. Any abnormal areas observed should be removed as described above for the lung.

The stomach is not smooth, but contains rugae (ridges; Fig. 94b). Unless a reptile has fed just prior to its death, the stomach should be empty and easy to examine. Be sure to check for parasites. Adult ascarids inhabit the stomach and are easily seen with the naked eye. If these parasites are present, remove them and place the intact parasites in preservative with the reptile's tissues. Also remove any stomach tissue that

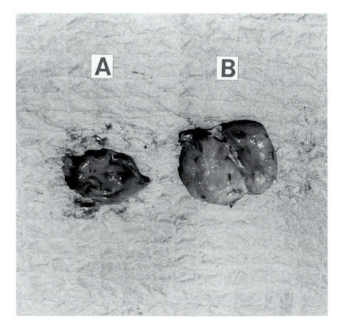

Fig. 89 A) gallbladder opened; B) pancreas cut in half. Photo courtesy of Gregory C. Greer.

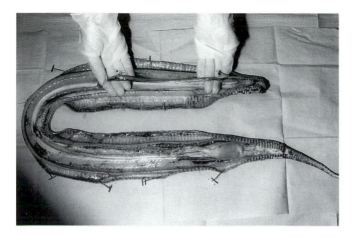

Fig. 90 Dissection of the lung. Photo courtesy of Gregory C. Greer.

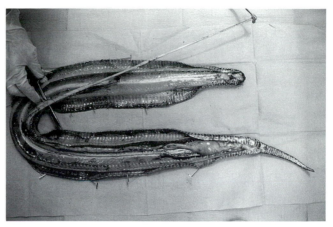

Fig. 92 Dissection of the gastrointestinal tract. Photo courtesy of Gregory C. Greer.

finger-like projections called villi; the large intestine (Fig. 94d) does not. Take sections from areas of intestine that have nodules or other signs of pathology. Even if no pathology is observed, take several small sections from both the large and small intestines. Pathologic conditions that may not be visible to the naked eye are often observed when examining the fixed tissues with a microscope.

The kidneys (Fig. 97) are paired and lobulated in most reptiles and usually lie dorsal and medial within the abdominal cavity. Take several representative sections from each kidney (Fig. 98). Most chelonians and lizards have a urinary bladder (not present in snakes). The

Fig. 91 A small section of lung cut for fixation. Photo courtesy of Gregory C. Greer.

bladder should be examined for urinary calculi (stones) which often appear when these animals are dehydrated or are fed artificial diets such as commercially-prepared dog food (Frye, 1984). Save any calculi in a dry slide-film canister.

Less obvious to the amateur prosector are the pituitary, adrenal, thyroid, and parathyroid glands. Rather than attempting to locate and collect the pituitary gland, remove the reptile's head and carefully open the skull longitudinally on the dorsal aspect (Fig. 99). This procedure allows proper fixation of all the cranial tissues. If a reptile is extremely small such as an *Anolis* lizard, it is not necessary to open the head prior to fixation. (Remember, when dissecting venomous snakes, the head is not examined. Remove the head BEFORE beginning the necropsy to prevent an accidental envenomation.)

The paired adrenal glands may be found caudomedial to the reptile's gonads. Their appearance may range from yellow-orange to darkly pigmented. The thyroid and parathyroid glands can be located cranial and dorsal to the base of the heart near the major vessels, or where the trachea bifurcates in those reptiles possessing paired lungs. Depending on the reptilian species, the thyroid gland may be single or paired and is usually pink. There may be from one to two pairs of parathyroid glands which may be cream to white. The glands vary in location, depending on the species. Frye (1981a) gave this description of their locations: "In most lizards the cranial pair lies adjacent to the bifurcation of the common carotid artery. In most snakes, the parathyroids are represented as two pairs of glands; the caudal pair is usually located between and often medial to the anterior and posterior thymic lobes. The cranial pair is adjacent to and often intimately associated with the common carotid artery. In the

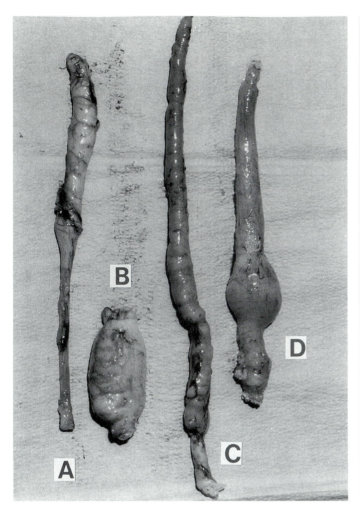

Fig. 93 A) section of esophagus; B) stomach; C) section of small intestine; D) section of large intestine. Photo courtesy of Gregory C. Greer.

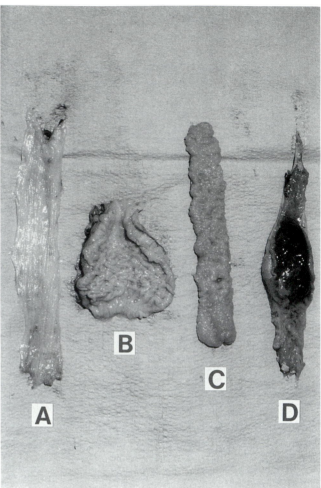

Fig. 94 To examine the mucosal surfaces of the gastrointestinal tract, cut the tissue longitudinally and open. A) esophagus; B) stomach; C) small intestine; D) large intestine. Photo courtesy of Gregory C. Greer.

crocodilians, there may be either one or two pairs, anterior to the heart base and very near the common carotid artery. Chelonians have two pairs. The anterior pair is within the thymus while the posterior pair is usually near the aortic arches and ultimobranchial body" (or lateral thyroids).

Other tissues that should be taken are thymus, spleen, lymph glands, muscle, and bone. The thymus usually is a paired gland located in the reptile's neck, cranial to the base of the heart near the great vessels. Lymph nodes are particularly difficult to find and may be confused in some cases with adipose tissue. Bone can be removed by cross-sectioning a piece of vertebral column with a sharp blade. Additional bone can be taken from a reptile's limb.

Disposal and Clean-up

Understandably, the temporary necropsy facility has been contaminated. To avoid spreading possible patho-

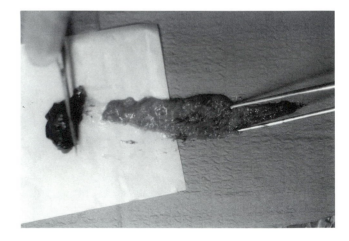

Fig. 95 Feces are commonly found in the intestines at necropsy. Scrape a sample from the large intestine for parasitology. Photo courtesy of Gregory C. Greer.

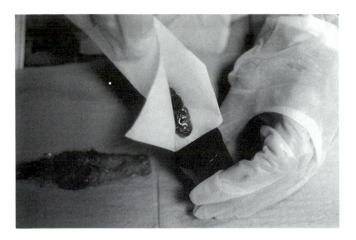

Fig. 96 Fecal samples can be placed in slide-film containers which contain 10% formalin. Photo courtesy of Gregory C. Greer.

Fig. 99 To fix cranial tissue properly, open the skull longitudinally on the dorsal aspect. Photo courtesy of Gregory C. Greer.

Fig. 97 Paired, lobulated kidneys. Photo courtesy of Gregory C. Greer.

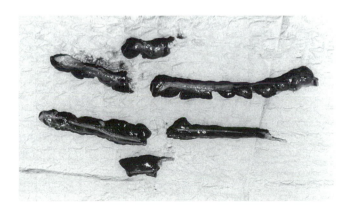

Fig. 98 Cut small sections from each kidney for fixation. Photo courtesy of Gregory C. Greer.

gens to unsuspecting individuals, thoroughly clean with soap and then disinfect the working area with 10% household bleach. After cleaning, soak dissecting instruments in a strong solution of household bleach for about 8 hours, then rinse and store for future necropsies.

If a toxicity is suspected, freeze small sections of liver, muscle and kidney. The remainder of the reptile's body should be sealed in a plastic bag and frozen for further tests that may be recommended by a veterinary pathologist.

Never contaminate indoor wastebaskets with a dead animal or disposable necropsy materials. Rather, double-bag and seal discarded material in heavy plastic containers, and place them in an outdoor trash can. For venomous reptiles, be ESPECIALLY cautious about proper disposal. Children and/or neighborhood pets may disturb trash cans. Be certain lids are secured properly. Whenever possible, make arrangements with a veterinarian to discard carcasses properly.

Submission of Samples

The veterinarian can best determine (after review of the history and gross findings) whether further diagnostic services are likely to be productive. The availability and cost of diagnostic laboratory services varies throughout the country and in most cases, submissions must be sent through a licensed veterinarian. Final interpretation of the results and their significance should also be done by the veterinarian. The reptile owner, however, by following careful necropsy procedures, has ensured that valuable information has been preserved for the benefit of the entire collection of animals.

Chapter 6

Reproduction and Egg Incubation

One of the most important considerations for successful propagation of any animal species is its state of health. Generally, reptiles should be lean. When preparing females for breeding, however, they should be maintained slightly overweight because tremendous energy is required for production of offspring. Also consider that birth defects may occur when reproductively active reptiles are fed nutritionally poor diets (Bellairs, 1981).

Most herpetologists prefer to restrict their efforts in reptilian reproduction to a few species. Such restrictions allow these professionals to concentrate on developing successful breeding techniques, especially when working with rare species or animals that do not reproduce easily in captivity. It is not possible to discuss specific breeding techniques here. Reproductive strategies, however, are widely published throughout the herpetological literature. Information presented in this chapter is general, and only covers the fundamentals of reptilian reproduction.

SEXING

It is important to observe any obvious secondary sex characteristics before pairing reptiles. These characteristics will often be apparent only in mature animals. In some lizards, sexual dimorphism may be apparent by the presence (male) or absence (female) of femoral pores, the thickness of the base of tails, the size of crests or the intensity of coloration. When sexual dimorphism is not apparent, it may be necessary to use a cloacal probe (Fig. 100) to distinguish the sexes.

Interestingly, some lizard species reproduce asexually, a process called parthenogenesis. Parthenogenetic genera include *Lacerta*, *Hemidactylus*, *Leiolepis*, *Brookesia*, *Cnemidophorus* and *Basiliscus* (Zimmerman, 1986).

Chelonians

The penis of male chelonians is singular and usually heavily pigmented (Fig. 101; also see Fig. 2, Chapter

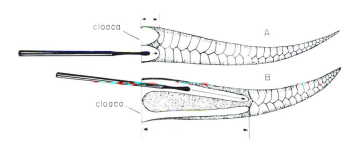

Fig. 100 The use of the Furmont reptile sexing probe for sex determination in snakes. After Laszlo, 1973.

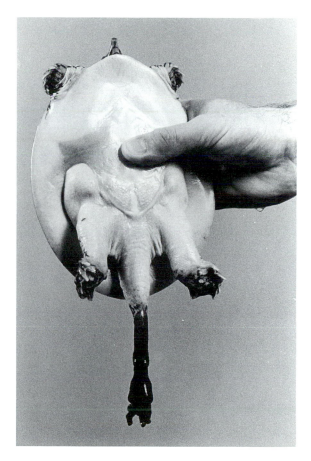

Fig. 101 Copulatory organ in a soft-shelled turtle, *Apalone* sp. (= *Trionyx*). Photo courtesy of BROMOfoto.

1). Adult males of many chelonians have a concave plastron (Fig. 102a), longer tails than females, and their cloacal vent is located more posteriorly than that of females. Females have a convex or flat plastron (Fig. 102b), a shorter tail than males and are usually larger in size. No probing should be necessary to determine the sex of an adult chelonian.

Crocodilians

Adult male crocodilians are usually larger than females. Male gavials have a bulb-like structure at the ends of their snouts (Fig. 103); females do not. To sex a crocodilian, gently insert a finger into the cloaca and palpate for the comparatively rigid penis of the male. This structure is absent in females, although in some species the clitoris may be large enough to be mistaken for a penis. The penis is late in developing and crocodilians must be relatively large (over 3 ft. in length) before accurate sexing is possible.

Lizards

Males of most species have bright colors (especially on their heads), crests and dewlaps, whereas females are usually plain in appearance. Males of most lizard species often have larger heads than females, and usually have pronounced preanal and femoral pores (Fig. 104b). These pores are either small or absent in females (Fig. 104a). Like snakes, male lizards possess paired penises called hemipenes (Fig. 12, Chapter 1) and during copulation only one hemipenis is used. With some exceptions (e.g., *Heloderma*, *Varanus*), no probing should be necessary to distinguish between the sexes of lizards.

Snakes

The ability to sex snakes by observing any secondary sex characteristics that may be present increases with experience. It is also necessary to observe many individuals of both sexes and of differing species. Males of many species have a swelling at the base of their tails where their hemipenes are located, and their tails are proportionately longer than those of females, with a larger number of subcaudal scutes. The tails of females taper sharply immediately behind the cloaca, and the shorter tails have fewer subcaudal scutes.

"Popping" is a method of sexing baby snakes as well as adults of small species. In fact, any snake in which the vent can be opened easily can be sexed in this manner. "Popping" is accomplished by holding the snake in the hand with its tail bent upwards in order to open its cloaca. If the snake is a male, pressure applied to the base of the animal's tail will cause the hemipenes

Fig. 102 Secondary sex characteristics in the spiny-shelled turtle, *Heosemys spinosa*. A) male with concave plastron; B) female with convex or flat plastron. Photo courtesy of BROMOfoto.

to evert. However, if the snake is a female, one will merely observe two dark red spots on the everted tissue.

Although stressful, and sometimes injurious when performed improperly, the most accurate method for sexing snakes under most circumstances is by probing the cloaca. Probing involves dipping a blunt, appropriately sized Furmont sexing probe (Fig. 100) in a lubricant (e.g., K.Y.® Jelly), gently inserting it into the animal's cloaca, and then gently pushing toward the base of the tail. Since all lubricants of this nature are spermacidal, sex determination by probing should be done well in advance of the breeding season. In males, the probe can be inserted many times deeper (to a

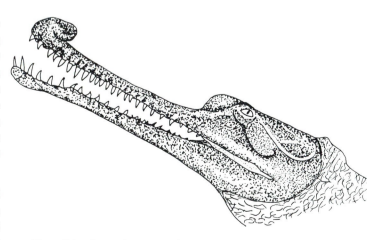

Fig. 103 Secondary sex characteristic in the male gavial (*Gavialis gangenticus*). Male gavials are ready to reproduce when the bulb-like structure at the end of their snouts has developed.

Fig. 104 Secondary sex characteristic in a lizard. A) female with small femoral pores; B) male with larger femoral pores. Photo courtesy of BROMOfoto.

depth of 5+ subcaudal scutes) than in females (to a depth of approximately 3 subcaudal scutes). Probes, however, can be obstructed by seminal plugs in the hemipenes (Mengden et al., 1980). Laszlo (1973) reported the use of the following Furmont probe sizes:

Snakes under 2 1/2 ft.	2–3 mm in diameter
3–3 1/2 ft. California Kingsnake (*Lampropeltis getulus californiae*)	2 mm
5 ft. ball python (*Python regius*)	4 mm
6 1/2 ft. Texas bull snake (*Pituophis melanoleucus sayi*)	3 mm

BREEDING STIMULI

Stimuli for inducing breeding may include feeding reptiles certain prey. Equally important is the provision for proper temperature and humidity (absolutely required by many species), light (photoperiod) and the opportunity to hibernate. Bustard (1980) reported that cycling ambient temperatures daily and seasonally helps to induce captive crocodiles to breed. A change in ambient temperature and water temperature also may be necessary for the successful propagation of semi-aquatic and aquatic reptiles. Water temperatures that are cooler than ambient temperatures provide reptiles with a range of temperatures for thermoregulation. However, if ambient temperatures drop below a reptile's selected body temperature (Table 1, Chapter 3) for long periods, the water temperature should be increased accordingly.

Most successful reptile breeders agree that there should be a cooling period prior to breeding. For temperate-zone specimens this may mean allowing sexual pairs to hibernate (see The Captive Environment, Chapter 3). Tropical specimens such as boids should not be allowed to hibernate, but should be cooled several weeks prior to breeding. This is simply a matter of reducing their temperatures from 31–32°C (88–90°F) to 18–21°C (65–70°F) at night (Ross and Marzec, 1990).

Huff (1980) reported changing husbandry routines, feeding schedules, and the types and quantities of food offered to potential breeders to avoid "captive stagnancy." In his opinion, it is not necessary to feed precisely on the same day each week. Huff suggested feeding a small amount one time, and instead of the usual amount the following week, perhaps waiting three or four more days and feeding a large meal.

Generally, temperate zone species breed in spring, subtropical animals in autumn, and equatorial animals breed anytime of the year. Separating the sexes prior to the breeding season has been known to stimulate copulation, as has introducing mates at the time of shedding. Rivalry between males may be necessary to stimulate courtship in some species. To avoid injurious conflicts, however, it may be necessary to have several breeding pairs. If the paired animals show no interest in each other, they can be rearranged. NEVER PAIR INCOMPATIBLE ANIMALS! Also, some species require more than one female per male.

Collins (1980) reported that three males and three females are a satisfactory breeding colony for Mediterranian tortoises. A breeding group of this size allows males to mate randomly with females without excessive combat, and also prevents the males from exhausting any single female. Most herpetologists agree that an excess of males to females in many species increases sexual competition and reduces the chances of inbreeding.

When a breeding group of crocodilians is established, introduction of additional adults could result in restructuring of the social hierarchy, thereby interfering with normal reproductive activities. Conversely, removing animals may be equally as disruptive, especially if the animal(s) in question are dominant members of the social group.

Regardless of the species of animals being paired for breeding, enclosures must be appropriately sized and should include territorial space for each animal. Also, avoid excessive human activity and cage maintenance.

COPULATION

Chelonians

Male tortoises fight with sexual rivals by ramming shells prior to copulating with a female (Fig. 105). Some

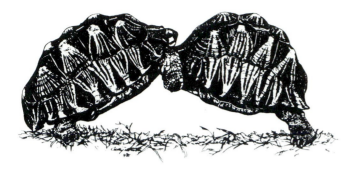

Fig. 105 Combat behavior between male radiated tortoises (*Testudo radiata*). Illustration by Cathy A. Taibbi.

species possess enlarged, scoop-like gular projections on their plastrons which they use to flip rivals onto their backs. Tortoise combat is noisy and relatively fierce.

The males of aquatic turtles (e.g., *Chrysemys, Graptemys, Pseudemys*), use their elongated front claws to stroke the faces of their intended mates. Courtship is often intense, and it is not uncommon for a female to be drowned during the act of copulation.

During mating, male chelonians mount females from behind (Figs. 106, 107). The male grasps the female's carapace with his forelegs (or hindlegs, in some species). In tortoise species, the proximity of the mating pair is made possible by the male's concave plastron (Fig. 102a). In box turtles (*Terrapene* spp.), the male will fall onto his back in order to effect intromission. In aquatic species (e.g., *Pseudemys* spp.), where the sexes have similar plastrons, intromission may be facilitated by the smaller size of the male. During mating, male tortoises may roar loudly, and the clicking of their plastrons against the females' carapaces is often equally as loud.

Crocodilians

Depending on the species, males court females by roaring, grunting, hissing, head and tail slapping, circular swimming and blowing bubbles in the water. A courting male grasps the female with his legs and mounts her while bringing their cloacae into apposition (Fig. 108).

Lizards

Lizard mating behaviors are as diverse as their appearances. Many species change or intensify their coloration, extend their dewlaps, crests or other structures, bob the head and/or body up and down, or perform other elaborate courtship rituals. Many males engage in combat during courtship with females, injuring them. Mating occurs as the male mounts the female, grasping

her with his forelimbs (or all limbs, in some species) (Fig. 109). In some taxa, the male will often grasp the back of the female's neck with his mouth. He then curls his tail under hers and brings their vents into apposition. Depending upon the side from which the male approaches, he protrudes the appropriate hemipenis and copulation begins.

Snakes

Pinney (1981) reported that male snakes rely primarily upon vision and scent to locate females. Sexually aroused males and females of many species may give

Fig. 106 Copulating position in tortoises. Photo courtesy of Ellen Nicol.

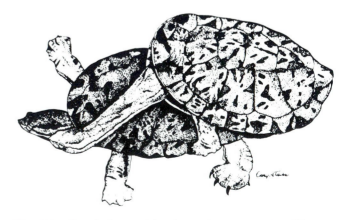

Fig. 107 Copulating position in semiaquatic turtles. Illustration by Cathy A. Taibbi.

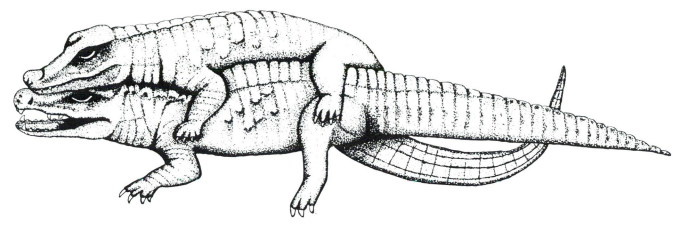

Fig. 108   Copulating position in the West African dwarf crocodile (*Osteolaemus tetraspis*). After Tryon, 1980.

the appearance of dancing. Both sexes may jerk and thrash their heads while undulating their bodies. Snakes have similar courtship behavior with some differences. For example, male boids stroke the females with their spurs. In some other species (e.g., crotalids), males enter into ritualized combat (Fig. 110) in an apparent show of dominance. Usually no harm is inflicted, and the dominant male will copulate with the female while the other departs.

Courtship in snakes proceeds with the male gliding along the female's body while jerking and rubbing his lower jaw along her back. Once the male brings his cloaca into apposition with the female's cloaca, he firmly presses or coils his tail against hers. Depending upon the side from which the male approaches, he protrudes the appropriate hemipenis and copulation begins.

PREGNANCY

Reptiles deliver their young in two ways, oviparously (egg layers) (Fig. 111) or viviparously (live bearers) (Fig. 112). Oviparous species include all chelonians and crocodilians, most lizards and snakes. The embryos of chelonians, crocodilians and some lizards derive most of the calcium required for bone development from the

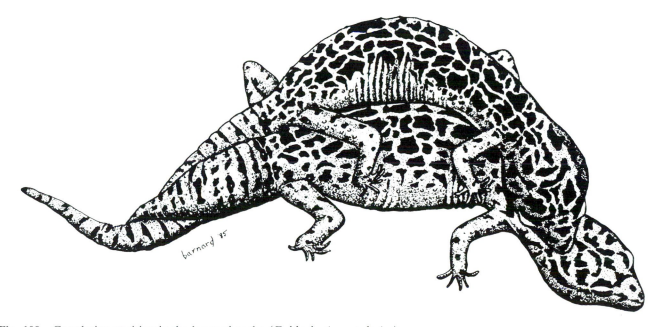

Fig. 109   Copulating position in the leopard gecko (*Eublepharis macularius*).

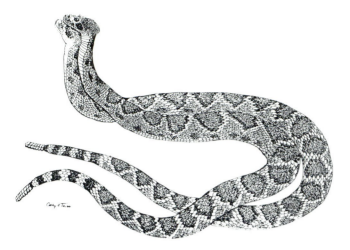

Fig. 110 Combat behavior between male rattlesnakes. Illustration by Cathy A. Taibbi.

Fig. 111 A female corn snake (*Elaphe guttata*) with eggs. Note the emergence of an egg from the female's cloaca. Photo courtesy of Manny V. Rubio.

inner surfaces of the calcareous egg shells. Females, therefore, must often be provided with calcium supplements; however, in species (most lizards and many snakes) that lay soft-shelled eggs, most of the calcium is derived from the yolk. Developing embryos of viviparous species also obtain their calcium from yolk.

Pregnant females may seek warmth to hasten development of embryos and may cease feeding. Also, they may shed prior to delivery of their eggs or young. Chelonians and lizards often increase digging and scratching activities during this period.

PARTURITION

On occasion, a gravid female may become egg-bound. There are several causes for this condition, and they may include the lack of a suitable place in which to lay eggs, shipping or acclimation stress in newly acquired reptiles, or poor husbandry practices. Dystocia is a serious problem and has caused many reptilian deaths. Progeny may be saved by caesarean section, even after the death of a pregnant female. After the eggs are recovered, they should be incubated artificially.

Nesting Requirements

Gravid females require the appropriate kinds and amounts of nesting material, such as peat and/or sphagnum moss. For example, some crocodilians build nest mounds (Fig. 113), some pythons carve indentations in the substrate, and chelonians and some lizards dig holes. Depending upon the species, nesting material must be provided well in advance of oviposition to allow the female reasonable time to construct her nest. Nesting material should be placed in one corner of the

Fig. 112 A female banded water snake (*Nerodia sipedon*) with neonates. Photo by R. L. Ditmars, neg. #16272; courtesy of the American Museum of Natural History, New York.

Fig. 113 Female alligator (*Alligator mississippiensis*) sitting on her nest. Photo courtesy of Manny V. Rubio.

female's enclosure in such a way as to maximize her privacy. For example, Wagner (1980) suggested placing nesting material in an enclosed box with a small hole. This method works well for all small lizard species. Wagner also described a method of collecting eggs laid by arboreal geckos. Laying sites constructed of pieces of hanging bark, or flowerpots with holes knocked into the sides can be provided. It is important not to remove the eggs from the object on which arboreal geckos lay their eggs, but rather place the object with attached eggs into the incubator.

Some serious tortoise breeders advocate the use of large, movable outdoor enclosures (see Frye, 1991a, Fig. 2–9), because sunlight and the opportunity to graze on natural vegetation seems to enhance breeding success. In such circumstances, however, consideration must be given to the provision for shaded areas, plant contamination, the danger of predators, and proper drainage. Tortoises bury their eggs and if drainage is not adequate, they may spoil before they hatch or before they can be retrieved for artificial incubation.

Artificial Incubation

With few exceptions, eggs should be removed for artificial incubation unless one is studying natural incubation behavior. This is necessary not only to meet specific temperature and humidity requirements (discussed below), but to prevent other ovipositing cage mates from uncovering eggs that have been left buried in the cage substrate. Some reptilian species are known to eat newly laid eggs or the newly emerging young. Eggs of some species may require environmental conditions that are deleterious to adults of the species, or vice versa. In nature, eggs are normally deposited in areas providing optimal incubating conditions, after which the female leaves the site. The environmental conditions necessary for incubation are often not beneficial for the free-living adults.

There are many appropriate media in which to incubate eggs. Sand-peat moss mixtures, sphagnum moss and vermiculite are all excellent media for artificial incubation. Some breeders do not place reptilian eggs in a medium, but prefer to suspend the eggs over water. This can be done by placing the eggs in a hardware cloth basket in such a way that the eggs never come in contact with the water. I prefer the use of one of the sterile media listed above. Most media used to incubate eggs are slightly acidic and thus inhibit the growth of bacteria or fungi. At Zoo Atlanta, eggs of rare reptilian species including Gila monsters (*Heloderma suspectum*), beaded lizards (*Heloderma horridum*), Morelet's crocodiles (*Crocodylus moreleti*), bog turtles (*Clemmys muhlenbergii*) and radiated tortoises (*Testudo radiata*) have been hatched successfully in various moss media.

When using a sand-peat moss mixture, moisten until the bolus of mixture compacts when it is squeezed in the hands. Vermiculite should be mixed with water in a 1:1 ratio by weight. Eggs should be partially buried in the substrate (Fig. 114). If some of the eggs are adhered to one another, do not separate them because this may damage the shells. Place adhered eggs into the incubator in the same manner that single eggs are placed.

Incubators can consist of an appropriately sized styrofoam container (Fig. 114), aquarium with a glass lid, or a plastic shoe box. The choice depends on the species, the number and/or size of the eggs that will be incubated, and the temperature required to hatch the eggs successfully. At Zoo Atlanta, eggs from venomous reptiles are placed in an aquarium with a sealed screen lid. A glass is placed over the lid to maintain humidity. The glass incubator allows keepers to observe the hatch, count the hatchlings and safely transfer them to their neonatal enclosure.

The incubator should have just a few airholes because too many holes cause rapid loss of humidity. An average incubation humidity for most reptilian species is between 75 and 85% (Frye, 1981a). However, some tropical species require humidities in excess of 85%, and the eggs of desert-dwelling reptiles require humidities below 75%. If eggs should begin to dimple, gentle misting with tepid water will usually restore their normal shape.

With some exceptions, most reptile eggs require incubation temperatures from 25 to 30°C (79 to 86°F). However, eggs of desert species may require temperatures exceeding this range, and tuatara (*Sphenodon*

Fig. 114 Turtle eggs being incubated artificially at Zoo Atlanta. Photo courtesy of Gregory A. George.

punctatus) eggs must be incubated at 21°C (70°F) (Frye, 1981a). A human infant or poultry chick incubator may be used to hatch reptile eggs, but most are incubated easily in the containers described above by placing a low-wattage lamp nearby to achieve the required temperature. Eggs incubated at the top end of their temperature range hatch more quickly than when incubated at the lower end of their range.

Some reptiles lack sex chromosomes, and incubation temperatures determine sex in these species (Bull and Vogt, 1979; Wagner, 1980; Yntema, 1976). For example, males are produced at higher temperatures in geckos, while lower temperatures produce males in many turtle species. It is advisable to split a clutch between the upper and lower temperature ranges required by the species in question to insure that both sexes will be produced. Zoos, however, may reverse this procedure and "put all their eggs in one incubator" to avoid surplusses of sexes or of common reptilian species.

Malformations may occur if eggs are incubated at improper temperatures and humidities (Bellairs, 1981; Bustard, 1969; Frye, 1981a).

Unlike avian eggs, those of reptiles should NEVER be rotated. Rotating can deform or kill the embryo.

Fertile eggs should not be affected by mold if the incubation humidity is proper for the species. Infertile eggs may become overgrown by contaminants (Ross, 1980), and they should be removed from the incubator when discovered.

Eggs in incubation are not necessarily free of bacteria. Feeley and Treger (1969) reported that *Salmonella* can penetrate turtle eggs, and Ross and Marzec (1984) reported culturing *Pseudomonas* from allantoic aspirations from two of three ball python (*Python regius*) eggs.

Hatchlings

Young reptiles rarely feed immediately after hatching. Feeding begins after their yolk has been absorbed, about 10 days for most species. Hatchling crocodilians have a large amount of residual yolk stored in their body cavities, and unless they are allowed to bask within the range of their selected body temperatures (Table 1, Chapter 3), these animals may not begin feeding for a month or more. Also, inadequate temperatures may predispose such hatchlings to disease, and unassimilated yolk can compact, causing infection.

Young snakes usually feed after their first shed, which takes approximately 10 days. This same time frame also applies to lizards and chelonians. Mehrtens (1984) reported that the umbilical scar of hatchling turtles is prone to fungal infections. This area should be checked periodically, and if infection is observed, administer a topical antifungal cream (Appendix XII).

When housing newborn reptiles, avoid overcrowding. It is best to separate these animals to prevent competition for food and other forms of stress. Plastic shoe and sweater boxes make excellent first homes for many species of newborn reptiles. Be sure they are well ventilated with small holes, which can be made with a small, heated nail.

A discussion on the various methods of encouraging neonates or hatchlings to begin feeding is covered in Feeding and Nutritional Disorders, Chapter 4.

Appendixes

Appendix I

Climates, Habits, Habitats, and Approximate Adult Sizes of the Reptiles of the World*

Reptile (species listed for monotypic genera)	Region of World Reptile Occurs (1,4)	"Native" Thermal Regimes (2,4)	Habits (3,4,6) & Habitats (3,4,6) (also refer to Glossary for habitat definitions)	Approximate Adult Sizes Feet ('); Inches (") (4,5,6)
Chelonians				
FAMILY CARETTOCHELYIDAE (New Guinean Plateless Turtle)				
Carettochelys insculpta (Fly River, Pig-nosed or Pitted-shelled Turtle)	Aus.	Tr.	(Aq.)—Slow-flowing rivers.	2' 3½" (70 cm)
FAMILY CHELIDAE (Side-necked Turtles)				
Acanthochelys (= *Platemys*, except *P. platycephala*) (South American Side-necked Swamp Turtles)	S.Am.	Te., S.Tr.	(Aq.)—Shallow, muddy bodies of fresh water.	6" to 8" (15–20 cm)
Chelodina (Snake-necked Turtles)	Aus., N.Z.	Te., S.Tr., Tr.	(Aq.)—Slow-flowing rivers, swamps, ponds, waterholes; introduced into New Zealand.	7" to 1' 6" (18–48 cm)
Chelus fimbriata (Matamata)	S.Am.	Tr.	(Aq.)—Swamps, lakes, ponds, stagnant pools, shallow areas of rivers.	1' 4" (41 cm)
Elseya (Australian Snapping Turtles)	Aus.	S.Tr., Tr.	(Aq.)—Large rivers, lagoons, lakes.	1' to 1' 6" (30–46 cm)
Emydura (Australian Short-necked Turtles)	Aus.	Te., S.Tr., Tr.	(Aq.)—Rivers, lagoons, lakes, waterholes, flood plains.	9" to 1' (23–30 cm)
Hydromedusa (South American Snake-necked Turtles)	S.Am.	Te.	(Aq.)—Rivers, lakes.	9½" to 1' 2" (24–36 cm)
Phrynops (Toad-headed Turtles)	S.Am.	Te., S.Tr.	(Aq.)—Lakes, ponds.	6" to 1' 6" (15–46 cm)
Platemys platycephala (Twist-necked Turtle)	S.Am.	Te., S.Tr.	(Aq.)—Shallow, muddy bodies of fresh water.	6" to 8" (15–20 cm)
Pseudemydura umbrina (Western Swamp Turtle)	Aus.	Te.	(Aq.)—Swamps.	6" (15 cm)
Rheodytes leukops (Fitzroy Turtle)	Aus.	Tr.	(Aq.)—Large, deep pools in Fitzroy River.	11" (28 cm)
FAMILY CHELONIDAE (True Sea Turtles)				
Caretta caretta (Loggerhead Turtle)	Worldwide	Te., S.Tr.	(Aq.)—Temperate and subtropical seas.	2' 8" to 3' 8" (81–112 cm)
Chelonia (Flatback and Green Turtles)	Worldwide	S.Tr., Tr.	(Aq.)—Warm, tropical and subtropical seas.	2' 4" to 4' 6" (71–137 cm)
Eretmochelys (Hawksbill Turtles)	Worldwide	Tr.	(Aq.)—Warm, tropical seas.	2' to 3' (61–91 cm)
Lepidochelys (Ridley Turtles)	Atlantic, Indian & Pacific Oceans	S.Tr., Tr.	(Aq.)—Warm waters of the southern Atlantic, Indian, and Pacific Oceans.	2' 6" (76 cm)
FAMILY CHELYDRIDAE (Snapping Turtles)				
Chelydra serpentina (Common Snapping Turtle)	N.Am., S.Am.	Te., S.Tr., Tr.	(Aq.)—Bottoms of streams, lakes, ponds, and in many other shallow aquatic situations.	1' (30 cm)
Macroclemys temminckii (Alligator Snapping Turtle)	N.Am.	Te.	(Aq.)—Bottoms of streams, lakes, ponds, and rivers.	1' 3" to 3' (38–91 cm)

Reptile (species listed for monotypic genera)	Region of World Reptile Occurs (1,4)	"Native" Thermal Regimes (2,4)	Habits (3,4,6) & Habitats (3,4,6) (also refer to Glossary for habitat definitions)	Approximate Adult Sizes Feet ('); Inches (") (4,5,6)
FAMILY DERMATEMYDIDAE				
Dermatemys mawii (Central American River Turtle)	N.Am., S.Am.	Tr.	(Aq.)—Rivers and lakes.	2' (61 cm)
FAMILY DERMOCHELYIDAE				
Dermochelys coriacea (Leatherback Turtle)	Worldwide	Te., S.Tr., Tr.	(Aq.)—Warm and temperate seas.	6' 10" (178 cm)
FAMILY EMYDIDAE (Pond Turtles)				
Annamemys annamensis (Annam Pond Turtle)	S.As.	Tr.	(Aq.)—Forest lakes and ponds.	7" to 10" (18–25 cm)
Batagur baska (River Terrapin)	E.I., S.As.	S.Tr., Tr.	(Aq.)—Primarily in larger rivers; also in brackish or salt water areas.	2' (61 cm)
Callagur borneoensis (Painted Terrapin)	E.I.	Tr.	(Aq.)—Brackish or salt water areas.	2' 6" (76 cm)
Chinemys (Chinese Pond Turtles)	E.As.	Te., S.Tr.	(Aq.)—Reservoirs, streams, ponds, canals, rice paddies.	4" to 1' 3" (10–38 cm)
Chrysemys (Painted Turtles)	N.Am.	Te.	(Aq.)—Lakes, ponds, streams, bogs, ditches.	5" to 1' (13–30 cm)
Cistoclemmys (Chinese Box Turtles)	Hainan Is., Ryuku Is., S.As.	Te., S.Tr., Tr.?	(S.Aq.)—Clear mountain streams, flooded rice fields.	8" (20 cm)
Clemmys (Pond Turtles)	N.Am.	Te., S.Tr.	(S.Aq., T)—Lakes, ponds, streams, rivers, bogs, marshes, other bodies of shallow, fresh water; wet meadows, moist forests.	3" to 8" (8–20 cm)
Cuora (Asian Box Turtles)	E.I., E.As., Pac., Phil.	Te., S.Tr., Tr.	(S.Aq.)—Clear mountain streams, swamps rivers, flooded rice fields, moist forest floors.	8" (20 cm)
Cyclemys (Asian Leaf Turtles)	Pac., Phil., S.As.	Tr.	(S.Aq.)—Adults: forests. Young: marshes.	8" to 10" (20–25 cm)
Deirochelys (Chicken Turtles)	N.Am.	Te., S.Tr.	(Aq., S.Aq.)—Shallow ponds, ditches.	7" (18 cm)
Emydoidea (Blanding's Turtles)	N.Am.	Te.	(S.Aq.)—Bodies of fresh water with dense vegetation.	9" (23 cm)
Emys (European Pond Turtles)	Eu., N.Af., W.As.	Te.	(Aq.)—Standing or slow-flowing water with dense shore vegetation.	5½" (14 cm)
Geoclemys hamiltonii (Spotted Pond Turtle)	S.As.	S.Tr.	(S.Aq.)—Large rivers, swamps, flood plains.	1' 2" (36 cm)
Geomyda spengleri (Black-breasted Leaf Turtle)	E.I., E.As., S.As.	S.Tr., Tr.	(S.Aq.)—Damp mountain forests and meadows near bodies of fresh water.	5" (13 cm)
Graptemys (Map Turtles)	N.Am.	Te.	(Aq.)—Rivers, lakes, ponds, flood plains.	4" to 1' (10–30 cm)
Hardella thurjii (Crowned River Turtle)	S.As.	S.Tr., Tr.	(Aq.)—Large streams, rivers.	1' 7" (48 cm)
Heosemys (Forest Turtles)	E.I., S.As.	Te., S.Tr., Tr.	(S.Aq., T)—Near streams at high and low altitudes; poor swimmer, no webbing between toes.	5" to 1' 5" (13–43 cm)
Hieremys annandalii (Yellow-headed Temple Turtle)	S.As.	Tr.	(Aq.)—Quiet, fresh waters with dense vegetation.	1' 6" (46 cm)
Kachuga (Indian Roofed or Tent Turtles)	S.As.	S.Tr.	(Aq.)—Large rivers, streams.	7" to 1' 4" (18–41 cm)
Malaclemys (Diamondback Terrapins)	N.Am.	Te., S.Tr.	(Aq.)—Brackish and saltwater marshes, estuaries, and protected lagoons.	8½" (22 cm)
Malayemys subtrijuga (Malayan Snail-eating Turtle)	E.I., S.As.	S.Tr., Tr.	(Aq.)—Marshes, canals, slow-flowing rivers.	1' (30 cm)
Mauremys (Stripe-necked Turtles)	E.As., Eu., N.Af., S.As., W.As.	Te., S.Tr.	(Aq.)—Bodies of fresh water with dense vegetation.	7" (18 cm)
Melanochelys (Indian Black Turtles)	S.As.	Te., S.Tr., Tr.	(S.Aq., T)—In and around still, fresh water in lowlands and hills.	6" to 1' 3" (15–38 cm)
Morenia (Eyed Turtles)	S.As.	S.Tr.	(Aq., S.Aq.)—Shallow freshwater pools.	9" (23 cm)

Reptile (species listed for monotypic genera)	Region of World Reptile Occurs (1,4)	"Native" Thermal Regimes (2,4)	Habits (3,4,6) & Habitats (3,4,6) (also refer to Glossary for habitat definitions)	Approximate Adult Sizes Feet ('); Inches (") (4,5,6)
Notochelys platynota (Malayan Flat-shelled or Purple-shelled Turtle)	E.I., S.As.	S.Tr., Tr.	(S.Aq.)—Swampy forests, ponds.	1' (30 cm)
Ocadia sinensis (Chinese Stripe-necked Turtle)	E.As.	S.Tr.	(Aq.)—Slow-flowing streams, ponds and canals in open country at low elevations.	6" to 10" (15–25 cm)
Orlitia borneensis (Malaysian Giant Turtle)	E.I.	Tr.	(Aq.)—Large lakes and rivers; also feeds out of water.	2' to 4" (71 cm)
Pseudemys (*P. scripta* = *Trachemys*) (Cooters and Red-bellied Turtles)	N.Am.	Te., S.Tr.	(Aq.)—Almost any body of fresh water; very aquatic.	8" to 1' 4" (20–41 cm)
Pyxidea mouhotii (Keeled Box Turtle)	Hainan Is., S.As.	S.Tr., Tr.	(S.Aq.)—Forest pools, moist forests, wet meadows, marshes bordering streams.	7" (18 cm)
Rhinoclemmys (Neotropical Wood Turtles)	N.Am., S.Am.	S.Tr., Tr.	(Aq., S.Aq., T)—Most terrestrial; others on banks of bodies of fresh water, rain puddles, etc.; in a wide variety of habitats including rain forests, thorn scrub, and thorn forests.	6" to 11" (15–28 cm)
Sacalia bealei (Four-eyed Turtle)	Hainan Is., E.As., S.As.	S.Tr.	(S.Aq.)—Mountain streams in wooded areas.	5" (13 cm)
Siebenrockiella crassicollis (Black Marsh Turtle)	E.I., S.As.	S.Tr., Tr.	(Aq.)—Canals, small streams.	1' 3" (38 cm)
Terrapene (Box Turtles)	N.Am., S.Am.	Te., S.Tr., Tr.	(T)—Sandy, semidry areas near fresh water to moist areas in woodlands.	4" to 7" (10–18 cm)
Trachemys (= *Pseudemys scripta*) (Slider Turtles)	N.Am., S.Am., W.I.	Te., S.Tr., Tr.	(Aq.)—In bodies of still or slow-flowing fresh water.	8" to 1' 4" (20–41 cm)
FAMILY KINOSTERNIDAE (Mud and Musk Turtles)				
Claudius angustatus (Narrow-bridged Musk Turtle)	N.Am., S.Am.	S.Tr., Tr.	(Aq.)—Marshy areas formed by slow-flowing rivers, shallow streams, mud puddles; estivates in dry seasons.	4½" (11 cm)
Kinosternon (American Mud Turtles)	N.Am., S.Am.	Te., S.Tr., Tr.	(Aq., S.Aq.)—Flooded Amazon basin, mud holes, ponds, ditches, other standing or slow-flowing fresh water.	3" to 7" (8–18 cm)
Staurotypus (Giant Musk Turtles)	N.Am., S.Am.	S.Tr., Tr.	(Aq.)—Bottom of standing or slow-flowing fresh water in lowland areas.	7" to 1' (18–30 cm)
Sternotherus (Common Musk Turtles)	N.Am.	Te., S.Tr.	(Aq.)—Bottom of standing, slow and fast-flowing fresh water with flat-rock bottoms.	3" to 6" (8–15 cm)
FAMILY PELOMEDUSIDAE (Side-necked Turtles)				
Erymnochelys madagascariensis (Madagascar Big-headed Turtle)	Mad.	S.Tr.	(Aq.)—Forest ponds and streams.	1' 5" (43 cm)
Pelomedusa (Helmeted Turtles)	S.Af.	S.Tr., Tr.	(Aq.)—Standing fresh water; estivate in dry season.	1' 5" (43 cm)
Peltocephalus dumerilianus (Big-headed Amazon River Turtle)	S.Am.	Tr.	(Aq.)—Shallow, muddy fresh water.	4" to 1' 3" (10–38 cm)
Pelusios (African Mud Turtles)	S.Af.	S.Tr., Tr.	(Aq.)—Adults: large rivers; some estivate during dry season. Young: streams.	1' 7" (48 cm)
Podocnemis (South American Side-necked River Turtles)	S.Am.	Tr.	(Aq.)—Small ponds and streams, forest pools near rivers.	1' (30 cm)
FAMILY PLATYSTERNIDAE				
Platysternon megacephalum (Big-headed Turtle)	S.As.	Te., S.Tr.	(Aq.)—Cool mountain streams.	10" (25 cm)
FAMILY TESTUDINIDAE (Land Tortoises)				
Chersine angulata (South African Bowsprit or Angulate Tortoise)	S.Af.	Te.	(T)—Sandy coastal areas.	5" (13 cm)
Geochelone (Typical Tortoises)	Galapagos Is., Mad., S.Af., S.Am., S.As.	Te., S.Tr., Tr., Ar.	(T)—Mountainous and low hilly areas, woodlands, tropical and scrub forests, grasslands, lava soil, grassy thickets.	11" to 4' 6" (28–137 cm)

Reptile (species listed for monotypic genera)	Region of World Reptile Occurs (1,4)	"Native" Thermal Regimes (2,4)	Habits (3,4,6) & Habitats (3,4,6) (also refer to Glossary for habitat definitions)	Approximate Adult Sizes Feet ('); Inches (") (4,5,6)
Gopherus (Gopher Tortoises)	N.Am.	Te., S.Tr., Ar.	(F, T)—Caliche, loam, clay, and sandy areas in bomas and desert flats.	6" to 10" (15–25 cm)
Homopus (Cape Tortoises)	S.Af.	Te.	(T)—Shady areas in coastal lowlands, mountainous terrain, plateaus, grassy areas, rocky semi-deserts.	6" to 1' 3" (15–38 cm)
Indotestudo (Asian Tortoises)	S.As.	S.Tr.	(T)—Low-lying areas of hilly regions.	4" (10 cm)
Kinixys (Hinged-back Tortoises)	Mad., S.Af.	S.Tr., Tr.	(T)—Partially fossorial; rocky terrain, semimoist bushy areas, rain forests, grasslands, marshes, shady banks of rivers.	8" to 1' (20–30 cm)
Malacochersus tornieri (Pancake Tortoise)	S.Af.	S.Tr.	(T)—Under rocks and in crevices of rocky outcrops; thorn bush areas, mountain ranges.	6" (15 cm)
Manouria (Indo-Chinese Tortoises)	S.As.	Tr.	(T)—Tropical forests near streams.	1' to 2' (30–61 cm)
Psammobates (Starred Tortoises)	S.Af.	Te., Ar.	(T)—Grasslands, arid bush.	6" (15 cm)
Pyxis (includes *Acinixys planicauda*) (Spider Tortoises)	Mad.	S.Tr.	(T)—Near rivers in humid forests.	6" (15 cm)
Testudo (Palearctic Tortoises)	C.As., Eu., N.Af., W.As.	Te., Ar.	(T)—Semimoist to arid conditions, sandy areas in woodlands, dry steppes, semi-deserts, grasslands on high plains; some cross deserts and estivate during hot, dry seasons.	5½" to 3' (14–91 cm)
FAMILY TRIONYCHIDAE (Soft-shelled Turtles)				
Amyda cartilaginea (= *Trionyx*) (Asiatic Soft-shelled Turtle)	E.I., S.As.	Tr.	(Aq.)—Under rocks, flat stones, sand or mud of rivers, streams, ponds, lakes, and swamps.	2' 4" (71 cm)
Apalone (= *Trionyx*) (Florida, Smooth and Spiny Soft-shelled Turtles)	N.Am.	Te., S.Tr.	(Aq.)—Under rocks, flat stones, sand, or mud of rivers, streams, ponds, lakes, and swamps; also found in brackish water.	7" to 14" (18–36 cm)
Aspideretes (= *Trionyx*) (Indian Soft-shelled Turtles)	S.As., W.As.	Te., S.Tr.	(Aq.)—Deep, turbid rivers to shallow waters.	2' to 2' 8" (61–81 cm)
Chitra indica (Narrow-headed Soft-shelled Turtle)	S.As.	S.Tr., Tr.	(Aq.)—Large rivers with sandy bottoms.	3' to 6' (91–183 cm)
Cyclanorbis (Sub-Saharan Flapshell Turtles)	S.Af.	Tr.	(Aq.)—Rivers.	2' (61 cm)
Cycloderma (Central African Flapshell Turtles)	S.Af.	Tr.	(Aq.)—Quiet rivers and muddy lakes in tropical rain forests.	2' (61 cm)
Dogania subplana (= *Trionyx*) (Malayan Soft-shelled Turtle)	E.I., S.As.	S.Tr., Tr.	(Aq.)—Under rocks and flat stones in muddy rivers and hill streams.	10" (25 cm)
Lissemys punctata (Indian Flapshell Turtle)	S.As.	S.Tr., Tr.	(Aq.)—In all types of fresh water including deep, rapidly flowing rivers, ponds, flooded rice fields, reservoirs, and sewage ponds.	6" to 1' (15–30 cm)
Nilssonia formosa (= *Trionyx*) (Burmese Peacock Soft-shelled Turtle)	S.As.	S.Tr., Tr.	(Aq.)—Rivers, lakes, canals, creeks.	1' 6" (46 cm)
Palea steindachneri (Wattle-necked Soft-shelled Turtle)	S.As.	S.Tr.	(Aq.)—Bodies of fresh water.	10" (25 cm)
Pelochelys bibroni (Asian Giant Soft-shelled Turtle)	Phil., S.As.	S.Tr., Tr.	(Aq.)—Deep, slow-flowing rivers, small inland inlets; salt and fresh water.	4' 2" (127 cm)
Pelodiscus sinensis (= *Trionyx*) (Chinese Soft-shelled Turtle)	E.As.	Te.	(Aq.)—Rivers, lakes, canals, creeks.	1' 8" (51 cm)
Rafetus (= *Trionyx*) (Asian Soft-shelled Turtles)	E.As., W.As.	Te., S.Tr.	(Aq.)—Rivers, lakes, canals, creeks.	1' 3½" (39 cm)

Reptile (species listed for monotypic genera)	Region of World Reptile Occurs (1,4)	"Native" Thermal Regimes (2,4)	Habits (3,4,6) & Habitats (3,4,6) (also refer to Glossary for habitat definitions)	Approximate Adult Sizes Feet ('); Inches (") (4,5,6)
Trionyx triunguis (African or Nile Soft-shelled Turtle)	N.Af., S.Af.	Te., S.Tr.	(Aq.)—Under rocks and flat stones on sandy or muddy bottoms of rivers, streams, ponds, lakes, swamps; also found in brackish and salt water.	3' (91 cm)

Lizards
FAMILY AGAMIDAE (Agamid Lizards)

Reptile (species listed for monotypic genera)	Region of World Reptile Occurs (1,4)	"Native" Thermal Regimes (2,4)	Habits (3,4,6) & Habitats (3,4,6) (also refer to Glossary for habitat definitions)	Approximate Adult Sizes Feet ('); Inches (") (4,5,6)
Acanthosaura (Flattened Plated Lizards)	E.I., S.As.	Te., S.Tr., Tr.	(A, T)—Mountain and rain forests.	3' (91 cm)
Agama	Eu., N.Af., S.Af., S.As., W.As.	Te., S.Tr., Ar.	(A, T)—Various habitats including rocky areas in mountains, grasslands, and deserts, around human dwellings.	1' to 1' 6" (30–46 cm)
Amphibolurus (Bearded Dragons)	Aus.	Te., S.Tr., Tr., Ar.	(S, T)—Under ground litter in wet and dry sclerophyll forests, woodlands, semi- and sandy deserts, grasslands, arid scrub, rocky areas Not found in tropical rain forests.	6" to 2' (15–61 cm)
Aphaniotis	E.I., S.As.	(6)	(A)–(6)	(6)
Calotes (Garden Lizards)	E.I., S.As., W.As.	Te., S.Tr., Tr.	(A)—Mountain forests in open shrubbery, rain forests, gardens, parks.	1' to 2' (30–61 cm)
Caimanops amphiboluroides	Aus.	Te., S.Tr., Ar.	(A, T)—Arid, scrubby areas, grasslands.	10" (25 cm)
Ceratophora (Horned Agamids)	S.As.	S.Tr., Tr.	(A, T)—Montane rain forests, near water on tea plantations.	8" to 1' (20–30 cm)
Chelosania brunnea (Chameleon Dragon)	Aus.	S.Tr.	(T)—Semiarid to humid savanna woodlands.	6½" (16 cm)
Chlamydosaurus kingii (Frilled Lizard)	Aus.	S.Tr.	(A)—Dry to humid woodlands.	2' (61 cm)
Cophotis (Deaf Agamids)	E.I., S.As.	Te., S.Tr., Tr.	(A)—Monsoon forests between elevations of 900 to 4,500 ft.	9" (23 cm)
Diporiphora	Aus.	Te., S.Tr., Ar.	(S, T)—Coastal sand dunes, under ground litter in savanna woodlands, grasslands, deserts, wet and dry sclerophyll forests.	1' (30 cm)
Draco (Flying Lizards)	E.I., S.As.	S.Tr., Tr.	(A)—Glides from tree to tree in rain forests, on plantations growing tropical rubber, kapok, coconut, arecanut, and other trees, mountains.	8" (20 cm)
Gonocephalus (Dragon Lizards or Angle-headed Agamids)	Aus., E.I., Pac., Phil., S.As.	Tr.	(A)—Monsoon and tropical rain forests.	1' to 2' (30–61 cm)
Harpesaurus (Hook-nosed Agamids)	E.I.	S.Tr. (?)	(A)—Mountains.	8" (20 cm)
Hydrosaurus (Water Lizards)	E.I., New Guinea, Phil.	Tr.	(A, S.Aq.)—Near rivers in tropical rain forests.	4' (122 cm)
Hylagama borneensis	E.I.	S.Tr. (?)	(A)—Mountains.	(6)
Japalura (Japalura Mountain Lizards)	E.I., S.As.	Te., S.Tr.	(S, T)—On rocks, bushes and tree stumps in montane rain forests.	1' 4" (41 cm)
Leiolepis (Butterfly Lizards, Butterfly Runners)	E.I., S.As.	S.Tr., Tr.	(F, T)—Along coasts and other sandy areas.	1' 6" (46 cm)
Lophocalotes	E.I.	S.Tr., Tr.	(A)—On open shrubbery in montane forests.	8" (20 cm)
Lophognathus	Aus., E.I.	Tr., Ar.	(A, T)—Coastal sand dunes, near streams and swamps, arid to semiarid grasslands, savanna woodlands.	1' 4" (41 cm)
Lyriocephalus scutatus (Lyre-headed Lizard)	Sri Lanka	Te., S.Tr., Tr.	(S, T)—Montane forests, open tropical rain forests.	11" to 1' 3" (28–38 cm)
Moloch horridus (Thorny Devil)	Aus.	Te., Ar.	(F, T)—Arid scrubs, sand and spinifex deserts, grasslands, woodlands.	8" (20 cm)
Oriocalotes paulus	S.As.	Te.	(A)—Montane forests.	8" (20 cm)
Otocryptis	S.As.	Tr.	(S, T)—Tropical rain forests, near streams, wooded river valleys of lowlands and hill country.	10" to 1' 8" (25–51 cm)

Reptile (species listed for monotypic genera)	Region of World Reptile Occurs (1,4)	"Native" Thermal Regimes (2,4)	Habits (3,4,6) & Habitats (3,4,6) (also refer to Glossary for habitat definitions)	Approximate Adult Sizes Feet ('); Inches (") (4,5,6)
Phoxophrys	E.I., S.As.	Tr.	(6)–(6)	8" (20 cm)
Phrynocephalus (Toad-headed Agamids)	W.As.	Te., S.Tr., Ar.	(F, T)—Hot to temperate habitats in dry sandy soil; hard, stony clay or rocky steppes almost devoid of plant life. Some species found at elevations over 15,000 ft.	4" to 10" (10–25 cm)
Physignathus (Water Dragons)	Aus., E.I.	S.Tr., Tr.	(A, S.Aq., T)—Humid, subtropical and tropical forests, tropical rain forests, wooded streams, rocky littoral.	3' (91 cm)
Psammophilus (Rock Agamas)	S.As.	S.Tr., Tr.	(T)—Low, hilly areas, rocky areas at elevations over 6,000 ft.	8" (20 cm)
Ptyctolaemus gularis (Blue-throated Lizard)	S.As.	S.Tr.	(6)—Hills.	10" (25 cm)
Salea (includes *Mictopholis*)	S.As.	S.Tr., Tr.	(S ?)—In bushes, hedges and gardens, open forests in hills at elevations up to 8,000 ft.	8" (20 cm)
Sitana ponticeriana (Sita's Lizard, Fan-throated Lizard)	S.As.	Tr.	(S, T)—Hot lowlands and dry habitats, but not in deserts.	5½" to 11" (14–28 cm)
Tympanocryptis (Lake Eyre Agamids, Earless Dragons)	Aus.	Te., S.Tr., Ar.	(T)—Arid, stony regions, deserts, open forests, woodlands, grasslands.	5" (13 cm)
Uromastyx (includes *Aporoscelis*) (Spiny-tailed Agamids)	N.Af., S.As., W.As.	S.Tr., Tr., Ar.	(F, T)—Rocky deserts.	2' 10" (86 cm)
FAMILY ANELYTROPSIDAE (Skink Relatives)				
Anelytropsis papillosus (Mexican Blind or American Snake Lizard)	N.Am.	S.Tr., Tr.	(F)—Subtropical and tropical deciduous forests.	9" (23 cm)
FAMILY ANGUIDAE (Anguid Lizards)				
Abronia (Tree Anguids)	N.Am., S.Am.	Te., S.Tr., Tr.	(A)—Humid and montane forests, orchards, thickets, bromeliads.	1' (30 cm)
Anguis fragilis (Slow Worm)	Eu., N.Af., W.As.	Te.	(F)—Moist areas in woodlands, open plains, meadows, cultivated areas rubbish dumps, wood piles, under soft soil, in rodent burrows.	1' 8" (51 cm)
Celestus	N.Am., S.Am., W.I.	S.Tr., Tr.	(F)—Under logs in and around cultivated areas.	8" (20 cm)
Coloptychon rhombifer	S.Am.	(6)	(6)–(6)	(6)
Diploglossus (Galliwasps)	S.Am., W.I.	S.Tr., Tr.	(T)—Subtropical and tropical rain forests, cultivated areas, human habitations.	10" to 1' 2" (25–36 cm)
Elgaria (= *Barisia* and *Gerrhonotus*) (Alligator Lizards)	N.Am., S.Am.	Te., S.Tr., Ar.	(T)—From sea level to high elevations, in coastal sand dunes, near lakes and creeks, under leaf litter in humid coniferous forests, pine forests, chaparral and open, semiwet grassy areas, ocotillo, tarbush and creosote-covered deserts.	2' (61 cm)
Ophiodes (South American Worm Lizards)	S.Am., W.I.	Tr.	(F, T)—From dry areas to tropical rain forests.	8" (20 cm)
Ophisaurus (Glass Lizards)	Eu., E.As., N.Af., N.Am., S.As.	Te.	(F, T)—Under moist, decaying vegetation near ponds and streams, under rocks, among hedges and bushes, sun-exposed areas in fields and paddocks.	1' 3" to 4' (38–122 cm)
Sauresia	W.I.	Tr.	(F)–(6)	4½" to 7" (11–18 cm)
Wetmorena haetiana	W.I.	Tr.	(F)–(6)	4½" to 7" (11–18 cm)
FAMILY ANNIELLIDAE (Legless Lizards)				
Anniella (Legless Lizards)	N.Am.	Te., S.Tr.	(F)—In a variety of habitats from beaches to dry, sandy regions, in pine forests.	8" (20 cm)

Reptile (species listed for monotypic genera)	Region of World Reptile Occurs (1,4)	"Native" Thermal Regimes (2,4)	Habits (3,4,6) & Habitats (3,4,6) (also refer to Glossary for habitat definitions)	Approximate Adult Sizes Feet ('); Inches (") (4,5,6)
FAMILY CHAMAELEONIDAE (True Chameleons)				
Bradypodion (Dwarf Chameleons), *Brookesia* (Stump-tailed Chameleons), *Chamaeleo* (Common Chameleons), *Rhampholeon* (Leaf Chameleons)	Eu., Mad., N.Af., S.Af., S.As.	Te., S.Tr., Tr.	(A, S, T)—In bushes and trees on plantations, humid, dry and evergreen forests, orchards, oases, mountain and sandy regions, wooded savannas.	10" to 1' 4" (25–41 cm)
FAMILY CORDYLIDAE (Sungazers or Girdle-tailed Lizards)				
Chamaesaura (South African Snake or Grass Lizards), *Cordylus* (Club-tailed or Girdled Lizards), *Platysaurus* (Flat Lizards), *Pseudocordylus* (False Club-tailed or Crag Lizards)	S.Af.	Te., S.Tr., Ar.	(T)—Under bark, among rocks in lush, open and arid grasslands, on ant hills and in rodent burrows, shady areas on wooded, grassy and rocky mountain slopes.	6" to 2' 6" (15–76 cm)
FAMILY DIBAMIDAE (Blind Lizards)				
Dibamus	E.I., Phil, S.As.	Tr	(F)—Under humus in tropical rain forests.	1' (30 cm)
FAMILY FEYLINIDAE (Worm-like Lizards)				
Chabanaudia boulengeri	S.Af.	(6)	(6)–(6)	(6)
Feylinia (African Snake Lizards)	S.Af.	Tr.	(F)—Tropical forests.	1' 1" (33 cm)
FAMILY GEKKONIDAE (Geckos)				
Afroedura (Flat Geckos)	S.Af.	Te., S.Tr., Ar.	(T)—Rocky areas, moist, arid, and montane grasslands.	2½" to 6" (6–15 cm)
Agamura	W.As.	Te., S.Tr.	(T)—Dry, rocky hillsides and plains.	4" (10 cm)
Ailuronyx	Mad.	S.Tr.	(6)–(6)	(6)
Alsophylax (Even-fingered Geckos)	Eu., N.Af., W.As.	Te.	(T)—Rocky areas around human dwellings at high elevations.	4½" (11 cm)
Aristelliger	N.Am., S.Am., W.I.	S.Tr., Tr.	(A, T)—Sparsely vegetated areas, gardens.	2" to 4" SVL (5–10 cm)
Bavayia	E.I.	Tr.	(A, T)—Damp areas.	4" (10 cm)
Bogertia	S.Am.	(6)	(6)–(6)	(6)
Briba	S.Am.	(6)	(6)–(6)	(6)
Bunopus	N.Af., W.As.	(6)	(6)–(6)	(6)
Carphodactylus laevis (Chameleon Gecko)	Aus.	Tr.	(S, T)—Under leaf litter in tropical rain forests.	4" to 6" (10–15 cm)
Chondrodactylus angulifer (Sand or Giant Ground Gecko)	S.Af.	S.Tr., Ar.	(F, T)—Under stones or in burrows they dig themselves in deserts, gravel plains, sandy flats, and interdune areas.	6" (15 cm)
Cnemaspis (Dwarf Geckos)	E.I., S.Af., S.As.	S.Tr., Tr.	(A, T)—Under ground litter and rocks around human dwellings, at bases of trees in various types of forests.	6" (15 cm)
Coleodactylus	S.Am.	Te., S.Tr., Tr.	(T)—Subtropical and tropical rain forests and forested mountain regions.	2" (5 cm)
Coleonyx (Banded Geckos)	N.Am., S.Am.	Te., S.Tr., Tr., Ar.	(T)—Under rocks, in rocky crevices or rodent burrows in deserts and canyons.	2" to 7" SVL (5–18 cm)
Colopus wahlbergii (Kalahari Ground Gecko)	S.Af.	Te.	(T)—In burrows in flat, sandy plains with scattered vegetation.	2½" to 3½" (6–9 cm)
Cosymbotus platyurus (Frilled House Gecko)	E.I., S.As.	S.Tr., Tr.	(A)—Around human dwellings.	5" (13 cm)
Crenadactylus ocellatus (Clawless Gecko)	Aus.	Te., Ar.	(T)—Sandy scrub, grasslands, woodlands.	2" SVL (5 cm)
Crossobamon eversmanni	C.As., W.As.	Te., S.Tr., Ar.	(S, T)—Deserts, semideserts.	6" (15 cm)
Cyrtodactylus (Bent-toed Geckos)	Aus., E.I., N.Af., Pac.,	Te., S.Tr., Tr., Ar.	(A, T)—Semiarid to humid areas, under litter and rocks in wet and dry forests in caves, on walls, around human dwellings.	4" to 7" SVL (10–18 cm)
Diplodactylus	Aus.	Te., S.Tr., Tr., Ar.	(A, T)—Forests, woodlands, grasslands, stony hills, sandy deserts.	2" to 4" SVL (5–10 cm)

Reptile (species listed for monotypic genera)	Region of World Reptile Occurs (1,4)	"Native" Thermal Regimes (2,4)	Habits (3,4,6) & Habitats (3,4,6) (also refer to Glossary for habitat definitions)	Approximate Adult Sizes Feet ('); Inches (") (4,5,6)
Dravidogecko anomallensis	S.As.	Tr.	(T ?)—Under rocks in scrub forests.	4″ (10 cm)
Ebenevia	Mad.	S.Tr.	(A ?)–(6)	4″ (10 cm)
Eublepharis (= *Goniurosaurus* in Japan and China) (Leopard Geckos)	S.As., W.As.	S.Tr., Tr.	(T)—Rocky habitats (*E. macularius*), urban areas, wet forests (*Eublepharis* native to Japan and China); because of habitat differences, do not house *E. macularius* with, or in the same manner as species from Japan and China.	1′ (30 cm)
Garthia	S.Am.	Te., Ar.	(6)—Deserts at elevations between 4,500 and 7,500 ft.	(6)
Geckolepis	Mad.	S.Tr.	(A ?)—Forests.	6″ (15 cm)
Geckonia chazaliae (Helmet-headed Gecko)	N.Af.	S.Tr.	(T)—Dry, often sandy areas.	4″ (10 cm)
Gehyra	As., Aus., E.I., Mad., N.Am., Pac., S.As.	Te., S.Tr., Tr.	(A, T)—Under bark in dry to humid habitats including forests, savanna woodlands, mangroves, grasslands, cultivated areas, caves, around human dwellings; introduced into Mexico.	4″ to 6″ (10–15 cm)
Gekko	E.I., S.As.	S.Tr., Tr.	(A)—In trees around human dwellings and cultivated areas.	8″ to 1′ 2″ (20–36 cm)
Gonatodes	N.Am., S.Am., W.I.	Tr.	(A)—Swamps, tropical rain and dry forests, forest edge situations, grasslands, around human dwellings.	1½″ to 4″ SVL (4–10 cm)
Gymnodactylus	E.I., Eu., N.Af., Pac., S.Am., S.As., W.As.	Te. (?), S.Tr., Tr.	(T)—On trees and rocks, under bark and dead trees in subtropical, tropical, and montane forests, around human dwellings.	5½″ (14 cm)
Hemidactylus (Tropical Geckos)	Aus., E.I., Eu., Pac., S.Af., S.Am., S.As., W.I.	Te., S.Tr., Tr., Ar.	(A, T)—Under loose bark in wet and dry forests, forest edge situations, arid and moist grasslands, caves, in and around human dwellings.	3″ to 6″ SVL (8–15 cm)
Hemiphyllodactylus	E.I., Pac., S.As.	S.Tr., Tr.	(A)—Under tree bark, rock piles and other debris, forested areas.	3½″ (9 cm)
Hemitheconyx (African Fat-tailed Geckos)	N.Af.	S.Tr., Tr.	(T)—Relatively dry habitats.	8″ (20 cm)
Heteronotia	Aus.	Te., S.Tr., Tr., Ar.	(T)—Under ground litter in wet forests, in rock crevices, and caves, grasslands, woodlands, arid deserts.	2¼″ SVL (6 cm)
Heteropholis	N.Z.	Te.	(A)—Scrubby and bushy areas, forests.	9″ (23 cm)
Holodactylus	N.Af.	S.Tr., Tr.	(T)—Dry habitats.	8″ (20 cm)
Homonota (includes *Wallsaurus*)	S.Am.	Te., S.Tr.	(T)—Rocky terrain in mountains and on plateaus.	2″ to 3″ (5–10 cm)
Homopholis (Velvet Geckos)	Mad., S.Af.	Te., S.Tr., Tr., Ar.	(A)—Under bark and rocks, in birds' nests, caves, coastal bush, moist and dry grasslands, in and around human dwellings.	4″ to 8″ (10–20 cm)
Hoplodactylus	N.Z.	Te.	(A, T)—Under stones, leaf litter and bark, in hollow trees and petrel burrows, coastal areas, cultivated fields, forests, forest edge situations.	10½″ (27 cm)
Kaokogecko vanzyli (Kaoko Web-footed Gecko)	S.Af.	Te.	(F, T)—Digs own burrow on gravel plains.	3″ to 4″ (8–10 cm)
Lepidoblepharis	S.Am.	Tr.	(T)—Tropical rain and dry forests.	1″ SVL (2 cm)
Lepidodactylus	Aus. E.As.(?), E.I., S.As.	Tr.	(A)—Humid, tropical woodlands, in crowns of palms and buildings.	2″ to 3½″ SVL (5–9 cm)

Reptile (species listed for monotypic genera)	Region of World Reptile Occurs (1,4)	"Native" Thermal Regimes (2,4)	Habits (3,4,6) & Habitats (3,4,6) (also refer to Glossary for habitat definitions)	Approximate Adult Sizes Feet ('); Inches (") (4,5,6)
Lophopholis scabriceps (Scaled Gecko)	S.As., Sri Lanka	Tr.	(F, T)—(6)	4" (10 cm)
Lucasium damaeum (Beaded Gecko)	Aus.	S.Tr., Tr., Ar.	(T)—Humid to arid conditions, savanna woodlands, sand hills, grasslands.	2¼" SVL (6 cm)
Lygodactylus (Dwarf Geckos)	Mad., S.Af., S.Am.	Te., S.Tr., Ar.	(A)—In trees and cracks of boulders in arid to moist areas including dry woodlands, rocky, arid grasslands and hillsides, montane forests, around human dwellings.	2" to 4" (5–10 cm)
Mediodactylus	Eu., N.Af., W.As.	(6)	(6)—(6)	(6)
Narudasia festiva (Festive Gecko)	S.Af.	Te., Ar.	(T)—Arid mountain slopes.	2½" (6 cm)
Naultinus (Green Tree Geckos)	N.Z.	Te.	(A)—Scrubby and bushy areas.	7" (18 cm)
Nephrurus (Kidney-tailed or Knob-tailed Geckos)	Aus.	Te., S.Tr. Tr., Ar.	(T)—Rocky habitats, deserts, grasslands, woodlands, forests.	6" (15 cm)
Oedura (Fat-tailed or Velvet Geckos)	Aus.	Te., S.Tr., Tr., Ar.	(A, S, T)—Humid to arid conditions, under ground litter, bark of fallen trees and human debris, in and around buildings, caves, rocky areas, grasslands, woodlands, forests.	7" (18 cm)
Pachydactylus (Thick-toed Geckos)	S.Af.	Te., S.Tr., Ar.	(T)—In rock crevices, under leaf litter and fallen trees in a wide variety of habitats including arid to moist grasslands, montane grasslands, rocky, semideserts, deserts, coastal dunes, woodlands, in and around human dwellings.	3" to 7" (8–18 cm)
Palmatogecko rangei (Web-footed Gecko)	S.Af.	Te., Ar.	(F, T)—Scrubby and coastal areas, deserts; digs own burrow.	5½" (14 cm)
Paragehyra petiti	Mad.	S.Tr.	(6)—(6)	(6)
Paroedura	Mad.	S.Tr., Ar.	(A, T)—Sandy deserts, stony hills, forests, woodlands.	(6)
Perochirus	Pac., Phil.	Tr.	(6)—Tropical forests.	6" (15 cm)
Phelsuma (Day Geckos)	E.I., Mad., Pac., S.Af., S.As., Seychelles	S.Tr., Tr.	(A)—In coconut palms, bamboo, banana plants, other trees in damp forests, edges of evergreen forests, bushlands, leafy foliage around human habitations, and interestingly, they have been observed under marginal scutes of tortoises (perhaps they feed on insects drawn to the tortoises' feces); introduced into Hawaii.	11" (28 cm)
Phyllodactylus (Leaf-toed Geckos)	Aus., Eu., Mad., N.Am., S.Af., S.Am., S.As., W.As., W.I.	S.Tr., Tr., Ar.	(A, T)—Semiarid to arid rocky terrain, thorn woodlands, dry forests, sand dunes, coastal deserts, savannas, montane grasslands; introduced into N.Am.	4" to 8" (10–20 cm)
Phyllopezus pollicaris	S.Am.	(6)	(6)—(6)	(6)
Phyllurus (Leaf-tailed Geckos)	Aus.	Te., S.Tr., Tr.	(A, T)—Forests, woodlands, sandstone caves, rocky crevices, buildings.	6" to 10" (15–25 cm)
Platyurus	E.I., S.As.	Tr.	(A)—On tree trunks and branches in lower forest canopy, cultivated areas, around human dwellings.	5" (13 cm)
Pristurus	N.Af., W.As.	S.Tr.	(T)—Dry rocky areas.	6" (10 cm)
Pseudogekko	Solomon Is.	Tr.	(A)—(6)	(6)
Pseudogonatodes	S.Am.	Te.(?), S.Tr., Tr.	(A (?), T)—Rain, mountain and dry forests, coastal deserts.	2½" (6 cm)
Pseudothecadactylus	Aus.	Tr.	(A, T)—Forests, woodlands, rocky areas, caves.	8" (20 cm)

Reptile (species listed for monotypic genera)	Region of World Reptile Occurs (1,4)	"Native" Thermal Regimes (2,4)	Habits (3,4,6) & Habitats (3,4,6) (also refer to Glossary for habitat definitions)	Approximate Adult Sizes Feet ('); Inches (") (4,5,6)
Ptenopus (Barking Geckos)	S.Af.	Te., S.Tr., Ar.	(F, T)—Barren gravel plains, sandy and sparsely vegetated deserts and semideserts.	5" (13 cm)
Ptychozoon (Flying Geckos)	E.I., S.As.	Tr.	(A)—On tree trunks and under bark in tropical rain forests.	7" (18 cm)
Ptyodactylus (House or Fan-footed Geckos)	N.Af., S.Af., W.As.	Te., Ar.	(A, T)—Deserts, rocky caves, rocky and thorny regions, on walls in human dwellings.	7" (18 cm)
Quedenfeldtia trachyblepharus (Atlas Day Gecko)	Morocco	Te.	(6)—Mountains.	4" (10 cm)
Rhacodactylus (Giant Geckos)	New Caledonia Pac.	Tr.,	(A)—Under bark and in tree hollows in forests.	1' 2" (35 cm)
Rhinogecko missonnei	W.As.	(6)	(6)—(6)	(6)
Rhoptropella ocellata	S.Af.	(6)	(6)—Rock dwellers.	(6)
Rhoptropus (Namib Day Geckos)	S.Af.	Te., S.Tr., Ar.	(A, T)—Rocky areas in deserts and semideserts.	3" to 6" (8–15 cm)
Rhynchoedura ornata (Beaked Gecko)	Aus.	Te., S.Tr., Tr., Ar.	(T)—Arid and semiarid areas, open savanna woodlands, grasslands.	3" (8 cm)
Saurodactylus (Lizard-finger Geckos)	N.Af.	S.Tr.	(T)—Stoney areas on mountain slopes and dry valleys.	2" (5 cm)
Sphaerodactylus (Least or Reef Geckos)	N.Am., S.Am., W.I.	Tr.	(T)—In bromeliads, under bark and dead leaves in tropical dry and rain forests, other wooded areas, under stones and logs along base of limestone cliffs, coastal areas, around human dwellings.	3½" (9 cm)
Stenodactylus	N.Af., W.As.	S.Tr., Ar.	(T)—Rocky areas in deserts and mountains.	4½" (11 cm)
Tarentola (Common Geckos)	Eu., N.Af., S.As., W.I.	Te., S.Tr., Tr.	(A)—On rocks, trees and walls of buildings in warm, dry coastal lowlands; one species in neotropics.	7" (18 cm)
Teratolepis fasciata (Banded Scaled Gecko)	S.As.	S.Tr., Ar.(?)	(F, T)—Deserts, bushland.	4" (10 cm)
Teratoscincus (Frog-eyed Geckos)	W.As.	Te., S.Tr.(?), Ar.	(F, T)—Deserts and dry habitats with sparse plant cover.	7" to 9" (18–23 cm)
Thecadactylus rapicauda (Smooth Gecko)	N.Am., S.Am., W.I.	S.Tr., Tr., Ar.	(A)—Subtropical and tropical rain and dry forests, thorn woodlands, grasslands, coastal deserts; introduced into N.Am	7" (18 cm)
Trachydactylus jolensis	W.As.	(6)	(6)—(6)	(6)
Trigonodactylus arabicus	W.As.	(6)	(6)—(6)	(6)
Tropiocolotes	N.Af., W.As.	Te., S.Tr.	(S, T)—Dry, sandy habitats.	4" (10 cm)
Underwoodisaurus	Aus.	Te., S.Tr., Ar.	(T)—Forests, savanna woodlands, arid scrubs, rocky outcrops and stony hills.	7" (18 cm)
Uroplatus (Leaf-tailed or Bark Geckos)	Mad.	S.Tr.	(A)—On tree trunks in rain forests.	9" (23 cm)

FAMILY GERRHOSAURIDAE (Gerrhosaurid Lizards)

Reptile	Region	Thermal	Habits & Habitats	Size
Angolosaurus skoogi (Desert Plated Lizard), *Cordylosaurus subtessellatus* (Dwarf Plated Lizard), *Gerrhosaurus* (Plated Lizards), *Tetradactylus* (South African Seps, Whip or Plated Snake Lizards), *Tracheloptychus* (Keeled Gerrhosaurids), *Zonosaurus* (Girdled Lizards)	Mad., S.Af.	Te., S.Tr., Tr.	(F, T)—Tropical rain and coastal forests, grasslands, sand dunes, near river banks, rocky regions, urban areas.	4" to 2' 6" (10–76 cm)

FAMILY HELODERMATIDAE (Venomous Lizards)

Reptile	Region	Thermal	Habits & Habitats	Size
Heloderma (Gila Monsters and Beaded Lizards)	N.Am., S.Am.	Te., S.Tr., Tr., Ar.	(T)—Desert floors or valleys, broad canyons in desert mountains.	2' 6" to 3' (76–91 cm)

FAMILY IGUANIDAE (Iguanid Lizards)

Reptile	Region	Thermal	Habits & Habitats	Size
Amblyrhynchus cristatus (Marine Iguana)	Galapagos Is.	S.Tr.	(Aq.)—On rocky coasts of equatorial islands in cold ocean currents.	4' 6" (137 cm)

Reptile (species listed for monotypic genera)	Region of World Reptile Occurs (1,4)	"Native" Thermal Regimes (2,4)	Habits (3,4,6) & Habitats (3,4,6) (also refer to Glossary for habitat definitions)	Approximate Adult Sizes Feet ('); Inches (") (4,5,6)
Anisolepis	S.Am.	Tr.	(6)—Tropical rain forests.	1' (30 cm)
Anolis (includes *Audantia, Deiroptyx, Mariguana, Norops* and *Xiphocercus*) (Anoles)	N.Am., S.Am., W.I.	Te., S.Tr., Tr., Ar.	(A)—On trees, shrubs, roots, vines and rocks in humid to arid areas including subtropical and tropical rain forests, other forested areas, sandy and grassy savannas, coastal deserts and desert scrub, thorn woodlands, agricultural areas, in and around human dwellings.	4" to 2' (10–60 cm)
Aptycholaemus longicauda	S.Am.	S.Tr.(?)	(A ?)—Closely related to *Anolis;* may be similar in habits.	(6)
Basiliscus (Basilisks)	N.Am., S.Am.	S.Tr., Tr.	(A, S.Aq., T)—Near bodies of fresh water in rain and dry forests.	3' (91 cm)
Brachylophus (Fijian Iguanids)	Fiji Is. Tonga Is.	Tr.	(A)—Wooded areas along edges of fresh water.	3' (91 cm)
Callisaurus (Zebra or Gridiron-tailed Lizards)	N.Am.	Te., S.Tr., Ar.	(T)—Semiarid regions in loose, sandy soil.	8" (20 cm)
Ceiolaemus	S.Am.	(6)	(6)—(6)	(6)
Chalarodon madagascariensis	Mad.	S.Tr.	(S, T)—Plateaus.	8" (20 cm)
Chamaeleolis (False Chameleons)	W.I.	Tr.	(A)—Shady, leafy forests and coffee plantations.	1' (30 cm)
Chamaelinorops (= *Hispaniolus*) *barbouri*	W.I.	S.Tr.	(A)—Mountains.	4" (10 cm)
Conolophus pallidus (Galapagos Land Iguana)	Galapagos Is.	Tr.	(F, T)—In burrows in rocky dry regions.	3' (91 cm)
Corytophanes (Helmeted Iguanids)	N.Am., S.Am.	S.Tr., Tr.	(A)—Subtropical and tropical rain forests.	1' 2" (35 cm)
Crotaphytus (Collared and Leopard Lizards)	N.Am.	Te., Ar.	(T)—Hilly, rocky or canyon banks of arroyos, other hilly terrain, desert lowlands, grasslands.	1' 4" (40 cm)
Ctenoblepharis (= *Phrynosaura*)	S.Am.	Te., S.Tr., Ar.	(A, T)—In and around trees in arid regions at elevations between 3,000 and 14,000 ft.	6" (15 cm)
Ctenosaura (Black Iguanids)	N.Am., S.Am.	S.Tr., Tr.	(A, T)—In trees in thorn forests, on rocks on coastal beaches.	4' (122 cm)
Cyclura (Ground Iguanids)	W.I.	Tr.	(T)—In burrows, rocky areas, bushlands.	5' (152 cm)
Diplolaemus	S.Am.	Te.	(T)—Plateaus, talus slopes, scrub areas.	8" (20 cm)
Dipsosaurus (Desert Iguanids)	N.Am.	Te., Ar.	(T)—In deserts under shrubs and in mammal burrows.	4" to 1' (10–30 cm)
Enyalioides	S.Am.	Tr.	(F, T)—In rotting stumps, under leaf litter and in small burrows in tropical rain forests.	1' (30 cm)
Enyaliosaurus (Spiny-tailed Swifts)	N.Am., S.Am.	Tr.	(T)—Scrubby areas.	1' 6" (46 cm)
Enyalius (Brazilian Tree Lizards)	S.Am.	Te., S.Tr.	(A)—Rain forests, coastal mountains on shady bushes.	1' (30 cm)
Gambelia (Leopard Lizards)	N.Am.	Te.	(T)—Sandy areas (but not dunes) on flat desert terrain where vegetation is sparse, rocky flats.	1' 4" (40 cm)
Garbesaura garbei	S.Am.	(6)	(6)—(6)	(6)
Holbrookia (Earless Lizards)	N.Am.	Te.	(T)—Sand dunes, deserts, chalk beds, flat gravel areas, rocky hills, mixed grasslands, plateaus.	8" (20 cm)
Hoplocercus (Weapon-tailed Iguanids)	S.Am.	S.Tr.	(F, T)—Dig holes under shrubbery in open grasslands.	6" (15 cm)
Iguana (True Iguanids)	N.Am. Pac.(?), S.Am., W.I.	S.Tr., Tr., Ar.	(A, S.Aq., T)—Dry forests, forest edge situations, woodlands, grasslands, desert scrub, coastal deserts; often perch in trees overhanging bodies of water.	6' (183 cm)

Reptile (species listed for monotypic genera)	Region of World Reptile Occurs (1,4)	"Native" Thermal Regimes (2,4)	Habits (3,4,6) & Habitats (3,4,6) (also refer to Glossary for habitat definitions)	Approximate Adult Sizes Feet ('); Inches (") (4,5,6)
Laemanctus (Casque-headed Lizards)	N.Am., S.Am.	Tr.	(A)—Edge of and in tropical rain forests.	2' 6" (76 cm)
Leiocephalus (Crested Keeled or Curly-tailed Lizards)	S.Am., W.I.	S.Tr., Tr., Ar.	(T)—Wide variety of habitats including open country, sandy coastal areas, rocky slopes, open coniferous forests, brush- and cactus-covered plains.	6" to 1' 2" (15–35 cm)
Leiosaurus	S.Am.	(6)	(6)—(6)	(6)
Liolaemus (Smooth-throated Lizards)	S.Am.	Te., S.Tr., Tr., Ar.(?)	(T)—In diverse climatic temperature zones at elevations up to 15,000 ft., subtropical and tropical rain forests, damp montane forests, coastal deserts.	6" to 1' (15–30 cm)
Morunasaurus	S.Am.	Tr.	(T)—Tropical rain forests.	(6)
Ophryoessoides	S.Am.	S.Tr., Tr.	(S, T)—Under leaf litter and on fallen logs in subtropical and tropical rain and dry forests, coastal scrub, dry rocky areas in mountains.	8" (20 cm)
Oplurus (= *Hoplurus*) (Madagascar Iguanids)	Mad.	S.Tr.	(A, S, T)—In dry rocky crevices and in trees.	10" (25 cm)
Pelusaurus cranwelli	S.Am.	(6)	(6)—(6)	(6)
Petrosaurus (Rock Lizards)	N.Am.	S.Tr., Ar.	(T)—Deserts, rocky areas, canyons.	4½" (11 cm)
Phenacosaurus (False Anoles)	S.Am.	Te.	(S)—On cool slopes at elevations between 5,400–11,000 ft.	10" (25 cm)
Phrynosoma (Horned Lizards)	N.Am.	Te., S.Tr., Ar.	(T)—Deserts, valleys, mesas, foothills, flat, rocky terrain in gravelly, sandy, or loamy soil, sand hills, grasslands.	3½" to 7½" SVL (9–19 cm)
Phymaturus palluma	S.Am.	Te.	(T)—Rocky areas on plateaus at high elevations.	9" (23 cm)
Plica (Harlequin Racerunners)	S.Am.	Tr.	(A)—Tropical rain forests and forest edge situations; avoid thin branches and isolated trees.	1' 4" (40 cm)
Polychrus (includes *Polychroides peruvianus*) (Long-legged Iguanids)	S.Am.	Te.(?), S.Tr., Tr.	(A)—Tropical rain forests, dry forests, forest edge situations, grasslands.	2' (61 cm)
Pristidactylus	S.Am.	Te.(?)	(6)—Forests.	(6)
Proctotretus	S.Am.	Te.	(T)—Rocky regions on plateaus at high elevations.	8" (20 cm)
Sator	N.Am.	S.Tr., Ar.	(T)—Forests, rocky deserts, scrub areas.	4" (10 cm)
Sauromalus (Chuckwallas)	N.Am.	Te., S.Tr., Ar.	(T)—Arid to semiarid conditions; dry bushland, paddocks, forests, rock outcrops in foothills, flat, sandy deserts, talus slopes.	5" to 1' 7" (13–48 cm)
Sceloporus (Spiny Lizards or Swifts)	N.Am., S.Am.	Te., S.Tr., Tr., Ar.	(A, T)—Arid conditions on sand dunes, desert floors, limestone bluffs, on mesquite and other scrubby trees, on cacti, in pine, tropical, deciduous and rain forests, under rocks and other ground litter, in mammal burrows and buildings.	4½" to 1' 4" (11–41 cm)
Stenocercus (Narrow-tailed Iguanids)	S.Am.	Tr.	(S)—Tropical rain forests.	8" (20 cm)
Streptosaurus (Collared Utas)	N.Am.	S.Tr.	(A, T)—Around large boulders in barren, rocky canyons.	8" (20 cm)
Strobilurus torquatus	S.Am.	Tr.	(S, T)—Tropical forests.	4¼" (11 cm)
Tapinurus semitaeniatus	S.Am.	(6)	(6)—(6)	(6)
Tropidodactylus onca	S.Am.	Tr.	(A)—Forests.	8" (20 cm)
Tropidurus (Lava Lizards)	Galapagos Is., S.Am.	Tr., Ar.	(S, T)—Wide variety of habitats including forests, forest edge situations, grasslands, other open country.	1' 2" (35 cm)

Reptile (species listed for monotypic genera)	Region of World Reptile Occurs (1,4)	"Native" Thermal Regimes (2,4)	Habits (3,4,6) & Habitats (3,4,6) (also refer to Glossary for habitat definitions)	Approximate Adult Sizes Feet ('); Inches (") (4,5,6)
Uma (Fringe-toed Lizards)	N.Am.	Te., Ar.	(F, T)—Very sandy soil in desert areas, sand dunes.	8" (20 cm)
Uracentron (Spiny-tailed Iguanids)	S.Am.	Tr.	(S)—Lower levels of trees in tropical rain and thorn forests.	5½" (14 cm)
Uranoscodon superciliosa (Mop-headed Iguana)	S.Am.	Tr.	(S, S.Aq., T)—Shady areas near water where forest begins close to banks of lakes, ponds, rivers, etc.	1' 8" (51 cm)
Urosaurus (Climbing Utas)	N.Am.	Te., S.Tr., Tr.	(A)—On trees, bushes, boulders, and cliffs in dry habitats.	6" to 8" (15–20 cm)
Urostrophus vautieri	S.Am.	Tr.	(T)—Tropical rain forests, steppes, semideserts.	10" (25 cm)
Uta (Ground Utas)	N.Am.	Te.	(T)—From sea level to at least an elevation of 7,000 ft, in grassy areas, rocky terrain, near river banks, in flat desert regions, on mountain slopes and canyon walls.	3" (8 cm)

FAMILY LACERTIDAE (Wall and Sand Lizards)

Reptile (species listed for monotypic genera)	Region of World Reptile Occurs (1,4)	"Native" Thermal Regimes (2,4)	Habits (3,4,6) & Habitats (3,4,6) (also refer to Glossary for habitat definitions)	Approximate Adult Sizes Feet ('); Inches (") (4,5,6)
Acanthodactylus (Fringe-toed Lacertids)	Eu., N.Af., S.As., W.As.	Te., Ar.	(F, T)—Rocky substrates on plateaus, sandy semideserts, deserts with sparse vegetation, near human habitations.	5½" to 10½" (14–27 cm)
Adolfus	S.Af.	Te.	(T)—Mountains.	8" (20 cm)
Algyroides (Keeled Lizards)	Eu.	Te.	(T)—Meadows, pine forests, damp areas in overgrown rock faces of mountains.	6" (15 cm)
Aporosaura anchietae (Shovel-snouted Lizard)	S.Af.	Te., Ar.	(F, T)—Loose, unstable desert sand dunes.	5½" (14 cm)
Bedriagaia tropidopholis	S.Af.	Tr.	(6)—Tropical forests.	1' (30 cm)
Cabrita (Indian Lacertids)	S.As.	S.Tr., Tr.	(T)—Open dry forests, sandy areas, plateaus.	6" (15 cm)
Eremias (Desert Lacertids)	C.As., Eu., N.Af., S.As., W.As.	Te., Ar.	(F, T)—Semideserts, deserts, plateaus.	6" to 1' (15–30 cm)
Gallotia	Canary Is.	Te.	(T)—(6)	6" to 2' (15–60 cm)
Gastropholis vittatus	S.Af.	Tr.	(A ?)—In trees and bushes.	1' (30 cm)
Heliobolus (Bushveld Lizards)	S.Af.	Te.(?), S.Tr.	(T)—Arid to humid grasslands.	6" to 1' (15–30 cm)
Holaspis guentheri (Fringe-tailed or Blue-tailed Tree Lizard)	S.Af.	Tr.	(A)—Tropical and coastal forests.	5" (13 cm)
Ichnotropis (Rough-scaled Lizards)	S.Af.	Te.(?), S.Tr.	(T)—Arid to humid grasslands.	7" (18 cm)
Lacerta (Mediterranean Lizards)	Eu., N.Af., S.Af., W.As.	Te., S.Tr.	(A, T)—Dry areas including woodland glades, mountain slopes, heaths, sand dunes, stony areas, around human habitations in gardens, lowlands to mountains, some species close to water; most species are good swimmers.	5½" to 3' (14–91 cm)
Latastia	N.Af., W.As.	Te., S.Tr.	(F, T)—In burrows on sand hills and semideserts.	8" (20 cm)
Meroles (Desert Lizards)	S.Af.	S.Tr., Ar.	(T)—Vegetated coastal dunes, arid grasslands, sparsely vegetated deserts.	5" to 9" (13–23 cm)
Mesalina	N.Af., W.As.	(6)	(6)—(6)	(6)
Nucras (Blunt-headed or Sandveld Lacertids)	S.Af.	Te., S.Tr.	(T)—A wide variety of grasslands including moist, dry and montane.	10½" (27 cm)
Ommateremias	W.As.	Te.	(6)—(6)	(6)
Ophisops (Snake-eyed Lizards)	Eu., N.Af., S.As., W.As.	Te., S.Tr.	(T)—Stony and scrubby areas, around thorny bushes in grasslands.	8" (20 cm)
Pedioplanis (Sand Lizards)	S.Af.	Te., Ar.	(T)—Rocky flats and montane grasslands, arid to moist grasslands, coastal dunes, deserts.	5" to 8" (13–20 cm)

Reptile (species listed for monotypic genera)	Region of World Reptile Occurs (1,4)	"Native" Thermal Regimes (2,4)	Habits (3,4,6) & Habitats (3,4,6) (also refer to Glossary for habitat definitions)	Approximate Adult Sizes Feet ('); Inches (") (4,5,6)
Philochortus	N.Af., W.As.	Te.(?), S.Tr.(?)	(T)—Semideserts.	(6)
Podarcis (Wall Lizards)	Eu., N.Af.	S.Tr.	(S)—Lowlands to plateaus, along walls, cliff faces, gardens and bushes.	11" (28 cm)
Poromera fordii	S.Af.	Tr.	(A)—Tropical rain forests, secondary forests.	8" (20 cm)
Psammodromus (Plated Lacertids)	Eu., N.Af.	S.Tr.	(T)—Dunes and salt marshes, beaches, urban areas in gardens and parks.	1' 1½" (34 cm)
Rhabderemias	W.As.	Te.(?)	(6)—(6)	(6)
Tachydromus or *Takydromus* (Long-tailed Grass Lacertids)	S.As., E.As.	Te., S.Tr., Tr.(?)	(S, T)—Runs on top of plants in damp forests, open grasslands, hill country and along river banks.	1' 3" (38 cm)
Tropidosaura (Mountain Lizards)	S.Af.	Te.(?), S.Tr.	(T)—Dense plant growth, crevices and rocky areas in mountains and on grassy slopes.	7" (18 cm)
FAMILY LANTHANOTIDAE (Earless Monitor)				
Lanthanotus borneensis (Earless Monitor)	Borneo	Tr.	(F, S.Aq)—Around human habitations including ditches in rice fields and other water-dependent areas.	1' 7½" (43 cm)
FAMILY PYGOPODIDAE (Flap-footed or Snake Lizards)				
Aclys concinna	Aus.	Te.	(F)—Subhumid, coastal heaths and woodlands on sandy substrates.	1' 4" (40 cm)
Aprasia (Blunt-tailed Scaley-foots)	Aus.	Te., Ar.	(F)—Semiarid to arid rocky habitats on sandy or loamy soils, woodlands, forests, grasslands.	1' 4" (40 cm)
Delma (Smooth-scaled Scaley-foots)	Aus.	Te., S.Tr., Tr., Ar.	(F, S, T)—Under logs, rocks and other debris, coastal monsoon and sclerophyll forests, rocky, sandy arid areas, woodlands, grasslands.	1' 8" (51 cm)
Lialis burtonis (Burton's Snake Lizard, Long-headed Scaley-foot)	Aus.	Te., S.Tr., Tr., Ar.	(T)—Under low vegetation or ground litter in coastal forests, woodlands, grasslands, desert areas.	2' 6" (76 cm)
Ophidiocephalus taeniatus (Bronzback)	Aus.	Te.	(F)—In loose soil covered by leaf litter overlying cracking clay loams, grasslands.	4" SVL (10 cm)
Paradelma orientalis	Aus.	Tr.	(T)—Rocky, gravel areas bordering forests.	1' (30 cm)
Pletholax gracilis	Aus.	Te.	(F)—Subhumid, sandy coastal woodland.	10" to 1' 2" (25–35 cm)
Pygopus (Scaley-foot Lizards)	Aus.	Te., S.Tr., Tr., Ar.	(T)—Wet sclerophyll forests, coastal heaths and dunes, grasslands, woodlands, deserts; occasionally burrow and climb.	2' 4" (70 cm)
FAMILY SCINCIDAE (True Skinks)				
Ablepharus (Lidless or Ocellated Skinks)	E.I., Eu., N.Af., Pac., S.As., W.As.	Te., S.Tr., Tr.	(T)—Under leaf litter and rocks in deciduous forests, grasslands, and on plateaus.	3" to 5½" (8–14 cm)
Acontias (African Dart or Greater Legless Lance Skinks)	S.Af.	S.Tr., Tr.	(F)—Under stones, loose leaf litter, and decaying logs, in sandy, arid soil at the base of bushes, in humic soils in damp areas, forested areas, a variety of grasslands from coastal areas to mountains, sparsely vegetated coastal dunes.	4" to 1' 6" (10–46 cm)
Acontophiops lineatus (Woodbush Legless Skink)	S.Af.	Tr.	(F)—Under stones on rocky hillsides, montane grasslands.	7" (18 cm)
Amphiglossus	Mad.	S.Tr.	(6)—(6)	(6)

Reptile (species listed for monotypic genera)	Region of World Reptile Occurs (1,4)	"Native" Thermal Regimes (2,4)	Habits (3,4,6) & Habitats (3,4,6) (also refer to Glossary for habitat definitions)	Approximate Adult Sizes Feet ('); Inches (") (4,5,6)
Anomalopus	Aus.	S.Tr., Tr.	(F)—Under decaying or fallen timber in wet and dry sclerophyll forests, rain forests and woodlands.	6" to 10" (15–26 cm)
Ateuchosaurus	E.As., S.As.	Te., S.Tr.	(T)—Under leaves in damp areas of forests.	8" (20 cm)
Barkudia	S.As.	Tr.	(F)—Burrow in loose soil under trees in open country.	6½" (17 cm)
Brachymeles (Philippine Short-legged Skinks)	Phil.	Tr.	(6)—(6)	6" to 1' (15–30 cm)
Carlia	Aus., E.I., Pac.	Tr.	(T)—Arid to humid habitats including stony hills, woodlands, forests.	8" (20 cm)
Chalcides (Cylindrical or Barrel Skinks)	Eu., N.Af., W.As.	Te., S.Tr.	(F, T)—On clay soil, under stones, open areas with shrubbery, grasslands, moist meadows, dry regions.	6" to 1' (15–30 cm)
Cophoscincopus durus	S.Af.	S.Tr., Tr.(?)	(S.Aq.)—Near water, under leaves, rocks and logs.	4" (10 cm)
Corucia zebrata (Giant Skink)	Pac.	Tr.	(A)—Tropical forests, around human dwellings.	2' (61 cm)
Cryptoblepharus	Aus., E.I., Mad., N.Af., S.Af.	Te., S.Tr., Tr., Ar.	(A, T)—In a variety of arid to humid habitats, under bark and in rocky crevices, mangrove swamps, beaches, grasslands, woodlands, forests, deserts.	4" (10 cm)
Crytoposcincus minimus	Mad.	S.Tr.	(6)—(6)	(6)
Ctenotus	Aus.	Te., S.Tr., Tr., Ar.	(T)—Arid to humid conditions, coastal areas, wet and dry sclerophyll forests, savanna woodlands, inland deserts, grasslands.	1' (30 cm)
Cyclodina	N.Z.	Te.	(T)—Under leaf litter, logs, rocks and tree roots, in seabird burrows.	10" (25 cm)
Dasia	E.I., S.As., Phil.	Tr.	(A)—Tropical forests.	11" (28 cm)
Egernia	Aus.	Te., S.Tr., Tr., Ar.	(A, F, T)—Arid to humid conditions, coastal heaths, wet and dry sclerophyll forests, rain forests, woodlands, grasslands, deserts.	6" to 1' 10" (15–55 cm)
Emoia	Aus., E.I., Pac., S.As.	Tr.	(A, S.Aq., T)—Coastal scrubs, rocky areas, grasslands, lowland forests, mangroves.	4" to 1' (10–30 cm)
Eremiascincus (Sand Swimmers)	Aus.	Te., S.Tr., Ar.	(F, T)—Under logs, stones and other debris in sandy and loamy soils, grasslands, woodlands, deserts.	3" to 4" SVL (8–10 cm)
Eugongylus	Aus., E.I., Pac.(?)	Tr.	(T)—Under fallen timber and leaf litter in monsoon and tropical rain forests.	8" to 2' (20–61 cm)
Eumeces	N.Af., N.Am., S.Am., S.As., W.As.	Te., S.Tr., Tr.	(A, F, T)—Humid conditions, under ground litter and rocks, in rotten logs, on trees, in sandy soil near coastal areas, in canyons, wooded areas, humid deserts, grassy hillsides, lava fields along streams and swamps.	1' 6" (45 cm)
Gongylomorphus bojeri	Mad.	S.Tr.	(6)—(6)	(6)
Grandidierina	Mad., Seychelles	S.Tr.	(6)—(6)	(6)
Hemiergis	Aus.	Te., S.Tr.	(F)—Under stones and fallen timber in woodlands, forests and scrubby areas.	1½" to 3" SVL (4–8 cm)
Janetaescincus	Mad.	S.Tr.	(6)—(6)	(6)

Reptile (species listed for monotypic genera)	Region of World Reptile Occurs (1,4)	"Native" Thermal Regimes (2,4)	Habits (3,4,6) & Habitats (3,4,6) (also refer to Glossary for habitat definitions)	Approximate Adult Sizes Feet ('); Inches (") (4,5,6)
Lampropholis	Aus., Pac.	Te., S.Tr., Tr.	(T)—Under ground litter and in open areas, temperate heaths, woodlands, subtropical rain forests; introduced into Hawaii.	6" (15 cm)
Leiolopisma	Aus., E.As., E.I., N.Af., N.Z., S.As.	Te., S.Tr., Tr.	(T)—Primarily humid habitats, under leaf litter, rock piles and fallen timber, subtropical and tropical rain forests, wet and dry sclerophyll forests, deciduous, pine and montane forests, grasslands, woodlands, cultivated areas.	4" to 1' 4" (10–40 cm)
Lerista (includes *Rhodona*)	Aus.	Te., S.Tr., Tr., Ar.	(F)—Under logs, stones and in termite mounds, in a variety of habitats including humid coastal areas, woodlands, grasslands, scrubby areas, arid inland deserts.	6" (15 cm)
Lygosoma (Ground, Metallic or Writhing Skinks)	Aus., E.As., E.I., Pac., S.Af., S.As.	Te., S.Tr., Tr.	(F, T)—Under leaf litter, fallen timber and stones, arid, sandy areas, well-drained hillsides, coastal and grassy plains, cultivated areas; introduced onto Christmas Island.	8" (20 cm)
Mabuya (Common or Brahminy Skinks)	E.I., N.Af., N.Am., S.AF., S.Am., S.As., W.As., W.I.	Te., S.Tr., Tr., Ar.	(T)—In a wide variety of habitats including mountains, arid to humid grasslands, rain forests, deciduous and evergreen forests, forest edge situations, mangrove swamps, coastal bush, in and around human dwellings.	5" to 1' (12–30 cm)
Macroscinicus cocteaui (Cape Verde Giant Skink)	Cape Verde Is.	S.Tr.	(T)—Barren, rocky areas.	1' 11" (58 cm)
Malacontias	Mad.	S.Tr.	(6)—(6)	(6)
Melanoseps	S.Af.	S.Tr.(?), Tr.(?)	(F ?)—(6)	(6)
Menetia	Aus.	Te., S.Tr., Tr., Ar.	(T)—In every type of habitat throughout the continent except those on the north and southeast coasts.	4" (10 cm)
Morethia	Aus.	Te., S.Tr., Tr., Ar.	(T)—Under ground litter and fallen timber in humid coastal areas, forests, woodlands, arid rocky hills and deserts.	6" (15 cm)
Neoseps reynoldsi (Florida Sand Skink)	N.Am.	Te., S.Tr.	(F)—Under fallen timber and in loose, dry soil in scrubby and high pine areas; has been recorded to burrow to a depth of about 2 ft.	4½" (11 cm)
Nessia (Singalese Skinks)	Sri Lanka	Tr.	(F)—Under decaying vegetation, stones and soil in cultivated areas and hill country.	3½" (9 cm)
Notoscincus	Aus.	S.Tr., Tr.	(T)—Under ground litter in semiarid to humid conditions in woodlands, grasslands and deserts.	4" (10 cm)
Ophiomorus (Asian Sand Skinks, Sandfishes)	Eu., S.As., W.As.	Te., S.Tr.	(F)—Sandy regions including coastal dunes, mountain slopes.	9½" (24 cm)
Ophioscincus (Asian Snake Skinks)	Aus., S.As.	Tr.	(T)—Forests.	8½" (19 cm)
Pamelaescincus gardini	Seychelles	Tr.	(6)—(6)	(6)
Panaspis (Snake-eyed Skinks)	S.Af.	S.Tr., Tr.	(T)—Also semiburrowing; under ground litter in tropical rain and evergreen forests and dry to damp grasslands.	8" (20 cm)
Paracontias	Mad.	S.Tr.	(6)—(6)	(6)

Reptile (species listed for monotypic genera)	Region of World Reptile Occurs (1,4)	"Native" Thermal Regimes (2,4)	Habits (3,4,6) & Habitats (3,4,6) (also refer to Glossary for habitat definitions)	Approximate Adult Sizes Feet ('); Inches (") (4,5,6)
Proablepharus	Aus.	S.Tr., Tr., Ar.	(T)—Under ground litter in woodlands, dry sclerophyll forests, grasslands and deserts.	4" (10 cm)
Proscelotes (Slender Skinks)	S.Af.	Te., S.Tr.	(T)—Under stones and other debris in montane grasslands and evergreen forests.	7' (18 cm)
Pseudacontias madagascariensis	Mad.	S.Tr.	(6)—(6)	(6)
Pseudemoia	Aus.	Te.	(T)—Under decaying timber and other ground litter in wet sclerophyll forests and woodlands.	6" (15 cm)
Pygomeles	Mad.	S.Tr.	(6)—(6)	(6)
Riopa (Snake Skinks)	E.I., Pac., S.Af., S.As.	S.Tr., Tr.	(T)—Open plains; one species lives in forests.	1' 3½" (39 cm)
Ristella (Indian Cat Skinks)	S.As.	Tr.	(S, T)—Hill and forested areas.	6" (15 cm)
Saiphos equalis	Aus.	Te., S.Tr.	(F)—Under logs, rocks and other ground litter in humid, coastal areas, moderately dry rocky areas and around human habitation.	6" (15 cm)
Scelotes (Dwarf Burrowing Skinks)	Mad., S.Af.	Te., S.Tr., Tr.(?)	(F)—Under loose ground litter and soil in relatively moist grasslands and coastal sand dunes.	4" to 1' 8" (10–50 cm)
Scincella laterale (Ground Skink)	N.Am.	Te.	(F, T)—Under leaf litter in humid forests, hardwood hammocks, dry, sandy pine areas.	5" (13 cm)
Scincopus fasciatus (Tunisian Night Skink)	N.Af.	S.Tr., Ar.	(T)—Under sand in deserts.	(6)
Scincus (Sand Skinks)	N.Af., W.As.	Te., Ar.	(T)—Dry, sandy areas including deserts.	9" (23 cm)
Sepsina (Savanna Burrowing Skinks)	S.Af.	Te., S.Tr.	(F)—From rocky arid to moderately moist grasslands.	3" to 8" (8–20 cm)
Sepsophis punctatus	S.As.	Tr.	(T)—Forests.	8" (20 cm)
Sphenomorphus (Forest Skinks)	Aus., E.I., Pac., S.As.	Te.(?), S.Tr., Tr.	(A, F, T)—Under stones and other ground litter around swamps, ponds, creeks in rain and dry forests, coastal dunes, savanna woodlands, and grasslands.	8" (20 cm)
Sphenops	N.Af.	S.Tr.	(F)—Sandy, scrub flats.	7" (18 cm)
Tiliqua (collectively called Blue-tongued Skinks)	Aus., E.I.	Te., S.Tr., Tr., Ar.	(T)—Under ground litter in a variety of humid to arid conditions, forests, rocky areas on low hills, deserts.	6" to 1' 8" (15–51 cm)
Trachydosaurus rugosus (Shingle-back, Double-headed or Stump-tailed Skink)	Aus.	Te., S.Tr., Ar.	(T)—Under ground litter in deserts, grasslands, woodlands and forests.	1' 2" (35 cm)
Tribolonotus (Casque-headed Skinks)	E.I.	Tr.	(T)—Under stones, tree stumps and fallen leaves in shady valleys and dense forests, near mountain brooks.	7" to 8½" (18–22 cm)
Tropidophorus (Keeled Skinks)	Aus., E.I., Phil., S.As.	S.Tr., Tr.	(S.Aq., T)—Under stones, decaying timber and in damp grass near running fresh water on stony ground and tropical forests.	6" to 1' (15–30 cm)
Typhlacontias (African Blind Dart or Western Burrowing Skinks)	S.Af.	Te., S.Tr., Ar.	(F)—In sandy soil and under leaf litter in sparsely vegetated deserts and plains.	3" to 5" (8–13 cm)
Typhlosaurus (Blind Legless Skinks)	S.Af.	Te., S.Tr., Tr., Ar.	(F)—Under stones, dead tree bark and fallen timber in a wide variety of habitats including coastal sand dunes, montane grasslands, evergreen forests, cultivated areas, and deserts.	5" to 1' (13–30 cm)

Reptile (species listed for monotypic genera)	Region of World Reptile Occurs (1,4)	"Native" Thermal Regimes (2,4)	Habits (3,4,6) & Habitats (3,4,6) (also refer to Glossary for habitat definitions)	Approximate Adult Sizes Feet ('); Inches (") (4,5,6)
FAMILY TEIIDAE (Whiptails and Racerunners)				
Alopoglossus	S.Am.	Tr.	(T)—Tropical rain forests, grassy fields, forest edge situations, in and around human dwellings.	8" (20 cm)
Ameiva (Jungle Runners)	N.Am., S.Am., W.I.	S.Tr., Tr.	(T)—Grasslands, cactus-covered plains, rocky coastal regions, mangrove swamps, dry and rain forests, forest edge situations, limestone hills, in and around human dwellings.	1' to 2' (30–61 cm)
Anadia (includes *Angalia*)	S.Am.	S.Tr., Tr.	(A)—In bromeliads and ferns in subtropical and tropical rain forests.	10" (25 cm)
Anotosaura	S.Am.	S.Tr., Tr.	(T)—Similar to *Bachia*.	(6)
Arthrosaura	S.Am.	S.Tr., Tr.	(T)—Under leaf litter in open areas of subtropical and tropical rain forests.	6" (15 cm)
Bachia (includes *Ophiognomon* and *Scolecosaurus*) (Earless, Worm and Snake Teiids)	S.Am., W.I.	S.Tr., Tr.	(F, T)—Under decaying leaf litter and fallen timber in rain and dry forests, thorn woodlands, coastal deserts.	8" (20 cm)
Callopistes (Dwarf or Monitor Tegus)	S.Am.	Te., S.Tr., Ar.	(F)—Rocky deserts and plateaus, arid lowlands and mountains.	1' 11" (58 cm)
Cercosaura ocellata	S.Am.	S.Tr., Tr.	(T)—Semimoist and sunny areas in rain and dry forests, grasslands.	8" (20 cm)
Cnemidophorus	N.Am., S.Am., W.I.	Te., S.Tr., Tr., Ar.	(T)—In a wide variety of habitats from below sea level to an elevation of over 7,000 ft., near streams in dry regions with sparse vegetation, deserts, sand dunes, sandy and grassy canyons, foothills, dry bush and paddocks, rocky terrain on semiarid mountain sides, dry forests, thorn woodlands.	6" to 1' 8" (15–51 cm)
Colobodactylus taunayi	S.Am.	S.Tr., Tr.	(T)—Subtropical and tropical rain forests.	(6)
Colobosaura	S.Am.	S.Tr., Tr.	(T)—Subtropical and tropical rain forests.	(6)
Crocodilurus	S.Am.	S.Tr., Tr.	(S.Aq.)—Swampy areas, near streams in rain forests.	2' (61 cm)
Dicrodon	S.Am.	Te., S.Tr., Tr.	(T)—Coastal areas and semideserts.	1' 4" (40 cm)
Dracaena (Caiman Lizards)	S.Am.	Tr.	(S.Aq.)—Flooded forests, tropical rain forests, forest edge situations, grasslands.	4' (122 cm)
Echinosaura (Little Rough Teiids)	S.Am.	S.Tr., Tr.	(T)—Subtropical and tropical rain forests.	7' (18 cm)
Ecpleopus	S.Am.	S.Tr., Tr.	(T)—Subtropical and tropical rain forests.	6" (15 cm)
Euspondylus	S.Am.	S.Tr., Tr.	(6)—Along river banks in sunny clearings in subtropical and tropical rain forests.	8" (20 cm)
Gymnophthalmus (Spectacled Teiids)	N.Am., S.Am., W.I.	Te., S.Tr., Tr.	(T)—In rotting tree stumps, under stones and fallen leaves in grasslands, dry forests, forest edge situations, coastal deserts and human habitations.	6" (15 cm)
Heterodactylus	S.Am.	S.Tr., Tr.	(T)—Subtropical and tropical rain forests.	(6)

Reptile (species listed for monotypic genera)	Region of World Reptile Occurs (1,4)	"Native" Thermal Regimes (2,4)	Habits (3,4,6) & Habitats (3,4,6) (also refer to Glossary for habitat definitions)	Approximate Adult Sizes Feet ('); Inches (") (4,5,6)
Iphisa elegans	S.Am.	S.Tr., Tr.	(T)—Near streams under damp leaf litter in subtropical and tropical rain forests, under dry ground litter at the summit of sand hills.	6" (15 cm)
Kentropyx	S.Am., W.I.	S.Tr., Tr.	(S, S.Aq., T)—River beaches, flooded lowlands, rain and dry forests, forest edge situations, grassy savannas.	4" to 1' 2" (10–35 cm)
Leposoma	S.Am.	S.Tr., Tr.	(S.Aq., T)—Near fresh water in rain and dry forests.	4" (10 cm)
Macropholidus	S.Am.	Te.	(T)—Cloud forests at an elevation of about 9,000 ft.	(6)
Microblepharus	S.Am.	(6)	(6)—(6)	(6)
Neusticurus (Water Teiids)	S.Am.	Te., S.Tr., Tr.	(S, S.Aq., T)—Rain forests, mountains at moderate elevations; some species near water holes along banks of rivers.	7" to 1' 1½" (18–34 cm)
Opipeuter xestus	S.Am.	Te.	(T)—Near rivers and streams in cloud forests at elevations between 3,000 and 9,000 ft.	(6)
Pantodactylus	S.Am.	S.Tr., Tr.	(F, T)—Rain forests.	4" (10 cm)
Pholidobolus	S.Am.	Te.	(T)—Dry forests, montane habitats at elevations between 6,000 and 12,000 ft.	2½" (6 cm)
Placosoma	S.Am.	S.Tr., Tr.	(T)—Subtropical and tropical rain forests.	(6)
Prionodactylus	S.Am.	S.Tr.(?), Tr.	(S, T)—Tropical rain forests, forest edge situations, mountain slopes.	6" (15 cm)
Proctoporus (Lightbulb Teiids)	S.Am., W.I.	S.Tr., Tr.	(T)—Under leaf litter on mountain slopes.	6" (15 cm)
Ptychoglossus	S.Am.	S.Tr., Tr.	(T)—Under leaf litter in subtropical and tropical rain forests.	4" (10 cm)
Stenolepis ridleyi	S.Am.	Tr.	(T)—Tropical rain forests.	(6)
Teius	S.Am.	Tr.	(T)—Among rotting leaves in grasslands, and brushlands.	1' 1½" (34 cm)
Tejovaranus flavipunctatus (False Monitor)	S.Am.	S.Tr., Ar.	(T)—Rocky deserts near the coast.	3' (91 cm)
Tretioscincus (includes *Calliscincopus*)	S.Am.	Tr.	(S, T)—Dry forests, thorn woodlands, coastal deserts, around human habitations.	6" (15 cm)
Tupinambis (Tegu Lizards)	S.Am., W.I.	S.Tr., Tr., Ar.	(A)—Rain and dry forests, cultivated areas, sand dunes in coastal deserts, sandy and grassy savannas.	4' (122 cm)
FAMILY VARANIDAE (Monitor Lizards)				
Varanus	Aus., E.I., N.Af., S.Af., S.As.	Te., S.Tr., Tr., Ar.	(A, Aq., S.Aq., T)—Many species in a wide variety of habitats including humid coastal woodlands and plains, wet and dry sclerophyll forests, monsoon, rain and palm forests, mangroves, around freshwater streams, rocky areas, grasslands, sandy and loamy desert areas, clay pans, caves.	9" to 12' (23–366 cm)
FAMILY XANTUSIIDAE (Night Lizards)				
Cricosaura typica (Cuban Night Lizard)	Cuba	Tr.	(T)—Rare, only found in an area 200 sq. Km; under rocks in sparse woods.	4" (13 cm)
Klauberina riversiana (Island Night Lizard)	N.Am.	S.Tr.	(T)—Grasslands, rubble slopes, cacti thickets.	8" (20 cm)
Lepidophyma (Central American Night or Bark Lizards)	S.Am.	S.Tr., Tr.	(F, T)—Subtropical and tropical flat lands and rain forests, rocky areas.	4" (10 cm)

Reptile (species listed for monotypic genera)	Region of World Reptile Occurs (1,4)	"Native" Thermal Regimes (2,4)	Habits (3,4,6) & Habitats (3,4,6) (also refer to Glossary for habitat definitions)	Approximate Adult Sizes Feet ('); Inches (") (4,5,6)
Xantusia	N.Am.	Te., Ar.	(T)—In deserts and dry forests under and around rotting trees, bushes, ground litter, boulders and in mammal burrows; range from almost sea level to an elevation of 9,300 ft.	4½" to 5½" (11–14 cm)
FAMILY XENOSAURIDAE (Xenosaurid and Shinisaurid Lizards)				
Shinisaurus crocodilus (Crocodile Lizard)	E.As.	Te.	(S, S.Aq., T)—In damp forests and on mountain sides along streams.	1' 4" (40 cm)
Xenosaurus	N.Am., S.Am.	Te.(?), S.Tr., Tr.	(A, S, T)—Under roots, in hollow tree stumps and rocky crevices, on trees and shrubs, tropical rain forests, cloud forests.	9" (23 cm)
Amphisbaenians (Worm Lizards)				
Agamodon, Amphisbaena, Ancylocranium, Anops, Aulura, Baikia, Bipes (Arizona Worm Snake), *Blanus, Bronia, Cadea, Chirindia, Cynisca, Dalophia, Diphalus, Diplometopon, Geocalamus, Leposternon, Loveridgea, Mesobaena, Monopeltis* (Central African Single-shield Worm Lizards), *Pachycalamus, Rhineura floridana* (Florida Worm Lizard) *Tomuropeltis, Trogonophis, Zygaspis*	Eu., N.Af., N.Am., S.Af., S.Am., W.I.	Te., S.Tr., Tr.	(F)—Rain and dry forests, high pine and mesophytic hammocks.	3½" to 3' (9–91 cm)
Rhynchocephalians				
Sphenodon punctatus (Tuatara)	Coastal Is. off N.Z.	Te.	(F, T)—In petrel burrows in open ground below forest canopy; often dig own burrows.	2' (61 cm)
Snakes				
FAMILY ACROCHORDIDAE (File or Elephant's Trunk Snakes)				
Acrocordus	Aus., E.I., Phil., S.As.	Tr.	(Aq.)—Burrow under sand, mud, leaves, and roots of trees in banks of rivers, streams and freshwater lagoons, estuaries, ocean.	3' 6" to 8' (107–244 cm)
FAMILY ANILIIDAE (Burrowing Snakes)				
Anilius (False Coral Snakes)	S.Am.	Tr.	(F, T)—Near water, in loose, sandy soil, under ground litter and fallen timber in tropical rain forests.	3' (91 cm)
Anomalochilus (White Spotted Snakes)	E.I., S.As.	Tr.	(F)—Tropical rain forests.	10" (25 cm)
Cylindrophis (Pipe Snakes)	E.I., S.As.	Tr.	(F, S.Aq.)—Under rocks, rotten logs, and other debris in marshy areas including paddy fields, mud flats, river deltas, swamps, and cultivated areas.	3' (91 cm)
FAMILY BOIDAE (Pythons and Boas)				
Acrantophis (Ground Boas)	Mad.	S.Tr.	(T)—Sparse, open woodland, dry ground near water, hot humid forests.	10' (305 cm)
Aspidites (Black-headed Pythons)	Aus.	S.Tr., Tr., Ar.	(T)—Wet coastal forests, woodlands, grasslands, marshes, swamps, semiarid to arid deserts.	4' 6" to 8' (122–244 cm)
Boa (Boa Constrictors)	N.Am., S.Am., W.I.	S.Tr., Tr.	(A, S.Aq., T)—Near bodies of fresh water in semidesert regions, coastal deserts, grasslands, thorn woodlands, rain and dry forests, forest edge situations and around human dwellings.	10' (305 cm)

Reptile (species listed for monotypic genera)	Region of World Reptile Occurs (1,4)	"Native" Thermal Regimes (2,4)	Habits (3,4,6) & Habitats (3,4,6) (also refer to Glossary for habitat definitions)	Approximate Adult Sizes Feet ('); Inches (") (4,5,6)
Bolyeria multicarinata	Round Is.	Tr.	(F, T)—Prefers moist soil in tropical rain forests.	3' to 5' (91–152 cm)
Calabaria reinhardtii (Calabar Ground Python)	S.Af.	Tr.	(F, T)—Under leaf litter and loose soil in humid tropical forests.	3' (91 cm)
Candoia (Pacific Boas)	Aus., E.I., Pac.	Tr.	(A, T)—Near bodies of fresh water in humid tropical forests, marshes, swamps.	1' 6" to 6' (46–183 cm)
Casarea dussumieri (Round Island Ground Boa)	Round Is.	Tr.	(F, T)—In sparse remnants of tropical forests.	5' (152 cm)
Charina (Rubber Boas)	N.Am.	Te.	(F, S, S.Aq., T)—Under fallen timber, in rock crevices and mammal burrows, along roads and open areas, in mountains, canyons, and conifer areas; prefer humid habitats.	1' to 2' 6" (30–76 cm)
Chondropython viridis (Green Tree Python)	Aus., E.I.	Tr.	(A)—In hollow trees, bushes, and shrubs in tropical rain forests.	6' (183 cm)
Corallus (Tree Boas)	S.Am., W.I.	S.Tr., Tr.	(A)—Near bodies of fresh water in rain and dry forests, forest edge situations, woodlands and grasslands, cane fields, swamps.	8' (244 cm)
Epicrates (West Indian and Rainbow Boas)	S.Am., W.I.	S.Tr., Tr.	(A)—Rain and dry forests, forest edge situations, rocky areas, grasslands, mangroves, around human dwellings; may estivate during dry periods.	10' (305 cm)
Eryx (includes *Gongylophis conicus*) (Sand Boas)	Eu., N.Af., S.Af., S.As., W.As.	Te., S.Tr., Tr., Ar.	(F)—In mammal burrows on sandy dry plains and scrubby grasslands, rock outcroppings, forests.	1' 6" to 2' 6" (46–76 cm)
Eunectes (Anacondas)	S.Am.	Tr.	(S, S.Aq.)—In and around sluggish rivers and streams in tropical rain and dry forests, grassy savannas, swamps, marshes.	30' (914 cm)
Exiliboa placata (Oaxacan Wood Snake)	N.Am., S.Am.	Te.	(T)—Under logs in montane cloud forests.	2' (61 cm)
Liasis (includes *Bothrochilus*) (Rock Pythons)	Aus., E.I.	S.Tr., Tr.	(A, T)—Near waterholes, streams and lagoons in monsoon forests, grasslands, woodlands and deserts, swamps; occasionally found under rock slabs, termite mounds and around human dwellings.	4' 6" to 21' (137–640 cm)
Lichanura (Rosy Boas)	N.Am.	Te., Ar.	(A, F, T)—Near ponds, creeks and river banks, in rocky terrain with brushy vegetation, barren mountains, foothills, cultivated fields, grassy areas, chaparral and scrubby deserts.	1' 6" to 4' (46–122 cm)
Morelia (Carpet and Diamond Pythons)	Aus., E.I., Phil., S.As.	Te., S.Tr., Tr., Ar.	(A, T)—In rock piles, mammal burrows, and in trees, rain forests, woodlands, mangroves, deserts, around human dwellings.	6' 6" to 13' (198–396 cm)
Python				
P. *anchietae* (Angolan Python)	S.Af.	Tr., S.Tr.	(S, T)—Rock outcroppings, grasslands, open brushy plains.	5' to 6' (152–182 cm)
P. *curtus* (Blood Python)	E.I.	Tr.	(S.Aq., T)—Under loose leaf litter in clearings of thick tropical rain forests, near swamps, lakes, and large bodies of fresh water.	10' (305 cm)

Reptile (species listed for monotypic genera)	Region of World Reptile Occurs (1,4)	"Native" Thermal Regimes (2,4)	Habits (3,4,6) & Habitats (3,4,6) (also refer to Glossary for habitat definitions)	Approximate Adult Sizes Feet ('); Inches (") (4,5,6)
P. molurus (Indian and Burmese Pythons)	E.I., S.As.	S.Tr., Tr.	(A, S.Aq., T)—In a wide variety of habitats usually near a permanent source of fresh water, in abandoned mammal burrows and hollow trees, forests, rocky slopes of hills at an elevation of about 8,000 ft., open rocky areas, grasslands, woodlands, swamps, marshes, river valleys, mangrove thickets, caves.	21' (640 cm)
P. regius (Royal or Ball Python)	S.Af.	Tr.	(S, T)—Often near fresh water in open forests, grasslands, and mountain regions.	3' to 5' (91–152 cm)
P. reticulatus (Reticulated Python)	E.I., Phil.(?), S.As.	Tr.	(A, T)—Dense, hot and humid forests, woodlands, swamps, occasionally around human habitations.	30' (914 cm)
P. sebae (African Rock Python)	S.Af.	S.Tr., Tr.	(S.Aq., T)—Slightly arboreal; occasionally near fresh water in dense forests, usually near fresh water in open scrub, rocky outcrops and grasslands, around human habitations in urban and suburban areas.	15' to 20' (457–610 cm)
P. timorensis (Timor Python)	Timor and Flores Is.	Tr.	(A, T)—Bush and dry forests.	10' (305 cm)
Sanzinia madagascariensis (Madagascar Tree Boa)	Mad.	S.Tr.	(A)—Trees and shrubs near bodies of fresh water in or adjacent to rain forests.	8' (244 cm)
Trachyboa (Rough Boas)	N.Am., S.Am.	S.Tr., Tr.	(T)—Under logs and other debris, usually near fresh water, tropical and montane rain forests, humid to wet lowland areas, garden walls, rocky ledges.	1' 6" (46 cm)
Ungaliophis (Central American Dwarf Boas)	S.Am.	S.Tr., Tr.	(S, T)—Under logs and other debris, often near fresh water, lower montane forests, rain forests.	3' (91 cm)
FAMILY COLUBRIDAE (Colubrid or Typical Snakes)				
Achalinus	E.As., S.As.	Te., S.Tr.	(F)—Hilly areas, under forest litter, roots of bushes and grasses.	1' 8" (51 cm)
Adelphicos quadrivirgatus	N.Am., S.Am.	S.Tr., Tr.	(T)—Subtropical and tropical wet forests.	1' 4" (40 cm)
Aeluroglena cucullata	Somalia	S.Tr.	(6)—(6)	(6)
Aftronatrix anoscopus (Brown Water Snake)	S.Af.	Tr.	(S.Aq.)—Forest pools and streams.	2' (61 cm)
Agrophis	E.I.	S.Tr.(?), Tr.(?)	(F)—Montane forests.	8" to 10" (20–25 cm)
Ahaetulla (= *Dryophis*) (Oriental Vine Snakes, Whipsnakes)	E.I., Phil., S.As.	S.Tr., Tr.	(A, S)—In trees and shrubs, lowlands, plains, deciduous, rain, submontane and evergreen forests, cultivated areas.	8" to 6' (20–183 cm)
Alluaudina	Mad.	S.Tr.	(T)—Forests.	1' to 1' 8" (30–51 cm)
Alsophis (West Indian Racers)	W.I.	Tr.	(S, T)—Arroyos, rocky areas, sand dunes, woodlands, cultivated areas.	2' to 7' (61–213 cm)
Amastridium (= *Phrydops*) *veliferum*	N.Am., S.Am., W.I.	S.Tr., Tr.	(T)—Subtropical and tropical forests.	1' 8" (51 cm)
Amblycephalus	E.As.(?), E.I., S.As.	S.Tr., Tr.	(A)—Moist cultivated areas.	2' (61 cm)
Amblyodipsas (Purple-glossed Snakes)	S.Af.	S.Tr., Tr.	(F)—Moist areas in rocky regions, forests, grasslands and deserts.	15" to 2' 6" (38–76 cm)

Reptile (species listed for monotypic genera)	Region of World Reptile Occurs (1,4)	"Native" Thermal Regimes (2,4)	Habits (3,4,6) & Habitats (3,4,6) (also refer to Glossary for habitat definitions)	Approximate Adult Sizes Feet ('); Inches (") (4,5,6)
Amphiesma	E.I., S.As.	Te., S.Tr., Tr.	(A, S.Aq., T)—In trees over-hanging or near freshwater streams, swamps and lagoons, under logs, leaves and other debris in lowlands, hilly country, mountains, wooded and grassy areas, sometimes near cultivated fields; may estivate in dry season.	1' 6" to 3' (46–91 cm)
Amplorhinus multimaculatus (Cape Many-spotted or Cape Reed Snake)	S.Af.	S.Tr.	(S.Aq., T)—Marshes, montane grasslands near fresh water.	1' 3" to 2' (38–61 cm)
Anoplohydrus aemulans	E.I.	Tr.	(T)—Tropical rain forests.	1' 6" (46 cm)
Antillophis	W.I.	Tr.	(T)—Tropical forests, scrub areas; similar to *Thamnophis*.	1' 2" (35 cm)
Aparallactus (Centipede-eating Snakes)	S.Af.	S.Tr., Tr.	(F)—Under logs, rocks and other debris, in termite mounds, sandy areas, coastal bush, evergreen forests, montane grasslands.	1' to 1' 8" (30–51 cm)
Aplopeltura (= *Haplopeltura*) (Blunt-headed Snakes)	E.I., S.As.	S.Tr., Tr.	(A, T)—Forests.	2' 6" (76 cm)
Apostolepis	S.Am.	S.Tr., Tr.	(F, T)—Subtropical and tropical rain and dry forests.	10" to 2' 2" (25–66 cm)
Argyrogena (Indian Racers, Indian Rat Snakes)	S.As.	Te., S.Tr., Tr.	(T)—In rodent burrows, on rock piles, high grassy areas, heavy brush, urban areas.	3' 6" (102 cm)
Arizona (Glossy Snakes)	N.Am.	Te., Ar.	(F, T)—Semiarid, sandy, grassy or wooded areas, plowed fields, chaparral, deserts.	2' 3" to 4' 8" (69–142 cm)
Arrhyton	W.I.	Tr.	(T ?)—In moist litter, under rocks, around human dwellings.	1' (30 cm)
Aspidura (Rough-sided Snakes)	Sri Lanka	S.Tr.(?), Tr.(?)	(F)—Under leaf litter and other debris, in dung heaps, montane forests.	8" to 1' 4" (20–41 cm)
Atractaspis (Mole Vipers, Burrowing Adders, Side-stabbing Snakes)	N.Af., S.Af., W.As.	S.Tr., Tr.	(F, T)—Tropical rain forests, grasslands.	1' to 1' 6" (30–46 cm)
Atractus (Spindle Snakes)	S.Am., W.I.	S.Tr., Tr.	(F, T)—Under leaf litter and fallen timber, tropical rain forests, forest edge situations, grasslands, cultivated fields.	2' (61 cm)
Atretium (Keelback Water Snakes)	S.As.	S.Tr., Tr.	(Aq., S.Aq.)—In crab holes, other holes, still waters.	1' 6" to 2' 6" (46–76 cm)
Balanophis ceylonensis	Sri Lanka	S.Tr. (?), Tr.(?)	(F ?, T ?)—Montane rain forests.	2' (61 cm)
Bitia hydroides	E.I., S.As.	Tr.	(Aq., S.Aq.)—In and around coastal waters.	1' 8" (51 cm)
Blythia reticulata	S.As.	Tr.	(6)—Tropical, montane rain forests.	1' 4" (41 cm)
Boaedon (House Snakes)	S.Af., Seychelles, W.As.	Tr., Ar.	(T)—Gallery forests, deserts, urban areas.	1' 8" to 3' 3" (51–99 cm)
Boiga (Cat or Tree Snakes)	Aus., E.I., Pac., Phil., S.Af., S.As., W.As.	Te., S.Tr., Tr.	(A, T)—In hollow trees and rock crevices, rain forests, woodlands, caves, around human dwellings.	4' to 8' (122–244 cm)
Bothrolycus lineatus	S.Af.	S.Tr., Tr.	(S)—Tropical gallery and rain forests, montane forests.	4' (122 cm)
Bothrophthalmus	S.Af.	Te., S.Tr., Tr.	(S.Aq. ?)—Rain forests, forest islands, lake-shore forests.	4' 9" (145 cm)
Brachyophis revoili	N.Af.	Tr.	(6)—(6)	(6)
Calamaria (Reed Snakes)	E.I., Phil., S.As.	S.Tr., Tr.	(F)—Under stones and fallen logs in forests.	11" to 1' 2" (28–36 cm)
Calamorhabdium	E.I.	Tr.	(F)—Under stones and fallen debris in wooded, hilly damp areas.	1' (30 cm)
Cantoria violacea (Cantor's Water Snake)	E.I., S.As.	Tr.	(Aq.)—Coastal waters, mouths of rivers.	3' (91 cm)

Reptile (species listed for monotypic genera)	Region of World Reptile Occurs (1,4)	"Native" Thermal Regimes (2,4)	Habits (3,4,6) & Habitats (3,4,6) (also refer to Glossary for habitat definitions)	Approximate Adult Sizes Feet ('); Inches (") (4,5,6)
Carphophis amoenus (Worm Snake)	N.Am.	Te.	(F)—Humid areas, under ground litter in woods or wooded areas, meadows, and agricultural areas.	7" to 1' (18–61 cm)
Cemophora (Scarlet Snakes)	N.Am.	Te.	(F)—Under ground litter in sandy or muddy areas, near swamps, creeks, streams, farming or construction sites.	8" to 2' (20–61 cm)
Cerberus (Oriental or Dog-faced Water Snakes)	Aus., E.I., Phil., S.As.	Tr.	(Aq., S.Aq.)—Coastal waters, coastal mangrove swamps, estuaries, tidal rivers and creeks, fresh water, and cultivated areas.	2' to 4' (61.0–121.9 cm)
Cercaspis carinatus	Sri Lanka	Tr.	(T)—(6)	2' 6" (76 cm)
Chamaelycus	S.Af.	Tr.	(F)—Tropical forests.	1' 2" (35 cm)
Chersodromus liebmanni	N.Am.,, S.Am.	S.Tr.	(T)—(6)	1' 2" (35 cm)
Chilomeniscus (Banded Sand Snakes)	N.Am.	Te.	(F, T)—Under ground litter and rocks, in sand, loose soil or stumps, highland deserts.	6" to 11" (15–28 cm)
Chilorhinophis (Striped or Black and Yellow Burrowing Snakes)	S.Af.	S.Tr., Tr.	(F)—Grasslands, ploughed fields; active after rain.	8" to 1' 4" (?) (20–41 cm)
Chionactis (Shovel-nosed Snakes)	N.Am.	Te., Ar.	(F)—Sandy areas, dunes in deserts and desert foothills, rocky hillsides, arroyos, creosote bush, and mesquite areas.	6" to 1' 5" (15–43 cm)
Chironius	S.Am., W.I.	S.Tr., Tr.	(S, T)—Rain and dry forests, forest edge situations, sandy scrubby terrain, coastal swamps.	1' to 6' (30–183 cm)
Chrysopelea (Flying Snakes)	E.I., S.As.	S.Tr., Tr.	(A, S)—In trees and bushes on hills and around human dwellings.	6' (183 cm)
Clelia clelia (Mussurana)	N.Am., S.Am., W.I.	S.Tr., Tr.	(T)—Under ground litter and in mammal burrows in a variety of habitats including rain and dry forests, forest edge situations and grasslands.	7' (213 cm)
Clonophis (Kirtland's Water Snakes)	N.Am.	Te.	(S.Aq., T)—Under ground litter, near water, around human habitations.	1' 2" to 1' 6" (36–46 cm)
Collorhabdium williamsoni	E.I.	Tr.	(6)—Highlands.	(6)
Coluber (Racers, Whipsnakes)	E.I., Eu., N.Af., N.Am., S.Am., S.As.	Te., S.Tr., Tr.	(A, T)—Virtually all land habitats; near streams, swamps and marshes, rocky and scrub areas, deciduous and coniferous forests, open fields, sand dunes, and near human dwellings.	2' to 9' (61–274 cm)
Compsophis albiventris	Mad.	S.Tr.	(T)—Montane forests ?	7" (18 cm)
Coniophanes (Black-striped Snakes)	N.Am. S.Am.	Te., S.Tr., Tr., Ar.	(F, T)—Under ground litter, in palm fronds and dead cacti, desert scrub, semiarid forests, tropical and subtropical wet forests, coastal thorn scrub.	1' to 1' 6" (30–46 cm)
Conophis (includes *Tomodon*)	N.Am., S.Am.	S.Tr., Tr.	(T)—Dry tropical forests, semiarid regions.	1' to 2' 3" (30–69 cm)
Conopsis	Mexico	Te., S.Tr., Tr.	(F, T)—Under rocks and fallen timber, tropical short-tree forests, montane forests, pine/oak woodlands.	4" to 1' (10–30 cm)
Contia (Sharp-tailed Snakes)	N.Am., S.Am.	Te.	(F, T)—Under ground litter, in redwood forests, hilly terrain, near streams and irrigation ditches.	5" to 1' 6" (13–46 cm)
Coronella (European Smooth or Crowned Snakes)	As., Eu., N.Af., W.As.	Te.	(T)—Under rocks and in crevices, dry rocky terrain with bushes.	2' 6" to 3' (76–91 cm)

Reptile (species listed for monotypic genera)	Region of World Reptile Occurs (1,4)	"Native" Thermal Regimes (2,4)	Habits (3,4,6) & Habitats (3,4,6) (also refer to Glossary for habitat definitions)	Approximate Adult Sizes Feet ('); Inches (") (4,5,6)
Crisantophis nevermanni (= *Conophis nevermanni*)	S.Am.	Tr.	(T)—Tropical dry forests.	1' 2" (36 cm)
Crotaphopeltis (African Herald or Southern Spot-striped Snakes)	S.Af.	S.Tr., Tr.	(A, S.Aq., T)—Under logs, leaf litter and rocks near fresh water, swamps, marshes, grasslands, open woodlands.	1' to 3' (30–91 cm)
Cryptolycus nanus (Dwarf Wolf Snake)	S.Af.	S.Tr.	(F)—Woodlands, flood plains.	1' (30 cm)
Cyclocorus	Phil.	Tr.	(6)—(6)	(6)
Darlingtonia haetiana	W.I.	Tr.	(T)—Semiarid scrub ?	1' (30 cm)
Dasypeltis (African Egg-eating Snakes)	S.Af., W.As.	Te., S.Tr., Tr.	(A, T)—In all types of habitats except deserts and rain forests.	1' 6" to 3' (46–91 cm)
Dendrelaphis (Tree Snakes)	Aus., E.I., Phil., S.As.	Te., S.Tr., Tr.	(A, S)—Monsoon, bamboo, montane and rain forests, woodlands, mangroves, around human habitation.	2' to 6' (61–183 cm)
Dendrolycus elapoides	S.Af.	Tr.	(A)—Tropical rain forests.	1' 8" (51 cm)
Dendrophidion	N.Am., S.Am.	S.Tr., Tr.	(S, T)—Subtropical and tropical rain forests.	4' (122 cm)
Diadophis (Ring-necked Snakes)	N.Am.	Te.	(T)—Under ground litter in a wide variety of habitats including coastal areas, mountains, deserts, urban areas.	10" to 2' 6" (25–76 cm)
Diaphorolepis wagneri	S.Am.	Te., S.Tr., Tr.	(F, T)—Tropical lowlands, montane and rain forests.	2' 3" (69 cm)
Dinodon (Big-toothed Snakes)	E.As., S.As.	Te., S.Tr.	(T)—Around small streams, in rice fields and wooded areas.	5' (152 cm)
Dipsadoboa (Cat-eyed Tree Snakes)	S.Af.	S.Tr., Tr.	(A)—Under bark and in hollow trees in gallery and tropical rain forests.	3' 6" (107 cm)
Dipsas (Thirst or Snail-eating Snakes)	N.Am., S.Am.	S.Tr., Tr.	(S, T)—Tropical montane and rain forests, cloud forests.	3' (91 cm)
Dipsina (Dwarf Beaked Snakes)	S.Af.	S.Tr., Tr.	(T)—Under loose stones or sand at the base of bushes in rocky areas.	1' to 1' 4" (30–41 cm)
Dispholidus typus (Boomslang)	S.Af.	Te., S.Tr., Tr.	(A, T)—In all types of habitats except deserts.	4' to 6' (122–183 cm)
Ditypophis vivax	Socotra	S.Tr.	(6)—(6)	(6)
Drepanoides anomalus	S.Am.	Tr.	(F)—Tropical rain forests, forest edge situations, mountain slopes, in and around human dwellings.	1' 2" (35 cm)
Dromicodryas	Mad.	S.Tr.	(T)—(6)	3' 6" (107 cm)
Dromicus (West Indian Ground Snakes)	S.Am., W.I.	S.Tr., Tr.	(T)—Semiarid scrub areas near fresh water.	1' 8" (51 cm)
Dromophis (Olympic Snakes)	S.Af.	S.Tr., Tr.	(S, S.Aq., T)—Swamps and marshes.	2' to 3' (61–91 cm)
Drymarchon (Indigo Snakes, Cribos)	N.Am., S.Am.	Te., S.Tr., Tr.	(T)—In tortoise and mammal burrows, near streams and ponds in sandy, palmetto-covered areas, pine barrens, hammocks, savanna woodlands, rain and dry forests, forest edge situations, coastal deserts.	3' to 8' (91–244 cm)
Drymobius (Speckled Racers)	N.Am., S.Am.	Te., S.Tr., Tr.	(T)—Near fresh water in rain and dry forests, plains and mountains.	1' 6" to 3' 6" (46–107 cm)
Drymoluber	S.Am.	Tr.	(T)—Open areas in tropical rain forests.	3' (91 cm)
Dryocalamus (Bridal Snakes)	E.I., Phil., S.As.	S.Tr., Tr.	(A, T)—Under ground litter in monsoon and rain forests, plains and hills.	1' 2" to 3' (35–91 cm)
Dryophiops rubescens	E.I., Phil., S.As.	S.Tr., Tr.	(A)—Trees and shrubs.	3' (91 cm)
Duberria (Slug-eating Snakes)	S.Af.	Te., S.Tr.	(T)—Under rocks and decaying timber, coastal bush, grasslands, mountain slopes, cultivated areas.	1' to 1' 6" (30–46 cm)

Reptile (species listed for monotypic genera)	Region of World Reptile Occurs (1,4)	"Native" Thermal Regimes (2,4)	Habits (3,4,6) & Habitats (3,4,6) (also refer to Glossary for habitat definitions)	Approximate Adult Sizes Feet ('); Inches (") (4,5,6)
Eirenis (Dwarf Snakes)	N.Af., W.As.	Te.	(T)—Under rocks, loose stones and in rocky crevices in mountain regions.	1' to 2' (30–61 cm)
Elaschistodon westermanni (Indian Egg-eating Snake)	S.As.	S.Tr.	(A)—Open forests.	3' (91 cm)
Elaphe (Rat or Trinket Snakes)	E.I., Eu., N.Am., S.Am., S.As., W.As.	Te., S.Tr., Tr., Ar.	(A, S, T)—In almost all types of habitats from mangrove swamps to inland deserts and everything in between, near human dwellings where rodents and other vertebrates are present.	1' 6" to 8' (46–244 cm)
Elapoides fuscus	E.I.	Tr.	(F)—Tropical, montane rain forests.	1' 8" (51 cm)
Elapomojus dimidiatus	S.Am.	(6)	(6)—(6)	(6)
Elapomorphus	S.Am.	S.Tr., Tr.	(F, T)—Subtropical and tropical rain forests.	8" to 1' (20–30 cm)
Emmochliophis fugleri	S.Am.	S.Tr.	(6)—(6)	(6)
Enhydris (Asian Water Snakes)	Aus., E.I., S.As.	S.Tr., Tr.	(Aq.)—Freshwater creeks, clear swamps, large rivers, water holes, wet cultivated areas.	1' 6" to 3' (46–91 cm)
Enulius	N.Am., S.Am.	S.Tr., Tr., Ar.	(F)—Tropical rain, dry and arid forests.	1' to 1' 4" (30–41 cm)
Eremiophis (includes Zaocys)	N.Af., S.As., W.As.	S.Tr.(?)	(S, T ?)—Perhaps mountain slopes, wooded and agricultural areas.	(6)
Erpeton (Tentacled Snakes)	E.I., S.As.	Tr.	(Aq.)—Flooded ditches and rice fields; fresh and brackish water.	2' (61 cm)
Erythrolamprus (False Coral Snakes)	S.Am.	S.Tr., Tr.	(T)—On rain forest floor; very secretive.	1' 6" to 3' (46–91 cm)
Farancia (Mud and Rainbow Snakes)	N.Am.	Te.	(Aq., F., S.Aq.)—Fresh and saltwater marshes, bogs, wet lowlands, freshly plowed fields, swamps, ditches, other muddy areas.	1' 8" to 5' (51–152 cm)
Ficimia (Mexican Hooknose Snakes)	N.Am., S.Am.	S.Tr., Tr.	(F)—Moist and dry forests, desert grasslands, rocky terrain.	10" to 1' 7" (25–48 cm)
Fimbrios klossi (Bearded Snake)	S.As.	S.Tr.	(T)—Under logs in montane forests.	1' 4" (41 cm)
Fordonia leucobalia (White-bellied Mangrove or Crab-eating Snake)	Aus., E.I., Phil., S.As.	Tr.	(Aq., S.Aq.)—Mudbanks, estuaries mangrove swamps.	1' 6" to 7' (46–213 cm)
Gastropyxis	S.Af.	Tr.	(A)—Tropical rain and gallery forests.	3' 6" (107 cm)
Geagras	S.Am.	Tr.	(F)—Dry forests to semideserts.	8" (20 cm)
Geodipsas	Mad., S.Af.	S.Tr., Tr.	(T)—Damp areas in rain and dry forests.	1' 2" to 2' 8" (36–81 cm)
Geophis	N.Am., S.Am.	S.Tr., Tr., Ar.(?)	(F, T)—Pine/oak, cloud, rain and dry forests, cactus-covered deserts.	10" to 1' 4" (25–41 cm)
Gerarda prevostiana (Gerard's Water Snake)	E.I., S.As.	Tr.	(Aq.)—Tidal rivers, estuaries, coastal waters.	2' (61 cm)
Gonionotophis	S.Af.	Tr.	(F, T)—Tropical forests.	1' 8" (51 cm)
Gonyophis margaritatus (Rainbow Tree Snake)	E.I.	Tr.	(T)—Near fresh water in lowland and montane forests.	5' 6" (168 cm)
Gonyosoma (Tree Racers)	E.I., Phil., S.As.	Tr.	(A)—Bamboo, mangrove, monsoon, and rain forests; also near brackish water.	7' 6" (229 cm)
Grayia (African Water Snakes)	S.Af.	Tr.	(Aq., S.Aq.)—Rivers, streams and lakes near or in forests and grasslands.	7' 6" (229 cm)
Gyalopion (Hook-nosed Snakes)	N.Am.	Te., S.Tr., Tr.	(F)—Mesquite/creosote and open short grassy areas on sandy or gravel terrain, tropical thorn scrubs.	6" to 1' 2" (15–36 cm)
Haemorrhois (includes Zamenis)	Eu., N.Af., W.As.	Te., S.Tr.	(T)—Dry, sparsely wooded areas, rocky hillsides, brush.	3' to 8' (91–244 cm)

Reptile (species listed for monotypic genera)	Region of World Reptile Occurs (1,4)	"Native" Thermal Regimes (2,4)	Habits (3,4,6) & Habitats (3,4,6) (also refer to Glossary for habitat definitions)	Approximate Adult Sizes Feet ('); Inches (") (4,5,6)
Haplocerus ceylonensis	Sri Lanka	Tr.	(F, T)—Hill country, montane forests.	1' 8" (51 cm)
Haplodon philippinensis	Phil.	Tr.	(T)—Tropical lowland forests.	2' 8" (81 cm)
Hapsidophrys lineatus (Green-lined Snake)	S.Af.	Tr.	(A)—Tropical rain, gallery, and montane forests.	4' (122 cm)
Helicops (South American Water Snakes)	S.Am.	Te., S.Tr., Tr.	(S.Aq., T)—Streams and small bodies of fresh water in rain and dry forests and grasslands; habits similar to *Nerodia*.	3' (91 cm)
Hemirhagerrhis (Bark or Mopane Snakes)	S.Af.	S.Tr., Tr.	(T)—Under loose bark of trees in dry, lowland grasslands and savanna woodlands, mountain areas.	8" to 1' 4" (20–41 cm)
Heterodon (Hognose Snakes)	N.Am.	Te., S.Tr.	(F, T)—Sandy areas on hills, dunes, and grasslands (occasionally found in wet or moist habitats).	1' to 4' (30–122 cm)
Heteroliodon torquatus (Shovel-nosed Burrowing Snake)	Mad.	S.Tr.	(F)—(6)	1' (30 cm)
Heurnia ventromaculata	E.I.	Tr.	(6)—(6)	(6)
Hologerrhum philippinum	Phil.	Tr.	(F)—(6)	1' 2" (36 cm)
Homalopsis buccata (Puff-faced or Dog-faced Water Snake)	E.I., S.As.	S.Tr., Tr.	(Aq.)—Fresh and salt waters; common in drainage ditches.	3' (91 cm)
Homoroselaps (Harlequin Snakes)	S.Af.	Te., S.Tr.	(F)—In termite mounds, under loose soil, in desert-like dry habitats.	8" to 1' 4" (20–41 cm)
Hormonotus modestus (Yellow Forest Snake)	S.Af.	S.Tr., Tr.	(T)—Rain forests.	2' 10" (86 cm)
Hydrablabes	E.I.	Tr.	(F)—Tropical rain forests.	1' 8" (51 cm)
Hydrodynastes (= *Cyclagras*, *Dugandia*) (False Water Cobras)	S.Am.	S.Tr., Tr.	(S.Aq., T)—In moist areas of thorn forests, grasslands.	6' 6" (198 cm)
Hydromorphus	S.Am.	Tr.	(Aq., S.Aq.)—In and around fresh water of tropical lowland forests.	2' 5" (74 cm)
Hydrops triangularis	S.Am.	Tr.	(Aq., S.Aq.)—Tropical rain and dry forests, in and around fresh water in grasslands.	1' 6" to 3' (46–91 cm)
Hypoptophis wilsoni	S.Af.	Tr.	(T)—(6)	(6)
Hypsiglena (Night Snakes)	N.Am., S.Am.	Te., S.Tr., Ar.	(F, T)—Under rocks, ground litter, and other debris in a wide variety of arid to humid habitats, including hot sagebrush and desert areas, mountain sides and river areas.	7" to 2' (18–61 cm)
Hypsirhynchus ferox	W.I.	Tr.	(T ?)—(6)	3' (91 cm)
Ialtris	W.I.	Tr.	(T)—(6)	2' 6" (76 cm)
Idiopholis	Borneo	Tr.	(6)—(6)	6" to 8" (15–20 cm)
Iguanognathus werneri	Sumatra	Tr.	(F ?)—Tropical rain forests?	1' (30 cm)
Imantodes (Big-headed, Chunk-headed or Blunt-headed Tree Snakes)	N.Am., S.Am.	S.Tr., Tr., Ar.	(A, S)—Trees and scrubs in rain and dry forests, grasslands.	3' 8" (112 cm)
Ithycyphus	Mad.	S.Tr.	(T)—Rain and dry forests.	3' (91 cm)
Lampropeltis (Kingsnakes and Milk Snakes)	N.Am., S.Am.	Te., S.Tr., Tr., Ar.	(T)—All types of habitats from arid to humid, from sea level to high elevations, coastal areas to inland areas; frequently seen around human dwellings.	7" to 6' (18–183 cm)
Lamprophis (Aurora Snakes)	S.Af., W.As.	Te., S.Tr., Tr.	(F, S.Aq., T)—Under ground litter and near bodies of fresh water in grasslands, woodlands, on scrub-covered hillsides, and around human dwellings.	1' to 4' (30–122 cm)
Langaha (Leafnose Snakes)	Mad.	S.Tr.	(A)—Rain and dry forests, dry scrub areas.	3' (91 cm)
Leimadophis	S.Am.	Te., S.Tr., Tr.	(S.Aq., T)—Wet areas and along bodies of fresh water in rain and dry forests, forest edge situations, grasslands.	2' (61 cm)

Reptile (species listed for monotypic genera)	Region of World Reptile Occurs (1,4)	"Native" Thermal Regimes (2,4)	Habits (3,4,6) & Habitats (3,4,6) (also refer to Glossary for habitat definitions)	Approximate Adult Sizes Feet ('); Inches (") (4,5,6)
Leptodeira (Cat-eyed Snakes)	N.Am., S.Am.	Te., S.Tr., Tr., Ar.	(A, T)—Semidesert areas, thorny grasslands, coastal plains, rain, dry and arid forests, forest edge situations, wooded banks of streams, ponds and rivers.	10" to 3' (25–91 cm)
Leptodrymus pulcherrimus	S.Am.	S.Tr., Tr.	(6)—Tropical and subtropical moist and dry forests, thornbush.	3' 4" (102 cm)
Leptophis (Parrot Snakes)	N.Am., S.Am.	S.Tr., Tr.	(A, S, T)—Near fresh water in rain and dry forests, forest edge situations, bushlands, grasslands.	5' (153 cm)
Lepturophis borneensis (Slender Wolf Snake)	E.I.	Tr.	(A, T)—Forests.	4' 10" (147 cm)
Limnophis bicolor (Striped Swamp Snake)	S.Af.	Te., S.Tr.	(S.Aq., T)—Marshy areas.	2' (61 cm)
Lioheterodon (Madagascar Hognose Snakes)	Mad.	S.Tr.	(F, T)—Grasslands, plains, rain forests, forest edge situations.	4' (122 cm)
Liopeltis	E.As., E.I., S.As.	Te., S.Tr., Tr.	(T)—Wooded and moist areas, bamboo, monsoon and rain forests, hilly regions, gardens.	1' to 2' 8" (30–81 cm)
Liophidium	Mad.	S.Tr.	(T)—Rain and dry forests.	1' to 1' 8" (30–51 cm)
Liophis (includes *Lygophis*)	S.Am., W.I.	S.Tr., Tr.	(S.Aq., T)—In and around bodies of fresh water, rain, dry and gallery forests, forest edge situations, grasslands.	1' 2" to 2' 8" (36–81 cm)
Liopholidophis	Mad.	S.Tr.	(6)—(6)	2' to 3' (61–91 cm)
Lycodon (Oriental Wolf Snakes)	E.I., Mad., S.As., W.As.	S.Tr., Tr.	(A, T)—In stone piles, hollows of trees, under bark and logs, and other secure areas, open areas, caves, various dry habitats, plateaus, forested and rocky mountain areas, cultivated fields, around human dwellings.	2' (61 cm)
Lycodonomorphus (includes *Abladophis*) (African or White-lipped Water Snakes)	S.Af.	Te., S.Tr., Tr.	(Aq., S.Aq.)—In and around flowing streams of wooded areas.	1' to 3' (30–91 cm)
Lycodryas	Mad.	S.Tr.	(A)—Rain and dry forests.	1' 3" to 3' (38–91 cm)
Lycognathophis seychellensis	Seychelles	Tr.	(T)—Dry habitats.	3' (91 cm)
Lycophidion (African Wolf Snakes)	S.Af., W.As.	Te.(?), S.Tr., Tr.	(F, T)—Grasslands, mountains.	10" to 2' 4" (25–71 cm)
Lystrophis (South American Hook-nosed Snakes)	S.Am.	S.Tr., Tr.	(F, T)—Grasslands, rain forests; similar to *Heterodon* in habits.	1' to 2' 6" (30–76 cm)
Lytorhynchus (Long-nosed or Leaf-nosed Snakes)	N.Af., W.As.	Te.	(F, T)—Dry habitats on plateaus, desert edges, grasslands, semiarid bush and mountains.	1' to 2' 6" (30–76 cm)
Macrelaps microlepidotus (Natal Black Snake)	S.Af.	Te.	(F)—Burrows in moist leaf litter and humic soil in damp localities including coastal bush and swamps, on banks of ponds; excellent swimmers.	2' to 3' (61–91 cm)
Macrocalamus	E.I., S.As.	S.Tr., Tr.	(F)—Under stones and fallen debris in mountain forests.	1' 3" to 2' 6" (38–76 cm)
Macropisthodon	E.I., S.As.	Te., S.Tr., Tr.	(T)—High elevations in thick vegetation of pine and deciduous forests, plains and other open areas, near human dwellings.	1' 10" to 2' 6" (86–76 cm)
Macropophis	E.I., New Guinea, Phil.	Tr.	(S.Aq.)—Lowlands.	2' 7" (79 cm)
Macroprotodon cucullatus (False Smooth or Hooded Snake)	Eu., N.Af.	Te., S.Tr.	(T)—Rocky terrain, grasslands, mountains.	2' (61 cm)
Madagascarophis colubrina	Mad.	S.Tr.	(A, T)—Rain and dry forests.	3' 6" (107 cm)

Reptile (species listed for monotypic genera)	Region of World Reptile Occurs (1,4)	"Native" Thermal Regimes (2,4)	Habits (3,4,6) & Habitats (3,4,6) (also refer to Glossary for habitat definitions)	Approximate Adult Sizes Feet ('); Inches (") (4,5,6)
Malpolon	Eu., N.Af., W.As.	Te., S.Tr., Tr.	(T)—Cool to warm arid regions covered with low scrub and thorny bushes.	6' (183 cm)
Manolepis (= *Tomodon*)	N.Am.	S.Tr., Tr.	(T)—A variety of dry habitats.	2' (61 cm)
Masticophis (North American Whipsnakes and Coachwhips)	N.Am., S.Am.	Te., S.Tr., Tr., Ar.	(A, T)—Around bodies of fresh water in a variety of habitats including deciduous, coniferous, and rain forests, thorn woodlands, mountains, and canyons, sandhills, open prairies, grasslands, chaparral, and deserts; occasionally, found far from water.	2' to 8' 6" (61–259 cm)
Mastigodryas (Tropical Racers)	N.Am., S.Am., W.I.	S.Tr., Tr.	(T)—Rain, dry and montane forests, forest edge situations, grasslands.	4' to 6' (123–183 cm)
Mehelya (File Snakes)	S.Af.	Te., S.Tr., Tr.	(T)—Forests, grasslands, rocky mountainous regions.	2' to 3' (61–91 cm)
Meizodon (African Smooth Snakes)	N.Af., S.Af.	S.Tr., Tr. (?)	(T)—Under stumps and ground litter in dry areas including grasslands, thornbush and plateaus.	1' 4" to 2' 4" (41–71 cm)
Micrelaps	S.Af., W.As.	Te., S.Tr.	(F, T)—Semiarid thornbush, mountains, semideserts.	1' 6" (46 cm)
Micropisthodon ochraceus	Mad.	S.Tr.	(6)—(6)	2' (61 cm)
Mimophis mahafalensis	Mad.	S.Tr.	(T)—Dry forests and grasslands.	3' (91 cm)
Myersophis alpestris	Phil.	Tr.	(6)—(6)	(6)
Myron richardsonii	Aus., E.I.	Tr.	(Aq., S.Aq.)—Mangrove creeks and estuaries.	1' 4" to 2' 4" (41–71 cm)
Natriciteres (African Marsh Snakes)	S.Af.	S.Tr., Tr.	(S.Aq.)—From lowlands to an elevation of 7,000 ft. near bodies of fresh water in grasslands and rain forests.	10" to 2' (25–61 cm)
Natrix (European Grass or Water Snakes)	E.I., Eu., N.Af., S.As., W.As.	Te., S.Tr., Tr.	(S.Aq., T)—Near ponds, ditches, streams, and rivers, along field boarders, open woods, on stony ground, low thickets, dried water courses, hilly slopes, and mountains.	2' 6" to 4' (61–122)
Nerodia (North American Water Snakes)	Cuba, N.Am.	Te., S.Tr., Tr.	(Aq., S.Aq.)—Shallow and deep-water habitats, under moist ground litter and brush, in salt and brackish water canals and estuaries, mangroves, swamps, marshes, lakes, roadside ditches, flooded rice fields, and bogs.	1' to 6' (30–183 cm)
Ninia (Ring-necked Coffee Snakes)	N.Am., S.Am.	S.Tr., Tr.	(F, T)—Rain, dry and lower montane moist forests.	1' 4" to 2' (41–61 cm)
Nothopsis rugosus	S.Am.	Tr.	(T)—Tropical rain forests.	2' 4" (71 cm)
Oligodon (Kukri Snakes)	E.I., Phil., S.As., W.As.	Te., S.Tr., Tr.	(T)—Damp areas on plains, in caves, rock crevices and hollow trees, desert-edge situations, rain forests, occasionally in termite mounds, around human dwellings.	1' to 3' (30–91 cm)
Opheodrys (Green Snakes)	E.I., N.Am., S.Am., S.As.	Te., S.Tr., Tr.	(A, T)—Under ground litter, in bushes, trees, vines and hedges, near creeks, streams, lakes, marshes, and swamps, in pastures, prairies, canyons, dry forests, and mountains.	1' to 3' (30–91 cm)
Opisthoplus (= *Aproterodon*) *degener*	S.Am.	Tr.	(T)—(6)	2' 2" (66 cm)
Opisthotropis (Mountain Water Snakes)	E.I., Phil., S.As.	S.Tr. (?), Tr.	(S.Aq.)—Under rocks and water plants in mountain streams, rain forests, forest edge situations, grasslands.	8" to 2' 8" (20–81 cm)

Reptile (species listed for monotypic genera)	Region of World Reptile Occurs (1,4)	"Native" Thermal Regimes (2,4)	Habits (3,4,6) & Habitats (3,4,6) (also refer to Glossary for habitat definitions)	Approximate Adult Sizes Feet ('); Inches (") (4,5,6)
Oreocalamus hanitschi (Hanitsch's Reed Snake)	E.I.	Tr.	(F)—Under rocks and fallen debris in tropical montane forests.	1' 4" (41 cm)
Oxybelis (Vine Snakes)	N.Am., S.Am.	S.Tr., Tr., Ar.	(A, S)—In shrubs of all wooded areas, including rain, dry, and arid forests, grasslands, coastal deserts, near creeks and streams.	3' 4" to 5' (91–152 cm)
Oxyrhabdium	Phil.	Tr.	(F, T)—Tropical lowland and montane rain forests.	2' to 2' 8" (61–81 cm)
Oxyrhopus	N.Am., S.Am.	S.Tr., Tr.	(T)—Under leaf litter and fallen logs in rain and dry forests, grasslands.	3' (91 cm)
Padangia pulchra	Sumatra	Tr.	(6)—(6)	(6)
Parahelicops	S.As.	(6)	(6)—(6)	(6)
Pararhabdophis chapaensis	S.As.	Tr.	(Aq.)—(6)	3' (91 cm)
Pararhadinaea melanogaster	Mad.	S.Tr.	(F)—Rain forests.	10" (25 cm)
Pareas (Slug Snakes)	E.I., S.As.	S.Tr., Tr.	(A, T)—Moist montane forests, cultivated areas.	1' to 2' 6" (30–76 cm)
Paroxyrhopus	S.Am.	Tr.	(T)—Various tropical forests.	2' 6" (76 cm)
Philodryas (South American Green Snakes)	S.Am.	Tr.	(A, T)—Tropical rain and dry forests.	3' (91 cm)
Philothamnus (African Green and Bush Snakes)	S.Af., W.As.	S.Tr., Tr.	(S, S.Aq.)—Near water in forested areas including rain, gallery, wet montane, and dry forests, coastal bush, grasslands, swamps, and marshes; also found near fresh water in arid regions.	2' 6" to 3' (76–91 cm)
Phimophis	S.Am.	Tr.	(T)—Grasslands, semideserts.	2' to 3' (61–91 cm)
Phyllorhynchus (Leaf-nosed Snakes)	N.Am.	Te., S.Tr., Ar.	(F)—Bushy areas, mesquite, salt bush, creosote, under stones in rocky, brushy, sandy, or barren deserts.	6" to 1' 8" (15–51 cm)
Pituophis (Bullsnakes, Pine and Gopher Snakes)	N.Am., S.Am.	Te., S.Tr., Tr., Ar.	(T)—In a wide variety of habitats, from sea level to high elevations, in arid to humid areas, near oceans, rivers, streams, and ponds, in mountains, deserts, forests, plains, around human dwellings, under ground litter in mammal burrows, trees, and at the base of bushes.	3' to 8' (91–244 cm)
Plagiopholis	S.As.	S.Tr.	(T)—Montane forests.	1' 4" (41 cm)
Platynion lividum	S.Am.	Tr.	(F)—Tropical rain forests.	2' 6" (76 cm)
Pliocercus (False Coral Snakes)	N.Am., S.Am.	Tr.	(T)—Under logs in damp lowland forests.	1' to 2' 8" (30–81 cm)
Polemon	S.Af.	Tr.	(F, T)—Tropical forests.	3' (1 cm)
Prosymna (Shovel-snouted Snakes)	S.Af.	Te., S.Tr., Tr., Ar.	(F)—Under ground litter in cultivated areas, coastal dunes, evergreen forests, woodlands, steppes, and grasslands, under rocks in arid regions.	6" to 1' 6" (15–46 cm)
Psammodynastes (Mock Vipers)	E.I., S.As.	S.Tr., Tr.	(A, T)—In lowland bushes and trees, monsoon and montane forests.	1' to 2' (30–61 cm)
Psammophis (African Sand Racers)	N.Af., S.Af., S.As., W.As.	Te., S.Tr., Tr., Ar.	(A, T)—In a wide variety of habitats including open forests, dry, hot thornbush, steppes, deserts, and paddy fields.	1' to 5' (30–152 cm)
Psammophylax (Skaapstekers or Grass Snakes)	S.Af.	Te., S.Tr.	(T)—Dry grasslands from the coast to high elevations in mountains, flood plains.	1' 6" to 3' (46–122 cm)
Pseudablabes agassizii	S.Am.	(6)	(F)—(6)	1' 4" (41 cm)
Pseudaspis cana (Mole Snake)	S.Af.	Te. (?), S.Tr., Ar.	(F)—Dry bush in sandy soil, deserts, mountains.	4' (122 cm)

Reptile (species listed for monotypic genera)	Region of World Reptile Occurs (1,4)	"Native" Thermal Regimes (2,4)	Habits (3,4,6) & Habitats (3,4,6) (also refer to Glossary for habitat definitions)	Approximate Adult Sizes Feet ('); Inches (") (4,5,6)
Pseudoboa	S.Am., W.I.	Tr.	(T)—Close to fresh water, under fallen logs and root systems of large trees in tropical rain, dry, and gallery forests, forest edge situations, grasslands.	3' (91 cm)
Pseudoboodon lemniscatus	N.Af.	(6)	(6)—(6)	(6)
Pseudoeryx (= *Dipsadoides*) *plicatilis*	S. Am.	Tr.	(S.Aq.)—Near fresh water in tropical rain forests with dense vegetation, grasslands.	2' 8" to 4' (81–122 cm)
Pseudorabdion	E.I., Phil., S.As.	S.Tr., Tr.	(F)—Under stones and fallen logs in forests.	9" (23 cm)
Pseudotarbophis gabesiensis	N.Af.	(6)	(6)—(6)	(6)
Pseudotomodon trigonatus	S.Am.	Te. (?), Ar.	(T)—Arid areas.	1' 6" (46 cm)
Pseudoxenodon	E.I., S.As.	S.Tr., Tr.	(T)—Monsoon, rain, bamboo, and montane forests.	1' 6" to 3' 6" (46–102 cm)
Pseudoxyrhopus	Mad.	S.Tr.	(S.Aq. ?)—Lightly wooded areas, grasslands, marshes, and rain forests?	1' to 3' 6" (30–102 cm)
Pseustes (Central American Chicken Snakes)	N.Am., S.Am.	Tr.	(A, S, T)—Tropical rain and dry forests, forest edge situations, grasslands.	5' to 7' (153–213 cm)
Ptyas (Asian Rat Snakes)	E.I., Phil., S.As., W.As.	S.Tr., Tr.	(A, T)—In trees, bushes, high grass, and decaying vegetation, paddy fields, lower mountain slopes, around human dwellings, near water.	2' to 10' (61–305 cm)
Ptychophis flavovingatus	S.Am.	Tr.	(6)—Tropical rain forests.	2' (61 cm)
Pythonodipsas carinata (Western Keeled Snake)	S.Af.	S.Tr., Ar.	(T)—Rocky desert.	2' (61 cm)
Rabdion (= *Rhabdophidium*) *forsteni*	Sulawesi	Tr.	(F)—(6)	1' 6" (46 cm)
Regina (Crayfish Snakes)	N.Am.	Te., S.Tr.	(Aq.)—In aquatic vegetation and mud banks in marshes, bogs and bay heads.	1' to 2' 8" (30–81 cm)
Rhabdophis (Rear-fanged Keelbacks)	E.As., E.I., Phil., S.As.	Te., S.Tr., Tr.	(S.Aq., T)—Slightly scansorial; from lowlands to mountains; some species live near fresh water in brush-covered grassy areas and rice fields.	3' (91 cm)
Rhabdops	S.As.	S.Tr., Tr.	(T)—Under rocks, logs, and other ground litter.	2' 6" (76 cm)
Rhachidelus brazili	S.Am.	Tr.	(T)—Tropical forests.	(6)
Rhadinaea (Pinewoods Snakes)	N.Am., S.Am.	Te., S.Tr., Tr.	(F, T)—Dry to humid areas near fresh water under ground litter in pine, deciduous, cloud and rain forests, cypress edges, swamps, cultivated fields.	1' 8" (51 cm)
Rhamphiophis (Sharp-nosed or Beaked Snakes)	S.Af.	Te. (?), S.Tr., Tr., Ar.	(T)—In mammal burrows and termite mounds, lightly wooded areas, damp grasslands, gallery forests, steppes, arid, sandy savannas, thornbush desert.	2' to 5' (61–152 cm)
Rhinobothryum	S.Am.	Tr.	(A)—Tropical lowland forests.	4' 6" (137 cm)
Rhinocheilus lecontei (Long-nosed Snake)	N.Am., S.Am.	Te., S.Tr., Ar.	(F, T)—From the ocean to an elevation of 5,400 ft., under ground litter and human debris in sandy and bushy deserts, rocky slopes, chaparral, and mountains.	1' 8" to 3' 4" (51–102 cm)
Rhynchocalamus	W.As.	S.Tr.	(T)—Under rocks in steppes, mountains, semidesert regions.	1' 4" (41 cm)
Rhynchophis boulengeri	S.As.	S.Tr., Tr.	(A, T)—Rocky areas, montane forests, grasslands.	1' 6" to 3' 6" (46–107 cm)
Salvadora (Patch-nosed Snakes)	N.Am., S.Am.	Te., S.Tr., Ar.	(T)—Under rocks in primarily arid deserts and adjacent areas, mountains.	1' 8" to 4' (51–122 cm)
Saphenophis	S.Am.	S.Tr., Tr.	(T)—Under stones in rain and dry forests, grasslands.	3' (91 cm)

Reptile (species listed for monotypic genera)	Region of World Reptile Occurs (1,4)	"Native" Thermal Regimes (2,4)	Habits (3,4,6) & Habitats (3,4,6) (also refer to Glossary for habitat definitions)	Approximate Adult Sizes Feet ('); Inches (") (4,5,6)
Scaphiodontophis (American Many-toothed Snakes)	N.Am., S.Am.	S.Tr., Tr.	(T)—Montane rain forests, dry forests, rocky areas near swamps and streams.	1' 8" to 2' 8" (51–81 cm)
Scaphiophis albopunctatus	S.Af.	S.Tr., Tr.	(F)—Dry grasslands around termite mounds.	6' (183 cm)
Scolecophis atrocinctus	S.Am.	S.Tr., Tr.	(T)—Tropical rain forests, dry forests, mountain slopes.	1' 4" (41 cm)
Seminatrix (Red-bellied Swamp Snakes)	N.Am.	Te., S.Tr.	(F, S.Aq.)—Under ground litter along creeks, ponds, lakes, marshes, and bogs.	9" to 1' 8" (23–51 cm)
Sibon (includes *Tropidodipsas*)	N.Am., S.Am.	Te., S.Tr., Tr.	(A, F, T)—Montane, rain, and dry forests, forest edge situations, grasslands, coastal deserts.	2' 9" (84 cm)
Sibynomorphus	S.Am.	Tr.	(A, T)—Tropical rain forests, dry lowlands.	1' 4" to 2' 10" (41–86 cm)
Sibynophis (Collared Snakes)	E.I., Phil., S.As.	Te., S.Tr., Tr.	(T)—Under ground litter in cultivated areas, montane, and lowland rain forests, monsoon, and bamboo forests, mountains.	2' 6" (76 cm)
Simophis	S.Am.	Tr.	(T)—Grasslands, forest edge situations.	2' 6" (76 cm)
Sinonatrix (Asiatic Water Snakes)	E.I., S.As.	Tr.	(S.Aq.)—Near water.	(6)
Siphlophis (includes *Alleidophis*)	S.Am.	Tr.	(A)—Tropical rain forests.	2' 4" to 3' (71–91 cm)
Sonora (Ground Snakes)	N.Am.	Te., Ar.	(F)—Under ground litter, on river banks and other freshwater areas in deserts, grasslands, and mountains.	8" to 1' 7" (20–48 cm)
Sordellina punctata	S.Am.	Tr.	(F, T)—Tropical lowland forests near water.	8" (20 cm)
Spalerosophis (includes *Zaocys*) (Desert Racers)	N.Af., S.As., W.As.	Te., S.Tr., Ar.	(T)—Under rocks, in rocky crevices and rodent burrows, from lowlands to mountains at elevations of 6,500 ft., deserts; excellent climbers.	6' (183 cm)
Spilotes pullatus (Mexican or Tiger Rat Snake)	N.Am., S.Am.	S.Tr., Tr.	(A, T)—In and around fresh water in rain and dry forests, forest edge situations, grasslands, coastal deserts, in and around human dwellings; excellent swimmers.	8' (244 cm)
Stegonotus	Aus., E.I., Phil.	Tr.	(S.Aq., S., T)—Coastal dunes, rocky creek-beds, streams, lagoons, tropical rain forests, woodlands, around human dwellings.	3' to 4' (91–122 cm)
Stenorrhina	N.Am., S.Am.	S.Tr., Tr.	(T)—Tropical and subtropical moist, wet and dry forests, lower montane wet forests.	2' 8" (81 cm)
Stilosoma extenuatum (Short-tailed Snake)	N.Am.	Te.	(F)—High pine, upland hammock, scrub areas, sphagnum beds.	1' to 2' (30–61 cm)
Stoliczkaia	E.I., S.As.	S.Tr.	(T)—Montane rain forests.	2' (61 cm)
Storeria (Brown and Red-bellied Snakes)	N.Am., S.Am.	Te., S.Tr.	(F, S.Aq., T)—Under ground litter and human debris in dry to wet urban and rural areas, sandy soil in meadows and desert foothills, in coniferous forests and all waterways.	8" to 1' 6" (20–46 cm)
Styporhynchus mairi	Aus.	S.Tr., Tr.	(Aq., S.Aq.)—In and around fresh water in forests and woodlands.	3' (91 cm)
Sympholis lippiens	N. Am.	Tr.	(F)—Tropical thorn scrub.	1' to 1' 8" (30–51 cm)
Synophis	S.Am.	Tr.	(Aq., S.Aq.)—In and around standing and slow-flowing waters in tropical rain forests.	2' 6" (76 cm)

Reptile (species listed for monotypic genera)	Region of World Reptile Occurs (1,4)	"Native" Thermal Regimes (2,4)	Habits (3,4,6) & Habitats (3,4,6) (also refer to Glossary for habitat definitions)	Approximate Adult Sizes Feet ('); Inches (") (4,5,6)
Tachymenis	S.Am.	Te., S.Tr., Tr., Ar.	(T)—Dry, scrubby to arid areas at elevations up to 14,000 ft.	2' (61 cm)
Tantilla (Black-headed, Flat-headed and Crowned Snakes)	N.Am., S.Am.	Te., S.Tr., Tr., Ar.	(F, T)—From sea level to high elevations, from desert regions and plains to moist, heavy vegetation in a variety of forest types, near bodies of fresh water.	6" to 2' (15–61 cm)
Tantillita lintoni	N.Am., S.Am.	(6)	(6)—May be similar to *Tantilla*.	(6)
Telescopus (Old World Cat-eyed or Tiger Snakes)	Eu., N.Af., S.Af., W.As.	Te., S.Tr.	(T)—Grasslands, dry mountain areas, dry rocky terrain with low bushes.	1' 3" to 3' (38–91 cm)
Tetralepis fruhstorferi	Java	Tr.	(T ?)—Tropical rain forests?	1' 8" (51 cm)
Thamnodynastes	S.Am.	S.Tr., Tr.	(S.Aq., S, T)—Near bodies of fresh water in thorn woodlands, rain and dry forests, forest edge situations, grasslands, and cultivated fields	2' 3" (69 cm)
Thamnophis (Garter and Ribbon Snakes)	N.Am., S.Am.	Te., S.Tr., Tr.	(S, S.Aq., T)—From sea level to high elevations, near bodies of fresh water in deserts, mountains, canyons, grasslands, and dense forests, around human dwellings.	10" to 5' (25–152 cm)
Thelotornis (African Bird Snakes)	S.Af.	S.Tr., Tr.	(A)—Near fresh water in tropical forests and grasslands.	3' to 5' (91–152 cm)
Thermophis baileyi	Tibet	Te.	(6)—(6)	(6)
Thrasops (= *Rhamnophis*) (Black Tree Snakes)	S.Af.	S.Tr., Tr.	(A)—Tropical and montane rain forests.	2' 6" to 4' (76–122 cm)
Toluca	N.Am.	S.Tr. (?)	(T)—Highlands.	1' 8" (51 cm)
Trachischium (Oriental Worm Snakes)	S.As.	S.Tr.	(T)—Under rocks and fallen trees in montane forests.	10" to 2' 6" (25–76 cm)
Tretanorhinus	N.Am., S.Am., W.I.	Tr.	(Aq., S.Aq.)—In and around creeks and ponds in rain and dry forests.	2' (61 cm)
Trimetopon	S.Am.	Tr.	(T)—Tropical rain forests.	1' (30 cm)
Trimorphodon (Lyre Snakes)	N.Am., S.Am.	S.Tr., Tr., Ar.	(S, T)—From sea coasts to an elevation of 5,000 ft. in deserts, rocky terrain, hillsides, mountains, and tropical dry forests.	2' to 4' (61–122 cm)
Tripanurgos compressus	S.Am.	Tr.	(A)—Tropical rain forests.	2' 6" (76 cm)
Tropidoclonion (Lined Snakes)	N.Am.	Te.	(F, T)—In urban and suburban areas, under ground litter, rocks and human debris, in clay banks, grasslands and flood plains.	9" to 2' (23–61 cm)
Tropidodryas (= *Philodryas pseudoserra* and *P. serra*)	S.Am.	Tr.	(6)—Tropical rain and dry forests.	6' 6" (198 cm)
Typhlogeophis brevis	Phil.	Tr.	(F)—(6)	1' 2" (36 cm)
Umbravaga	S.Am.	Tr.	(T)—Grasslands, forests.	1' 4" (41 cm)
Uromacer (West Indian Racers)	W.I.	Tr.	(A)—Partially terrestrial; forests, dry scrub, cultivated areas.	6' 6" (198 cm)
Uromacerina ricardinii	S.Am.	Tr.	(A)—Tropical forests.	3' to 6' (91–183 cm)
Virginia (Earth Snakes)	N.Am.	Te.	(F)—Under moist ground litter and human debris in a variety of habitats.	4" to 1' (10–30 cm)
Wallophis (includes *Zaocys*)	S.As.	Tr.	(T)—Grassy, wooded areas, agricultural areas, lower mountain slopes.	(6)
Xenelaphis (Asian Brown Snakes)	E.I., S.As.	Tr.	(S.Aq., T)—Near fresh water.	4' to 6' (121–213 cm)
Xenocalamus (Quill-snouted Snakes)	S.Af.	S.Tr., Tr.	(F)—Sandy soil.	2' 6" (76 cm)
Xenochrophis (Fishing Keelbacks)	E.I., S.As., W.As.	S.Tr., Tr.	(Aq., S.Aq., T)—Near bodies of fresh water in lowlands and hilly country, cultivated fields.	4' (122 cm)

Reptile (species listed for monotypic genera)	Region of World Reptile Occurs (1,4)	"Native" Thermal Regimes (2,4)	Habits (3,4,6) & Habitats (3,4,6) (also refer to Glossary for habitat definitions)	Approximate Adult Sizes Feet ('); Inches (") (4,5,6)
Xenodermus javanicus (Strange-scaled Snake)	E.I., S.As.	Tr.	(S.Aq.)—Near bodies of fresh water in tropical forests, swamps, cultivated areas, other wet, humid areas.	2' 2" (66 cm)
Xenodon (includes *Waglerophis*) (False Vipers)	N.Am., S.Am.	S.Tr., Tr.	(T)—In extremely humid habitats including rain forfests, also found in dry forests, forest edge situations, and grasslands.	3' (91 cm)
Xenopholis scalaris	S.Am.	Tr.	(T)—Under leaf litter and other fallen debris in tropical rain forests.	5" to 1' (13–30 cm)
Xylophis	S.As.	S.Tr. (?), Tr.	(6)—Mountains.	10" to 2' (25–60 cm)
FAMILY ELAPIDAE (Cobras and their Relatives)				
Acanthophis (Death Adders)	Aus., E.I.	Te., S.Tr., Tr.	(T)—Under ground litter, around bases of shrubs and trees in a variety of semiarid to semihumid habitats (not found in central desert regions), rain forests, dry scrub areas, woodlands, grasslands.	1' 6" to 3' 3" (46–99 cm)
Aspidelaps (African Coral Snakes or Shield-nose Cobras)	S.Af.	S.Tr., Ar.	(F, T)—Dry, sandy soil in grasslands or open woodlands (burrowing habits require loose soil).	1' 6" (46 cm)
Aspidomorphus (Crowned Snakes)	E.I., New Guinea	Tr.	(T)—Primarily sandstone areas, tropical and montane rain forests.	1' 6" to 2' 6" (46–76 cm)
Austrelaps superbus (Australian Copperhead)	Aus.	Te., S.Tr.	(S.Aq., T)—Marshes, swamps, forests, woodlands.	4' to 6' (122–183 cm)
Boulengerina (Water Cobras)	S.Af.	Tr.	(S.Aq.)—Brushy or wooded banks of bodies of fresh water, tropical rain forests.	8' (244 cm)
Bungarus (Kraits)	E.I., S.As., W.As.	Te., S.Tr., Tr., Ar.	(T)—Primarily plains, also have been found in termite mounds, mammal burrows, arid, wooded, and grassy areas, tropical forests, hills, and mountains near rivers, streams, and lakes, around human dwellings.	4' to 6' (122–183 cm)
Cacophis (Australian Crowned Snakes)	Aus.	Te., S.Tr., Tr.	(T)—Under stones, logs and leaf litter in semihumid to humid forests and woodlands.	8" to 2' (20–61 cm)
Calliophis (Oriental Spotted Coral Snakes)	E.I., Phil., S.As.	Tr.	(F, T)—Under ground litter in low hilly regions, forests, and coastal scrub; avoid dry terrain.	1' to 2' (30–61 cm)
Cryptophis (Small-eyed Snakes)	Aus.	Te., S.Tr., Tr.	(T)—Under rocks, logs and ground litter, in rock crevices in coastal heathland, woodlands, forests.	1' 6" to 4' (46–122 cm)
Demansia (Australian Whipsnakes)	Aus.	Te., S.Tr., Tr., Ar.	(T)—In a variety of habitats including agricultural areas, semiarid, stony areas, coastal dunes, savanna woodlands, arid interior of the continent and monsoon forests.	1' 6" to 3' (46–91 cm)
Dendroaspis (Mambas)	S.Af.	S.Tr., Tr.	(A, T)—Tropical rain forests, other forests, open bushy areas.	6' to 14' (183–427 cm)
Denisonia	Aus.	Te., S.Tr., Tr.	(T)—Under ground litter in a variety of habitats including woodlands, grasslands and coastal mountain swamps.	1' 6" to 5' (46–153 cm)
Drysdalia	Aus.	Te., S.Tr.	(T)—Forests, woodlands, shrubby areas.	1' 6" (46 cm)

Reptile (species listed for monotypic genera)	Region of World Reptile Occurs (1,4)	"Native" Thermal Regimes (2,4)	Habits (3,4,6) & Habitats (3,4,6) (also refer to Glossary for habitat definitions)	Approximate Adult Sizes Feet ('); Inches (") (4,5,6)
Echiopsis	Aus.	Te.	(T)—Dry habitat in woodlands, grasslands and shrubby areas.	1' 2" to 1' 8" (36–51 cm)
Elapognathus minor (Little Brown Snake)	Aus.	Te.	(T)—Dry coastal areas.	1' 6" (46 cm)
Elapsoidea (African Garter Snakes)	S.Af.	S.Tr., Tr.	(F, T)—Widespread on grass-lands, forest edge situations, light woodlands and bushy areas.	2' to 4' (61–122 cm)
Furina (Red- and orange-naped Snakes)	Aus.	S.Tr., Tr.	(T)—Under ground litter in ar-eas inhabited by termites in-cluding shrubby areas, wood-lands, and forests.	1' 6" (46 cm)
Glyphodon (Australian Collared Snakes)	Aus.	Tr.	(T)—In loose earth and earth cracks in forests and wood-lands.	1' 6" to 3' (46–91 cm)
Hemachatus haemachatus (Ringhals or Rinkals)	S.Af.	S.Tr.	(T)—Grasslands and other open country.	5' (153 cm)
Hemiaspis	Aus.	S.Tr., Tr.	(T)—Coastal, marshy, and rocky areas, beach dunes, woodlands, forests.	1' 6" (46 cm)
Hemibungarus	E.I., S.As.	Tr.	(T)—Wooded mountainous areas.	2' (61 cm)
Hoplocephalus (Australian Broad-headed Snakes)	Aus.	Te., S.Tr., Tr.	(A, S, T)—In a wide range of habitats from rain or wet for-ests to dry eucalypt forests, woodlands, and sandstone ar-eas under rocks and loose bark, in tree hollows.	1' 6" to 2' (46–61 cm)
Loveridgelaps elapoides	Solomon Is.	Tr.	(T)—Under leaf litter and other fallen debris in tropical forests.	3' 3" (99 cm)
Maticora (Long-glanded Coral Snakes)	E.I., Phil., S.As.	S.Tr. (?), Tr.	(F, T)—Under ground litter and loose soil on tropical and montane rain forest floors.	2' to 4' (61–121 cm)
Melanelaps	S.As.	(6)	(6)—(6)	(6)
Micropechis ikaheka (Pacific Coral Snake)	Pac., New Guinea	Tr.	(F, T)—Tropical forests, swamps.	4' (121 cm)
Micruroides euryxanthus (Western Coral Snake)	N.Am.	Te., Ar.	(T)—Under rocks and other ground cover in open dry ar-eas including semidesert and desert areas, around human habitations.	1' 3" to 2' (38–61 cm)
Micrurus (Coral Snakes)	N.Am., S.Am.	Te., S.Tr., Tr.	(F, S.Aq., T)—In a wide variety of habitats under ground lit-ter, coastal pine forests, plains, wet and dry ham-mocks, grasslands, and grass swamps, rain and dry forests, forest edge situations, thorn woodlands, coastal deserts.	1' 8" to 4' 6" (51–137 cm)
Naja (Cobras)	E.I., N.Af., S.Af., S.As., W.As.	Te., S.Tr., Tr., Ar.	(A, T)—Thick growth of trees in forests, open areas with or without vegetation, sandy, des-ert areas, grasslands, gardens, and other cultivated fields, woodpiles, under rubbish, crevices of walls, mammal bur-rows, around human dwell-ings, drainage areas; excellent swimmers.	3' to 9' (91–274 cm)
Neelaps (Black-naped Snakes)	Aus.	Te., S.Tr., Ar.	(F, T)—Forests, woodlands, schrubby areas, deserts.	8" to 1' 4" (20–41 cm)
Notechis (Tiger Snakes)	Aus.	Te.	(T)—In a wide range of habitats that include dry, rocky areas and sclerophyll forests, marshes, coastal dunes, grass-lands, woodlands, river flood plains, and temperate rain forests.	5' 3" (160 cm)

Reptile (species listed for monotypic genera)	Region of World Reptile Occurs (1,4)	"Native" Thermal Regimes (2,4)	Habits (3,4,6) & Habitats (3,4,6) (also refer to Glossary for habitat definitions)	Approximate Adult Sizes Feet ('); Inches (") (4,5,6)
Ogmondon vitianus (Fiji Snake)	Fiji	Tr.	(F, T)—(6)	1' 4" (41 cm)
Ophiophagus hannah (King Cobra)	E.I., Phil., S.As.	Tr.	(T)—Dense forests, agricultural areas.	18' (549 cm)
Oxyuranus scutellatus (Taipan)	Aus.	Te., S.Tr., Tr.	(S, T)—In a wide variety of habitats that include wet and dry sclerophyll forests and open savanna woodlands, around rocks and boulders where it lives in rodent burrows.	6' to 12' (183–366 cm)
Parademansia microlepidota (Fierce Snake)	Aus.	S.Tr., Tr., Ar.	(T)—Arid shrubby areas, grasslands.	7' (213 cm)
Paranaja multifasciata (Burrowing Cobra)	S.Af.	Tr.	(F ?)—Tropical forests?	4' (122 cm)
Parapistocalamus hedigeri (Hediger's Snake)	New Guinea, Solomon Is.	Tr.	(F)—Tropical forests.	1' 8" (51 cm)
Pseudechis (Australian Black and Mulga Snakes)	Aus., E.I.	Te., S.Tr., Tr., Ar.	(T)—Rocky hillsides, forests, woodlands, grasslands, deserts, scrubby and shrubby areas, river flood plains, streams, swamps and lagoons.	7' (213 cm)
Pseudohaje (Tree or Forest Cobras)	S.Af.	Tr.	(A)—Tropical forests; good swimmers.	9' (274 cm)
Pseudonaja (Brown Snakes)	Aus.	Te., S.Tr., Tr., Ar.	(T)—Tropical sclerophyll forests, central deserts, rocky hillsides and scrubby grasslands, woodlands.	1' 6" to 5' 3" (46–160 cm)
Rhinoplocephalus bicolor (Muller's Snake)	Aus.	Te.	(T)—Coastal swamps.	1' 6" (46 cm)
Salomonelaps par	New Guinea, Solomon Is.	Tr.	(T ?)—Tropical forests.	2' (61 cm)
Simoselaps (Australian Coral Snakes)	Aus.	Te. (?), S.Tr., Tr., Ar.	(F, T)—Under ground litter on stony hills, open grasslands, interior scrubby areas and deserts, coastal and sclerophyll forests, woodlands.	1' 8" (51 cm)
Suta suta (Myall or Curl Snake)	Aus.	Te. (?), S.Tr., Tr., Ar.	(T)—Under ground litter in grasslands, woodlands, sandy arid scrubs, stony hills, and deserts.	2' (61 cm)
Toxicocalamus (Short-fanged or Elongate Snakes)	E.I., New Guinea	Tr.	(F)—Montane forests.	1' 2" to 3' 4" (36–102 cm)
Tropidechis carinatus (Rough-scaled Snake)	Aus.	S.Tr., Tr.	(T)—Wet sclerophyll or rain forests, other forest types near water.	4' (122 cm)
Unechis	Aus.	Te., S.Tr., Tr.	(T)—Forests, woodlands, shrubby, and scrubby areas.	8" to 1' (20–30 cm)
Vermicella (Bandy-bandy Snakes)	Aus.	Te., S.Tr., Tr., Ar.	(F)—Wet coastal forests, shrubby and scrubby areas, desert sand hills.	1' 3" (38 cm)
Walterinnesia aegyptia (Desert Black Cobra)	N.Af., W.As.	S.Tr., Tr., Ar.	(T)—Gardens, oases and irrigated areas, barren, rocky mountain hillsides, sandy deserts with sparse bushes.	4' (122 cm)
FAMILY HYDROPHIDAE (Sea Snakes)				
Acalyptophis peronii	Waters off Aus., S.As.	Tr.	(Aq.)—On surface of reef waters.	3' (91 cm)
Aipysurus	Waters off Aus., E.I., Pac., S.As.	Tr.	(Aq.)—Shallow reef and deep sea areas.	1' 6" to 6' 5" (46–198 cm)
Astrotia stokesii (Stoke's Sea Snake)	Waters off Aus., E.I., S.As.	Tr.	(Aq.)—Surface of turbid coastal or reef waters, estuaries.	3' 6" to 4' (107–122 cm)
Disteira	Waters off Aus., E.I., S.As., W.As.	Tr.	(Aq.)—Deep coastal waters, estuaries.	3' 8" to 5' (112–152 cm)
Emydocephalus annulatus	Waters off Aus., Pac., S.As.	Tr.	(Aq.)—Aggregate in large numbers in shallow or reef waters.	2' 6" (76 cm)
Enhydrina schistosa	Waters off Aus., E.I., Mad., Phil., S.As., W.As.	Tr.	(Aq.)—Shallow water in rivers and estuaries with sand or mud bottoms.	3' 8" (112 cm)

Reptile (species listed for monotypic genera)	Region of World Reptile Occurs (1,4)	"Native" Thermal Regimes (2,4)	Habits (3,4,6) & Habitats (3,4,6) (also refer to Glossary for habitat definitions)	Approximate Adult Sizes Feet ('); Inches (") (4,5,6)
Ephalophis greyi	Waters off Aus.	Tr.	(Aq.)—Partially terrestrial; coastal waters, estuaries.	1' 6" (46 cm)
Hydrelaps darwiniensis	Waters off Aus.	Tr.	(Aq.)—Partially terrestrial; mangrove swamps, estuaries.	1' 6" (46 cm)
Hydrophis	Waters off Aus., E.I., Pac., Phil., S.As., W.As.	S.Tr., Tr.	(Aq.)—Reef and deep waters, river estuaries.	1' 8" to 6' (51–183 cm)
Kerilia	Waters off E.I. S.As.	Tr.	(Aq.)—Coastal waters.	3' 4" (102 cm)
Lapemis	Waters off Aus., E.I., Phil., S.As., W.As.	Tr.	(Aq.)—Shallow, clear reef waters to silted waters.	3' (91 cm)
Parahydrophis mertoni	Waters off Aus.	Tr.	(Aq.)—Partially terrestrial; coastal waters, estuaries.	1' 8" (51 cm)
Pelamis platurus (Yellow-bellied or Parti-colored Sea Snake)	Waters off Mad., N.Af., N.Am., Pac., S.Af., S.Am., S.As., W.As.	S.Tr., Tr.	(Aq.)—open seas, coastal waters.	3' (91 cm)
Thalassophina viperina	Waters off E.I., S.As., W.As.	S.Tr., Tr.	(Aq.)—Open seas, coastal waters, mangrove swamps.	3' 4" (102 cm)
Thalassophis anomalus	Waters off E.I.	Tr.	(Aq.)—Coastal waters, mangrove swamps.	2' 8" (81 cm)
FAMILY LATICAUDIDAE *Laticauda* (Banded Sea Kraits)	Waters off Aus., E.I., Pac., Phil., N.Am., S.Am., S.As.	Tr.	(Aq.)—Partially terrestrial; rocky or coral crevices along shores, mangrove swamps, lagoons, estuaries, island forests.	4' 6" (137 cm)
FAMILY LEPTOTYPHLOPIDAE (Thread Snakes) *Leptotyphlops, Rhinoleptus*	N.Af., N.Am., S.Af., S.Am., S.As., W.As., W.I.	Te., S.Tr., Tr.	(F)—Under rocks and roots of bushes in a wide variety of habitats that include moderately sandy, semiarid grasslands, with or without trees, chaparral-covered mountains, coastal areas, rain forests.	4" to 1' 6" (10–46 cm)
FAMILY LOXOCEMIDAE *Loxocemus bicolor* (Mexican Dwarf or Burrowing Python)	N.Am., S.Am.	Tr., S.Tr., Ar.	(F, T)—Under loose sandy soil, ground litter and in mammal burrows in tropical moist, dry, and arid forests.	3' (91 cm)
FAMILY TROPIDOPHIIDAE *Tropidophis* (West Indian Dwarf Boas)	N.Am., S.Am., W.I.	Tr.	(T)—In between and under rocks, rotting wood and other debris, near fresh water in woodlands, forest edges and rocky hillsides.	3' (91 cm)
FAMILY TYPHLOPIDAE (Blind Burrowing Snakes) *Anomalepis, Helminthophis, Liotyphlops, Rhamphotyphlops, Rhinotyphlops, Typhlophis, Typhlops*	Aus., E.I., Eu., Mad., N.Am., Pac., Phil., S.Af., S.Am., S.As., Seychelles, W.As., W.I.	Te., S.Tr., Tr., Ar.	(F)—Humid to arid conditions; in decaying logs which termites inhabit, in human dwellings where ants invade, beneath rocks, gravel, and roots of plants, in flower pots, rain and dry forests, grasslands, coastal deserts.	5" to 3' (13–91 cm)
FAMILY UROPELTIDAE (Rough-tailed Snakes) *Melanophidium, Platyplectrurus, Plectrurus, Pseudotyphlops, Rhinophis, Teretrurus, Typhlina, Uropeltis*	S.As.	S.Tr., Tr.	(F)—Under rocks, logs, and other ground litter, in mammal burrows, damp, hilly, and wooded areas, gardens and other cultivated fields, rain, monsoon, and montane forests, around human dwellings.	1' to 2' (30–61 cm)

Reptile (species listed for monotypic genera)	Region of World Reptile Occurs (1,4)	"Native" Thermal Regimes (2,4)	Habits (3,4,6) & Habitats (3,4,6) (also refer to Glossary for habitat definitions)	Approximate Adult Sizes Feet ('); Inches (") (4,5,6)
FAMILY VIPERIDAE (Vipers)				
(PIT VIPERS)				
Agkistrodon	E.As., Eu., C.As., N.Am., S.Am., W.I.	Te., S.Tr., Tr., Ar.	(S.Aq., T)—Under ground litter, in hollow trees and caves, near fresh and coastal waters, mangrove swamps, marshes, flood plains and wet cultivated areas, upland woods, open pine and other forested areas, rocky deserts, thorn scrub, mountains, around human dwellings.	1' 6" to 6' (46–183 cm)
Bothrops (New World Lance-headed Vipers)	N.Am., S.Am., W.I.	S.Tr., Tr.	(A ?, T)—Primarily rain forests, dry forests, forest edge situations, plantations and grasslands, along streams, ponds, lakes, and ditches.	7' (213 cm)
Bothriechis (= *Bothrops*) (Arboreal Pit Vipers)	N.Am., S.Am.	S.Tr., Tr.	(A)—Rain forests, shrubs adjacent to streams and rivers.	2' (61 cm)
Bothriopsis (= *Bothrops*) (South American Pit Vipers)	S.Am.	Te., S.Tr., Tr.	(A)—Trees and shrubs adjacent to bodies of fresh water.	2' 6" (76 cm)
Calloselasma (= *Agkistrodon*)	E.I., S.As.	S.Tr., Tr.	(T)—Coastal forests, forest edge situations, bamboo thickets, plantations.	2' 6" (76 cm)
Crotalus (Rattlesnakes)	N.Am., S.Am.	Te., S.Tr., Tr., Ar.	(T)—In every type of habitat.	1' to 7' 6" (30–229 cm)
Deinagkistrodon (= *Agkistrodon*) *acutus* (Sharp-nosed Viper or Hundred Pacer)	E.As., S.As.	Te., S.Tr., Tr.	(T)—Wooded mountain slopes, rocky hillsides, valleys.	4' (122 cm)
Gloydius (= *Agkistrodon*)	C.As., E.As., S.As., W.As.	Te., S.Tr., Tr., Ar.	(T)—Marshy river valleys, lowland forests, rocky bluffs, steppes, mountains, grasslands, deserts, cultivated areas, around human dwellings.	8" to 1' 2" (20–36 cm)
Hypnale (= *Agkistrodon*)	S.As.	S.Tr., Tr.	(S, T)—Tropical and montane forests, areas of dense vegetation, cultivated fields in hilly areas.	1' 8" (51 cm)
Lachesis mutus (Bushmaster)	S.Am.	Tr.	(S, T)—Rain and dry forests, forest edge situations.	12' (366 cm)
Ophryacus (= *Bothrops*) (New World Bush Vipers)	N.Am.	S.Tr., Tr.	(S, T)—Rocky outcrops and shrubby terrain adjacent to streams, cloud forests.	1' 2" to 1' 6" (36–46 cm)
Ovophis (= *Trimeresurus*)	E.I., S.As.	Te., S.Tr., Tr.	(S, T)—Wooded mountainous areas at elevations up to 8,000 ft., palm, rain, dry, and montane forests, cultivated fields, around human dwellings.	3' to 6' (91–183 cm)
Porthidium (= *Bothrops*) (New World Hog-nosed and Jumping Vipers)	N.Am., S.Am.	S.Tr., Tr.	(T)—Cloud, pine/oak, and rain forests, forest edge situations, plantations, rocky and sandy hillsides, and adjacent flats.	2' (61 cm)
Protobothrops (= *Trimeresurus*)	E.As., S.As.	Te., S.Tr., Tr.	(S, T)—Sparse, hilly and forested areas, palm, rain, and monsoon forests, forest edge situations, caves, cultivated fields, around human dwellings.	4' to 6' (122–183 cm)
Sistrurus (Pigmy Rattlesnakes and Massasaugas)	N.Am.	Te., S.Tr.	(T)—In a wide variety of habitats that include elevated patches of marshy areas, near rivers and streams in hammocks, grasslands and meadows, pine forests, dry sandy ridges, and cultivated fields.	1' 3" to 3' 4" (38–102 cm)

Reptile (species listed for monotypic genera)	Region of World Reptile Occurs (1,4)	"Native" Thermal Regimes (2,4)	Habits (3,4,6) & Habitats (3,4,6) (also refer to Glossary for habitat definitions)	Approximate Adult Sizes Feet ('); Inches (") (4,5,6)
Trimeresurus	E.I., Phil., S.As.	S.Tr., Tr.	(A, T)—In a wide variety of habitats including montane, rain, and dry forests, mangrove swamps, semideserts, cultivated fields, and around human dwellings.	2' to 6' (61–183 cm)
Tropidolaemus (= *Trimeresurus*) *wagleri* (Wagler's or Temple Viper)	Phil., S.As.	S.Tr., Tr.	(A)—Montane, rain, bamboo, and mangrove forests.	2' 6" (76 cm)
(TRUE VIPERS)				
Adenorhinos barbouri (Worm-eating Viper)	S.Af.	S.Tr.	(A, T)—Woodlands, forests, swamps.	3' (91 cm)
Atheris (African Bush Vipers)	S.Af.	Tr.	(A, S, T)—Tropical rain forests, humid valleys, mountain areas, around lakes and upland swamps.	3' (91 cm)
Azemiops feae (Fea's Viper)	S.As.	Tr.	(F, T)—Mountains, roadsides, cultivated fields, around human dwellings.	3' (91 cm)
Bitis (African Vipers)	N.Af., S.Af., W.As.	S.Tr., Tr., Ar.	(T)—Tropical rain forests, river banks, and other moist areas including swamps, lightly forested habitats, grasslands, deserts.	4' (122 cm)
Causus (Night Adders)	S.Af.	Te., S.Tr.	(T)—Damp areas associated with forests at elevations up to 7,000 ft.	3' (91 cm)
Cerastes (Horned or Desert Vipers)	N.Af., W.As.	Te. (?), Ar.	(F, T)—Under stones and in rodent burrows in sandy, rocky outcroppings, deserts, and oases.	1' to 2' (30–61 cm)
Echis (Saw-scaled Vipers)	N.Af., S.Af., W.As.	Te., S.Tr., Tr., Ar.	(T)—Semideserts and deserts in sandy arid soil from seacoasts to elevations of 6,000 ft.	2' (61 cm)
Eristocophis macmahoni (McMahon's Viper)	W.As.	Te., Ar.	(T)—Sandy areas in deserts.	2' (61 cm)
Pseudocerastes persicus (Desert or False Horned Viper)	W.As.	Te., S.Tr., Ar.	(T)—Under rocks and in rodent burrows in sandy, rocky deserts and mountain regions.	3' (91 cm)
Vipera (Old World Vipers)	Eu., E.I., N.Af., S.As., W.As.	Te., S.Tr., Tr.	(T)—Woodlands, rocks, and cliffs, mountain slopes, around human dwellings; primarily dry habitats, but some species found near fresh water.	1' 6" to 5' 6" (46–168 cm)
FAMILY XENOPELTIDAE				
Xenopeltis unicolor (Sunbeam Snake)	E.I., Phil., S.As.	S.Tr., Tr.	(F, T)—Entirely under soil except when hunting prey; lowland river valleys, rice fields, gardens, and similar areas with damp soil, mountains.	4' (122 cm)

Crocodilians

FAMILY ALLIGATORIDAE
(Alligators and Caimans)

Reptile	Region	Thermal	Habits & Habitats	Size
Alligator	N.Am., S.As.	Te., S.Tr., Tr.	(S.Aq.)—Nearly all bodies of fresh water including swamps, marshes, ponds, rivers, lakes, flood plains, and occasionally near brackish water.	4' 6" to 18' (137–549 cm)
Caiman	N.Am., S.Am., W.I.	Tr.	(S.Aq.)—Nearly all bodies of fresh water including swamps, marshes, ponds, rivers, lakes, and streams; introduced into U.S.	6' (183 cm)
Melanosuchus niger (Black Caiman)	S.Am.	Tr.	(S.Aq.)—Nearly all bodies of fresh water including swamps, marshes, ponds, lakes, and streams.	10' to 12' (305–366 cm)
Paleosuchus (Dwarf Caimans)	S.Am.	Tr.	(S.Aq.)—Still or flowing fresh water in tropical rain forests.	4' (122 cm)

Reptile (species listed for monotypic genera)	Region of World Reptile Occurs (1,4)	"Native" Thermal Regimes (2,4)	Habits (3,4,6) & Habitats (3,4,6) (also refer to Glossary for habitat definitions)	Approximate Adult Sizes Feet ('); Inches (") (4,5,6)
FAMILY CROCODYLIDAE (True Crocodiles)				
Crocodylus	Aus., Mad., N.Am., Phil., S.Af., S.Am., S.As., W.I.	S.Tr., Tr.	(S.Aq.)—Nearly all bodies of water including swamps, marshes, ponds, rivers, lakes, streams, waterholes, estuaries, coastal brackish lagoons, the sea, and in forested areas.	6' to 30' (183–914 cm)
Osteolaemus tetraspis (African Dwarf Crocodile)	S.Af.	Tr.	(S.Aq.)—Quiet fresh waters in forested areas.	3' 6" to 6' (107–183 cm)
FAMILY GAVIALIDAE				
Gavialis gangeticus (Gavial, Gharial)	S.As.	S.Tr., Tr.	(S.Aq.)—Large freshwater rivers.	12' to 21' (366–640 cm)
Tomistoma schlegeli (False Gavial or Gharial)	E.I.	Tr.	(S.Aq.)—Quiet fresh waters.	10' (305 cm)

* Bellairs, 1970; Branch, 1988; Breen, 1974; Burquez et al., 1986; Campbell and Lamar, 1989; Campden-Main, 1970; Carr, 1952; Cochran, 1941; Cogger, 1975; Cogger et al., 1983; Conant, 1975; Daniel, 1983; Deoras, 1978; Dixon and Soini, 1986; Duellman, 1979; Ehmann, 1980; Freiberg, 1982; Gharpurey, 1962; Goin et al., 1978; Greer, 1989; Grenard, 1991; Grzimek, 1975; Guyer and Savage, 1986; Heatwole, 1987; Henderson and Binder, 1980; Isemonger, 1962; Iverson, 1985; Karsen et al., 1986; Khalaf, 1959; Kuntz, no date; Lee, 1980; Leutscher, 1961; Loveridge, 1946; Marais, 1992; Mattison, 1986; Mehrtens, 1987; Meylan, 1987; NAVMED, 1965; Newman, 1987; Obst et al., 1988; Peters and Donoso-Barros, 1970; Peters and Orejas-Miranda, 1986; Pinney, 1981; Pitman, 1974; Pope, 1935; Pritchard, 1979; Robb, 1986; de Rooij, 1917; Schmidt, 1928; Schmidt and Inger, 1957; Schwartz and Henderson, 1985; Shine, 1986; Smith, 1946; Smith, 1935; Stebbins, 1966; Switak, 1984; Tanaka, 1986; Taylor, 1963; Trutnau, 1986; Tweedie, 1983; Weigel, 1988; Welch, 1982, 1983, 1988; Whitaker, 1978; Wilson and Meyer, 1985; Wright and Wright, 1957; Zappalorti, 1976; Zimmermann, 1986.

1. As. = Asia; Aus. = Australasia; C.As. = Central Asia; E.As. = East Asia, primarily China; E.I. = East Indies including southern Malaysia, Borneo, and Indonesia; Eu. = Europe; Mad. = Madagascar; N.Af. = Africa north of and including the Sahara; N.Am. = North America including Mexico; N.Z. = New Zealand; Pac. = Pacific Islands east of Australasia; Phil. = Philippines; S.Af. = Sub-Sahara Africa; S.Am. = Southern America including Central America south of Mexico; S.As. = Southern Asia including India, Sri Lanka, Burma, Indochina, and part of southern China; W.As. = Western Asia including the Arabian Peninsula, Iran, and Pakistan; W.I. = West Indies.

2. Thermal regimes were extrapolated from range maps according to latitude and elevation.

For the captive care of those species whose natural climatic conditions vary, the reader should consult the above references.

Ar. = Arid; S.Tr. = Subtropical; Te. = Temperate; Tr. = Tropical.

3. For the captive care of those species in which the habits or natural environments listed vary greatly, the reader should consult the above references.

A = Arboreal; Aq. = Aquatic; F = Fossorial; S = Scansorial; S.Aq. = Semiaquatic; T = Terrestrial.

4. Depending on species and/or sex.

5. SVL = Snout-vent-length, otherwise sizes given are for total length.

6. Information not found.

Appendix II

Maintenance of Selected Insect Colonies

Insectivorous reptiles normally forage for a variety of insects, providing them with the well-balanced diet necessary for good health and reproduction. Unfortunately, when these animals become captives, it is difficult to provide a similar variety. Although insects are rich in proteins and fats and contain B complex vitamins (Lint, 1961), commercially raised insects are deficient in calcium. Many captive reptiles therefore may suffer nutritional problems.

Most bait stores sell the food items that will be discussed in this chapter, and insects purchased in this manner can be refrigerated until needed. Mealworms may survive 2 to 3 months under refrigeration, waxworms about 1 to 3 weeks and crickets approximately 24 to 60 hours. When purchasing insects, do not freeze them because they will not move, and reptiles may not feed upon them.

In addition to offering captive reptiles a combination of several commercially grown insects, their diets also can be varied by feeding them insects from net-sweepings. Alternatively, many insects can be attracted to a black light or a sunlamp. Wild-caught insects, however, may contain pesticide residues, and many varieties serve as intermediate hosts for numerous parasites. Feeding captive reptiles net-sweepings sparingly to balance their diet outweighs the risks involved. For this reason, fecal examinations should be performed about every six months to check for parasites. Also, avoid feeding reptiles insects that have been exposed to toxins that are used to control weeds and insects. Sublethal levels of toxic residues may be ingested by the insects and concentrated in reptiles' tissues. As time passes the toxic residues may become fatal to the reptiles as they continue to feed upon the contaminated insects. Also, do not allow cockroaches, ants or other undesirable pests to gain access to a reptile's enclosure.

Raising insects, rather than buying them as needed, provides the insectivorous reptile with nutrients it may otherwise do without. This method is less expensive than buying insects as they are needed, and requires little time and effort for maintenance.

The following insects are maintained easily as food sources for all species of captive insect-eating animals, and when fed on an enriched medium, and in combination with other insects, they can provide an insectivorous reptile with a reasonably balanced diet.

I. Mealworm (*Tenebrio molitor*) Colony

Materials:

1 wide-mouth gallon jar or other appropriately sized container (Fig. 115).

Enough medium (equal parts of oat bran and wheat bran) to fill jar half-way.

½ cup vitamin-mineral powder containing vitamin D$_3$ (e.g., Vionate®).

1,000 mealworms (preferably of mixed sizes).

½ potato or apple (necessary for moisture).

Cheesecloth.

String or rubber band.

1 appropriately sized bowl with tap water.

10-inch forceps.

Place the brans and vitamin-mineral powder in the jar and mix them thoroughly. Place the mealworms in the jar and gently swirl them into the medium. Place ½ potato on top of the medium and secure the cheesecloth cover with a piece of string or a rubberband. Place the jar and its contents into an appropriate-sized bowl of water.

Ground monkey chow, powdered dry dog food or laboratory rodent chow, chick starter, etc., have been used for growing mealworms, but these commercial animal diets often contain arthropod pests that can contaminate the mealworm culture. The use of a medium intended for human consumption is less likely to contain such contaminants. Nevertheless, grain mites (*Tyrophagus* spp.) are almost always a potential problem because their eggs may adhere to the mealworms at the

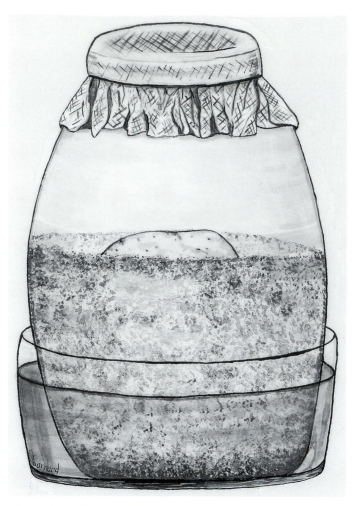

Fig. 115 Wide-mouth gallon jar containing mealworm colony. Placing jar with mealworm colony in a container of water will help prevent the colony from becoming contaminated with invading arthropod pests. Likewise, the proliferation of pests purchased with the growing medium will remain contained. Reprinted with permission from Barnard 1986c.

time of purchase. These mites are commonly found in stored food. Once gaining access to an insect colony, these mites can build up large populations. Placing the jar that contains a mealworm colony into a bowl of water, reduces access to the colony by invading mites. At the same time, mites that may have been on purchased mealworms or within the oatmeal will be contained and prevented from dispersing into the surrounding area. If mites or other pests are observed, one may wish to discard the mealworm colony, although these contaminants are not known to be harmful to reptiles.

To change a mealworm colony to fresh medium, first pour all contents from the old jar into a clean one, and discard only the moist, hard sediment on the bottom. Add enough fresh medium to fill the clean jar half-way. Mix in ⅛ cup multivitamin powder and ⅛ cup bone meal. Place ½ fresh potato or apple on top of the new

medium. A fresh potato or apple should be added when the old one no longer provides moisture for the mealworms. When changing a colony to a clean jar, never throw away old potatoes or apples because mealworms lay their eggs in these items.

Mealworms are easily removed from the jar with 10-inch forceps. Note: reptiles should never be fed mealworms exclusively. The mealworms' chitinous exoskeleton may cause intestinal impaction.

II. Wax Moth (*Galleria mellonella*) Colony

Materials:

1 5-gal. plastic container with tightly sealing lid (cut hole in lid and screen) (Fig. 116).

Starter culture.

½ lb. artificial diet*.

Appropriately sized pan with water.

Lamp with 60–100 W incandescent bulb.

*Artificial diet (Dutky et al., 1962):

Ingredients:

1 lb. box mixed Gerber's baby cereal.

¾ cup glycerine

½ cup sugar.

½ cup tap water (Once preparation is completed, never add water to colony or food will spoil).

0.6 ml (cc) Poly-Vi-Sol® baby vitamins (comes with an 0.6 ml dropper)**.

**To the above ingredients also add 2 Tbsp. bone meal powder.

Place the starter culture on the bottom of the container with the artificial diet. Cover the container and place it in a pan of water to prevent the colony from becoming contaminated by undesirable arthropods, and to prevent the wax moth larvae (waxworms) from migrating accidently outside of the container. Set the lamp about 6 to 8 in. from the pan (do not allow the lamp to melt the plastic container or pan). Waxworms develop most rapidly at temperatures between 26.7–32.2°C (80–90°F).

Periodically check the culture for the appropriate-sized larvae to feed to reptiles. Do not feed reptiles too many moths because they are necessary to continue the culture, and because they are not as nourishing as the larvae. Add more food when the artificial diet appears to be riddled with larvae and cocoons. If parts of the container's contents become moldy, remove immediately. Surplus wax moth food can be stored in the refrigerator for several months if sealed tightly in a plastic bag.

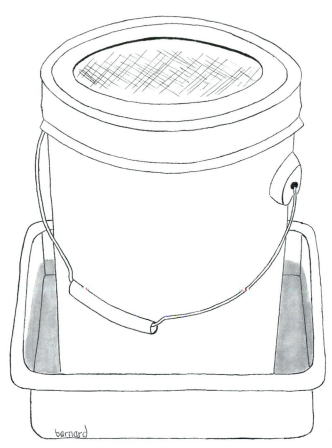

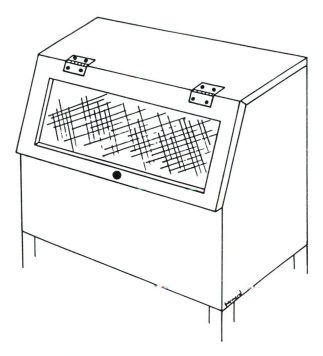

Fig. 117 Plywood box with screened lid typically used to house crickets. Reprinted with permission from Barnard 1986c.

Fig. 116 Five-gallon plastic container with tightly sealing lid provides convenient housing for wax moth colonies. Since moisture is produced as larvae metabolize their food, be sure to cut a large opening in lid and cover with screening. Placing the colony in a container of water will reduce the chances of contamination by invading arthropod pests, and will prevent wax moth larvae from escaping into the environment. Reprinted with permission from Barnard 1986c.

Excess wax moths should never be released intentionally into the environment because they are parasites of bee hives. When a wax moth culture becomes too large, one may wish to give part of it to zoological organizations or pet owners housing reptiles or other insect-eating animals. If a surplus colony should be refused, it can be destroyed by soaking in hot water.

III. Cricket (*Acheta domestica*) Colony

Materials:

> 1 wooden box (approx. 2 ft. wide × 1 ft. deep) with screen lid (Fig. 117).
>
> Enough peat moss to cover bottom, about 2 to 3 inches deep.
>
> Chick starter or game bird chow.
>
> 1-pint poultry water dispenser (Fig. 118).

> Paper towels.
>
> Fresh leafy greens (collards, parsley, clover, grass, etc.).
>
> Cardboard egg containers (these dividers are usually shipped with crickets from farm).
>
> Lamp with 60–100 W incandescent bulb.
>
> Appropriately sized collecting jar and funnel.
>
> Use 1,000 or more crickets for large culture*.
>
> Use 1 or 2 dozen crickets for small culture*.
>
> *For available sizes see Fig. 119

When ordering 1,000 or more crickets, the cricket bin can be made of ½-in. plywood. Carefully sand the inside walls smooth to about 4 in. from the top of the container and apply glossy paint (crickets cannot walk on this surface). Spread dry peat moss over the bottom of the box, and place the chick starter, water and greens in the center. The (poultry) water dispenser should be lined with 2 or 3 paper towels to prevent the crickets from drowning. These insects drink water from the soaked towels. Place the crickets in the bin and cover with a screened top. Place the lamp over the screened top to provide warmth (23.9°C; 75°F). To prevent the cricket bin from becoming contaminated with invading arthropod pests, it may be necessary to place each leg of the bin into a container of water, or to ring each leg abundantly with vasoline.

Fig. 118 Poultry water dispenser is used to provide moisture for crickets. Paper towels prevent crickets from drowning, yet allow these insects to receive water necessary for survival. Reprinted with permission from Barnard 1986c.

The water jar should be cleaned and paper towels replaced when necessary. Remove old greens and replace with fresh material every 2 to 3 days, and replenish the chow as needed. The peat-moss bedding should be kept dry and changed every 1 to 2 weeks. To do this, remove the water, greens and chow, and place the egg cartons at one end of the bin and wait until the crickets have migrated to the cartons. Change one half of the bedding; place the egg cartons at the opposite end of the bin, and proceed as before. Replace the water, greens and chow when finished. When collecting crickets from the bin, insert a funnel into a collecting jar and shake the crickets from cardboard egg containers. Since adult crickets live about 2 weeks, use them as soon as possible.

When breeding and raising crickets, it will be necessary to have on hand additional supplies. They are as follows:

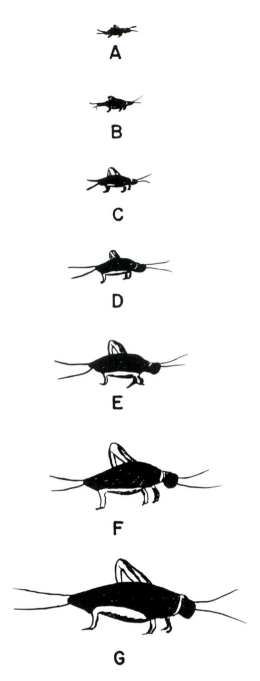

Fig. 119 Available cricket sizes that can be purchased at any cricket farm. A) "pinhead," 1/8"; B) 1 week old, 3/16"; C) 2 weeks old, 1/4"; D) 3 weeks old, 3/8"; E) 4 weeks old, 1/2"; F) 5 weeks old, 3/4"; G) adult, 1". Reprinted with permission from Barnard, 1986c.

2 10-gal. aquariums.

Misting bottle.

2 lamps with 25–40 W incandescent bulbs.

4 jar lids or Petri dishes.

2 cardboard egg containers.

Potting soil or peat moss.

Newspaper.

2 small sponges.

1 bowl.

Line one aquarium with newspaper and the other with about 1 to 2 inches of potting soil or peat moss. Into the aquarium lined with newspaper, place about 2 to 3 dozen crickets (females have long ovipositors protruding posteriorly from their abdomens). Also place a cardboard egg container into each aquarium. Use one Petri dish for food (feed with diet discussed earlier) and the other for water for the breeding crickets. Hold the other two in reserve for the hatchling crickets. Into the Petri dish that is to contain water, place one sponge and soak it well. In a corner of the breeding aquarium, place a bowl filled with potting soil or peat moss. Be sure the soil or moss is kept damp, not wet. This can be done with the misting bottle. Cover the aquarium with a lid, and place it next to the lamp to maintain the temperature at 26.7°C (80°F). Remove moistened soil or moss containing the eggs from the bowl weekly, and add it to the other aquarium reserved for raising the hatchlings.

After the first eggs have been placed into the second aquarium, maintain it in the same manner as the "feed-off" and breeding containers. The substrate containing eggs must be kept damp. It is important not to mix the hatchlings with adults, as the adults may eat them. This problem can be avoided by offering the adult crickets meat in their diet (e.g., a small amount of canned dog food).

Eggs require 3 to 4 weeks to hatch, and young mature within 3 to 4 months. Additional aquaria can be used to separate hatchlings according to size. When hatchlings approach adult size, they can be placed into the "feed off" bin. Feed crickets to reptiles in combination with mealworms and waxworms.

Appendix III

Composition of Raw Fruits and Berries, 100 grams Edible Portion*

Description	Water %	Food Energy Cal.	Protein Gr.	Fat Gr.	Carbohydrate Total Gr.	Carbohydrate Fiber Gr.	CA:P Ratio	Iron Mg.	Sodium Mg.	Potassium Mg.	Magnesium Mg.	Vitamin A I.U.	Thiamine Mg.	Riboflavin Mg.	Niacin Mg.	Vitamin C Mg.
Apples (not pared)	84.4	58	0.2	0.6	14.5	1.0	0.70:1	0.3	1	110	8	90	0.03	0.02	0.1	4
Apricots	85.3	51	1.0	0.2	12.8	0.6	0.74:1	0.5	1	281	12	2,700	0.03	0.04	0.6	10
Bananas	75.7	85	1.1	0.2	22.2	0.5	0.30:1	0.7	1	370	33	190	0.05	0.06	0.7	10
Blackberries	84.5	58	1.2	0.9	12.9	4.1	1.68:1	0.9	1	170	30	200	0.03	0.04	0.4	21
Blueberries	83.2	62	0.7	0.5	15.3	1.5	1.15:1	1.0	1	81	6	100	0.03	0.06	0.5	14
Canteloup	91.1	30	0.9	0.1	7.2	0.5	0.88:1	0.4	12	251	16	3,400	0.04	0.03	0.6	23
Cherries																
Sour Red	83.7	58	1.2	0.3	14.3	0.2	1.16:1	0.4	2	191	14	1,000	0.05	0.06	0.4	10
Sweet	80.4	70	1.3	0.3	17.4	0.4	1.16:1	0.4	2	191	9	110	0.05	0.06	0.4	10
Cranberries	87.9	46	0.4	0.7	10.8	1.4	1.14:1	0.5	2	82	8	40	0.03	0.02	0.1	11
Dates (dry)	22.5	274	2.2	0.5	72.9	2.3	0.93:1	3.0	1	648	58	50	0.09	0.10	2.2	0
Elderberries	79.8	72	2.6	0.5	16.4	7.0	1.36:1	1.6	—	300	—	600	0.07	0.06	0.5	36
Figs (raw)	77.5	80	1.2	0.3	20.3	1.2	1.59:1	0.6	2	194	20	80	0.06	0.05	0.4	2
(dried, uncooked)	23.0	274	4.3	1.3	69.1	5.6	1.63:1	3.0	34	640	71	80	0.10	0.10	0.7	0
Grapefruit																
All varieties	88.4	41	0.5	0.1	10.6	0.2	1.00:1	0.4	1	135	12	80	0.04	0.02	0.2	38
Grapes																
American	81.6	69	1.3	1.0	15.7	0.6	1.33:1	0.4	3	158	13	100	0.05	0.03	0.3	4
European	81.4	67	0.6	0.3	17.3	0.5	0.60:1	0.4	3	173	6	100	0.05	0.03	0.3	4
Guavas																
Common	83.0	62	0.8	0.6	15.0	5.6	0.55:1	0.9	4	289	13	280	0.05	0.05	1.2	242
Strawberry	81.8	65	1.0	0.6	15.8	6.4	0.55:1	0.9	4	289	—	90	0.03	0.03	0.6	37
Loganberries	83.0	62	1.0	0.6	14.9	3.0	2.06:1	1.2	1	170	25	200	0.03	0.04	0.4	24
Mangos	81.7	66	0.7	0.4	16.8	0.9	0.77:1	0.4	7	189	18	4,800	0.05	0.05	1.1	35
Nectarines	81.8	64	0.6	Trace	17.1	0.4	0.17:1	0.5	6	294	13	1,650	—	—	—	13
Oranges (with peel)	82.3	40	1.3	0.3	15.5	—	3.18:1	0.8	2	196	11	250	0.10	0.05	0.5	71
Papayas	88.7	39	0.6	0.1	10.0	0.9	1.25:1	0.3	3	234	—	1,750	0.04	0.04	0.3	56
Peaches	89.1	38	0.6	0.1	9.7	0.6	0.47:1	0.5	1	202	10	1,330	0.02	0.05	1.0	7
Pears (with skin)	83.2	61	0.7	0.4	15.3	1.4	0.73:1	0.3	2	130	7	20	0.02	0.04	0.1	4
Persimmons																
Japanese or Kaki	78.6	77	0.7	0.4	19.7	1.6	0.23:1	0.3	6	174	8	2,710	0.03	0.02	0.1	11
Native	64.4	127	0.8	0.4	33.5	1.5	1.04:1	2.5	1	310	—	—	—	—	—	66
Pineapple	85.3	52	0.4	0.2	13.7	0.4	2.13:1	0.5	1	146	13	70	0.09	0.03	0.2	17
Plums																
Damson	81.1	66	0.5	Trace	17.8	0.4	1.06:1	0.5	2	299	9	300	0.08	0.03	0.5	—
Japanese & Hybrid	86.6	48	0.5	0.2	12.3	0.6	0.67:1	0.5	1	170	9	250	0.03	0.03	0.5	6
Prune-type	78.7	75	0.8	0.2	19.7	0.4	0.67:1	0.5	1	170	9	300	0.03	0.03	0.5	4
Prunes (dehydrated)	2.5	344	3.3	0.5	91.3	2.2	0.84:1	4.4	11	940	40	2,170	0.12	0.22	2.1	4
Raisins	18.0	289	2.5	0.2	77.4	0.9	0.61:1	3.5	27	763	35	20	0.11	0.08	0.5	1
Raspberries																
Black	80.8	73	1.5	1.4	15.7	5.1	1.36:1	0.9	1	199	30	Trace	0.03	0.09	0.9	18
Red	84.2	57	1.2	0.5	13.6	3.0	1.00:1	0.9	1	168	20	130	0.03	0.09	0.9	25
Strawberries	89.9	37	0.7	0.5	8.4	1.3	1.00:1	1.0	1	164	12	60	0.03	0.07	0.6	59
Tangerines	87.0	46	0.8	0.2	11.6	0.5	2.22:1	0.4	2	126	—	420	0.06	0.02	0.1	31
Watermelon	92.6	26	0.5	0.2	6.4	0.3	0.70:1	0.5	1	100	8	590	0.03	0.03	0.2	7

* From United States Department of Agriculture, Handbook No. 8.
—Value not known.

Appendix IV

Composition of Raw Garden Vegetables, 100 grams Edible Portion*

Description	Water %	Food Energy Cal.	Protein Gr.	Fat Gr.	Carbohydrate Total Gr.	Carbohydrate Fiber Gr.	CA:P Ratio	Iron Mg.	Sodium Mg.	Potassium Mg.	Magnesium Mg.	Vitamin A I.U.	Thiamine Mg.	Riboflavin Mg.	Niacin Mg.	Vitamin C Mg.
Asparagus	91.7	26	2.5	0.2	5.0	0.7	0.35:1	1.0	2	278	20	900	0.18	0.20	1.5	33
Beets (with tops)	87.3	43	1.6	0.1	9.9	0.8	0.48:1	0.7	60	335	25	20	0.03	0.05	0.4	10
Broccoli Spears	89.1	32	3.6	0.3	5.9	1.5	1.32:1	1.1	15	382	24	2,500	0.10	0.23	0.9	113
Carrots	88.2	42	1.1	0.2	9.7	1.0	1.03:1	0.7	47	341	23	11,000	0.06	0.05	0.6	8
Cauliflower	91.0	27	2.7	0.2	5.2	1.0	0.45:1	1.1	13	295	24	60	0.11	0.10	0.7	78
Celery	94.1	17	0.9	0.1	3.9	0.6	1.39:1	0.3	126	341	22	240	0.03	0.03	0.3	9
Chives	91.3	28	1.8	0.3	5.8	1.1	1.57:1	1.7	—	250	32	5,800	0.08	0.13	0.5	56
Corn	72.7	96	3.5	1.0	22.1	0.7	0.03:1	0.7	Trace	280	48	400	0.15	0.12	1.7	12
Cucumbers (not pared)	95.1	15	0.9	0.1	3.4	0.6	0.93:1	1.1	6	160	11	250	0.03	0.04	0.2	11
Egg Plant	92.4	25	1.2	0.2	5.6	0.9	0.46:1	0.7	2	214	16	10	0.05	0.05	0.6	5
Green (snap) Beans	90.9	24	2.2	0.3	4.6	1.3	1.27:1	0.8	7	243	32	600	0.08	0.11	0.5	19
Leeks (bulb, lower Leaf)	85.4	52	2.2	0.3	11.2	1.3	1.14:1	1.1	5	347	23	40	0.11	0.06	0.5	17
Lima Beans	67.5	123	8.4	0.5	22.1	1.8	0.37:1	2.8	2	650	67	290	0.24	0.12	1.4	29
Okra	88.9	36	2.4	0.3	7.6	1.0	1.80:1	0.6	3	249	41	520	0.17	0.21	1.0	31
Onions																
Mature	89.1	38	1.5	0.1	8.7	0.6	0.75:1	0.5	10	157	12	40	0.03	0.04	0.2	10
Welsh	90.5	34	1.9	0.4	6.5	1.0	0.37:1	—	—	—	—	—	0.05	0.09	0.4	27
Young, green bulb with top	89.4	36	1.5	0.2	8.2	1.2	1.31:1	1.0	5	231	—	2,000	0.05	0.05	0.4	32
Peas																
edible podded	83.3	53	3.4	0.2	12.0	1.2	0.69:1	0.7	—	170	—	680	0.28	0.12	—	21
green immature	78.0	84	6.3	0.4	14.4	2.0	0.23:1	1.9	2	316	35	640	0.35	0.14	2.9	27
Potatoes (not peeled)	79.8	76	2.1	0.1	17.1	0.5	0.01:1	0.6	3	407	34	Trace	0.10	0.04	1.5	20
Pumpkin	91.6	26	1.0	0.1	6.5	1.1	0.48:1	0.8	1	340	12	1,600	0.05	0.11	0.6	9
Radishes	94.5	17	1.0	0.1	3.6	0.7	0.96:1	1.0	18	322	15	10	0.03	0.03	0.3	26
Squash																
summer	94.0	19	1.1	0.1	4.2	0.6	0.97:1	0.4	1	202	16	410	0.05	0.09	1.0	22
winter	85.1	50	1.4	0.3	12.4	1.4	0.58:1	0.6	1	369	17	3,700	0.05	0.11	0.6	13
Sweet Potatoes	70.6	114	1.7	0.4	26.3	0.7	0.68:1	0.7	10	243	31	8,800	0.10	0.06	0.6	21
Tomatoes																
green	93.0	24	1.2	0.2	5.1	0.5	0.48:1	0.5	3	244	14	270	0.06	0.04	0.5	20
ripe	93.5	22	1.1	0.2	4.7	0.5	0.48:1	0.5	3	244	14	900	0.06	0.04	0.7	23
Turnips	91.5	30	1.0	0.2	6.6	0.9	1.30:1	0.5	49	268	20	Trace	0.04	0.07	0.6	36
Yams	73.5	101	2.1	0.2	23.2	0.9	0.29:1	0.6	—	600	—	Trace	0.10	0.04	0.5	9

* From United States Department of Agriculture, Handbook No. 8.
—Value not known.

Appendix V

Composition of Raw Green Leafy Vegetables, 100 grams Edible Portion*

Description	Water %	Food Energy Cal.	Protein Gr.	Fat Gr.	Carbohydrate Total Gr.	Carbohydrate Fiber Gr.	CA:P Ratio	Iron Mg.	Sodium Mg.	Potassium Mg.	Magnesium Mg.	Vitamin A I.U.	Thiamine Mg.	Riboflavin Mg.	Niacin Mg.	Vitamin C Mg.
Beet Greens	90.9	24	2.2	0.3	4.6	1.3	2.7:1	3.3	130	570	106	6,100	0.10	0.22	0.40	30
Brussels Sprouts	85.2	45	4.9	0.4	8.3	1.6	0.45:1	1.5	14	390	29	550	0.10	0.16	0.90	102
Cabbage	92.4	24	1.3	0.2	5.4	0.8	1.69:1	0.4	20	233	13	130	0.05	0.05	0.30	47
Collard Greens (without stems)	85.3	45	4.8	0.8	7.5	1.2	3.05:1	1.5	—	450	57	9,300	0.16	0.31	1.70	152
Dandelion Greens	85.6	45	2.7	0.7	9.2	1.6	2.83:1	3.1	76	397	36	14,000	0.19	0.26	—	35
Garden Cress	89.4	32	2.6	0.7	5.5	1.1	1.06:1	1.3	14	606	—	9,300	0.08	0.26	1.00	69
Kale (without stems)	82.7	53	6.0	0.8	9.0	—	2.68:1	2.7	75	378	37	10,000	0.16	0.26	2.10	186
Lettuce Bunching Varieties (Grand Rapids, Simpson, etc.)	94.0	18	1.3	0.3	3.5	0.7	2.72:1	1.4	9	264	—	1,900	0.05	0.08	0.40	18
Butterhead Varieties	95.1	14	1.2	0.2	2.5	0.5	1.35:1	2.0	9	264	—	970	0.06	0.06	0.30	8
Iceberg	95.5	13	0.9	0.1	2.9	0.5	0.90:1	0.5	9	175	11	330	0.06	0.06	0.30	6
Romaine	94.0	18	1.3	0.3	3.5	0.7	2.72:1	1.4	9	264	—	1,900	0.05	0.08	0.40	18
Mustard Greens	89.5	31	3.0	0.5	5.6	1.1	3.66:1	3.0	32	377	27	7,000	0.11	0.22	0.80	97
Parsley	85.1	44	3.6	0.6	8.5	1.5	3.22:1	6.2	45	727	41	8,500	0.12	0.26	1.20	172
Spinach	90.7	26	3.2	0.3	4.3	0.6	1.82:1	3.1	71	470	88	8,100	0.10	0.20	0.60	51
Swiss Chard	91.1	25	2.4	0.3	4.6	0.8	2.26:1	3.2	147	550	65	6,500	0.06	0.17	0.50	32
Turnip Greens Leaves & Stems	90.3	28	3.0	0.3	5.0	0.8	4.24:1	1.8	—	—	58	7,600	0.21	0.39	0.80	139
Watercress (leaves & stems)	93.3	19	2.2	0.3	3.0	0.7	2.80:1	1.7	52	282	20	4,900	0.08	0.16	0.90	79

* From United States Department of Agriculture, Handbook No. 8.
—Value not known.

Appendix VI

Composition of Raw Miscellaneous Foods, 100 grams Edible Portion*

Description	Water %	Food Energy Cal.	Protein Gr.	Fat Gr.	Carbohydrate Total Gr.	Carbohydrate Fiber Gr.	CA:P Ratio	Iron Mg.	Sodium Mg.	Potassium Mg.	Magnesium Mg.	Vitamin A I.U.	Thiamine Mg.	Riboflavin Mg.	Niacin Mg.	Vitamin C Mg
Eggs	73.7	163	12.9	11.5	0.9	0.0	0.26:1	2.3	122	129	11	1,180	0.11	0.30	0.1	0
Mushrooms	90.4	28	2.7	0.3	4.4	0.8	0.05:1	0.8	15	414	13	Trace	0.10	0.46	4.2	3
Seaweeds																
Agar	16.3	—	—	0.3	—	0.7	25.77:1	6.3	—	—	—	—	—	—	—	—
Dulse	16.6	—	—	3.2	—	1.2	1.11:1	—	2,085	8,060	—	—	—	—	—	—
Irishmoss	19.2	—	—	1.8	—	2.1	5.64:1	8.9	2,892	2,844	—	—	—	—	—	—
Kelp	21.7	—	—	1.1	—	6.8	4.55:1	—	3,007	5,273	—	—	—	—	—	—
Laver	17.0	—	—	0.6	—	11.0	—	—	—	—	—	—	—	—	—	—
Sprouted Seeds	86.3	46	6.2	1.4	5.3	0.8	0.72:1	1.0	—	—	—	80	0.23	0.20	0.8	13
Water Chestnuts	93.3	19	2.2	0.3	3.0	0.7	2.80:1	1.7	52	282	12	4,900	0.08	0.16	0.9	79

* From United States Department of Agriculture, Handbook No. 8.
—Value not known.

Composition of Raw Food Animals, 100 grams Edible Portion*

Description	Water %	Food Energy Cal.	Protein Gr.	Fat Gr.	Carbohydrate Total Gr.	Carbohydrate Fiber Gr.	CA:P Ratio	Iron Mg.	Sodium Mg.	Potassium Mg.	Magnesium Mg.	Vitamin A I.U.	Thiamine Mg.	Riboflavin Mg.	Niacin Mg.	Vitamin C Mg.
Catfish (freshwater)	78.0	103.0	17.6	3.1	0.0	0.0	—	0.4	60	330	—	—	0.04	0.03	1.7	—
Chicken**																
Day Old	73.0	162.3	16.8	6.4	—	0.3	0.80:1	3.3	—	—	—	—	0.36	—	—	—
Adult	66.5	198.6	19.0	9.0	—	0.7	1.40:1	4.9	122*	129*	—	1,180*	0.28	0.30*	0.1*	0*
Clams																
Meat & Liquid	85.8	54.0	8.6	1.0	2.0	—	—	—	—	—	—	—	—	—	—	—
Meat Only	80.8	82.0	14.6	1.9	1.3	—	—	3.4	36	235	—	—	—	—	—	—
Cod	81.2	78.0	17.6	0.3	0.0	0.0	0.05:1	0.4	70	382	28	0.0	0.06	0.07	2.2	2
Crappie (white)	81.8	79.0	16.8	0.8	0.0	0.0	—	—	—	—	—	—	Trace	0.03	1.4	—
Crickets***	—	—	—	—	—	—	0.33:1	—	—	—	—	—	—	—	—	—
Drum																
Freshwater	77.0	121.0	17.3	5.2	0.0	0.0	—	—	70	286	—	—	—	—	—	—
Red	80.2	80.0	18.0	0.4	0.0	0.0	—	—	55	273	—	—	0.15	0.05	3.5	—
Earthworms***	—	—	—	—	—	—	0.71:1	—	—	—	—	—	—	—	—	—
Eel (American)	64.6	233.0	15.9	18.3	0.0	0.0	0.09:1	0.7	—	—	—	1,610	0.22	0.36	1.4	—
Fly Larvae***	—	—	—	—	—	—	0.10:1	—	—	—	—	—	—	—	—	—
	—	—	—	—	—	—	0.33:1	—	—	—	—	—	—	—	—	—
Herring																
Atlantic	69.0	17.6	17.3	11.3	0.0	0.0	—	1.1	—	—	—	110	0.02	0.15	3.6	—
Pacific	79.4	98.0	17.5	2.6	0.0	0.0	—	1.3	74	420	—	100	0.02	0.16	3.5	3
Lake	79.7	96.0	17.7	2.3	0.0	0.0	0.06:1	0.5	47	319	—	—	0.09	0.10	3.3	—
Locusts***	—	—	—	—	—	—	0.13:1	—	—	—	—	—	—	—	—	—
Mealworms***	—	—	—	—	—	—	0.07:1	—	—	—	—	—	—	—	—	—
	—	—	—	—	—	—	0.33:1	—	—	—	—	—	—	—	—	—
Mouse**	64.6	207.7	19.8	8.8	—	0.6	1.33:1	8.5	—	—	—	—	—	—	—	—
Mussels (Atlantic and Pacific)	83.8	66.0	9.6	1.4	3.1	—	—	—	—	—	23	—	—	—	—	—
Oysters (meat only)																
Eastern	84.6	66.0	8.4	1.8	3.4	—	0.66:1	5.5	73	121	32	310	0.14	0.18	2.5	—
Pacific and Western	79.1	91.0	10.6	2.2	6.4	—	0.55:1	7.2	—	—	—	—	0.12	—	1.3	30
Pike																
Northern	80.0	88.0	18.3	1.1	0.0	0.0	—	—	—	—	—	—	—	—	—	—
Walleyed	78.3	93.0	19.3	1.2	0.0	0.0	—	0.4	51	319	—	—	0.25	0.16	2.3	—
Rat**	65.6	198.8	21.6	7.6	—	0.8	1.40:1	5.9	—	—	—	—	0.46	—	—	—
Salmon																
Atlantic	63.6	217.0	22.5	13.4	0.0	0.0	0.42:1	0.9	—	—	—	—	—	0.08	7.2	9
Chinook (king)	64.2	222.0	19.1	15.6	0.0	0.0	—	—	45	399	27	310	0.10	0.23	—	—
Chum	70.8	—	—	—	—	—	—	—	53	429	30	—	0.10	0.06	—	—
Coho (silver)	—	—	—	—	—	—	0.76:1	—	48	421	30	—	0.09	0.11	—	1
Pink (humpback)	76.0	119.0	20.0	3.7	0.0	0.0	—	—	64	306	30	—	0.14	0.05	—	—
Sockeye (red)	—	—	—	—	—	—	—	—	48	391	29	150	0.14	0.07	—	—
Shad (American)	70.4	170.0	18.6	10.0	0.0	0.0	0.08:1	0.5	54	330	—	—	0.15	0.24	8.4	—
Shrimp	78.2	91.0	18.1	0.8	1.5	—	0.38:1	1.6	140	220	42	—	0.02	0.03	3.2	—
Smelt (Atlantic, Jack, and Bay)	79.0	98.0	18.6	2.1	0.0	0.0	—	0.4	—	—	—	—	0.01	0.12	1.4	—
Snail	79.2	90.0	16.1	1.4	2.0	—	—	3.5	—	—	—	—	—	—	—	—
Trout																
Lake	70.6	168.0	18.3	10.0	0.0	0.0	—	0.8	—	—	—	—	0.09	0.12	2.7	—

Description	Water %	Food Energy Cal.	Protein Gr.	Fat Gr.	Carbohydrate Total Gr.	Carbohydrate Fiber Gr.	CA:P Ratio	Iron Mg.	Sodium Mg.	Potassium Mg.	Magnesium Mg.	Vitamin A I.U.	Thiamine Mg.	Riboflavin Mg.	Niacin Mg.	Vitamin C Mg.
Siscowet (< 6.5 lbs.)	64.9	241.0	14.3	19.9	0.0	0.0	—	—	—	—	—	—	—	—	—	—
Siscowet (> 6.5 lbs.)	36.8	524.0	7.9	54.4	0.0	0.0	—	—	—	—	—	—	—	0.07	—	—
Brook	77.7	101.0	19.2	2.1	0.0	0.0	—	—	—	—	—	—	0.08	0.20	8.4	—
Rainbow	66.3	195.0	21.5	11.4	0.0	0.0	—	—	—	—	—	—	—	—	—	—
Weakfish	76.7	121.0	16.5	5.6	0.0	0.0	—	—	75	317	—	—	0.09	0.06	2.7	—
Whitefish (lake)	71.7	155.0	18.9	8.2	0.0	0.0	—	0.4	52	299	—	2,260	0.14	0.12	3.0	—

* From United States Department of Agriculture, Handbook No. 8.
** Extrapolated from Bird and Ho (1976).
*** From Jackson and Cooper (1981).
—Value not known.

Appendix VIII

Preferred Foods of Captive Reptiles* (1,5)

Reptile (species listed for monotypic genera)	Small Mammals	Birds	Other Reptiles	Amphibians	Fish	Arthropods	Fruits & Berries	Vegetables	Other Foods/Comments
Chelonians									
FAMILY CARETTOCHELYIDAE (New Guinean Plateless Turtle) (2,4)	X	?			X	X	X		Worms, snails, carrion
FAMILY CHELIDAE (Side-necked Turtles) (2)									
Acanthochelys (= Platemys except P. platycephala) (South American Side-necked Turtles)	X			X	X	X			
Chelodina (Snake-necked Turtles)	X			X	X	X			Freshwater plants, snails, carrion
Chelus fimbriata (Matamata)					X				
Elseya (Australian Snapping Turtles)				X	X	X	X	X	Worms, crustaceans, freshwater plants, carrion
Emydura (Australian Short-necked Turtles) (3)				X	X	X	X	X	Crustaceans, mollusks, freshwater plants, carrion
Hydromedusa (South American Snake-necked Turtles)				X	X				Snails
Phrynops (Toad-headed Turtles)				X	X	X			Snails
Platemys platycephala (Twist-necked Turtle)	X			X	X	X			
Pseudemydura umbrina (Western Swamp Turtle)	X			X	X	X			
Rheodytes leukops (Fitzroy Turtle)					O	X and Larvae			Sponges
FAMILY CHELONIDAE (True Sea Turtles)									
Caretta caretta (Loggerhead Turtle)									Mollusks, crabs, coelenterates
Chelonia (Flatback and Green Turtles)									Crustaceans, marine plants
Eretmochelys (Hawksbill Turtles)									Sponges
Lepidochelys (Ridley Turtles)					X				Crustaceans, mollusks, jellyfish
FAMILY CHELYDRIDAE (Snapping Turtles) (2,4)	X	X	Turtles	X	X	X		O	Worms, crustaceans, freshwater plants, mollusks, carrion; cannibalistic
FAMILY DERMATEMYDIDAE Dermatemys mawii (4)							X	X	Freshwater plants, worms, crustaceans
FAMILY DERMOCHELYIDAE Dermochelys coriacea (2,4)					X and Eggs				Mollusks, jellyfish, marine plants, tunicates
FAMILY EMYDIDAE (Pond Turtles)									
Annamemys annamensis (Annam Pond Turtle)								X	Freshwater plants
Batagur baska (River Terrapin)							X	X	Freshwater plants
Callagur borneoensis (Painted Terrapin)							X	X	Freshwater plants

153

Reptile (species listed for monotypic genera)	Small Mammals	Birds	Other Reptiles	Amphibians	Fish	Arthropods	Fruits & Berries	Vegetables	Other Foods/Comments
Chinemys (Chinese Pond Turtles)						X		O	Freshwater plants, worms, snails, mussels
Chrysemys (Painted Turtles)				Tadpoles	X				Freshwater plants
Cistoclemmys (Chinese Box Turtles)						X		O	Freshwater plants, crustaceans
Clemmys (Pond Turtles) (3)	X			X	X	X	O		Freshwater plants, fungi, crustaceans, slugs
Cuora (Asian Box Turtles)				X	X	X	X	O	Freshwater plants, crustaceans, carrion
Cyclemys (Asian Leaf Turtles)						X		O	Freshwater plants
Deirochelys (Chicken Turtles)						O			Crustaceans
Emydoidea (Blanding's Turtles)				Tadpoles		X			Crustaceans
Emys (European Pond Turtles)				O	O	X		O	Crustaceans
Geoclemys hamiltonii (Spotted Pond Turtle)						X	X		Freshwater plants, snails
Geoemyda spengleri (Black-breasted Leaf Turtle)	O			X	X	X		X	Freshwater plants
Graptemys (Map Turtles) (2)						X		X	Mollusks
Hardella thurjii (Crowned River Turtle)							X	X	Freshwater plants
Heosemys (Forest Turtles)	Babies				X	X	X	X	Freshwater plants, fungi
Hieremys annandalii (Yellow-headed Temple Turtle)									Freshwater plants
Kachuga (Indian Roofed or Tent Turtles)					X	X	X	X	Crustaceans
Malaclemys (Diamondback Terrapins)									Crustaceans, mollusks
Malayemys subtrijuga (Malayan Snail-eating Turtle)									Snails
Mauremys (Stripe-necked Turtles)						X			Crustaceans
Melanochelys (Indian Black Turtles)	O					X		X	Freshwater plants
Morenia (Eyed Turtles)								X	Freshwater plants
Notochelys platynota (Malayan Flat-shelled or Purple-shelled Turtle)							X	X	Freshwater plants, carrion
Ocadia sinensis (Chinese Stripe-necked Turtle)	O			Frogs	X			X	Freshwater plants
Orlitia borneensis (Malaysian Giant Turtle)	X	O		X	X				O-Ripe bananas
Pseudemys (*P. scripta* = *Trachemys*) (Cooters and Red-bellied Turtles)	X	O		X	X			X	Freshwater plants
Pyxidea mouhotii (Keeled Box Turtle)	X					X	X	X	Natural vegetation, worms, fungi
Rhinoclemys (Neotropical Wood Turtles)						X		X	Freshwater plants, worms
Sacalia bealei (Four-eyed Turtle)	O			X	X	X		X	Freshwater plants
Siebenrockiella crassicollis (Black Marsh Turtle)									Carnivorous
Terrapene (Box Turtles)	X					X	X	X	Natural vegetation, worms, fungi
Trachemys (= *Pseudemys*) *scripta* (Slider Turtles) (2)	X	O		X	X	X		X	Freshwater plants
FAMILY KINOSTERNIDAE (Mud and Musk Turtles) (2,4)				X	X	X	O	O	Mollusks, crayfish, carrion
FAMILY PELOMEDUSIDAE (Side-necked Turtles) (2)									
Erymnochelys madagascariensis (Madagascar Big-headed Turtle)	X			X	X	X			Worms
Pelomedusa (Helmeted Turtles)	X			X	X	X			Worms
Peltocephalus dumerilianus (Big-headed Amazon River Turtle)									Freshwater plants
Pelusios (African Mud Turtles)						X and Larvae			Freshwater plants
Podocnemis (South American Side-necked River Turtles) (3)	X	X			X	X			Freshwater plants, worms, mollusks

Reptile (species listed for monotypic genera)	Small Mammals	Birds	Other Reptiles	Amphibians	Fish	Arthropods	Fruits & Berries	Vegetables	Other Foods/Comments
FAMILY PLATYSTERNIDAE *Platysternon megacephalum* (2,4)	X	X			X	X			Aquatic vegetation, worms, crustaceans
FAMILY TESTUDINIDAE (Land Tortoises) (4)						O	X	X	Natural vegetation, fungi
FAMILY TRIONYCHIDAE (Soft-shelled Turtles) (2,4)	X	X		Tadpoles	X	X	X	X	Freshwater plants, worms, crustaceans, mollusks

Lizards

Reptile (species listed for monotypic genera)	Small Mammals	Birds	Other Reptiles	Amphibians	Fish	Arthropods	Fruits & Berries	Vegetables	Other Foods/Comments
FAMILY AGAMIDAE (Agamid Lizards)									
Acanthosaura (Flattened-plated Lizards)						X			
Agama (3)						X	X	X	Natural vegetation
Amphibolurus (Bearded Dragons)	O		O			X		O	O-Natural vegetation
Aphaniotis (6)									
Calotes (Garden Lizards)	X	X	X			X			
Caimanops amphiboluroides						X			
Ceratophora (Horned Agamids)						X			Worms, slugs
Chelosania brunnea (Chameleon Dragon)						X			Small vertebrates
Chlamydosaurus kingii (Frilled Lizard)	X	?				X			Small vertebrates
Cophotis (Deaf Agamids)						X			Worms, slugs
Diporiphora						X			
Draco (Flying Lizards)						X			Prefer ants
Gonocephalus (Angle-headed Agamids)						X			
Harpesaurus (Hook-nosed Agamids)	?	?	?			X			
Hydrosaurus (Water Lizards)						X		X	Natural vegetation, mollusks
Hylagama borneensis (6)									
Japalura (Japalura or Mountain Lizards)						X			
Leiolepis (Butterfly Lizards or Butterfly Runners)			Lizards			X and Larvae		X	Natural vegetation; require lots of drinking water
Lophocalotes	?	?	?			X			
Lophognathus						X			
Lyriocephalus scutatus (Lyre-headed Lizard)						X		X	Natural vegetation
Moloch horridus (Thorny Devil)						Exclusively Ants			Feed approximately 1800 ants per day
Oriocalotes paulus (6)									
Otocryptis						X			Natural vegetation
Phoxophrys (6)									
Phrynocephalus (Toad-headed Agamids)		Eggs				X	X	X	Natural vegetation
Physignathus (Water Dragons)	X	X	Lizards	Frogs		X	X		Worms, crabs
Psammophilus (Rock Agamas)							X		
Ptyctolaemus gularis (Blue-throated Lizard) (6)									
Salea (includes *Mictopholis*)							X		
Sitana ponticeriana (Sita's or Fan-throated Lizard)							X		
Tympanocryptis (Lake Eyre Agamids or Earless Dragons)						X			
Uromastyx (includes *Aporoscelis*) (Spiny-tailed Agamids); adults							X	X	Natural vegetation
Juveniles						X			
FAMILY ANELYTROPSIDAE (Skink Relatives) (4)						Ants			
FAMILY ANGUIDAE (Anguid Lizards)									
Abronia (Tree Anguids)						X			Worms, snails
Anguis fragilis (Slow Worm)						X			Worms, slugs
Celestus						X			
Coloptychon rhombifer (6)									
Diploglossus (Galliwasps)	O				X	X			

Reptile (species listed for monotypic genera)	Small Mammals	Birds	Other Reptiles	Amphibians	Fish	Arthropods	Fruits & Berries	Vegetables	Other Foods/Comments
Elgaria (= *Barisia, Gerrhonotus*) (Alligator Lizards)			Lizards			X			Cannibalistic in captivity
Ophiodes (South American Worm Lizard)						X			
Ophisaurus (Glass Lizards) (3)	X	O	X and Eggs			X			Worms, snails
Sauresia						?			
Wetmorena haetiana						?			
FAMILY ANNIELLIDAE (Legless Lizards) (4)						Larvae			Crickets in captivity
FAMILY CHAMAELEONIDAE (True Chameleons)									
Bradypodion (Dwarf Chameleons)						X			
Brookesia (Stump-tailed Chameleons)						X			
Chamaeleo (Common Chameleons) (3)	X	X	X			X			
Rhampholeon (Leaf Chameleons)						X			
FAMILY CORDYLIDAE (Sungazers or Girdle-tailed Lizards) (3,4)	O	O				X		O	O-Natural vegetation
FAMILY DIBAMIDAE (Blind Lizards) (4)									Carnivorous
FAMILY FEYLINIDAE (Worm-like Lizards) (4)						Termites			
FAMILY GEKKONIDAE (Geckos) (3,4)	Babies		Lizards			X	X		Sweet plant foods, strained baby fruits with multivitamins and calcium carbonate or bonemeal, nectar
FAMILY GERRHOSAURIDAE (Gerrhosaurid Lizards)									
Angolosaurus skoogi (Desert Plated Lizard)						X			Seeds, grass, other dry plant matter
Cordylosaurus subtessellatus (Dwarf Plated Lizard)						X			
Gerrhosaurus (Plated Lizards)	Babies		X			X	X	X	Slugs, snails
Tetradactylus (Seps, Whip, or Plated Snake-Lizards)						X			
Tracheloptychus (Keeled Gerrhosaurids)						X			
Zonosaurus (Girdled Lizards)						X	X		
FAMILY HELODERMATIDAE (Venomous Lizards) (4)	X	Eggs	O-Lizards						
FAMILY IGUANIDAE (Iguanid Lizards)									
Amblyrhynchus cristatus (Marine Iguana)									Exclusively kelp
Anisolepis (6)									
Anolis (includes *Audantia, Deiroptyx, Mariguana, Norops, Xiphocercus*) (Anoles)			Lizards			X			
Aptycholaemus longicauda						?			
Basiliscus (Basilisks)	X	X				X	X		
Brachylophus (Fijian Iguanids)							X	X	Natural vegetation
Callisaurus (Zebra or Gridiron-tailed Lizards)			Lizards			X		O	O-Natural vegetation
Ceiolaemus (6)									
Chalarodon madagascariensis						X			
Chamaeleolis (False Chameleons)						X			
Chamaelinorops (= *Hispaniolus*) *barbouri*						?			
Conolophus (Crested Iguanids)								X	Cacti
Corytophanes (Helmeted Iguanids)						X and Larvae	O		O-Worms
Crotaphytus (Collared and Leopard Lizards)			X-Lizards O-Snakes			X	O	O	O-Natural vegetation; cannibalistic
Ctenoblepharis (= *Phrynosaura*)						?			

Reptile (species listed for monotypic genera)	Small Mammals	Birds	Other Reptiles	Amphibians	Fish	Arthropods	Fruits & Berries	Vegetables	Other Foods/Comments
Ctenosaura (Black Iguanids)		X				X	X	X	Natural vegetation
Cyclura (Ground Iguanids)	X	X				X	X	X	Natural vegetation
Diplolaemus						?			
Dipsosaurus (Desert Iguanids)						X	X	X	Natural vegetation, carrion; coprophagous
Enyalioides						?			
Enyaliosaurus (Spiny-tailed Swifts)	X	X					X	X	Natural vegetation
Enyalius (Brazilian Tree Lizards)						X			Require lots of drinking water; fee at temperatures between 70°F and 80°F (21.1–26.7°C)
Gambelia (Leopard Lizards)			Lizards			X			
Garbesaura garbei (6)									
Holbrookia (Earless Lizards)						X	?	?	Natural vegetation (?)
Hoplocercus (Weapon-tailed Iguanids)						X	?	X	Natural vegetation
Iguana (True Iguanids)						O	X	X	Natural vegetation
Laemanctus (Casque-headed Lizards)	Babies					X			
Leiocephalus (Crested Keeled or Curly-tailed Lizards)						X		X	Natural vegetation
Leiosaurus (6)									
Liolaemus (Smooth-throated Lizards)						X		X	Natural vegetation, worms
Morunasaurus						?		?	
Ophryoessoides						X			
Oplurus (= *Hoplurus*) (Madagascar Iguanids)						X			
Pelusaurus cranwelli (6)									
Petrosaurus (Rock Lizards)						X			Flowers and buds
Phenacosaurus (False Anoles)						X			
Phrynosoma (Horned Lizards)						X			Prefer ants
Phymaturus palluma						X		X	Dandelion flowers and leaves; difficult to feed in captivity
Plica (Harlequin Racerunners)						X			
Polychrus (includes *Polychroides peruvianus*) (Long-legged Iguanids)						X	O		
Pristidactylus (6)									
Proctotretus						?			
Sator						X			
Sauromalus (Chuckwallas)	O					O	X	X	Natural vegetation
Sceloporus (Spiny Lizards or Swifts)	O					X		O	O-Natural vegetation
Stenocercus (Narrow-tailed Iguanids)						X		?	Natural vegetation (?)
Streptosaurus (Collared Utas)						X		X	Natural vegetation (esp. blossoms)
Strobilurus torquatus						?			
Tapinurus semitaeniatus (6)									
Tropidodactylus onca						?			
Tropidurus (Lava Lizards)						X			
Uma (Fringe-toed Lizards)			Lizards ?			X		O	
Uracentron (Spiny-tailed Iguanids)						X			Prefer ants, termites and spiders
Uranoscodon superciliosa (Mop-headed Iguanid)	Babies					X			Worms; feeds at temperatures as low as 59°F (15°C)
Urosaurus (Climbing Utas)						X		O	O-Natural vegetation
Urostrophus vautieri									Natural vegetation (?), worms (?)
Uta (Ground Utas)						X			

Reptile (species listed for monotypic genera)	Small Mammals	Birds	Other Reptiles	Amphibians	Fish	Arthropods	Fruits & Berries	Vegetables	Other Foods/Comments
FAMILY LACERTIDAE (Wall and Sand Lizards) (3,4)	O	O	O-Lizards	O	O	X	X	X	Natural vegetation, crustaceans, worms, eggs
FAMILY LANTHANOTIDAE (Earless Monitor) (4)						X			Worms, eggs
FAMILY PYGOPODIDAE (Flap-footed or Snake Lizards (3,4)			Lizards			X	O		Grubs; cannibalistic
FAMILY SCINCIDAE (True Skinks) (3,4)	X	X and Eggs	X	X	X	X	X	X	In addition to the foods listed, large skinks may feed on other items including natural vegetation, crustaceans, carrion, snails, slugs, and worms; small skinks usually feed on insects
FAMILY TEIIDAE (Whiptails and Racerunners) (3,4)	X	X	X		X	X	X	X	O-Eggs, snails, crustaceans
FAMILY VARANIDAE (Monitor Lizards) (3,4);									
Adults	X	X	X	X	X	X			O-Eggs, carrion, crustaceans
Young						X			Slugs, snails, crustaceans
FAMILY XANTUSIIDAE (Night Lizards) (3)						X	X	X	Natural vegetation (including seeds)
FAMILY XENOSAURIDAE (Xenosaurid and Shinisaurid Lizards (3,4)	Babies		X		X	X			Aquatic larvae, snails
Amphisbaenians (Worm Lizards) (3,4)						X and Larvae			Worms; many take up water from moist soil via cilia located in their mouths

Rhynchocephalians

Reptile	Small Mammals	Birds	Other Reptiles	Amphibians	Fish	Arthropods	Fruits & Berries	Vegetables	Other Foods/Comments
Sphenodon punctatus (Tuatara)	O	O	O-Lizards			X			O-Eggs, worms, snails; cannibalistic toward own young

Snakes

Reptile	Small Mammals	Birds	Other Reptiles	Amphibians	Fish	Arthropods	Fruits & Berries	Vegetables	Other Foods/Comments
FAMILY ACROCHORDIDAE (File or Elephant's Trunk Snakes) (3,4)					X				Crabs
FAMILY ANILIIDAE (Burrowing Snakes) (3,4)			X		Eels	X			Amphisbaenids, worms, grubs
FAMILY BOIDAE (Pythons and Boas)									
Acrantophis (Ground Boas)	X	X							
Aspidites (Black-headed Pythons)	X	X	X	X					
Boa (Boa Constrictors)	X	X							
Bolyeria multicarinata	X		Lizards	Frogs					
Calabaria reinhardtii (Calabar Ground Python)	X								Worms
Candoia (Pacific Boas)	X	X	Lizards						
Casarea dussumieri (Round Island Ground Boa)	X		Lizards	Frogs					
Charina (Rubber Boas)	X		Lizards			X			
Chondropython viridis (Green Tree Python)	X	X	X						
Corallus (Emerald Tree Boas)	X	X	O						
Epicrates (West Indian and Rainbow Boas)	X	X							
Eryx (includes *Gongylophis conicus*) (Sand Boas) (3)	X	X	X	X		X			
Eunectes (Anacondas)	X	X	Crocs, Turtles		X				
Exiliboa placata (Oaxacan Wood Snake)	O		Lizards	Frogs					

Reptile (species listed for monotypic genera)	Small Mammals	Birds	Other Reptiles	Amphibians	Fish	Arthropods	Fruits & Berries	Vegetables	Other Foods/Comments
Liasis (includes *Bothrochilus*) Rock Pythons)	X	X	Lizards						
Lichanura (Rosy Boas)	X	X	Lizards						
Morelia (Carpet and Diamond Pythons)	X	X	X						
Python (3)	X	X	X						
Sanzinia madagascariensis (Madagascar Tree Boa)	X	X							
Trachyboa (Rough Boas)	O		Lizards	Frogs	X				
Ungaliophis (Central American Dwarf Boas)	O		Lizards	O					
FAMILY COLUBRIDAE (Colubrid or Typical Snakes)									
Achalinus						X			Worms, slugs; may refuse food in captivity
Adelphicos quadriviragatus			Lizards			Larvae			Worms
Aeluroglena cucullata (6)									
Aftronatrix anoscopus (Brown Water Snakes)			X		X				
Agrophis (6)									
Ahaetulla (= *Dryophis*) Oriental Vine Snakes or Whipsnakes)	X	X and Eggs	X	X	X	X			Prefer lizards
Alluaudina (6)									
Alsophis (West Indian Racers)	X	X	Lizards	Frogs					
Amastridium (= *Phrydops*) *veliferum* (6)									
Amblycephalus						X			Slugs
Amblyodipsas (Purple-glossed Snakes)			X						Amphisbaenids
Amphiesma			Lizards	X	X				Worms, slugs
Amplorhinus multimaculatus (Cape Many-spotted or Cape Reed Snake)			Lizards	X					
Anoplohydrus aemulans (6)									
Antillophis	X		Lizards	Frogs					
Aparallactus (Centipede-eating Snakes)						Centipedes			Also feed on scorpions and termites
Aplopeltura (= *Haplopeltura*; Blunt-headed Snakes)			Lizards						
Apostolepis			Lizards			X			Worms
Argyrogena (Indian Rat Snakes or Racers)	X			Frogs		X			
Arizona (Glossy Snakes)	X		X						
Arrhyton	?		?	?					
Aspidura (Rough-sided Snakes)						X and Larvae			Worms
Atractaspis (Mole Vipers, Burrowing Adders or Side-stabbing Snakes)	X		X						
Atractus (Spindle Snakes)			Lizards			Larvae			Worms
Atretium (Keelback Water Snakes)				X	X	Mosquito Larvae			
Balanophis ceylonensis (6)									
Bitia hydroides					X				
Blythia reticulata (6)									
Boaedon (House Snakes)	X	X and Eggs	X	X					
Boiga (Cat or Tree Snakes) (3)	X	X and Eggs	X	X	O				
Bothrolycus lineatus	X								
Bothrophthalmus	X								
Brachyophis revoili (6)									
Calamaria (Reed Snakes)			Lizards			X			Worms
Calamorhabdium			Lizards			X and Larvae			Worms
Cantoria violacea (Cantor's Water Snake)					X				
Carphophis amoenus (Worm Snakes)			Snakes ?			X			Worms; cannibalistic ?
Cemophora (Scarlet Snakes)	O		O and X-Eggs	O		X			Slugs

Reptile (species listed for monotypic genera)	Small Mammals	Birds	Other Reptiles	Amphibians	Fish	Arthropods	Fruits & Berries	Vegetables	Other Foods/Comments
Cerberus (Oriental or Dog-faced Water Snakes)				X	X				Prefer eels; also feed on crabs
Cercaspis carinatus (6)									
Chamaelycus			Lizards						
Chersodromus liebmanni (6)									
Chilomeniscus (Banded Sand Snakes)						X and Pupae			
Chilorhinophis (Stripped or Black and Yellow Burrowing Snakes)			X						Also amphisbaenids
Chionactis (Shovel-nosed Snakes)			O			X			Also feed on chrysalids and cocoons of butterflies and moths
Chironius		X	Lizards	X					
Chrysopelea (Flying Snakes)	X	X	X			X			
Clelia clelia (Mussurana)	O	O	X						Prefers snakes; carrion
Clonophis (Kirtland's Snakes)	Babies		Lizards	X					Worms, slugs
Collorhabdium williamsoni (6)									
Coluber (Racers, N. Am.; Whipsnakes, Eu.)	X	X	X	X		X			
Compsophis albiventris (6)									
Coniophanes (Black-striped Snakes)	X		X	X					
Conophis (includes *Tomodon*)						X			Worms, small vertebrates
Conopsis (6)									
Contia (Sharp-tailed Snakes)									Slugs
Coronella (European Smooth or Crowned Snakes)	X	X	X	Frogs		O			
Crisantophis nevermanni (= *Conophis nevermanni*)									Slugs
Crotaphopeltis (African Herald or Southern Spot-striped Snakes)	X		Lizards	X					
Cryptolycus nanus (Dwarf Wolf Snake)									Amphisbaenids
Cyclocorus (6)									
Darlingtonia haetiana				Frogs					
Dasypeltis (African Egg-eating Snakes)									Exclusively eggs
Dendrelaphis (Tree Snakes)	X	X and Eggs	X	X					
Dendrolycus elapoides			Lizards	Frogs					
Dendrophidion				Frogs					
Diadophis (Ring-necked Snakes)			X	Salamanders		X			Worms, slugs
Diaphorolepis wagneri				Frogs					
Dinodon (Big-toothed Snakes)			X	X					Cannibalistic ?
Dipsadoboa (Cat-eyed Tree Snakes)			Geckos	Tree Frogs					
Dipsas (Thirst or Snail-eating Snakes)									Land mollusks
Dipsina (Dwarf Beaked Snakes)			Lizards						
Dispholidus typus (Boomslang)	X	X and Eggs	Lizards						
Ditypophis vivax (6)									
Drepanoides anomalus		X							Lizard eggs
Dromicodryas (6)									
Dromicus (West Indian Ground Snakes)			Lizards	X	X				
Dromophis (Olympic Snakes)	X		Lizards ?	X					
Drymarchon (Indigo Snakes, Cribos)	X	X	Snakes	Frogs					Cannibalistic
Drymobius (Speckled Racers)	X		Lizards	Frogs					
Drymoluber			Lizards	Frogs					
Dryocalamus (Bridal Snakes)			Lizards	Frogs	X				
Dryophiops rubescens	?	X	Lizards	?					
Duberria (Slug-eating Snakes)			X						Prefer slugs and snails; cannibalistic
Eirenis (Dwarf Snakes)			O-Lizards			X			
Elachistodon westermanni (Indian Egg-eating Snake)		Eggs							

Reptile (species listed for monotypic genera)	Small Mammals	Birds	Other Reptiles	Amphibians	Fish	Arthropods	Fruits & Berries	Vegetables	Other Foods/Comments
Elaphe (Rat Snakes) (3) (in Asia, Trinket Snakes)	X	X	X	X		X			Worms, O-eggs
Elapoides fuscus (6)									
Elapomojus dimidiatus (6)									
Elapomorphus			X			X			Worms; cannibalistic
Emmochliophis fugleri (6)									
Enhydris (Asian Water Snakes)				X	X				Other aquatic vertebrates
Enulius									
Eremiophis (includes *Zaocys*) (6)									
Erpeton (Tentacled Snakes)					X				Crayfish
Erythrolamprus (Flase Coral Snakes)	X		X	Frogs					Cannibalistic
Farancia (Mud and Rainbow Snakes) (3)				X	X				Worms, salaman- ders, eels
Ficimia (Mexican Hooknose Snakes)						Spiders			O-Centipedes
Fimbrios klossi (Bearded Snake)				Frogs					Worms, slugs
Fordonia leucobalia (White-bellied Mangrove or Crab-eating Snake)				Frogs	X				Crabs
Gastropyxis			Lizards	Frogs					
Geagras						X			
Geodipsas				Frogs					
Geophis									Worms
Gerarda prevostiana (Gerard's Wa- ter Snake)					X				
Gonionotophus			Lizards	Frogs					Cannibalistic ?
Gonyophis margaritatus (Rainbow Tree Snake)				Frogs					
Gonyosoma (Tree Racers)	X	X	Lizards	Frogs					
Grayia (African Water Snakes)				Frogs	X		X		
Gyalopion (Hooknosed-Snakes)						Spiders			O-Scorpions and centipedes
Haemorrhois (includes *Zamenis*)	X		Lizards	O-Frogs		O			
Haplocerus ceylonensis (6)									
Haplodon philippiensis (6)									
Hapsidophrys lineatus (Green-lined Snake)			Lizards ?	Frogs					
Helicops (South American Water Snakes)				X	X				
Hemirhagerrhis (Bark or Mopane Snakes)			Lizards and Eggs	Frogs					
Heterodon (Hognose Snakes) (3)	O	O	O	X	O	X			Worms
Heteroliodon torquatus (Shovel- nosed Burrowing Snake) (6)									
Heurnia ventromaculata (6)									
Hologerrhum philippinum (6)									
Homalopsis buccata (Puff-faced or Dog-faced Water Snake)				Frogs	X				
Homoroselaps (Harlequin Snakes)			X						Prefer amphisbaenians
Hormonotus modestus (Yellow For- est Snake)	X		Lizards						
Hydrablabes (6)									
Hydrodynastes (= *Cyclagras*, *Du- gandia*) (False Water Cobras)	X		X	X	X				
Hydromorphus				Frogs	X				
Hydrops triangularis				Frogs	X				Aquatic caecilians
Hypotophis wilsoni (6)									
Hypsiglena (Night Snakes)			Lizards	Frogs		X			
Hypsirhynchus ferox	?	?	Lizards?	?					
Ialtris (6)									
Idiopholis (6)									
Iguanognathus werneri (6)									
Imantodes (Big-headed, Chunk- headed or Blunt-headed Tree Snakes)			Lizards						
Ithycyphus			Lizards	Frogs					
Lampropeltis (Kingsnakes and Milk Snakes)	X	X and Eggs	X and Eggs	Frogs					Cannibalistic

Reptile (species listed for monotypic genera)	Small Mammals	Birds	Other Reptiles	Amphibians	Fish	Arthropods	Fruits & Berries	Vegetables	Other Foods/Comments
Lamprophis (Aurora Snakes)	X	X	X	Frogs					
Langaha (Leafnose Snakes)		X	Lizards	Tree Frogs					
Leimadophis	O		Lizards	X	X				
Leptodeira (Cat-eyed Snakes)	X		X	X					
Leptodrymus pulcherrimus		O	Lizards	X					
Leptophis (Parrot Snakes)	O-Babies	O	Lizards	Frogs					
Lepturophis borneensis (Slender Wolf Snake)				Frogs	X				
Limnophis bicolor (Striped Swamp Snake)				X	X				
Lioheterodon (Madagascar Hognose Snakes)	X	O		X					
Liopeltis		X	Lizards			X			Worms
Liophidium	(6)								
Liophis (includes *Lygophis*)				X	X	X			Worms, other small prey
Liopholidophis (6)									
Lycodon (Oriental Wolf Snakes)	X		X	Frogs		X			
Lycodonomorphus (includes *Ablabophis*) (African or White-lipped Water Snakes)				X	X				
Lycodryas			Lizards	Frogs					
Lycognathophis seychellensis (6)									
Lycophidion (Wolf Snakes)	X		X	Frogs					
Lystrophis (South American Hook-nosed Snakes)			X	X					Worms
Lytorhynchus (Long-nosed or Leaf-nosed Snakes)			Lizards and Eggs			X			
Macrelaps microlepidotus (Natal Black Snake)	X		X	Frogs					
Macrocalamus			Lizards			X and Larvae			
Macropisthodon		X		X					
Macropophis				X	X				
Macroprotodon cucullatus (False Smooth or Hooded Snake)			Lizards						
Madagascarophis colubrina	X		Lizards	Frogs					
Malpolon	X	X	X						
Manolepis (= *Tomodon*)			Lizards						
Masticophis (North American Whipsnakes and Coachwhips)	X	O	X			X			O-Eggs
Mastigodryas (Tropical Racers)	X	X	Lizards	Frogs					
Mehelya (File Snakes)			X	X					Cannibalistic
Meizodon (African Smooth Snakes)	X		Lizards	Frogs					
Micrelaps (6)									
Micropisthodon ochraceus (6)									
Mimophis mahafalensis	O		Lizards						
Myersophis alpestris (6)									
Myron richardsonii					X				Crabs
Natriciteres (African Marsh Snakes)				X	X	X			
Natrix (European Grass or Water Snakes)	O	X and Eggs	O	X	X				Crayfish
Nerodia (North American Water Snakes)	O		O	X	X				Crayfish, other crustaceans
Ninia (Ringnecked Coffee Snakes)						Crickets			Worms, mealworms
Nothopsis rugosus (6)									
Oligodon (Kukri Snakes)	X	X	X and Eggs	X		X and Larvae			
Opheodrys (Green Snakes) (3)				X		X and Larvae			Slugs, snails, worms
Opisthoplus (= *Aproterodon*) degener						X			
Opisthotropis (Mountain Water Snakes)				X		X			Worms, crustaceans
Oreocalamus hanitschi (Hanitsch's Reed Snake)			Lizards			X and Larvae			Worms
Oxybelis (Vine Snakes)	O	X	Lizards	Frogs		X			
Oxyrhabdium				Frogs		X			Worms
Oxyrhopus	X		Lizards						Worms
Padangia pulchra (6)									

Reptile (species listed for monotypic genera)	Small Mammals	Birds	Other Reptiles	Amphibians	Fish	Arthropods	Fruits & Berries	Vegetables	Other Foods/Comments
Parahelicops (6)									
Pararhabdophis chapaensis				Frogs ?	?				
Pararhadinaea melanogaster (6)									
Pareas (Slug Snakes)									Slugs, snails
Paroxyrhopus			?	?					
Philodryas (South American Green Snakes)	X	X		Frogs					
Philothamnus (African Green and Bush Snakes)		X	X	X					
Phimophis			Lizards						
Phyllorhynchus (Leaf-nosed Snakes)			Lizards and Eggs			Larvae			
Pituophis (Bullsnakes, Pine, and Gopher Snakes) (3)	X	X and Eggs	O-Snakes X-Lizards						
Plagiopholis				?					Worms ?
Platynion lividum (6)									
Pliocercus (False Coral Snakes)			Lizards	Frogs	X				
Polemon			Snakes						
Prosymna (Shovel-snouted Snakes)			X			X			Variety of reptiles' eggs
Psammodynastes (Mock Vipers)			X	X					
Psammophis (African Sand Racers)	X		X	X					
Psammophylax (Skaapstekers or Grass Snakes)	X		Lizards	O					
Pseudablabes agassizii (6)									
Pseudaspis cana (Mole Snake)	X	Eggs	Eggs						
Pseudoboa	X		Lizards						
Pseudoboodon lemniscatus (6)									
Pseudoeryx (= *Dipsadoides*) *plicatilis*				O-Frogs	X				
Pseudorabdion			Lizards		X and Larvae			Worms	
Pseudotarbophis gabesiensis (6)									
Pseudotomodon trigonatus (6)									
Pseudoxenodon			Lizards	X					
Pseudoxyrhopus			?						
Pseustes (Central American Chicken Snakes)	X	X and Eggs	Lizards						
Ptyas (Asian Rat Snakes)	X	X	X	X					
Ptychophis flavovirgatus (6)									
Pythonodipsas carinata (Western Keeled Snake)	X		Lizards						
Rabdion (= *Rhabdophidium*) *forsteni* (6)									
Regina (Crayfish Snakes)			Snakes						Crayfish
Rhabdophis (Rear-fanged Keelbacks)	X	X	Lizards	X	X	X			
Rhabdops									Worms, slugs
Rhachidelus brazili		X							
Rhadinaea (Pinewoods Snakes)			X	X					
Rhamphiophis (Sharp-nosed or Beaked Snakes)	X		X	Frogs		X			
Rhinobothryum	O		Lizards						
Rhinocheilus lecontei (Long-nosed Snake)	X		X and Eggs			X			
Rhynchocalamus			Lizards			X			
Rhynchophis boulengeri			Lizards	Frogs					
Salvadora (Patch-nosed Snakes)	X	X	Lizards and Eggs						
Saphenophis						X			Other small prey
Scaphiodontophis (American Many-toothed Snakes)			X	Frogs ?					
Scaphiophis albopunctatus	X					X			Worms
Scolecophis atrocinctus (6)									
Seminatrix (Red-bellied Swamp Snakes)				X	X				Leeches, worms
Sibon (includes *Tropidodipsas*)	O		Lizards	X					Land mollusks
Sibynomorphus (3)				?					Land mollusks
Sibynophis (Collared Snakes)			X			Grass-hoppers			
Simophis	X								
Sinonatrix (Asiatic Water Snakes)	?		?	?	?				

Reptile (species listed for monotypic genera)	Small Mammals	Birds	Other Reptiles	Amphibians	Fish	Arthropods	Fruits & Berries	Vegetables	Other Foods/Comments
Siphlophis (includes *Alleidophis*)			Lizards	Frogs					
Sonora (Ground Snakes)						X			Prefer ants and their eggs
Sordellina punctata				Frogs					
Spalerosophis (includes *Zaocys*) (Desert Racers)	X	X	X						
Spilotes pullatus (Mexican or Tiger Snake)	X	X and Eggs	O	O					
Stegonotus				Frogs	X				
Stenorrhina						Scorpions			
Stilosoma extenuatum (Short-tailed Snakes)			X						
Stoliczkaia			Lizards ?	Frogs					Worms
Storeria (Brown and Red-bellied Snakes)				X		X			Worms, snails, slugs
Styporhynchus mairi					X				
Sympholis lippiens						Termites			
Synophis				Frogs	X				
Tachymenis			Lizards						
Tantilla (Black-headed, Flat-headed, and Crowned Snakes)			Lizards			X			Worms, slugs, centipedes
Tantillita lintoni			?			?			Worms ?, slugs ?
Telescopus (Old World Cat-eyed or Tiger Snakes)	O	O	Lizards			X			
Tetralepis fruhstorferi (6)									
Thamnodynastes	X			X					
Thamnophis (Garter and Ribbon Snakes) (3)	X	X	Lizards	X	X and Eggs	X			Worms, slugs, mollusks, leeches, carrion
Thelotornis (African Bird Snakes)		O and Eggs	X	X					
Thermophis baileyi (6)									
Thrasops (= *Rhamnophis*) (Black Tree Snakes)	X	X and Eggs	Lizards	Frogs					
Toluca (6)									
Trachischium (Oriental Worm Snakes)						X			Worms
Tretanorhinus				Frogs	X				
Trimetopon (6)									
Trimorphodon (Lyre Snakes) (3)	X	X	Lizards	?					
Tripanurgos campressus			Lizards	Frogs					
Tropidoclonion (Lined Snakes)						X and Larvae			Worms
Tropidodryas (= *Philodryas pseudoserra* and *P. serra*)	?	?		?					
Typhlogeophis brevis (6)									
Umbravaga (6)									
Uromacer (West Indian Racers)			Lizards	Frogs					
Uromacerina ricardinii			?	?					
Virginia (Earth Snakes)						X and Larvae			Worms
Wallophis (includes *Zaocys*) (6)									
Xenelaphis (Asian Brown Snakes)	O			Frogs					
Xenocalamus (Quill-snouted Snakes)			X						Prefer amphisbaenians
Xenochrophis (Fishing Keelbacks) (3)	?			X	X				
Xenodermus javanicus (Strange-scaled Snake)				Frogs					
Xenodon (includes *Waglerophis*) (False Vipers)	X	X	X	X		X			
Xenopholis scalaris (6)									
Xylophis (6)									
FAMILY ELAPIDAE (Cobras and their Relatives)									
Acanthophis (Death Adders)	X	O	X						
Aspidelaps (African Coral Snakes or Shield-nose Cobras)	X								
Aspidomorphus (Crowned Snakes) (6)									
Austrelaps superbus (Australian Copperhead)	O		X	X					
Boulengerina (Water Cobras)					X				

Reptile (species listed for monotypic genera)	Small Mammals	Birds	Other Reptiles	Amphibians	Fish	Arthropods	Fruits & Berries	Vegetables	Other Foods/Comments
Bungarus (Kraits)	X		X	X	X				
Cacophis (Australian Crowned Snakes)			Lizards			X			
Calliophis (Oriental Spotted Coral Snakes)			Snakes						
Cryptophis (Small-eyed Snakes)			Lizards	Frogs					
Demansia (Australian Whipsnakes)	X		X	Frogs					Cannibalistic
Dendroaspis (Mambas)	X	X							
Denisonia			Lizards	X					Other vertebrates
Drysdalia			Lizards	Frogs		X			
Echiopsis			Lizards	Frogs		X			
Elapognathus minor (Little Brown Snake)			Skinks	Frogs					
Elapsoidea (African Garter Snakes)			X	Frogs					
Furina (Red-naped or Orange-naped Snakes)			Lizards			X			Prefer termites and ants
Glyphodon (Australian Collared Snakes) (6)									
Hemachatus haemachatus (Ringhals or Rinkals)	X								
Hemiaspis			Lizards	Frogs					
Hemibungarus (6)									
Hoplocephalus (Australian Broad-headed Snakes) (3)	X	X	Lizards	X					Prefer skinks
Loverridgelaps elapoides			X	Frogs					
Maticora (Long-glanded Coral Snakes)			X	Frogs					
Melanelaps (6)									
Micropechis ikaheka (Pacific Coral Snake)			Snakes						
Micruroides euryxanthus (Western Coral Snake)	O		X	Frogs		X			Prefers smooth-scaled snakes
Micrurus (Coral Snakes)			O-Lizards X-Snakes	Frogs					Amphisbaenids
Naja (Cobras) (3)	X	O	X	X	X				Birds' eggs
Neelaps (Black-naped Snakes)			Lizards						
Notechis (Tiger Snakes)	X	X	X	Frogs					
Ogmondon vitianus (Fiji Snake)						X			
Ophiophagus hannah (King Cobra)			Snakes						
Oxyuranus scutellatus (Taipan)	X	X							
Parademansia microlepidota (Fierce Snake)	X	O	O	O					
Paranaja multifasciata (Burrowing Cobra) (6)									
Parapistocalamus hedigeri (Hediger's Snake)									Snail eggs
Pseudechis (Australian Black and Mulga Snakes)	X		X	Frogs					
Pseudohaje (Tree or Forest Cobras)				X					
Pseudonaja (Brown Snakes) (3)	X	O	X	X					
Rhinoplocephalus bicolor (Muller's Snake)			Skinks						
Salomonelaps par			Lizards	Frogs					
Simoselaps (Australian Coral Snakes)			Lizards						
Suta suta (Myall or Curl Snake)	X	O	Lizards?						
Toxicocalamus (Short-fanged or Elongate Snakes) (6)									
Tropidechis carinatus (Rough-scaled Snake)	X	O	X	Frogs					
Unechis			Lizards			X			
Vermicella (Bandy-bandy Snakes)			Snakes						Primarily typhlopids
Walterinnesia aegyptia (Desert Black Cobra)	X		Geckos	Toads					
FAMILY HYDROPHIDAE (Sea Snakes) (3,4)					X				Fish eggs
FAMILY LATICAUDIDAE (Banded Sea Kraits) (4)					X				Fish eggs
FAMILY LEPTOTYPHLOPIDAE (Thread Snakes) (4)				Salamanders		X			Insect pupae
FAMILY LOXOCEMIDAE (Mexican Dwarf or Burrowing Python) (4)	X		O-Lizards						

Reptile (species listed for monotypic genera)	Small Mammals	Birds	Other Reptiles	Amphibians	Fish	Arthropods	Fruits & Berries	Vegetables	Other Foods/Comments
FAMILY TROPIDOPHIIDAE (West Indian Dwarf Boas) (4)	O		O-Lizards	X					
FAMILY TYPHLOPIDAE (Blind Burrowing Snakes) (4)						X & Larvae			Worms, slugs
FAMILY UROPELTIDAE (Rough-tailed Snakes) (4)						X			Worms, grubs
FAMILY VIPERIDAE (Vipers)									
PIT VIPERS:									
Agkistrodon (3)	X	X	X	X	X	X			
Bothrops (New World Lance-headed Vipers)	X	X	Lizards						
Bothriechis (= *Bothrops*) (Arboreal Pit Vipers)	X	X	Tree Frogs						
Bothriopsis (= *Bothrops*) (South American Pit Vipers)	X		X						
Calloselasma (= *Agkistrodon*)	X		Lizards	Frogs					
Crotalus (Rattlesnakes) (3)	X	X	Lizards						
Deinagkistrodon acutus (= *Agkistrodon*) (Sharp-nosed Viper or Hundred Pacer)	X	X		Frogs					
Gloydius (= *Agkistrodon*) (6)									
Hypnale (= *Agkistrodon*) (Hump-nosed Vipers)	X		Lizards	X					
Lachesis mutus (Bushmaster)	X	X							
Ophryacus (= *Bothrops*) (New World Bush Vipers)	X	X	O						
Ovophis (= *Trimeresurus*)	X	X	Lizards	Frogs					
Porthidium (= *Bothrops*) (New World Hog-nosed and Jumping Vipers)	X	X	Lizards						
Protobothrops (= *Trimeresurus*)	X	X	Lizards	Frogs					
Sistrurus (Pigmy Rattlesnakes and Massasaugas) (3)	X	X	Lizards	X	X	X			Crayfish
Trimeresurus	X	X	Lizards	Frogs					
Tropidolaemus wagleri (= *Trimeresurus*) (Wagler's or Temple Viper)	X	X	Lizards	Frogs					
TRUE VIPERS:									
Adenorhinos barbouri (Worm-eating Viper)									Worms
Atheris (African Bush Vipers)	X		Lizards	X					
Azemiops feae (Fea's Viper)	X			Frogs ?					
Bitis (African Vipers)	X		Lizards						
Causus (Night Adders)				X					
Cerastes (Horned or Desert Vipers)	X		Lizards						
Echis (Saw-scaled Vipers)	X		X	Frogs		X			
Eristocophis macmahoni (McMahon's Viper)	X		Lizards						
Pseudocerastes persicus (Desert or False Horned Viper)	X		Lizards						
Vipera (Old World Vipers) (3)	X	X	Lizards	O					Birds' eggs
FAMILY XENOPELTIDAE (Sun-beam Snake) (4)	X	O	Snakes	X					
Crocodilians									
FAMILY ALLIGATORIDAE (Alligators and Caimans) (4)	X	X	X	X	X	X			Crustaceans
FAMILY CROCODYLIDAE (True Crocodiles) (4)	X	X	X	X	X	X			Crustaceans, snails
FAMILY GAVIALIDAE (Gavial, False Gavial) (4)	O-Skinned	O			X				

* Bellairs, 1970; Branch, 1988; Burquez et al., 1986; Carr, 1952; Cogger, 1975; Cogger et al., 1983; Dixon and Soini, 1986; Duellman, 1979; Gharpurey, 1962; Goin et al., 1978; Grzimek, 1975; Henderson and Binder, 1980; Isemonger, 1962; Iverson, 1985; Karsen et al., 1986; Kuntz, no date; Leutscher, 1961; Loveridge, 1946; Marais, 1992; Mattison, 1986; Mehrtens, 1987; NAVMED, 1965; Obst et al., 1988; Pinney, 1981; Pritchard, 1979; Robb, 1986; Schmidt, 1928; Schmidt and Inger, 1957; Shine, 1986; Smith, 1946; Stebbins, 1966; Switak, 1984; Trutnau, 1986; Tweedie, 1983; Wright and Wright, 1957; Zappalorti, 1976; Zimmermann, 1986.

1. X = Usual Food, O = Occasional Food.
2. In captivity, animals will also feed on trout chow (available in most pet stores), Frog Brittle ® and canned dog food.
3. Depending on the species. The reader should research the dietary requirement of the particular species.
4. See Appendix I for a listing of the genera.
5. Avoid feeding poisonous plants and fungi (see Appendix IX). Freeze prey that serve as parasitic hosts before feeding to a reptile.
6. Information not found.

Appendix IX

Poisonous Plants (1,2)

Abrus precatorius (CRAB'S EYE, JEQUIRITY BEAN, PRECATORY BEAN, ROSARY PEA); seeds; gastrointestinal tract affected by toxalbumins.

Acacia spp. (CATCLAW, GUAJILLO); foliage; plant is cyanogenetic.

ACKEE (*Blighia sapida*); pink raphe attaching aril to seed, arils in immature fruit; gastrointestinal tract and nervous system affected by toxins.

Acokanthera spp. (BUSHMAN'S POISON, WINTERSWEET); seeds; cardiovascular system affected by cardiac glycosides.

ACONITE (*Aconitum* spp.); entire plant, esp. leaves and roots; cardiovascular system affected by alkaloid toxins.

Aconitum spp. (ACONITE, MONKSHOOD); entire plant, esp. leaves and roots; cardiovascular system affected by alkaloid toxins.

Actaea spp. (BANEBERRY, DOLL'S EYES); foliage, berries, roots; gastrointestinal tract and nervous system affected by the toxin protoanemonin.

Adenium spp. (DESERT ROSE, MOCK AZALEA); entire plant; cardiovascular system affected by digitalis-like glycosides.

Adonis spp. (PHEASANT'S EYE); entire plant; cardiovascular system affected by cardiac glycosides.

Aesculus spp. (BUCKEYES, HORSE CHESTNUT); nuts, immature growths; gastrointestinal tract affected by saponins.

Aethusa cynapium (FOOL'S PARSLEY, LESSER HEMLOCK); entire plant; gastrointestinal tract affected by alkaloid toxins.

Agave lecheguilla (LECHUGUILLA); plant is hepatogenic.

Agrostemma githago (CORNCOCKLE, PURPLECOCKLE); seeds; gastrointestinal tract affected by saponins.

Aleurites spp. (CANDLEBERRY, CANDLENUT, TUNG NUT, TUNG TREE); entire plant; gastrointestinal tract affected by saponins and toxalbumins.

Allamanda cathartica (ALLAMANDA, CANARIO, GOLDEN TRUMPET VINE, YELLOW ALLAMANDA); bark, leaves, fruit, seeds, sap; plant contains cathartic toxins; plant also causes dermatitis.

Allium spp. (CHIVES, GARLIC, LEEKS, ONIONS); bulbs, bulblets, flowers, stems; gastrointestinal tract affected by plant toxins.

Alocasia spp. (ELEPHANT'S EAR, TARO); leaves, stems; mouth irritated by plant raphides.

AMARANTH (*Amaranthus hybridus*); plant may contain toxic levels of nitrates.

Amaranthus hybridus (AMARANTH, CARELESS WEED, TUMBLEWEED); plant may contain toxic levels of nitrates.

Amaryllis spp. (AMARYLLIS, NAKED-LADY LILLY); bulbs; gastrointestinal tract affected by alkaloid toxins.

Amianthemum muscaetoxicum (FLY-POISON, STAGGERGRASS); leaves, underground parts of plant; alkaloid toxins may cause respiratory failure.

Ammi majus (BISHOP'S WEED); plant may contain toxic levels of nitrates.

Amsinckia intermedia (FIDDLENECK, TARWEED); seed-like nutlets; plant may contain toxic levels of nitrates.

Anemone spp. (includes *Pulsatilla* spp.) (ANEMONE, PASQUE FLOWER, WINDFLOWER); entire plant; gastrointestinal tract affected by the toxin protoanemonin; plant also causes dermatitis.

ANGEL TRUMPET TREE (*Brugmansia* x *candida*); entire plant, esp. seeds; nervous system affected by belladonna alkaloids; plant contains hallucinogens.

Aplopappus spp. (GOLDENRODS, JIMMY WEED, RAYLESS); leaves; plant may contain toxic levels of nitrates.

Apocynum spp. (DOGBANE, INDIAN HEMP, SPREADING DOGBANE); leaves; plant contains cardiac glycosides.

APPLES (*Malus* spp.); seeds; plant is cyanogenetic.

APRICOTS (*Prunus* spp.); seeds; plant is cyanogenetic.

Aquilegia vulgaris (COLUMBINE); entire plant; cardiovascular system affected by plant toxins.

Areca catechu (ARECA PALM, BETEL NUT); entire plant.

ARECA PALM (*Areca catechu*); entire plant.

Argemone spp. (MEXICAN POPPY, PRICKLY POPPY); entire plant; isoquinoline alkaloid causes "epidemic dropsy" in humans.

Arisaema spp. (GREEN DRAGON, INDIAN TURNIP, JACK-IN-THE-PULPIT); entire plant; gastrointestinal tract affected by plant toxins; mouth irritated by plant raphides; plant also causes dermatitis.

Arnica montana (ARNICA); rhizomes, flowers; gastrointestinal tract and cardiovascular system affected by plant toxins; plant also causes dermatitis.

ARROWGRASS (*Triglochim maritima*); leaves; plant is cyanogenetic.

Arum spp. (CUCKOO-PINT, ITALIAN ARUM, LORDS & LADIES); entire plant; gastrointestinal tract affected by plant toxins; mouth irritated by plant raphides; plant also causes dermatitis.

Asclepias spp. (MILKWEEDS, WHORLED BUTTERFLY); leaves, stems; plant contains toxic resins.

Astragalus spp. (LOCOWEEDS, POISON-VETCHES); entire plant; plant may absorb toxic levels of selenium.

Atropa belladonna (BELLADONNA, DEADLY NIGHTSHADE); entire plant; nervous system affected by the alkaloids jasciamine, atropine, and belladonnin.

AUTUMN CROCUS (*Colchicum autumnale,* other *Colchicum* spp.); entire plant; gastrointestinal tract affected by the toxin colchicine and other alkaloids; plant also causes dermatitis.

Avena sativa (OATS); plant is nontoxic unless contaminated with smut or fungi.

AZALEAS (*Rhododendron* spp.); leaves, nectar; cardiovascular system affected by the resinoid andromedotoxin.

BAGPOD (*Sesbania* spp.); seeds; gastrointestinal tract affected by saponins.

Bahia oppositifolia (BAHIA); entire plant; plant is cyanogenetic.

BALSAM APPLE (*Momordica balsamina*); outer rind of ripe fruit, seeds; gastrointestinal tract affected by toxalbumins.

BALSAM PEAR (*Momordica charantia*); outer rind of ripe fruit, seeds; gastrointestinal tract affected by toxalbumins.

BANEBERRY (*Actaea* spp.); berries, roots; gastrointestinal tract and nervous system affected by the toxin protoanemonin.

BARILLA (*Halogeton glomeratus*); leaves, stems; plant contains soluble oxalates.

BARNYARD GRASS (*Echinochloa crusgalli*); plant may contain toxic levels of nitrates.

BEAD TREE (*Melia azedarach*); fruit, bark; plant contains convulsants.

BEGGAR-TICK (*Bidens frondosa*); plant may contain toxic levels of nitrates.

BELLADONNA (*Atropa belladonna*); entire plant; nervous system affected by the alkaloids jasciamine, atropine, and belladonnin.

BELLYACHE BUSH (*Jatropha gossypiifolia*); seeds; gastrointestinal tract affected by toxalbumins and cathartic oils; plant also causes dermatitis.

BERMUDA BUTTERCUP, BERMUDA OXALIS (*Oxalis pes-caprae*); leaves; plant contains soluble oxalates.

Beta vulgaris (MANGOLD, SUGAR BEET); leaves; plant contains soluble oxalates and may contain toxic levels of nitrates.

Bidens frondosa (BEGGAR-TICK); plant may contain toxic levels of nitrates.

BINDWEED (*Ipomea* spp.); entire plant; plant contains LSD-related hallucinogens and may contain toxic levels of nitrates.

BIRD-OF-PARADISE (*Caesalpinia gilliesii*); seeds; gastrointestinal tract affected by plant toxins.

BIRDSFOOT TREFOIL (*Lotus corniculatus*); entire plant; plant is cyanogenetic.

BISHOP'S WEED (*Ammi majus*); plant may contain toxic levels of nitrates.

BITTER GOURD (*Momordica charantia*); outer rind of ripe fruit, seeds; gastrointestinal tract affected by toxalbumins.

BITTERSWEET (*Celastrus scandens*—do not confuse with *Solanum dulcamara*); entire plant; plant is reputed to be toxic.

BITTERWEED (*Helenium* spp.); plant causes dermatitis.

BLACK BRUSH (*Flourensia cernua*); fruit; gastrointestinal tract affected by plant toxins.

BLACK BRYONY (*Tamus communis*); toxic principles similar to *Bryonia dioica*.

BLACK LOCUST (*Robinia pseudoacacia*); bark, seeds, leaves; gastrointestinal tract affected by toxalbumins.

BLACK NIGHTSHADE (*Solanum nigrum*); leaves, berries; gastrointestinal tract affected by solanin glycoalkaloids; plant also causes dermatitis.

BLEEDING HEART (*Dicentra formosa*); entire plant, esp. bulbs; plant contains convulsants including isoquinoline; plant also causes dermatitis.

Blighia sapida (ACKEE); pink raphe attaching aril to seed, arils in immature fruit; toxins affect gastrointestinal tract and nervous system.

BLOODROOT (*Sanguinaria canadensis*); juices from stems and rootstocks cause dermatitis.

BLUEBONNETS (*Lupinus subcarnosus*); leaves, esp. seeds; plant contains numerous alkaloid toxins including quinolizidine and piperidine.

BLUE RUSH (*Juncus inflexus*); plant causes convulsions in cattle.

BLUE TARO (*Xanthosoma* spp.); leaves; mouth irritated by plant raphides; plant also causes dermatitis.

BOUNCING BET (*Saponaria officinalis*); seeds; gastrointestinal tract affected by saponins.

BOX, BOXWOOD (*Buxus sempervirens*); entire plant; gastrointestinal tract affected by plant toxins; plant also causes dermatitis.

BRACKEN FERN, BRAKE FERN (*Pteridium* sp.); fronds; plant contains thiaminase.

Brassica spp. (CABBAGE, KALE, MUSTARD); leaves; plant is goitrogenic; may contain toxic levels of nitrates; *B. napus* (CULTIVATED RAPE) is hepatogenic.

Bromus spp. (RESCUE GRASS, SMOOTH BROMEGRASS); plant may contain toxic levels of nitrates.

BROOMCORN (*Sorghum* sp.); leaves; plant is cyanogenetic.

Brugmansia x *candida* (ANGEL TRUMPET TREE); entire plant, esp. seeds; nervous system affected by belladonna alkaloids; plant contains hallucinogens.

Bryonia dioica (DEVIL'S TURNIP, WHITE BRYONY); gastrointestinal tract affected by the glycosides bryonin and bryonidin; plant also causes dermatitis.

BUCKEYES (*Aesculus* spp.); nuts, immature growths; gastrointestinal tract affected by saponins.

BUCKTHORN (*Karwinskia humboldtiana*—do not confuse with the mildly toxic *Rhamnus* spp.); fruit; toxins affect nervous system.

BUCKWHEAT (*Fagopyrum esculentum*); plant causes photosensitization and contact dermatitis.

BUFFALO BUR (*Solanum* sp.); immature growths; gastrointestinal tract affected by solanine glycoalkaloids; plant may contain toxic levels of nitrates; also causes dermatitis.

BULL NETTLE (*Solanum* sp.); immature growths; gastrointestinal tract affected by solanine glycoalkaloids; plant may contain toxic levels of nitrates; also causes dermatitis.

BUNCH-GRASS (*Nolina texana*); foliage; hepatogenic.

BUR CLOVER (*Medicago denticulata*); plant causes photosensitization.

BURNING BUSH (*Euonymus* spp.); fruit; cardiovascular system affected by the glycosides evobioside, evomonoside, and evonoside.

BUSHMAN'S POISON (*Acokanthera* spp.); seeds; cardiovascular system affected by cardiac glycosides.

BUTTERCUPS (*Ranunculus* spp.); sap; toxin, protoanemonin, affects gastrointestinal tract and nervous system; plant also causes dermatitis.

BUTTONBUSH (*Cephalanthus occidentalis*); entire plant, esp. leaves.

Buxus sempervirens (BOX, BOXWOOD); entire plant; gastrointestinal tract affected by plant toxins; plant also causes dermatitis.

CABBAGE (*Brassica* sp.); leaves; plant is goitrogenic.

CACTI (numerous genera); certain species are toxic.

Caesalpina gilliesii (BIRD-OF-PARADISE); seeds; gastrointestinal tract affected by plant toxins.

Caladium spp. (CALADIUM, also see *Xanthosoma* spp.); leaves; mouth irritated by plant raphides.

CALEY PEA (*Lathyrus* spp.); stems, seeds; nervous system affected by plant toxins.

CALICO BUSH (*Kalmia* sp.); leaves, nectar; gastrointestinal tract, cardiovascular and nervous systems affected by the toxins andromedotoxin and arbutin.

CALIFORNIA CHICORY (*Rafinesquia californica*); plant may contain toxic levels of nitrates.

CALLA LILY (*Zantedeschia aethiopica*); leaves; mouth irritated by plant raphides.

Calotropis spp. (CROWN FLOWER); entire plant; cardiovascular system affected by cardiac glycosides.

Caltha palustris (COWSLIP, MARSH MARIGOLD); entire plant; gastrointestinal tract affected by the toxin protoanemonin; plant also causes dermatitis.

CALTROP (*Tribulus terrestris*); plant may contain toxic levels of nitrates; plant is also hepatogenic.

CALYCANTH (*Calycanthus* spp.); seeds; cardiovascular and nervous systems affected by plant toxins.

Calycanthus spp. (CALYCANTH, CAROLINA ALLSPICE); seeds; cardiovascular and nervous systems affected by plant toxins.

Campsis spp. (TRUMPET VINE); plant causes dermatitis.

CANADA THISTLE (*Cirsium arvense*); plant may contain toxic levels of nitrates.

CANARIO (*Allamanda cathartica*); bark, leaves, fruit, seeds, sap; plant contains cathartic toxins; plant also causes dermatitis.

CANDLEBERRY, CANDLENUT (*Aleurites molluccana*); entire plant; gastrointestinal tract affected by saponins and toxalbumins.

Cannabis sativa (MARIJUANA); leaves, flower bracts; plant contains the hallucinogens tetrahydro-cannabinols.

CARDINAL FLOWER (*Lobelia* spp.); leaves, stems, fruit; nervous system affected by the toxin pyridine; plant also causes dermatitis.

Carduus sp. (PLUMELESS THISTLE); plant may contain toxic levels of nitrates.

CARELESS WEED (*Amaranthus hybridus*); plant may contain toxic levels of nitrates.

CAROLINA ALLSPICE (*Calycanthus* spp.); seeds; cardiovascular and nervous systems affected by plant toxins.

CASSAVA (*Manihot esculenta*); leaves, esp. roots; plant is cyanogenetic.

Cassia spp. (COFFEE SENNA, GOLDEN SHOWER, INDIGO, SENNA, SICKLE POD); entire plant; gastrointestinal tract affected by toxalbumins.

CASTOR BEAN (*Ricinus communis*); seeds; gastrointestinal tract affected by toxalbumins; plant also causes dermatitis.

CATCLAW (*Acacia greggi*); foliage; plant is cyanogenetic.

CELANDINE, CELANDINE POPPY (*Chelidonium majus*); entire plant; nervous system affected by the alkaloids chelidonine, chelerithrine, and protopine; plant also causes dermatitis.

Celastrus scandens (BITTERSWEET); entire plant; plant is reputed to be toxic.

Cephalanthus occidentalis (BUTTONBUSH); entire plant, esp. leaves; plant is reputed to be toxic.

Cercocarpus montanus (MOUNTAIN-MAHOGANY); wilted leaves; plant is cyanogenetic.

Cestrum spp. (DAY-BLOOMING JESSAMINE, JASMINE, NIGHT-BLOOMING JESSAMINE); fruit, sap; gastrointestinal tract affected by solanine glycoalkaloids; nervous system affected by atropine-like toxins.

CHEESEWEED (*Malva parviflora*); plant may contain toxic levels of nitrates.

Chelidonium majus (CELANDINE, CELANDINE POPPY); entire plant; nervous system affected by the alkaloids chelidonine, chelerithrine, and protopine; plant also causes dermatitis.

Chenopodium spp. (GOOSEFOOT, LAMB'S QUARTERS, PIGWEED, WORMSEED); plant may contain toxic levels of nitrates.

CHERRIES (*Prunus* spp.); kernels in pits; plant is cyanogenetic.

CHERRY LAUREL (*Prunus* sp.); entire plant; plant is cyanogenetic.

CHICKWEED (*Stellaria media*); plant may contain toxic levels of nitrates.

CHINABERRY TREE (*Melia azedarach*); fruit, bark; plant contains convulsants.

CHINESE LANTERN (*Physalis* spp.); unripe berries; gastrointestinal tract affect by solanine glycoalkaloids.

CHIVES (*Allium* spp.); bulbs, bulblets, flowers, stems; toxins affect gastrointestinal tract; plant also causes dermatitis.

CHRISTMAS-BERRY (*Heteromeles artbutifolia*); leaves; plant is cyanogenetic.

CHRISTMAS ROSE (*Helleborus niger*); entire plant; cardiovascular system affected by the cardiac glycosides helleborin and helleborein; plant also causes dermatitis.

Cicuta spp. (WATER HEMLOCK); entire plant, esp. roots; nervous system affected by the convulsant cicutoxin.

Cirsium arvense (CANADA THISTLE); plant may contain toxic levels of nitrates.

Claviceps spp. (ERGOT); an ascomycetous fungus which grows on small grain (e.g., rye); also contains the alkaloid indole.

Clematis spp. (CLEMATIS, TRAVELLER'S JOY, VIRGIN'S BOWER); entire plant; gastrointestinal tract and nervous system affected by plant toxins; plant also causes dermatitis.

Cleome serrulata (ROCKY MT. BEE PLANT); plant may contain toxic levels of nitrates.

CLIMBING LILY (*Gloriosa* spp.); entire plant, esp. tubers; gastrointestinal tract affected by the toxin colchicine.

CLOVERS (*Trifolium* spp.); plant causes photosensitization and contact dermatitis (also see WHITE CLOVER).

COAL-OIL BRUSH (*Teradymia glabrata*); leaves; plant is hepatogenic.

COAST GOLDENBUSH (*Haplopappus venetus*); plant may contain toxic levels of nitrates.

COCKLEBUR (*Xanthium orientale*); leaves at sprouted two-leaf stage, germinating seeds; plant contains hydroquinone; also causes dermatitis.

COFFEE SENNA (*Cassia occidentalis*); entire plant; gastrointestinal tract affected by toxalbumins.

COFFEEWEED (*Sesbania* spp.); seeds; gastrointestinal tract affected by saponins.

Colchicum autumnale (AUTUMN CROCUS, MEADOW SAFFRON); entire plant; gastrointestinal tract affected by the toxin colchicine and other alkaloids; plant also causes dermatitis.

Colocasia esculenta (ELEPHANT'S EAR, TARO); leaves; mouth irritated by plant raphides.

COLUMBINE (*Aquilegia vulgaris*); entire plant; cardiovascular system affected by plant toxins.

COMMON LANTANA (*Lantana camara*); immature berries; nervous system affected by the atropine-like toxin lantodene; plant is also hepatogenic.

COMMON PRIVET (*Ligustrum vulgare*); entire plant; gastrointestinal tract affected by the glycoside ligustrin.

COMMON VETCH (*Vicia sativa*); seeds, moldy parts; plant is cyanogenetic; plant also causes photosensitization.

Conium maculatum (HEMLOCK, POISON HEMLOCK); entire plant, esp. roots and seeds; nervous system affected by alkaloids including coniine, coniceine, and conidrine; may contain toxic levels of nitrates; plant also causes dermatitis.

Convallaria majalis (LILY-OF-THE-VALLEY); entire plant; cardiovascular system affected by the glycosides convallarin and convallamarin.

COONTIE (*Zamia pumila*); roots, trunk; gastrointestinal tract and nervous system affected by plant toxins.

COPPERWEED (*Oxytenia acerosa*); leaves; toxic principle unknown.

CORAL PLANT (*Jatropha multifida*); seeds; gastrointestinal tract affected by toxalbumins and cathartic oils; plant also causes dermatitis.

Coriaria myrtifolia (no trivial name in U.S.); fruit; plant contains convulsants.

CORNCOCKLE (*Agrostemma githago*); seeds; gastrointestinal tract affected by saponins.

Corydalis spp. (FITWEED); entire plant; plant contains convulsants including isoquinoline.

Corynocarpus laevigatus (no trivial name in U.S.); fruit; plant contains convulsants.

COWCOCKLE (*Saponaria vaccaria*); seeds; gastrointestinal tract affected by saponins.

COWSLIP (*Caltha palustris*), entire plant; gastrointestinal tract affected by the toxin protoanemonin; plant also causes dermatitis.

COYOTILLO (*Karawinskia humboldtiana*); fruit; nervous system affected by plant toxins.

CRAB'S EYE (*Abrus precatorius*); seeds; gastrointestinal tract affected by toxalbumins.

CREEPING CHARLIE (*Glechoma hederacea*); plant contains a variety of volatile oils.

Crotalaria spp. (RATTLEBOX); entire plant; pyrrolizidine alkaloids cause hepatic veno-occlusive disease (Budd-Chiari syndrome) in humans.

CROWFOOTS (*Ranunculus* spp.); gastrointestinal tract and nervous system affected by the toxin protoanemonin; plant also causes dermatitis.

CROWNBEARD (*Verbesina encelioides*); plant may contain toxic levels of nitrates.

CROWN FLOWERS (*Calotropis* spp.) entire plant; cardiovascular system affected by cardiac glycosides.

Crytostegia spp. (RUBBER VINE, PURPLE ALLAMANDA); entire plant; cardiovascular system affected by digitalis-like glycoside.

CUCKOO-PINT (*Arum maculatum*); entire plant; gastrointestinal tract affected by plant toxins; mouth irritated by plant raphides; plant also causes dermatitis.

CULTIVATED RAPE (*Brassica napus*); plant is hepatogenic.

CURCAS BEAN (*Jatropha curcas*); seeds; gastrointestinal tract affected by toxalbumins and cathartic oils; plant also causes dermatitis.

Cypripedium spp. (LADY SLIPPER, MOCCASIN FLOWER, SHOWY LADY SLIPPER, YELLOW LADY SLIPPER); plant causes dermatitis.

Cytisus scoparious (SCOTCH BROOM); seeds; plant contains quinolizidine alkaloid toxins.

DAFFODIL (*Narcissus* spp.); bulbs; gastrointestinal tract affected by alkaloid toxins; plant also causes dermatitis.

Daphne spp. (DAPHNE, MEZEREON, SPURGE LAUREL, WOOD LAUREL); entire plant, esp. fruit and seeds; gastrointestinal tract and kidneys affected by coumarin glycosides; plant also causes dermatitis.

Datura stramonium (DEVIL'S TRUMPET, JIMSON WEED, THORNAPPLE); entire plant; nervous system affected by the alkaloids atropine, scopolamine, and hyoscyamine; may contain toxic levels of nitrates; plant also causes dermatitis.

DAY-BLOOMING JESSAMINE (*Cestrum diurnum*); fruit, sap; gastrointestinal tract affected by solanine glycoalkaloids; nervous system affected by atropine-like toxins.

DEADLY NIGHTSHADE (*Atropa belladonna*); entire plant; nervous system affected by the alkaloids jasciamine, atropine, and belladonnin.

DEATH CAMAS (*Zigadenus* spp.); entire plant; cardiovascular system affected by alkaloid toxins.

Delphinium spp. (LARKSPUR); cardiovascular system affected by alkaloids including delphinine; plant also causes dermatitis.

DESERT ROSE (*Adenium* spp.); entire plant; cardiovascular system affected by digitalis-like glycosides.

DEVIL'S CLUB (*Echinopanax horridum*); plant causes dermatitis.

DEVIL'S TRUMPET (*Datura stramonium*); entire plant; nervous system affected by the alkaloids atropine, scopolamine, and hyoscyamine; may contain toxic levels of nitrates; plant also causes dermatitis.

DEVIL'S TURNIP (*Bryonia dioica*); gastrointestinal tract affected by the glycosides bryonin and bryonidin; plant also causes dermatitis.

Dicentra spp. (BLEEDING HEART, DUTCHMAN'S BREECHES, GOLDEN EAR-DROPS, SQUIRREL CORN, STAGGER WEED, STEER'S HEAD); entire plant, esp. bulbs; plant contains convulsants including isoquinoline; plant also causes dermatitis.

Dieffenbachia spp. (DUMBCANE); leaves; mouth irritated by plant raphides; plant also causes dermatitis.

Digitalis purpurea (FOXGLOVE, PURPLE FOXGLOVE); entire plant; cardiovascular system affected by the glycosides digitalin and digitoxin; gastrointestinal tract affected by saponins.

Dionaea sp. (VENUS FLYTRAP); entire plant.

DOCKS (*Rumex* spp.); leaves; plant contains soluble oxalates and may contain toxic levels of nitrates; plant also causes dermatitis.

DOGBANE (*Apocynum cannabinum*); plant contains cardiac glycosides.

DOG HOBBLE (*Leucothoe* spp.); leaves, nectar; cardiovascular and nervous systems affected by plant toxins.

DOLL'S EYES (*Actaea* spp.); foliage, berries, roots; gastrointestinal tract and nervous system affected by the toxin protoanemonin.

DUMBCANE (*Dieffenbachia* spp.); leaves; mouth irritated by plant raphides; plant also causes dermatitis.

DUTCHMAN'S BREECHES (*Dicentra cucullaria*); entire plant, esp. bulbs; plant contains convulsants including isoquinoline; plant also causes dermatitis.

EAGLE FERN (*Pteridium* sp.); fronds; plant contains thiaminase.

Echinochloa crusgalli (BARNYARD GRASS); plant may contain toxic levels of nitrates.

Echinopanax horridum (DEVIL'S CLUB); plant causes dermatitis.

Echium vulgare (VIPER'S BUGLOSS); entire plant; pyrrolizidine alkaloid causes hepatic veno-occlusive disease (Budd-Chiari syndrome) in humans.

ELDERBERRY (*Sambucus* spp.); entire plant; plant is cyanogenetic and may contain toxic levels of nitrates.

ELEPHANT'S EAR (*Alocasia* sp., *Colocasia esculenta*); leaves, stems; mouth irritated by plant raphides.

ENGLISH IVY (*Hedera helix*); berries, leaves; gastrointestinal tract affected by saponins; plant also causes dermatitis.

Equisetum spp. (FOXTAILS, HORSETAILS, SCOURING RUSH); stems; toxic principles uncertain; fungus growing on plant may cause toxicity.

ERGOT (*Claviceps* spp.); an ascomycetous fungus which grows on small grain (e.g., rye); also contains the alkaloid indole.

Eriobotrya japonica (LOQUAT, JAPAN PLUM); kernel in pit; plant is cyanogenetic.

Euonymus spp. (BURNING BUSH, SPINDLE TREE, STRAWBERRY BUSH, WAHOO); fruit; cardiovascular system affected by the glycosides evobioside, evomonoside, and evonoside.

Eupatorium spp. (JOE-PYE WEED, THOROUGHWORT, WHITE SNAKEROOT); leaves; plant may contain toxic levels of nitrates.

Euphorbia spp. (EUPHORBIA, MILK BUSH, POINSETTIA, SNOW-ON-THE-MOUNTAIN, SPURGES); latex; gastrointestinal tract affected by the toxin euphorbin; may contain toxic levels of nitrates; plant also causes dermatitis.

EUROPEAN BEECH (*Fagus sylvatica*); seeds; gastrointestinal tract affected by saponins.

EUROPEAN MISTLETOE (*Viscum album*); leaves, stems; gastrointestinal tract affected by toxalbumins.

Fagopyrum spp. (BUCKWHEAT, INDIA WHEAT); plant causes photosensitization and contact dermatitis.

Fagus sylvatica (EUROPEAN BEECH); seeds; gastrointestinal tract affected by saponins.

FALSE HELLEBORE (*Veratrum* spp.); entire plant; cardiovascular system affected by alkaloid toxins; plant also causes dermatitis.

FALSE JESSAMINE (*Gelsemium* sempervirens); leaves, roots; plant contains convulsants including indole; plant also causes dermatitis.

FALSE SAGO PALM (*Zamia pumila*); trunk, roots; gastrointestinal tract and nervous system affected by plant toxins.

FANWEED (*Thlaspi arvensi*); seeds; gastrointestinal tract affected by mustard oil.

FESCUE, TALL (*Festuca arundinacea*); considered nontoxic unless contaminated with ERGOT (*Claviceps* sp.) or other fungi.

Festuca arundinacea (FESCUE, TALL); considered nontoxic unless contaminated with ERGOT (*Claviceps* sp.) or other fungi.

FETTERBUSH (*Pieris* spp.); leaves, nectar; cardiovascular and nervous systems affected by plant toxins.

FIDDLENECK (*Amsinckia intermedia*); seed-like nutlets; plant may contain toxic levels of nitrates.

FIREBALL (*Kochia scoparia;* plant may contain toxic levels of nitrates.

FITWEED (*Corydalis* spp.); entire plant; plant contains convulsants including isoquinoline.

FLAG (*Iris* spp.); rootstocks; toxins affect gastrointestinal tract; plant also causes dermatitis.

FLAX (*Linum usitatissimus*); entire plant, esp. immature seed pods; plant is cyanogenetic and goitrogenic; may contain toxic levels of nitrates.

Florensia cernua (BLACK BRUSH, TARBUSH); fruit; gastrointestinal tract affected by plant toxins.

Florestina tripteris (FLORESTINA); entire plant; plant is cyanogenetic.

FLORIDA ARROWROOT (*Zamia pumila*); trunk, roots; gastrointestinal tract and nervous system affected by plant toxins.

FLY-POISON (*Amianthemum muscaetoxicum*); leaves, underground parts of plant; alkaloids cause respiratory failure.

FOOL'S PARSLEY (*Aethusa cynapium*); entire plant; gastrointestinal tract affected by alkaloid toxins.

FOUR O'CLOCK (*Mirabilis* sp.); entire plant; gastrointestinal tract affected by the alkaloid trigonelline.

FOWL MANNAGRASS (*Glyceria striata*); entire plant; plant is cyanogenetic.

FOXGLOVE (*Digitalis purpurea*); entire plant; cardiovascular system affected by the glycosides digitalin and digitoxin; gastrointestinal tract affected by saponins.

FOXTAILS (*Equisetum* spp.); stems; toxic principles uncertain; fungus growing on plant may cause toxicity.

FRIJOLITO (*Sophora secundiflora*); seeds; nervous system affected by nicotine-like, quinolizidine alkaloids.

Fritillaria meleagris (SNAKE'S HEAD BULB); cardiovascular system affected by alkaloid toxins.

Galanthus nivalis (SNOWDROP); gastrointestinal tract affected by the alkaloids lycorine and galantamine.

GARLIC (*Allium* spp.); bulbs, bulblets, flowers, stems; gastrointestinal tract affected by plant toxins.

Gelsemium sempervirens (FALSE JESSAMINE, YELLOW JESSAMINE); flowers, leaves, roots; plant contains convulsants including indole; plant also causes dermatitis.

GILL-OVER-THE-GROUND (*Glechoma hederacea*); plant contains a variety of volatile oils.

Glechoma hederacea (CREEPING CHARLIE, GILL-OVER-THE-GROUND, GROUND IVY); plant contains a variety of volatile oils.

Gloriosa spp. (CLIMBING LILY, GLORIOSA LILY, GLORY LILY); entire plant, esp. tubers; gastrointestinal tract affected by the toxin colchicine.

GLORY LILY (*Gloriosa* spp.); entire plant, esp. tubers; gastrointestinal tract affected by the toxin colchicine.

Glyceria striata (FOWL MANNAGRASS); entire plant; plant is cyanogenetic.

Glycine max (SOYBEAN); plant is goitrogenic and may contain toxic levels of nitrates.

GOATHEAD (*Tribulus terrestris*); plant is hepatogenic and may contain toxic levels of nitrates.

GOAT WEED (*Hypericum perforatum*); entire plant; plant causes photosensitization and contact dermatitis.

GOLDENCHAINTREE (*Laburnum* x *watereri*); entire plant, esp. seeds; nervous system affected by the alkaloid cytisine.

GOLDEN EAR-DROPS (*Dicentra chrysantha*); entire plant, esp. bulbs; plant contains convulsants including isoquinoline; plant also causes dermatitis.

GOLDENRODS (*Aplopappus* spp.); leaves; plant may contain toxic levels of nitrates.

GOLDEN SHOWER (*Cassia fistula*); pulp of pods, leaves, bark; plant contains cathartic toxins.

GOLDEN TRUMPET VINE (*Allamanda cathartica*); bark, leaves, fruit, seeds, sap; gastrointestinal tract affected by plant toxins; plant also causes dermatitis.

GOLDENWEEDS (*Oonopsis* spp.); entire plant; plant may absorb toxic levels of selenium.

GOOSEFOOT (*Chenopodium glaucum*); plant may contain toxic levels of nitrates.

GOOSEGRASS (*Triglochin maritima*); leaves; plant is cyanogenetic.

GOUT STALK (*Jatropha podagrica*); seeds; gastrointestinal tract affected by toxalbumins and cathartic oils; plant also causes dermatitis.

GREASEWOOD (*Sarcobatus vermiculatus*); plant contains soluble oxalates; also causes dermatitis.

GREEN DRAGON (*Arisaema dracontium*); entire plant; gastrointestinal tract affected by plant toxins; mouth irritated by plant raphides; plant also causes dermatitis.

GROUND CHERRY (*Physalis* spp.); unripe berries; gastrointestinal tract affected by solanine glycoalkaloids.

GROUND IVY (*Glechoma hederacea*); plant contains a variety of volatile oils.

GROUNDSEL (*Senecio* spp.); entire plant; pyrrolizidine alkaloid causes hepatic veno-occlusive disease (Budd-Chiari syndrome) in humans.

GUAJILLO (*Acacia ber landieri*); foliage; plant is cyanogenetic.

Gymnocladus dioicus (KENTUCKY COFFEE TREE); seeds; nervous system affected by nicotine-like toxins.

Halogeton glomeratus (BARILLA, HALOGETON); leaves, stems; plant contains soluble oxalates.

Haplopappus venetus (COAST GOLDENBUSH); plant may contain toxic levels of nitrates.

Hedera helix (ENGLISH IVY); berries, leaves; gastrointestinal tract affected by saponins; plant also causes dermatitis.

Helenium spp. (BITTERWEED, PINGUE, RUBBERWEED, SNEEZEWEED); plant causes dermatitis.

Helianthus annuus (WILD ARTICHOKE, WILD SUNFLOWER); plant may contain toxic levels of nitrates.

HELIEBORE (*Ranunculus* spp.); sap; gastrointestinal tract and nervous system affected by the toxin protoanemonin; plant also causes dermatitis.

HELIOTROPE (*Heliotropium* spp.); entire plant; pyrrolizidine alkaloid causes hepatic veno-occlusive disease (Budd-Chiari syndrome) in humans.

Heliotropium spp. (HELIOTROPE); entire plant; pyrrolizidine alkaloid causes hepatic veno-occlusive disease (Budd-Chiari syndrome) in humans.

HELLEBORE (*Helleborus niger*); entire plant; cardiovascular system affected by the glycosides helleborin and helleborein; plant also causes dermatitis.

Helleborus niger (CHRISTMAS ROSE, HELLEBORE); entire plant; cardiovascular system affected by the glycosides helleborin and helleborein; plant also causes dermatitis.

HEMLOCK (*Conium maculatum*); entire plant, esp. roots and seeds; nervous system affected by the alkaloids coniine, conidrine, and coniceine; may contain toxic levels of nitrates; plant also causes dermatitis.

HENBANE (*Hyoscyamus niger*); seeds; nervous system affected by the alkaloids atropine, scopolamine, and hyoscyamine.

Heteromeles artbutifolia (CHRISTMAS-BERRY); leaves; plant is cyanogenetic.

HIGUERETA (*Ricinus communis*); seeds; gastrointestinal tract affected by toxalbumins; plant also causes dermatitis.

Hippobroma longiflora (HORSE POISON, MADAM FATA); entire plant; plant contains convulsants.

Hippomane mancinella (MANCHINEEL); latex; gastrointestinal tract affected by plant toxins; plant also causes dermatitis.

Holcus lanatus (VELVET GRASS, MESQUITE GRASS); fresh or wilted plant; plant is cyanogenetic.

HOLLY (*Ilex* spp.); berries; gastrointestinal tract affected by saponins.

HONEYSUCKLE BUSH (*Lonicera* spp); berries; gastrointestinal tract, cardiovascular and nervous systems affected by plant toxins.

HORSEBEAN (*Parkinsonia aculeata*); plant may contain toxic levels of nitrates.

HORSEBRUSH (*Tetradymia glabrata*); leaves; plant is hepatogenic.

HORSE CHESTNUT (*Aesculus* sp.); nuts, immature growths; gastrointestinal tract affected by saponins.

HORSE NETTLE (*Solanum* sp.); immature growths; gastrointestinal tract affected by solanine glycoalkaloids; may contain toxic levels of nitrates; plant also causes dermatitis.

HORSE POISON (*Hipponbroma longiflora*); entire plant; plant contains convulsants.

HORSETAILS (*Equisetum* spp.); stems; toxic principles uncertain; fungi growing on plant may cause toxicity.

Hura crepitans (MONKEY PISTOL, JAVILLO, SANDBOX TREE); seeds; gastrointestinal tract affected by toxalbumins; plant also causes dermatitis.

HYACINTH (*Hyacinthus orientalis*); bulbs; gastrointestinal tract affected by alkaloid toxins; plant also causes dermatitis.

Hyacinthus orientalis (HYACINTH); bulbs; gastrointestinal tract affected by alkaloid toxins; plant also causes dermatitis.

Hydrangea spp. (HYDRANGEA); flower buds; plant is cyanogenetic; plant also causes dermatitis.

Hyoscyamus niger (HENBANE); seeds; nervous system affected by the alkaloids atropine, scopolamine, and hyoscyamine.

Hypericum perforatum (GOAT WEED, KLAMATH WEED, ST. JOHNSWORT); entire plant; plant causes photosensitization and contact dermatitis.

Ilex spp. (HOLLY, YAUPON); berries; gastrointestinal tract affected by saponins.

INDIAN HEMP (*Apocynum cannabinum*); leaves; plant contains cardiac glycosides.

INDIAN KALE (*Xanthosoma* spp.); leaves; mouth affected by irritant raphides; plant also causes dermatitis.

INDIAN POKE (*Veratrum* sp.); entire plant; cardiovascular system affected by alkaloid toxins; plant also causes dermatitis.

INDIAN TOBACCO (*Lobelia inflata*); leaves, stems, fruit; nervous system affected by pyridine, a nicotine-like toxin; plant also causes dermatitis.

INDIAN TURNIP (*Arisaema triphyllum*); entire plant; gastrointestinal tract affected by plant toxins; mouth irritated by plant raphides; plant also causes dermatitis.

INDIA WHEAT (*Fagopyrum tataricum*); plant causes photosensitization.

INDIGO (*Cassia* sp.); entire plant; gastrointestinal tract affected by toxalbumins.

Ipomea spp. (BINDWEED, MORNING GLORIES, SWEET POTATO VINES); entire plant; plant contains LSD-related hallucinogens; may contain toxic levels of nitrates.

Iris spp. (IRIS, FLAG); rootstocks; gastrointestinal tract affected by the glycoside iridin; plant also causes dermatitis.

ITALIAN ARUM (*Arum italicum*); entire plant; gastrointestinal tract affected by plant toxins; mouth irritated by plant raphides; plant also causes dermatitis.

JACK-IN-THE-PULPIT (*Arisaema triphyllum*, other species); entire plant; gastrointestinal tract affected by plant toxins; mouth irritated by plant raphides; plant also causes dermatitis.

JAPANESE LANTERN (*Physalis* spp.); unripe berries; gastrointestinal tract affected by solanine glycoalkaloids.

JAPAN PLUM (*Eriobotrya japonica*); kernel in pit; plant is cyanogenetic.

JASMINE (*Cestrum* spp.); fruit, sap; gastrointestinal tract affected by solanine glycoalkaloids; nervous system affected by atropine-like toxins.

Jatropha spp. (BELLYACHE BUSH, CORAL PLANT, CURCAS BEAN, GOUT STALK, JICAMILLA, PEREGRINA, PHYSIC NUT, PURGE NUT); seeds; gastrointestinal tract affected by toxalbumins and cathartic oils; plant also causes dermatitis.

JAVA BEAN (*Phaseolus lunatus*); entire plant; plant is cyanogenetic.

JAVILLO (*Hura crepitans*); seeds; gastrointestinal tract affected by toxalbumins; plant also causes dermatitis.

JEQUIRITY BEAN (*Abrus precatorius*); seeds; gastrointestinal tract affected by toxalbumins.

JERUSALEM CHERRY (*Solanum pseudocapsicum*);

immature growths; gastrointestinal tract affected by solanine glycoalkaloids; may contain toxic levels of nitrates; plant also causes dermatitis.

JETBEAD (*Rhodotypos scandens*); berries; plant is reputed to contain a cyanogenic glycoside.

JICAMILLA (*Jatropha* spp.); seeds; gastrointestinal tract affected by toxalbumins and cathartic oils; plant also causes dermatitis.

JIMMY WEED (*Aplopappus heterophyllus*); leaves; plant may contain toxic levels of nitrates.

JIMSON WEED (*Datura stramonium*); entire plant; nervous system affected by the alkaloids atropine, scopolamine, and hyoscyamine; may contain toxic levels of nitrates; plant also causes dermatitis.

JOE-PYE WEED (*Eupatorium* sp.); plant may contain toxic levels of nitrates.

JOHNSON GRASS (*Sorghum halepense*); leaves; plant is cyanogenetic.

JONQUIL (*Narcissus* sp.); bulbs; gastrointestinal tract affected by alkaloid toxins; plant also causes dermatitis.

Juncus inflexus (BLUE RUSH); plant causes convulsions in cattle.

KALE (*Brassica* sp.); leaves; plant is goitrogenic.

Kalmia spp. (CALICO BUSH, LAMBKILL, MOUNTAIN LAUREL, SHEEP LAUREL); leaves, nectar; gastrointestinal tract, cardiovascular and nervous systems affected by the toxins andromedotoxin and arbutin.

Karwinskia humboldtiana (BUCKTHORN, COYOTILLO); fruit; nervous system affected by plant toxins.

KENTUCKY COFFEE TREE (*Gymnocladus dioicus*); seeds; nervous system affected by nicotine-like toxins.

KLAMATH WEED (*Hypericum perforatum*); entire plant; plant causes photosensitization and contact dermatitis.

Kochia scoparia (FIREBALL, MEXICAN FIREWOOD, SUMMER CYPRESS); plant may contain toxic levels of nitrates.

LABRADOR TEA (*Ledum* spp.); leaves; plant contains toxic resins.

Laburnum x *watereri* (GOLDENCHAINTREE, LABURNUM); entire plant, esp. seeds; nervous system affected by cytisine, a nicotine-like alkaloid.

Lactuca sariola (PRICKLY LETTUCE); plant may contain toxic levels of nitrates.

LADY SLIPPER (*Cypripedium spectabiles*); plant causes dermatitis.

LADY'S THUMB (*Polygonum persicaria*); plant may contain toxic levels of nitrates; plant also causes photosensitization and contact dermatitis.

LAMBKILL (*Kalmia augustifolia*); leaves, nectar; gastrointestinal tract, cardiovascular and nervous systems affected by andromedotoxin and arbutin.

LAMB'S QUARTERS (*Chenopodium album*); plant may contain toxic levels of nitrates.

Lantana camara (COMMON LANTANA); immature berries; nervous system affected by lantodene, an atropine-like toxin; plant is also hepatogenic.

LARKSPUR (*Delphinium* spp.); leaves; cardiovascular system affected by alkaloids including delphinine; plant also causes dermatitis.

Lathyrus spp. (CALEY PEA, SINGLETARY PEA, SWEET PEA, VETCHLING, WILD PEA); stems, seeds; nervous system affected by plant toxins.

LAUREL (*Rhododendron* spp.); leaves; cardiovascular system affected by the resinoid andromedotoxin.

LECHUGUILLA (*Agave lecheguilla*); plant is hepatogenic.

Ledum spp. (LABRADOR TEA); leaves; plant contains toxic resins.

LEEK (*Allium tricoccum*); bulbs, bulblets, flowers, stems; gastrointestinal tract affected by plant toxins; plant also causes dermatitis.

LESSER HEMLOCK (*Aethusa cynapium*); entire plant; gastrointestinal tract affected by alkaloid toxins.

Leucothoe spp. (DOG HOBBLE, PEPPER BUSH, SWEET BELLS, WHITE OSIER); leaves, nectar; cardiovascular and nervous systems affected by plant toxins.

Ligustrum vulgare (COMMON PRIVET, PRIVET); entire plant; gastrointestinal tract affected by the glycoside ligustrin.

LILY-OF-THE-FIELDS (*Anemone* spp.); entire plant; gastrointestinal tract affected by the toxin protoanemonin.

LILY-OF-THE-VALLEY (*Convallaria majalis*); entire plant; cardiovascular system affected by the glycosides convallarin and convallamarin.

LIMA BEAN (*Phaseolus lunatus*); entire plant; plant is cyanogenetic.

LINSEED (*Linum usitatissimus*); entire plant, esp. immature seed pods; plant is cyanogenetic and goitrogenic.

Linum spp. (FLAX, LINSEED, YELLOW PINE FLAX); entire plant, esp. immature seed pods; plant is cyanogenetic; FLAX and LINSEED (*L. usitatissimus*) may contain toxic levels of nitrates, and plants are goitrogenic; YELLOW PINE FLAX (*L. neomexicanum*) contains saponins which affect gastrointestinal tract.

Lobelia spp. (CARDINAL FLOWER, LOBELIA, INDIAN TOBACCO); leaves, stems, fruit; nervous system affected by pyridine, a nicotine-like toxin; plant also causes dermatitis.

LOCOWEEDS (*Astragalus* spp., *Oxytropis* spp.); entire plant; may absorb toxic levels of selenium.

Lonicera spp. (HONEYSUCKLE BUSH); berries;

gastrointestinal tract, cardiovascular and nervous systems affected by plant toxins.

LOQUAT (*Eriobotrya japonica*); kernel in pit; plant is cyanogenetic.

LORDS & LADIES (*Arum maculatum*); entire plant; gastrointestinal tract affected by plant toxins; mouth irritated by plant raphides; plant also causes dermatitis.

Lotus corniculatus (BIRDSFOOT TREFOIL); entire plant; plant is cyanogenetic.

LUPINES (*Lupinus* spp.); leaves, esp. seeds; plant contains numerous alkaloid toxins including quinolizidine and piperidine.

Lupinus spp. (BLUEBONNETS, LUPINES, PURSH, SILKY LUPINE); leaves, esp. seeds; plant contains numerous alkaloid toxins including quinolizidine and piperidine.

Lycium spp. (MATRIMONY VINE); leaves; gastrointestinal tract affected by plant toxins.

Lycospersicon esculentum (TOMATO); vines, suckers; gastrointestinal tract affected by solanine glycoalkaloids.

Lygodesmia juncea (SKELETONWEED); plant may contain toxic levels of nitrates.

MADAM FATE (*Hippobroma longiflora*); entire plant; plant contains convulsants.

MALANGA (*Xanthosoma* spp.); leaves; mouth affected by irritant raphides; plant also causes dermatitis.

MALLOW (*Malva parviflora*); plant may contain toxic levels of nitrates.

Malus spp. (APPLES); seeds; plant is cyanogenetic.

Malva parviflora (CHEESEWEED, MALLOW); plant may contain toxic levels of nitrates.

MANCHINEEL (*Hippomane mancinella*); latex; toxins affect gastrointestinal tract; plant also causes dermatitis.

Mandragora officinarum (MANDRAKE); nervous system affected by the toxins hyoscyamine and mandragorin.

MANDRAKE (*Mandragora officinarum*); nervous system affected by the toxins hyoscyamine and mandragorin.

MANGOLD (*Beta vulgaris*); leaves; plant contains soluble oxalates; may contain toxic levels of nitrates.

Manihot esculenta (CASSAVA); leaves, esp. roots; plant is cyanogenetic.

MARIJUANA (*Cannabis sativa*); leaves, flower bracts; plant contains the hallucinogens tetrahydro-cannabinols.

MARSH MARIGOLD (*Caltha palustris*); entire plant; gastrointestinal tract affected by the toxin protoanemonin; plant also causes dermatitis.

MARVEL OF PERU (*Mirabilis jalapa*); entire plant; gastrointestinal tract affected by the alkaloid trigonelline; plant also causes dermatitis.

MATRIMONY VINE (*Lycium* spp.); leaves; gastrointestinal tract affected by plant toxins.

MAY APPLE (*Podophyllum peltatum*); entire plant except fruit; nervous system affected by plant toxins; also cause hematological abnormalities; powdered root may cause conjunctivitis and keratitis.

MEADOW BRAKE (*Onoclea sensibilis*); leaves; nervous system affected by plant toxins.

MEADOW SAFFRON (*Colchicum autumnale*); entire plant; gastrointestinal tract affected by colchicine and other alkaloids; plant also causes dermatitis.

Medicago denticulata (BUR CLOVER); plant causes photosensitization.

Melia azedarach (BEAD TREE, CHINABERRY TREE, PRIDE-OF-INDIA); fruit, bark; plant contains convulsants.

Melilotus spp. (WHITE OR YELLOW SWEETCLOVERS); plant may contain toxic levels of nitrates.

Menispermum canadense (MOONSEED); fruit; plant contains convulsants.

Menziesia ferruginea (RUSTYLEAF); leaves; plant contains toxic resins.

MESCAL BEAN (*Sophora secundiflora*); seeds; nervous system affected by the nicotine-like, quinolizidine alkaloids.

MESQUITE GRASS (*Holcus lanatus*); fresh or wilted plant; plant is cyanogenetic.

Metopium toxiferum (POISON WOOD); plant causes dermatitis.

MEXICAN FIREWOOD (*Kochia scoparia*); plant may contain toxic levels of nitrates.

MEXICAN POPPY (*Argemone mexicana*); entire plant; isoquinoline alkaloid causes "epidemic dropsy" in humans.

MEZEREON (*Daphne mezereum*); entire plant, esp. fruit and seeds; gastrointestinal tract and kidneys affected by coumarin glycosides; plant also causes dermatitis.

MILK BUSH (*Euphorbia* spp.); latex; gastrointestinal tract affected by the toxin euphorbin; may contain toxic levels of nitrates; plant also causes dermatitis.

MILKWEEDS (*Asclepias* spp.); leaves, stems; plant contains toxic resins.

MINER'S LETTUCE (*Montia perfoliata*); plant may contain toxic levels of nitrates.

Mirabilis jalapa (FOUR O'CLOCK, MARVEL OF PERU); entire plant; gastrointestinal tract affected by the alkaloid trigonelline; plant also causes dermatitis.

MISTLETOES (*Phoradendron* spp.); leaves, stems, berries; gastrointestinal tract affected by toxalbumins; plant also causes dermatitis.

MOCCASIN FLOWER (*Cypripedium spectabiles*); plant causes dermatitis.

MOCK AZALEA (*Adenium* spp.); entire plant; cardiovascular system affected by digitalis-like glycosides.

MOCK ORANGE (*Poncirus trifoliata*); fruit; gastrointestinal tract affected by plant toxins.

Momordica spp. (BALSAM APPLE, BALSAM PEAR, BITTER GOURD, WHITE BALSAM APPLE); seeds; gastrointestinal tract affected by toxalbumins.

MONKEY PISTOL (*Hura crepitans*); seeds; gastrointestinal tract affected by toxalbumins.

MONKEY POD (*Samonia samon*); gastrointestinal tract affected by saponins; plant also causes dermatitis.

MONKSHOOD (*Aconitum* spp.); entire plant, esp. leaves and roots; cardiovascular system affected by alkaloid toxins.

Montia perfoliata (MINER'S LETTUCE); plant may contain toxic levels of nitrates.

MOONSEED (*Menispermum canadense*); fruit; plant contains convulsants.

MORNING GLORIES (*Ipomea* spp.); entire plant; plant contains LSD-related hallucinogens; may contain toxic levels of nitrates.

MOUNTAIN LAUREL (*Kalmia latifolia*); leaves, nectar; gastrointestinal tract, cardiovascular and nervous systems affected by the toxins andromedotoxin and arbutin.

MOUNTAIN-MAHOGANY (*Cercocarpus montanus*); wilted leaves; plant is cyanogenetic.

MUSHROOMS (many wild varieties); see appropriate literature for toxicities.

MUSTARD (*Brassica* sp.); leaves; plant is goitrogenic; may contain toxic levels of nitrates.

Myoporum laetum (no trivial name in U.S.); fruit, esp. leaves; plant contains convulsants.

NAKED-LADY LILY (*Amaryllis* sp.); bulbs; gastrointestinal tract affected by alkaloid toxins.

Narcissus spp. (DAFFODIL, JONQUIL); bulbs; gastrointestinal tract affected by alkaloid toxins; plant also causes dermatitis.

Nerium oleander (OLEANDER); entire plant, and water used for cut plants; cardiovascular system affected by the glycosides oleandrin, oleandroside, and nerioside; plant also causes dermatitis.

NETTLE (*Urtica procera*); plant may contain toxic levels of nitrates.

Nicotiana spp. (TOBACCO, TREE TOBACCO); leaves; nervous system affected by the alkaloids nicotine and pyridine.

NIGHT-BLOOMING JESSAMINE (*Cestrum nocturnum*); fruit, sap; gastrointestinal tract affected by solanine glycoalkaloids; nervous system affected by atropine-like toxins.

NIGHTSHADES (*Solanum* spp.); immature growths; gastrointestinal tract affected by solanine gly-

coalkaloids; may contain toxic levels of nitrates; plant also causes dermatitis.

Nolina texana (BUNCH GRASS, SACAHUISTA); foliage; plant is hepatogenic.

NUX-VOMICA TREE (*Strychnos nux-vomica*); entire plant; nervous system affected by the alkaloid strychnine.

OAKS (*Quercus* spp); buds, leaves; oak tannin causes gastritis and nephritis.

OATS (*Avena sativa*); nontoxic unless contaminated with smut or fungi.

Oenanthe crocata (WATER DROPWORT); entire plant; plant contains the convulsant oenanthetoxin.

OLEANDER (*Nerium oleander,* other species); entire plant, and water used for cut plants; cardiovascular system affected by the glycosides oleandrin, oleandroside, and nerioside; plant also causes dermatitis.

ONION (*Allium cepa*); bulbs, bulblets, flowers, stems; gastrointestinal tract affected by plant toxins; plant also causes dermatitis.

Onoclea sensibilis (MEADOW BRAKE, POLYPODY BRAKE, SENSITIVE FERN); leaves; nervous system affected by plant toxins.

Oonopsis spp. (GOLDENWEEDS); entire plant; plant may absorb toxic levels of selenium.

OPIUM POPPY (*Papaver somniferum*); unripe seedpods; plant contains a wide variety of alkaloids including morphine, codeine, papaverine, narcotine, and isoquinoline.

Ornithogalum spp. (STAR-OF-BETHLEHEM, WONDER FLOWER); entire plant, esp. bulbs; gastrointestinal tract affected by alkaloid toxins.

Oxalis pes-caprae (BERMUDA BUTTERCUP, BERMUDA OXALIS, SORREL, SOURSOB); leaves; plant contains soluble oxalates.

Oxytenia acerosa (COPPERWEED); leaves; toxic principle unknown.

Oxytropis spp. (LOCOWEEDS, POINT VETCH); entire plant; plant is reputed to be toxic.

Panicum capillare (PANIC-GRASS, WITCHGRASS); plant is hepatogenic; may contain toxic levels of nitrates.

Papaver somniferum (OPIUM POPPY); unripe seedpods; plant contains a wide variety of alkaloids including morphine, codeine, papaverine, narcotine, and isoquinoline.

Parkinsonia aculeata (HORSEBEAN); plant may contain toxic levels of nitrates.

PASQUE FLOWER (*Anemone* spp.; includes *Pulsatilla* spp.); entire plant; gastrointestinal tract affected by the toxin protoanemonin; plant also causes dermatitis.

Pastinaca sativa (WILD PARSNIP); plant causes dermatitis.

PEACH (*Prunus* spp.); seeds; plant is cyanogenetic.

Pedilanthus tithymaloides (SLIPPER FLOWER); latex; gastrointestinal tract affected by plant toxins.

PEPPER BUSH (*Leucothoe* spp.); leaves, nectar; cardiovascular and nervous systems affected.

PEREGRINA (*Jatropha integerrima*); seeds; gastrointestinal tract affected by toxalbumins and cathartic oils; plant also causes dermatitis.

PERIWINKLE (*Vinca* spp.); entire plant; plant contains hallucinogens.

Pernettya spp. (no trivial names in U.S.); leaves, nectar; cardiovascular system affected by plant toxins.

Phaseolus lunatus (JAVA BEAN, LIMA BEAN); entire plant; plant is cyanogenetic.

PHEASANT'S EYE (*Adonis* spp.); entire plant; cardiovascular system affected by cardiac glycosides.

Philodendron spp. (PHILODENDRON); leaves; mouth irritated by plant raphides.

Phoradendron spp. (MISTLETOES); leaves, stems, berries; gastrointestinal tract affected by toxalbumins; plant also causes dermatitis.

Physalis spp. (CHINESE LANTERN, GROUND CHERRY, JAPANESE LANTERN, POHA); unripe berries; gastrointestinal tract affected by solanine glycoalkaloids.

PHYSIC NUT (*Jatropha curcas*); seeds; gastrointestinal tract affected by toxalbumins and cathartic oils; plant also causes dermatitis.

Phytolacca americana (PIGEONBERRY, POKEBERRY, POKEWEED); leaves, roots; gastrointestinal tract affected by saponins.

Pieris spp. (FETTERBUSH); leaves, nectar; cardiovascular and nervous systems affected by plant toxins.

PIGEONBERRY (*Phytolacca americana*); all parts, esp. roots; gastrointestinal tract affected by saponins.

PIG-LILLY (*Zantedeschida* spp.); leaves; mouth irritated by plant raphides.

PIGWEED (*Chenopodium* spp.); entire plant; may contain toxic levels of nitrates.

PINGUE (*Helenium* spp.); plant causes dermatitis.

Plagiobothrys sp. (POPCORN FLOWER); plant may contain toxic levels of nitrates.

PLUM (*Prunus* spp.); seeds; plant is cyanogenetic.

PLUMELESS THISTLE (*Carduus* sp.); plant may contain toxic levels of nitrates.

Podophyllum peltatum (MAY APPLE); entire plant except fruit; plant toxins affect nervous system and cause hematological abnormalities; powdered root may cause conjunctivitis and keratitis.

POHA (*Physalis* spp.); unripe berries; gastrointestinal tract affected by solanine glycoalkaloids.

POINSETTIA (*Euphorbia pulcherrima*); latex; gastrointestinal tract affected by the toxin euphorbin;

may contain toxic levels of nitrates; plant also causes dermatitis.

POINT VETCH (*Oxytropis* spp.); entire plant; plant is reputed to be toxic.

POISON HEMLOCK (*Conium maculatum*); entire plant, esp. roots and seeds; nervous system affected by alkaloids including coniine, conidrine, and coniceine; may contain toxic levels of nitrates; plant also causes dermatitis.

POISON IVY (*Toxicodendron radicans*); leaves, bark, and fruit cause dermatitis.

POISON OAK (*Toxicodendron* spp.); leaves, bark, and fruit cause dermatitis.

POISON SUCKLEYA (*Suckleya suckleyana*); leaves; plant is cyanogenetic.

POISON SUMAC (*Toxicodendron vernix*); leaves, bark, and fruit cause dermatitis.

POISONVETCHES (*Astragalus* spp.); entire plant; may absorb toxic levels of selenium.

POISON WOOD (*Metopium toxiferum*); plant causes dermatitis.

POKEBERRY, POKEWEED (*Phytolacca americana*); leaves, roots; gastrointestinal tract affected by saponins.

Polygonum spp. (LADY'S THUMB, SMARTWEEDS); plant may contain toxic levels of nitrates; also causes photosensitization and contact dermatitis.

POLYPODY BRAKE (*Onoclea sensibilis*); leaves; nervous system affected by plant toxins.

Poncirus trifoliata (MOCK ORANGE, TRIFOLIATE ORANGE); fruit; gastrointestinal tract affected by plant toxins.

POPCORN FLOWER (*Plagiobothrys* sp.); plant may contain toxic levels of nitrates.

POTATO (*Solanum tuberosum*); immature growths; gastrointestinal tract affected by solanine glycoalkaloids; may contain toxic levels of nitrates; plant also causes dermatitis.

PRECATORY BEAN (*Abrus precatorius*); seeds; gastrointestinal tract affected by toxalbumins.

PRICKLY LETTUCE (*Latuca sariola*); plant may contain toxic levels of nitrates.

PRICKLY POPPY (*Argemone mexicana*); entire plant; isoquinoline toxin causes "epidemic dropsy" in humans.

PRIDE-OF-INDIA (*Melia azedarach*); fruit, bark; plant contains convulsants.

PRIMROSE (*Primula* spp.); leaves cause dermatitis.

Primula spp. (PRIMROSE); leaves cause dermatitis.

PRINCESS'S PLUME (*Stanleya pinnata*); entire plant; may absorb toxic levels of selenium.

PRIVET (*Ligustrum vulgare*); entire plant; gastrointestinal tract affected by the glycoside ligustrin.

Prunus spp. (APRICOT, CHERRY, CHERRY LAU-

REL, PLUM, PEACH); seeds; plant is cyanogenetic.

Ptelea baldwinii (WAFER ASH); plant causes photosensitization and contact dermatitis.

Pteridium spp. (BRACKEN FERN, BRAKE FERN, EAGLE FERN); fronds; plant contains thiaminase.

PUNCTURE VINE (*Tribulus terrestris*); plant is hepatogenic; may contain toxic levels of nitrates.

PURGE NUT (*Jatropha* spp.); seeds; gastrointestinal tract affected by toxalbumins and cathartic oils; plant also causes dermatitis.

PURPLE ALLAMANDA (*Cryptostegia* sp.); entire plant; cardiovascular system affected by digitalislike glycosides.

PURPLECOCKLE (*Agrostemma githago*); seeds; gastrointestinal tract affected by saponins.

PURPLE FOXGLOVE (*Digitalis purpurea*); entire plant; cardiovascular system affected by the glycosides digitalin and digitoxin; gastrointestinal tract affected by saponins.

PURSH (*Lupinus* sp.); leaves, esp. seeds; plant contains numerous alkaloid toxins including quinolizidine and piperidine.

QUEEN'S DELIGHT (*Stillingia treculeana*); leaves, stems; plant is cyanogenetic.

Quercus spp. (OAKS); buds, leaves; oak tannin causes gastritis and nephritis.

Rafinesquia californica (CALIFORNIA CHICORY); plant may contain toxic levels of nitrates.

RAGWORT (*Senecio jacobaea*); entire plant; pyrrolizidine alkaloids cause hepatic veno-occlusive disease (Budd-Chiari syndrome) in humans.

RAIN TREE (*Samonia samon*); gastrointestinal tract affected by saponins; plant also causes dermatitis.

Ranunculus spp. (BUTTERCUPS, CROWFOOTS, HELIEBORE); sap; gastrointestinal tract and nervous system affected by the toxin protoanemonin; plant also causes dermatitis.

RATTLEBOX (*Crotalaria* sp.); entire plant; pyrrolizidine alkaloids cause hepatic veno-occlusive disease (Budd-Chiari syndrome) in humans.

RATTLEBUSH, RATTLEBOX (*Sesbania* spp.); seeds; gastrointestinal tract affected by saponins.

RAYLESS (*Aplopappus heterophyllus*); leaves; plant may contain toxic levels of nitrates.

RED PUCCOON (*Sanguinaria canadensis*); juices from stems and rootstocks cause dermatitis.

RED SQUILL (*Urginea maritima*); bulbs; cardiovascular system affected by cardiac glycosides.

RESCUE GRASS (*Bromus* sp.); plant may contain toxic levels of nitrates.

Rhamnus spp. (BUCKTHORN, also see *Karwinskia humboldtiana*); fruit, bark; gastrointestinal tract affected by plant toxins.

Rheum rhaponticum (RHUBARB); leaf blades; plant contains cathartic toxins, including oxalic acid.

Rhododendron spp. (AZALEAS, LAUREL, RHODODENDRON); leaves; cardiovascular system affected by the resinoid andromedotoxin.

Rhodotypos scandens (JETBEAD); berries; plant is reputed to contain a cyanogenic glycoside.

RHUBARB (*Rheum rhaponticum*); leaf blades; plant contains cathartic toxins including oxalic acid.

RICINO (*Ricinus communis*); seeds; gastrointestinal tract affected by toxalbumins; plant also causes dermatitis.

Ricinus communis (CASTOR BEAN, HIGUERETA, RICINO); seeds; gastrointestinal tract affected by toxalbumins; plant also causes dermatitis.

Rivina humilis (ROUGE PLANT); leaves, roots; gastrointestinal tract affected by plant toxins.

Robinia pseudoacacia (BLACK LOCUST); bark, seeds, leaves; gastrointestinal tract affected by toxalbumins.

ROCKY MT. BEE PLANT (*Cleome serrulata*); plant may contain toxic levels of nitrates.

ROSARY PEA (*Abrus precatorius*); seeds; gastrointestinal tract affected by toxalbumins.

ROUGE PLANT (*Rivina humilis*); leaves, roots; gastrointestinal tract affected by toxalbumins.

RUBBER VINE (*Cryptostegia* sp.); entire plant; cardiovascular system affected by digitalis-like glycosides.

RUBBERWEED (*Helenium* spp.); plant causes dermatitis.

RUE (*Ruta graveolens*); gastrointestinal tract affected by the toxins furocoumarins, tannins, and xantotoxins; plant also causes photosensitization.

Rumex spp. (DOCKS, SHEEP SORREL); leaves; plant contains soluble oxalates; may contain toxic levels of nitrates; plant also causes dermatitis.

RUSTYLEAF (*Menziesia ferruginea*); leaves; plant contains toxic resins.

Ruta graveolens (RUE); gastrointestinal tract affected by the toxins furocoumarins, tannins, and xantotoxins; plant also causes photosensitization.

SACAHUISTA (*Nolina texana*); foliage; plant is hepatogenic.

SAGE (*Salvia reflexa*); leaves of certain varieties contain toxic levels of nitrates.

Salvia reflexa (SAGE); leaves of certain varieties contain toxic levels of nitrates.

Sambucus spp. (ELDERBERRY); entire plant; plant is cyanogenetic; may contain toxic levels of nitrates.

Samonia samon (MONKEY POD, RAIN TREE); gastrointestinal tract affected by saponins; plant also causes dermatitis.

SANDBOX TREE (*Hura crepitans*); seeds; gastrointestinal tract affected by toxalbumins; plant also causes dermatitis.

Sanguinaria canadensis (BLOODROOT, RED PUC-COON); juices from stems and rootstocks cause dermatitis.

Saponaria spp. (BOUNCING BET, COWCOCKLE); seeds; gastrointestinal tract affected by saponins.

Sarcobatus vermiculatus (GREASEWOOD); plant contains soluble oxalates; also causes dermatitis.

SCARLET PIMPERNEL (*Anagallis arvensis*); leaves; plant causes dermatitis.

SCOTCH BROOM (*Cytisus scoparious*); seeds; plant contains quinolizidine alkaloid toxins.

SCOURING RUSH (*Equisetum* spp.); stems; toxic principles unknown; fungi growing on plants may cause toxicity.

SEA ONION (*Urginea maritima*); bulbs; cardiovascular system affected by cardiac glycosides.

Senecio spp. (GROUNDSEL, RAGWORT); entire plant; pyrrolizidine alkaloids cause hepatic veno-occlusive disease (Budd-Chiari syndrome) in humans.

SENNA (*Cassia occidentalis*); entire plant; plant contains cathartic toxins.

SENSITIVE FERN (*Onoclea sensibilis*); leaves; nervous system affected by plant toxins.

Sephora secundiflora (FRIJOLITO, MESCAL BEAN); seeds; nervous system affected by nicotine-like quinolizidine alkaloids.

Sesbania spp. (BAGPOD, COFFEEWEED, RATTLEBOX, RATTLEBUSH); seeds; gastrointestinal tract affected by saponins.

SHEEP LAUREL (*Kalmia augustifolia*); leaves, nectar; gastrointestinal tract, cardiovascular and nervous systems affected by the toxins andromedotoxin and arbutin.

SHEEP SORREL (*Rumex acetosella*); leaves; plant contains soluble oxalates; may contain toxic levels of nitrates; plant also causes dermatitis.

SHOWY LADY SLIPPER (*Cypripedium reginae*); plant causes dermatitis.

SICKLEPOD (*Cassia* sp.); entire plant; gastrointestinal tract affected by toxalbumins.

SILKY LUPINE (*Lupinus* spp.); leaves, esp. seeds; plant contains numerous alkaloid toxins including quinolizidine and piperidine.

Silybum marianum (VARIEGATED THISTLE); plant may contain toxic levels of nitrates.

SINGLETARY PEA (*Lathyrus* spp.); stems, seeds; nervous system affected by the plant toxins.

SKELETONWEED (*Lygodesmia juncea*); plant may contain toxic levels of nitrates.

SKUNK CABBAGE (*Symplocarpus foetidus*); leaves; gastrointestinal tract affected by plant toxins.

SLIPPER FLOWER (*Pedilanthus tithymaloides*); latex; gastrointestinal tract affected by plant toxins; mouth irritated by plant raphides.

SMARTWEEDS (*Polygonum* spp.); plant may contain toxic levels of nitrates; plant causes photosensitization and contact dermatitis.

SMOOTH BROMEGRASS (*Bromus* sp.); plant may contain toxic levels of nitrates.

SNAKE'S HEAD (*Fritillaria meleagris*); bulb; cardiovascular system affected by alkaloid toxins.

SNEEZEWEED (*Helenium* spp.); plant causes dermatitis.

SNOWBERRY (*Symphoricarpos albus*); gastrointestinal tract affected by saponins; plant also causes dermatitis.

SNOWDROP (*Galanthus nivalis*); gastrointestinal tract affected by the alkaloids lycorine and galantamine.

SNOW-ON-THE-MOUNTAIN (*Euphorbia marginata*); latex; gastrointestinal tract affected by the toxin euphorbin; may contain toxic levels of nitrates; plant also causes dermatitis.

Solanum spp. (BITTERSWEET, BUFFALO BUR, BULL NETTLE, HORSE NETTLE, JERUSALEM CHERRY, NIGHTSHADES, POTATO); immature growths; gastrointestinal tract affected by solanine glycoalkaloids; may contain toxic levels of nitrates; plant also causes dermatitis.

Sonchus spp. (SOW THISTLE); plant may contain toxic levels of nitrates.

Sophora secundiflora (FRIJOLITO, MESCAL BEAN); seeds; nervous system affected by nicotine-like, quinolizidine alkaloids.

Sorghum spp. (BROOMCORN, JOHNSON GRASS, SORGHUM, SUDAN GRASS); leaves; plant is cyanogenetic; may contain toxic levels of nitrates.

SORRELS (*Oxalis pes-caprae*, *Rumex* spp.); leaves; plant contains soluble oxalates; plant also causes dermatitis.

SOURGRASS (*Triglochin maritima*); leaves; plant is cyanogenetic.

SOURSOB (*Oxalis pes-caprae*); leaves; plant contains soluble oxalates.

SOW THISTLE (*Sonchus* spp.); plant may contain toxic levels of nitrates.

SOYBEAN (*Glycine max*); may contain toxic levels of nitrates; plant is goitrogenic.

SPATHE FLOWER (*Spathiphyllum* spp.); entire plant; gastrointestinal tract affected by plant toxins; plant also causes dermatitis.

Spathiphyllum spp. (SPATHE FLOWER, WHITE ANTHURIUM); entire plant; gastrointestinal tract affected by plant toxins; plant also causes dermatitis.

Spigelia spp. (WEST INDIAN PINKROOT); entire plant; nervous system affected by the toxin spigeline.

SPINDLE TREE (*Euonymus europaeus*); fruit; cardiovascular system affected by the glycosides evobioside, evomonoside, and evonoside.

SPINELESS HORSEBRUSH (*Tetradymia canescens*); leaves, buds; plant causes photosensitization.

SPREADING DOGBANE (*Apocynum androsaemifolium*); leaves; plant contains cardiac glycosides.

SPRING RABBITBUSH (*Tetradymia glabrata*); leaves, buds; plant is hepatogenic.

SPURGE LAUREL (*Daphne laureola*); entire plant, esp. fruit and seeds; gastrointestinal tract and kidneys affected by coumarin glycosides; plant also causes dermatitis.

SPURGE NETTLE (*Jatropha* spp.); seeds; gastrointestinal tract affected by toxalbumins and cathartic oils; plant also causes dermatitis.

SPURGES (*Euphorbia* spp.); leaves, stems, latex; gastrointestinal tract affected by the toxin euphorbin; may contain toxic levels of nitrates; plant also causes dermatitis.

SQUILL (*Urginea maritima*); bulbs; cardiovascular system affected by cardiac glycosides.

SQUIRREL CORN (*Dicentra cucullaria*); entire plant, esp. bulbs; plant contains convulsants including isoquinoline; plant also causes dermatitis.

STAGGERGRASS (*Amianthemum muscaetoxicum*); leaves, underground parts; alkaloids cause respiratory failure.

STAGGER WEED (*Dicentra cucullaria*); entire plant, esp. bulbs; plant contains convulsants including isoquinoline; plant also causes dermatitis.

Stanleya pinnata (PRINCES'S PLUME); entire plant; plant may absorb toxic levels of selenium.

STAR-OF-BETHLEHEM (*Ornithogalum umbellatum*); entire plant, esp. bulbs; gastrointestinal tract affected by alkaloid toxins.

STEER'S HEAD (*Dicentra uniflora*); entire plant, esp. bulbs; plant contains convulsants including isoquinoline; plant also causes dermatitis.

Stellaria media (CHICKWEED); plant may contain toxic levels of nitrates.

Stillingia treculeana (QUEEN'S DELIGHT); leaves, stems; plant is cyanogenetic.

ST. JOHNSWORT (*Hypericum perforatum;* entire plant causes photosensitization and contact dermatitis.

STRAWBERRY BUSH (*Euonymus americanus*); fruit; cardiovascular system affected by the glycosides evobioside, evomonoside, and evonoside.

STRYCHNINE (*Strychnos nux-vomica*); entire plant; nervous system affected by the alkaloid strychnine.

Strychnos nux-vomica (NUX-VOMICA TREE, STRYCHNINE); entire plant; nervous system affected by the alkaloid strychnine.

Suckleya suckleyana (POISON SUCKLEYA); leaves; plant is cyanogenetic.

SUDAN GRASS (*Sorghum* sp.); leaves; plant is cyanogenetic; may contain toxic levels of nitrates.

SUGAR BEET (*Beta vulgaris*); leaves; plant contains soluble oxalates; may contain toxic levels of nitrates.

SUMMER CYPRESS (*Kochia scoparia*); plant may contain toxic levels of nitrates.

SWEET BELLS (*Leucothoe* spp.); leaves, nectar; cardiovascular and nervous systems affected by plant toxins.

SWEETCLOVERS; WHITE, YELLOW (*Melilotus* spp.); plant may contain toxic levels of nitrates.

SWEET PEA (*Lathyrus* spp.); stems, seeds; nervous system affected by plant toxins.

SWEET POTATO VINES (*Ipomea* spp.); entire plant; plant contains LSD-related hallucinogens; may contain toxic levels of nitrates.

Symphoricarpus albus (SNOWBERRY); gastrointestinal tract affected by saponins; plant also causes dermatitis.

Symplocarpus foetidus (SKUNK CABBAGE); leaves; gastrointestinal tract affected by plant toxins; mouth irritated by plant raphides.

Tamus communis (BLACK BRYONY); toxic principles similar to *Bryonia dioica.*

Tanacetum vulgare (TANSY); leaves, stems; plant toxins may cause gastritis and convulsions; plant also causes dermatitis.

TANSY (*Tanacetum vulgare*); leaves, stems; plant toxins may cause gastritis and convulsions; plant also causes dermatitis.

TARBUSH (*Flourensia cernua*); fruit; gastrointestinal tract affected by plant toxins.

TARO (*Alocasis* sp., *Colocasia esculenta*); leaves, stems; mouth irritated by plant raphides.

TARWEED (*Amsinckia intermedia*); seed-like nutlets; plant may contain toxic levels of nitrates.

Taxus spp. (YEWS); entire plant, except red aril; gastrointestinal tract and cardiovascular system affected by volatile oils, and the alkaloids taxine and ephedrine.

Tetradymia glabrata (COAL-OIL BRUSH, HORSE-BRUSH, SPRING RABBITBUSH); leaves; plant is hepatogenic.

Thevetia peruviana (YELLOW-BE-STILL-TREE, YELLOW OLEANDER); entire plant, esp. seeds; cardiovascular system affected by cardiac glycosides.

Thlaspi arvensi (FANWEED); seeds; gastrointestinal tract affected by mustard-oil.

THORNAPPLE (*Datura stramonium*); entire plant; nervous system affected by the alkaloids atropine, scopolamine, and hyoscyamine; may contain toxic levels of nitrates; plant also causes dermatitis.

THOROUGHWORT (*Eupatorium* sp.); plant may contain toxic levels of nitrates.

TOBACCO, TREE TOBACCO (*Nicotiana* spp.); leaves; nervous system affected by the alkaloids nicotine and pyridine.

TOMATO (*Lycospersicon esculentum*); vines, suckers;

gastrointestinal tract affected by solanine glycoalkaloids.

Toxicodendron spp. (POISON IVY, POISON OAK, POISON SUMAC); leaves, bark and fruit cause dermatitis.

TRAVELLER'S JOY (*Clematis* spp.); entire plant; gastrointestinal tract and nervous system affected by plant toxins; plant also causes dermatitis.

TREFOIL (*Lotus corniculatus*); entire plant; plant is cyanogenetic.

Tribulus spp. (CALTROP, GOATHEAD, PUNCTURE VINE); plant is hepatogenic; may contain toxic levels of nitrates.

TRIFOLIATE ORANGE (*Poncirus trifoliata*); fruit; toxins affect gastrointestinal tract.

Trifolium spp. (CLOVERS); plant causes photosensitization and contact dermatitis; *T. repens* (WHITE CLOVER) is cyanogenetic.

Triglochin maritima (ARROWGRASS, GOOSEGRASS, SOURGRASS); leaves; plant is cyanogenetic.

Triticum aestivum (WHEAT); nontoxic unless contaminated with fungi.

TRUMPET VINE (*Campsis* spp.); leaves, flowers; plant also causes dermatitis.

Tulipa spp. (TULIPS); bulbs; plant causes dermatitis.

TUMBLEWEED (*Amaranthus hibridus*); plant may contain toxic levels of nitrates.

TUNG NUT, TUNG TREE (*Aleurites fordii*); entire plant; gastrointestinal tract affected by saponins and toxalbumins.

Urechites lutea (YELLOW NIGHTSHADE); leaves; cardiovascular system affected by the cardiac glycoside urechitoxin.

Urginea maritima (RED SQUILL, SEA ONION, SQUILL); bulbs; cardiovascular system affected by cardiac glycosides.

Urtica procera (NETTLE); plant may contain toxic levels of nitrates.

VELVET GRASS (*Holcus lanatus*); entire plant; plant is cyanogenetic.

VENUS FLYTRAP (*Dionaea* sp.); entire plant.

Veratrum spp. (FALSE HELLEBORE, INDIAN POKE); entire plant; cardiovascular system affected by alkaloid toxins; plant also causes dermatitis.

Verbesina encelioides (CROWNBEARD); plant may contain toxic levels of nitrates.

VETCH (*Vicia* spp.); seeds, moldy parts; plant causes photosensitization.

VETCHLING (*Lathyrus* spp.); seeds, stems; nervous system affected by plant toxins.

Vicia sativa (COMMON VETCH); seeds, moldy parts; plant is cyanogenetic; plant also causes photosensitization.

Vinca spp. (PERIWINKLE); entire plant; contains hallucinogens.

VIPER'S BUGLOSS (*Echium plantagineum*); entire plant; pyrrolizidine alkaloids cause hepatic veno-occlusive disease (Budd-Chiari syndrome) in humans.

VIRGIN'S-BOWER (*Clematis* sp.); entire plant; gastrointestinal tract and nervous system affected by plant toxins; plant also causes dermatitis.

Viscum album (EUROPEAN MISTLETOE); leaves, stems; gastrointestinal tract affected by toxalbumins.

WAFER ASH (*Ptelea baldwinii*); plant causes photosensitization and contact dermatitis.

WAHOO (*Euonymus atropurpureus*); fruit; cardiovascular system affected by the glycosides evobioside, evomonoside, and evonoside.

WATER DROPWORT (*Oenanthe crocata*); entire plant; plant contains the convulsant oenanthetoxin.

WATER HEMLOCK (*Cicuta* spp.); entire plant, esp. roots; nervous system affected by the convulsant cicutoxin.

WEST INDIAN PINKROOT (*Spigelia* spp.); entire plant; nervous system affected by the toxin spigeline.

WHEAT (*Triticum aestivum*); nontoxic unless contaminated with fungi.

WHITE ANTHURIUM (*Spathiphyllum* spp.); entire plant; gastrointestinal tract affected by plant toxins; plant also causes dermatitis.

WHITE ARUM-LILY (*Zantedeschia aethiopica*); leaves; mouth irritated by plant raphides.

WHITE BRYONY (*Bryonia dioica*); gastrointestinal tract affected by the glycosides bryonin and bryonidin; plant also causes dermatitis.

WHITE CALLA (*Zantedeschia aethiopica*); leaves; mouth irritated by plant raphides.

WHITE CLOVER (*Trifolium repens*); plant is cyanogenetic.

WHITE OZIER (*Leucothoe* spp.); leaves, nectar; cardiovascular and nervous systems affected by plant toxins.

WHITE SNAKEROOT (*Eupatorium* sp.); leaves; plant may contain toxic levels of nitrates.

WHITE SWEETCLOVER (*Melilotus* sp.); plant may contain toxic levels of nitrates.

WHORLED BUTTERFLY (*Asclepias* sp.); leaves, stems; plant contains toxic resins.

WILD ARTICHOKE (*Helianthus annuus*); plant may contain toxic levels of nitrates.

WILD BALSAM-APPLE (*Momordica charantia*); seeds; gastrointestinal tract affected by toxalbumins.

WILD PARSNIP (*Pastinaca sativa*); plant causes dermatitis.

WILD PEA (*Lathyrus* spp.); stems, seeds; nervous system affected by plant toxins.

WILD SUNFLOWER (*Helianthus annuus*); plant may contain toxic levels of nitrates.

WINDFLOWER (*Anemone* spp., includes *Pulsatilla*); entire plant; gastrointestinal tract affected by the toxin protoanemonin; plant also causes dermatitis.

WINTERSWEET (*Acokanthera* spp.); seeds; cardiovascular system affected by cardiac glycosides.

Wisteria spp. (WISTERIA); entire plant; gastrointestinal tract affected by alkaloid toxins.

WITCHGRASS (*Panicum capillare*); plant is hepatogenic; may contain toxic levels of nitrates.

WONDER FLOWER (*Ornithogalum thyrsoides*); entire plant, esp. bulbs; gastrointestinal tract affected by alkaloid toxins.

WOOD LAUREL (*Daphne* sp.); entire plant esp. fruit and seeds; gastrointestinal tract and kidneys affected by coumarin glycosides; plant also causes dermatitis.

WOODY ASTERS (*Xylorrhiza* spp.); entire plant; plant may absorb toxic levels of selenium.

WORMSEED (*Chenopodium ambrosioides*); plant may contain toxic levels of nitrates.

Xanthium orlentale (COCKLEBUR); leaves at sprouted two-leaf stage, germinating seeds; plant contains hydroquinone; plant also causes dermatitis.

Xanthosoma spp. (BLUE TARO, CALADIUM, INDIAN KALE, MALANGA); leaves; mouth irritated by plant raphides; plant also causes dermatitis.

Xylorrhiza spp. (WOODY ASTERS); entire plant; plant may absorb toxic levels of selenium.

YAUPON (*Ilex vomitoria*); berries; gastrointestinal tract affected by saponins.

YELLOW ALLAMANDA (*Allamanda cathartica*); leaves, bark, fruit, sap, seeds; plant contains catharatic toxins.

YELLOW-BE-STILL TREE (*Thevetia peruviana*); entire plant, esp. seeds; cardiovascular system affected by cardiac glycosides.

YELLOW JESSAMINE (*Gelsemium sempervirens*); flowers, leaves, roots; plant contains convulsants, including indole; plant also causes dermatitis.

YELLOW LADY SLIPPER (*Cypripedium parviflorum*); leaves, stems; plant causes dermatitis.

YELLOW NIGHTSHADE (*Urechites lutea*); leaves; cardiovascular system affected by the cardiac glycoside urechitoxin.

YELLOW OLEANDER (*Thevetia peruviana*); entire plant, esp. seeds; cardiovascular system affected by cardiac glycosides.

YELLOW PINE FLAX (*Linum neomexicanum*); entire plant; plant is cyanogenetic.

YELLOW SWEETCLOVER (*Melilotus* sp.); plant may contain toxic levels of nitrates.

YEWS (*Taxus* spp.); entire plant, except red aril; gastrointestinal tract and cardiovascular system affected by volatile oils and the alkaloids taxine, and ephedrine.

Zamia pumila (COONTIE, FALSE SAGO PALM, FLORIDA ARROWROOT); roots, trunk; gastrointestinal tract and nervous system affected by plant toxins.

Zantedeschia aethiopica (CALLA LILY, PIG LILY, WHITE ARUM LILY, WHITE CALLA); leaves; mouth irritated by plant raphides.

Zigadenus spp. (DEATH CAMAS); entire plant; cardiovascular system affected by alkaloid toxins.

1. Kingsbury, 1964; Lampe and McCann, 1985; Muenscher, 1970; Ruhr, 1986; Woodward, 1985.

2. Plants are listed by scientific and common names for the reader's convenience.

Appendix X

Plants Causing Mechanical Injury (1,2)

Anemone patens (ANEMONE).
Aplopappus spp. (GOLDENRODS, JIMMY WEED, RAYLESS).
Arctium lappa (BURDOCK).
Aristida spp. (POVERTY GRASS, TRIPPLE AWN, WIRE GRASS).
Avena fatua (WILD OATS).
BARLEY, WILD BARLEY (*Hordeum* spp.).
Bidens spp. (SPANISH NEEDLES, STICK-TIGHTS).
Bromus tectorum (DOWNY BROME-GRASS).
BURDOCK (*Arctium lappa*).
CACTI (many genera).
CALTROP (*Tribulus* sp.).
Cenchrus spp. (SANDBURS).
Centaurea spp. (KNAPWEED, STARTHISTLE).
COCKLEBURS (*Xanthium* spp.).
CRIMSON CLOVER (*Trifolium* sp.).
DOWNY BROME-GRASS (*Bromus tectorum*).
Eremocarpus setegerus (TURKEY MULLEIN).
Equisetum spp. (FOXTAILS, HORSETAILS, SCOURING RUSH).
FOXTAIL GRASS (*Setaria lutescens*).
FOXTAILS (*Equisetum* spp.).
GOATHEAD (*Tribulus* sp.).
GOLDENRODS (*Aplopappus* spp.).
Hordeum spp. (BARLEY, WILD BARLEY, SQUIRREL-TAIL GRASS).
HORSETAILS (*Equisetum* spp.).
JIMMY WEED (*Aplopappus* sp.).
KNAPWEED (*Centaurea* sp.).
MESQUITE (*Prosopis chilensis*).
MULLEIN (*Verbascum thapsus*).
NEEDLE GRASS (*Stipa* sp.).
NIGHSHADES (*Solanum* spp.).
PEA STRAW HAY (*Pisum sativum*).
Pisum sativum (PEA STRAW HAY).

Platanus occidentalis (SYCAMORE).
PORCUPINE GRASS (*Stipa* sp.).
POVERTY GRASS (*Aristida* sp.).
Prosopis chilensis (MESQUITE).
PUNCTURE VINE (*Tribulus* sp.).
Pyracantha sp. (PYRACANTHA).
RABBIT-FOOT CLOVER (*Trifolium* sp.).
RASPBERRIES (*Rubus* spp.).
RAYLESS (*Aplopappus* sp.).
Rubus spp. (RASBERRIES).
SANDBURS (*Cenchrus* spp.).
SCOURING RUSH (*Equisetum* sp.).
Setaria lutescens (FOXTAIL GRASS, YELLOW BRISTLE GRASS).
SPANISH NEEDLES (*Bidens* sp.).
SQUIRREL-TAIL GRASS (*Hordeum* spp.).
STARTHISTLE (*Centaurea* spp.).
STICK-TIGHTS (*Bidens* sp.).
Stipa spp. (NEEDLE GRASS, PORCUPINE GRASS).
SYCAMORE (*Platanus occidentalis*).
Tribulus spp. (CALTROP, GOATHEAD, PUNCTURE VINE).
Trifolium spp. (CRIMSON CLOVER, RABBIT-FOOT CLOVER).
TRIPLE AWN (*Aristida* sp.).
TURKEY MULLEIN (*Eremocarpus setegerus*).
Verbascum thapsus (MULLEIN).
WILD OATS (*Avena fatua*).
WIRE GRASS (*Aristida* sp.).
Xanthium spp. (COCKLEBURS).
YELLOW BRISTLE GRASS (*Setaria lutescens*).

1. Kingsbury, 1964; Muenscher, 1970; Ruhr, 1986.
2. Plants are listed by scientific and common names for the reader's convenience.

Appendix XI

Therapeutics Used to Treat Nutritional Deficiencies*

Deficiency	Therapeutic	Dosage	Reference	Administration	Comments
Vitamin A	Aquasol-A®	10–10,000 I.U.	Frye, 1991a	Not established	Dosage depends on body weight and severity of the problem; frequency of administration not established.
		100 I.U./300 g body wt.	K. Fowler (pers. comm.)	IM	Administer 1 to 2 times first week; repeat in 1 week if necessary.
Vitamin B-1 (Thiamine)	Vitamin B-1 (Thiamine)	33 mg/Kg of thiaminase-containing fish consumed.	Jackson and Cooper, 1981	In Food	Place inside fish's body before feeding to reptile.
		1.5 mg/Kg body wt.	Frye, 1981a	IM	Daily, for 2 weeks.
	Thiamin HCl Tablets	25 mg/Kg body wt.	Frye, 1991a	In Food	Daily, until problem is corrected. Place inside fish's body before feeding to reptile.
Vitamin C	Vitamin C (Sodium Ascorbate)	30 mg/Kg body wt.	B. W. Richie (pers. comm.)	SC	Buffer in saline. Administer daily or as needed.
Vitamin E (Steatitis)	Vitamin E	50 I.U./Kg body wt.	K. Fowler (pers. comm.)	IM	Daily, until problem is corrected; use slightly higher dose if problem is severe.
Vitamin K	Vitamin K-1	0.25–0.50 mg/Kg body wt.	K. Fowler (pers. comm.)	IM	Single dose; frequency of administration not established (Frye, 1991a).
Calcium	Calcium Gluconate	500 mg/Kg body wt.	Frye, 1991a	IV, IM	Divided doses; intravenous administration may produce cardiac irregularities due to rapid uptake.
Cobalt (Anemia)	Vitamin B-12 (Cyanocobalamin)	10–2,000 I.U. depending on body wt.	Frye, 1991a	IM, SC	Single dose; frequency of administration not established.
Iodine (Hypothyroidism)	Sodium-iodide	0.25–3 ml as required.	Frye and Dutra, 1974	On Food	To reduce bitter taste, administer on day-old bread several times weekly until problem is corrected.
	Kelp Tablets	1–2 mg	Frye, 1991a,b	On Food	Powder and sprinkle on food. Administer daily for 2–3 weeks, followed by 1 time per week as a maintenance dose.
	Iodized Salt	0.5% of total wt. of diet.	Wallach, 1969	On Food	With each meal.

*For availability, see Appendix XIII.

Appendix XII

Miscellaneous Therapeutics Used In Reptiles*

Therapeutic (1)	Trade Name	Dosage	Administration (2)	Comments
ANTIBIOTICS				
Acylovir	Zovirax®		Topical	s.i.d., b.i.d.
		80 mg/Kg	Oral	s.i.d.
Amikacin	Amikin®	2.5 mg/Kg	Injectable	LIZARDS/SNAKES: IM, s.i.d. every 72 hrs.
		2.25 mg/Kg		CROCODILIANS: IM, s.i.d. every 96 hrs. Potentially nephrotoxic; fluid therapy recommended.
Amoxicillin	Amoxi-Drop®	22 mg/Kg	Oral	s.i.d., b.i.d.
Ampicillin trihydrate	Polyflex®	3–6 mg/Kg	Oral	s.i.d.
			Injectable	IM, SC; b.i.d.
Bacitracin, Neomycin sulfate, Polymixin B sulfate	Triple Antibiotic Ointment		Topical	As needed.
Benzathine penicillin	Flocillin®	1,000 units total penicillin activity/ Kg of body wt.	Injectable	IM; s.i.d. every 48–96 hrs; varies with temperature.
Cefotaxime	Claforan®	20–40 mg/Kg	Injectable	IM; s.i.d.
Cephaloridine	Loridine®	10 mg/Kg	Injectable	IM, SC; b.i.d.; potentially nephrotoxic; fluid therapy recommended.
Chloramphenicol	Chloromycetin®	10–15 mg/Kg	Injectable	IM, IV; b.i.d., or s.i.d. if multiple dose is stressful; potentially nephrotoxic; fluid therapy recommended.
	Chloromycetin® palmitate suspension	100 mg/Kg	Oral	Daily; may fail to produce therapeutic plasma levels.
Dihydrostreptomycin sulfate		5 mg/Kg	Injectable	IM; s.i.d., b.i.d.; potentially nephrotoxic; fluid therapy recommended.
Enrofloxacin	Baytril®	2.5–5.0 mg/Kg	Oral or Injectable	b.i.d.
Furazolidone	Furox®		Topical	As needed.
	Furoxone®	24–40 mg/Kg	Oral	s.i.d.; effective against *Salmonella* spp.
Gentamicin sulfate	Gentocin®	2.5 mg/Kg	Injectable	LIZARDS/SNAKES (except blood pythons): IM, SC; s.i.d. every 72 hrs.;
		2.5 mg/Kg		BLOOD PYTHONS: IM, SC; s.i.d. loading dose, then reduce dosage to . . .
		1.0 mg/Kg		. . . s.i.d. every 96 hrs.
		10 mg/Kg		CHELONIANS: IM; s.i.d. every 48 hrs.
		1.75 mg/Kg		CROCODILIANS: IM; s.i.d. every 96 hrs. Potentially nephrotoxic; fluid therapy recommended. Maintain reptiles at selected body temperatures; (see Table 1, Chapter 3).
	Gentocin®-Durafilm®	1–2 drops each eye	Opthalmic	2–4 times daily; contains a corticosteroid.
	Gentafair®	1–2 drops each eye	Opthalmic	2–4 times daily.
Hydrogen peroxide			Soak	As necessary for the removal of adhered sheds.
Kanamycin sulfate	Kantrim®	10–15 mg/Kg	Injectable	IV, s.i.d.; IM, b.i.d.; b.i.d. as a wound-flushing agent; potentially nephrotoxic, fluid therapy recommended.
Lincomycin HCl	Lincocin®	6 mg/Kg	Injectable	IM; s.i.d., b.i.d.; potentially nephrotoxic; fluid therapy recommended.

Therapeutic (1)	Trade Name	Dosage	Administration (2)	Comments
Mafenide acetate cream (8.5%)	Sulfamylon® Cream		Topical	As needed; excellent as a burn dressing.
Nitrofurazone	Furacin® Cream		Topical	As needed.
Nystatin-Neomycin sulfate-Thiostrepton-Triamcinolone-acetonide	Panalog® ointment		Topical	As needed.
Oxytetracycline	Liquamycin®	6–10 mg/Kg	Injectable	IV, IM; s.i.d.; may cause inflammation at injection site.
		6–12 mg/Kg	Oral	Higher doses may be required for *Salmonella* spp. infections. Suggested use with tetramisole in the treatment of *Rhabdias* spp. infections (also see Parasiticides below).
Piperacillin	Pipracil®	50–100 mg/Kg	Injectable	IM; s.i.d.; fluid therapy recommended.
Polymyxin B-Bacitracin	Polysporin® ointment		Topical	As needed.
Povidone iodine	Betadine®		Topical	As needed; for use in the treatment of open wounds.
Streptomycin sulfate	Many names	10 mg/Kg	Injectable	IM; s.i.d., b.i.d.; potentially nephrotoxic; fluid therapy recommended.
Sulfadimethoxine	Albon® Bactrovet®	90 mg/Kg 45 mg/Kg	Oral or Injectable	Day 1; IV, IM, O; s.i.d. Days 2–6; IV, IM, O; s.i.d.
Tetracycline	Many names	25–50 mg/Kg	Injectable	IM, SC; s.i.d.
Ticarcillin	Ticar®	50–100 mg/Kg	Injectable	IM; s.i.d.; fluid therapy recommended.
Tobramycin	Nebcin®	3–7.5 mg/Kg 10 mg/Kg	Injectable	AQUATIC/SEMIAQUATIC TURTLES . . . TERRESTRIAL TURTLES . . . Administer IM, s.i.d. every 48 hrs.; potentially nephrotoxic; fluid therapy recommended.
Trimethoprim-sulfadiazine	Ditrim® Tribrissen® (24% Suspension)	15–30 mg/Kg	Injectable	IM; s.i.d.; fluid therapy recommended.
Trimethoprim-sulfamethoxazole	Bactrim™	15–30 mg/Kg	Oral	s.i.d.; fluid therapy recommended.
Tylosin	Tylan®	25–75 mg/Kg	Injectable	IM, SC; s.i.d.
ANALGESICS				
Flunixin meglumine	Banamine®	0.1–0.5 mg/Kg	Injectable	IV; s.i.d., b.i.d. for 1–2 days; for the alliviation of inflammation and pain associated with musculoskeletal disorders.
ANTIFUNGAL PREPARATIONS				
Tolnaftate cream	Tinavet®		Topical	As needed; continue use for 2 weeks after disappearance of symptoms.
Miconazole nitrate cream (2%)	Monistat®-Derm		Topical	As needed.
ANTIHISTAMINES				
Tripelennamine hydrochloride	Re-Covr®	1.1 mg/Kg (0.25 ml/4.5 Kg)	Injectable	IM; s.i.d. as needed.
CORTICOSTEROIDS				Use should be avoided; there may be the possibility of immunosuppressive effects even from a single dose.
FLUIDS & ELECTROLYTES				
Electrolyte powder	8X		Topical	As needed; for use in reducing swelling of cloacal prolapses.
Dextrose (glucose)		3.3 g/Kg	Injectable	SC; s.i.d. every 48–72 hours until symptoms reverse. For treatment of hypoglycemia shock in crocodilians. Dilute with lactated Ringer's solution; do not administer at a concentration greater than 5%.
Dextrose (glucose) saline		2–4% of body wt.	Injectable	SC, IP; as needed.
Lactated Ringer's solution		15–30 ml/Kg	Injectable	SC, IP; as needed; for use with diuretics and nephrotoxic drugs and in the treatment of dehydration.

Therapeutic (1)	Trade Name	Dosage	Administration (2)	Comments
DIURETICS Furosemide	Lasix®	5 mg/Kg	Injectable	IM, IV; as needed; fluid therapy recommended.
PROTEOLYTIC ENZYMES	Dermaaid™		Topical	As needed; for use in the treatment of necrotic wounds.
	Granulex®		Topical	As needed; for use in the treatment of necrotic wounds.
PARASITICIDES (3,4) Dichlorvos	Task®	12.5 mg/Kg	Oral	Daily, for 2 days; repeat in 1 wk. if necessary. Effective against ascarids, hookworms, whipworms, and pinworms. Avoid excessive heat in cages. Remove all dichlorvos pest strips 24 hours before dosing.
	Pest strips	0.6 cm length per 0.28 cm of cage space	Aerosol	Hang in cage for 5 days; remove for 5 days. Repeat this cycle 2–3 more times.
Diethyl-carbamazine	Nemacide®-C	6 mg/Kg	Oral	Daily, for 1–2 months; dose is recommended for microfilariae.
		50–100 mg/Kg		Single dose, effective against ascarids, repeat in 2–3 weeks.
Di-phenthane-7-methylbenzene	Vermiplex®	70% of recommended mammalian dose	Oral	Effective against ascarids, hookworms, and as an aid in the removal of tapeworms. Higher dose may produce convulsions, possibly resulting in the death of snakes. Avoid breaking capsule in reptile's mouth; drug is caustic.
Emetine HCl		0.5 mg/Kg	Injectable	IM, SC; s.i.d., b.i.d. for 10 days; effective against some amebae and trematodes.
Fenbendazole	Panacur®	50 mg/Kg 100 mg/Kg	Oral	Single dose by stomach tube; repeat in 2 wks. Single dose mixed with food; repeat in 2 wks. Effective against ascarids, hookworms, and pinworms. Ovicidal; may reduce risk of reinfection during treatment period.
Ivermectin	Ivomec®	0.2 mg/Kg	Injectable	Single dose SC; paste available for oral administration. Effective against a wide variety of nematodes and some ectoparasites. DO NOT USE IN CHELONIANS; contraindicated in animals that have been given diazepam or that will be given diazepam within 10 days after being dosed with this anthelmintic (Frye, 1991a).
Levamisole HCl	Tramisol®	5–10 mg/Kg	Injectable	Single dose IP; repeat in 2–3 wks. Effective against ascarids, hookworms, and possibly lungworms.
Levamisole phosphate	Ripercol®	8–10 mg/Kg	Injectable	Single dose IP, SC; repeat in 2–3 wks. Effective against ascarids, hookworms, and possibly lungworms.
Mebendazole	Telmin®	20–25 mg/Kg	Oral	Single dose; repeat in 2 wks. Effective against ascarids, hookworms, whipworms, and pinworms.
Metronidazole (5)	Flagyl®	125–250 mg/Kg	Oral	Daily, for 3 days at 125 mg/Kg; do not exceed 400 mg total daily use.
		275 mg/Kg		A single dose may be substituted in cases where stress is to be reduced or when administering to venomous reptiles; repeat in 7–10 days.
		40–100 mg/Kg		Single dose; repeat in 2 wks. For the treatment of amebiasis and intestinal flagellate infections.
Niclosamide	Niclocide®	150 mg/Kg (132–200 mg/Kg)	Oral	Single dose; repeat in 3–4 wks. Effective against tapeworms.
Paromomycin		33–55 mg/kg 25–100 mg/Kg	Oral	Single dose; repeat in 1 wk. Single dose.
Praziquantel	Droncit®	7.5 mg/Kg (5–8 mg/Kg)	Oral or Injectable	Single dose; O, SC; repeat in 2–3 wks if necessary. Effective against tapeworms and some flukes. Safe in young chelonians; not necessary to halve dose (E. Jacobson, pers. comm.).

Therapeutic (1)	Trade Name	Dosage	Administration (2)	Comments
Pyrantel pamoate	Strongid-T® Nemex®	25 mg/Kg	Oral	Daily, for 2–4 doses. Effective against ascarids, hookworms, and pinworms.
Sulfamethazine	Many	1 oz/gal 75 mg/Kg 40 mg/Kg 90 mg/Kg 45 mg/Kg	Oral Injectable	*Ad libitum* in drinking water for 10 days. Day 1; IV, IM; b.i.d., Day 2–6; s.i.d. Day 1; s.i.d., Day 2–5; s.i.d. Effective against coccidia; fluid therapy recommended.
Sulfadimethoxine	Albon® Bactrovet®	90 mg/Kg 45 mg/Kg	Oral	Day 1; b.i.d. Days 2–6; b.i.d. Effective against coccidia. Fluid therapy recommended. An injectable form is also available for IM & IV administrations.
Thiabendazole	Equizole® Thibenzole® Mintezol®	50–100 mg/Kg	Oral	Single dose; repeat in 2 wks.; redose as needed. Effective against ascarids, hookworms, pinworms, *Strongyloides* spp., and possibly capillarids. Hydroscopic; administer with adequate water.
Trichlorphon	Neguvon®	0.1–0.2% sol. at 0.5 liter per cu. meter of cage space	Topical	Spray in cage and on reptile.

MISCELLANEOUS

Therapeutic (1)	Trade Name	Dosage	Administration (2)	Comments
Activated charcoal		5 heaping tsp. per 200 ml water	Oral	Via stomach tube as needed. For use in the treatment of plant and chemical poisoning.
Atropine sulfate		0.04 mg/Kg	Oral or Injectable	IM, IV, SC, O; for use in the treatment of plant and chemical poisoning.
Calcium gluconate		500 mg/Kg	Injectable	IM; intravenous administration may produce cardiac irregularities due to rapid uptake; for use in the treatment of plant and chemical poisoning. Administer at room temperature, in several sights, and rub bolus into muscle.
	Kaopectate®	Scale to body wt. of animal	Oral	Usually a single dose; repeat if necessary; for the treatment of diarrhea.
Malachite green			Topical	As needed; for use in the treatment of ulcerative shell disease.
Potassium permanganate			Topical	As needed; for use in the treatment of ulcerative shell disease.
Sodium biphosphate			In aquatic environment	Amount necessary to maintain water at pH 6.0; for use in the treatment of septicemic cutaneous ulcerative disease.

*Barnard, 1985b, pers. obs.; Bernstein, 1972; Bush, 1974; Bush et al., 1980; Deakins, 1973; Donaldson et al., 1975; Fletcher, 1979; Frye, 1973; 1981a, 1991a; Funk, 1988; Glenn et al., 1973; Holt, 1981; Jackson, 1974; Jacobson, 1976, pers. comm.; Marcus, 1981; Mirtschin and Ormerod, 1990; Murphy, 1973; Norton and Jacobson, 1989; Ross (pers. comm.); Ross and Marzec, 1984; Schweinfurth, 1970; Soifer, 1978; Wallach, 1969; Weber, 1973; Zwart, 1977; Zwart and Jansen, 1969.

1) For availability, see Appendix XIII.

2) Injections should not be given in tails or hind limbs to prevent metabolism of drugs by portal-renal system (Walshaw, 1983).

3) Dosages given should be halved for turtles.

4) Because reptiles drink water only intermittently, drugs used orally to treat them are more effective if administered via stomach tube rather than in the drinking water.

5) Also see Frye (1991a) for treatment with Flaganase 400.

Appendix XIII

Products Mentioned in Text

Product	Manufacturer/Available*
Activated charcoal (Toxiban®)	Vet-A-Mix, Inc. 604 W. Thomas Avenue Shenandoah, IA 51601
Acylovir (Zovirax®)	Burroughs Wellcome Co. 3030 Cornwallis Road Research Triangle Park, NC 27709
Amikacin (Amikin®)	Apthecon, Bristol-Myers Squibb Co. P.O. Box 4500 Princeton, NJ 08543-4500
Amoxicillin (Amoxi-Drop®)	SmithKline Beecham Animal Health 812 Springdale Drive Exton, PA 19341
Ampicillin trihydrate (Polyflex®)	Fort Dodge Laboratories, Inc. 800 Fifth St., NW Fort Dodge, IA 50501
Aquasol-A® (Vitamin A)	Astra USA, Inc. 50 Otis Street Westboro, MA 01581-4500
Atropine sulfate	Several pharmaceutical supply houses including Med-Tech, Inc. P.O. Box 338 Elwood, KS 66024
Benzathine penicillin (Flocillin®)	Fort Dodge Laboratories, Inc. 800 Fifth St., NW Fort Dodge, IA 50501
Bone meal	Several suppliers including United Pharmacal Co., Inc. 3705 Pear St., Box 969 St. Joseph, MO 64502
Calcium gluconate	Several pharmaceutical supply houses including Durvet, Inc. P.O. Box 279 24010 Highway 40 Eastbound Blue Springs, MO 64015
Catheter (feeding)	Several suppliers including veterinary clinics.
Cefotaxime (Claforan®)	Hoecht-Roussel Pharmaceuticals Inc. Route 202-206, P.O. Box 2500 Somerville, NJ 00876-1258
Cephaloridine (Loridine®)	Elanco Products Company Lilly Corporation Center Indianapolis, IN 46285
Cheesecloth	See suppliers of chemicals and general labware listed below; also may be available in supermarkets.
Chick starter	Feed and seed stores.
Chloramphenicol (Chlormycetin®)	Park-Davis Division of Warner-Lambert Co. 201 Tabor Rd. Morris Plains, NJ 07950
Colortone® 25-W lightbulb	Several suppliers including supermarkets.
Cork bark	Several suppliers including Hogtown Herpetological Supply, Inc. 1801 N.E. 23rd Avenue Gainesville, FL 32609

Product	Manufacturer/Available*
Crickets	Several suppliers including Fluker Farms, Inc. P.O. Box 378 Baton Rouge, LA 70821
Dermaaid™	PanAmerican™ Pharmaceuticals, Inc. Grand Rapids, MI 49508
Dextrose (glucose) (injectable)	Sanofi Animal Health, Inc. 7101 College Boulevard Overland Park, KS 66210
Dextrose (glucose) saline	Sanofi Animal Health, Inc. 7101 College Boulevard Overland Park, KS 66210
Dichlorvos (Task)	Fermenta Animal Health 10150 North Executive Hills Blvd. Kansas City, MO 64153
Dichlorvos (pest strip)	ACE Hardware Stores
Diethylcarbamazine (Nemacide®-C)	Fermenta Animal Health 10150 North Executive Hills Blvd. Kansas City, MO 64153
Dihydrostreptomycin sulfate	Several pharmaceutical supply houses including The Upjohn Company Animal Health Division 7000 Portage Road Kalamazoo, MI 49001
Di-phenthane-7-methylbenzene (Vermiplex®)	Pitman-Moore, Inc. 421 E. Hawley Street Mundelein, IL 60060
Electrolyte powder (8X)	Phoenix Pharmaceuticals, Inc. 4621 Easton Road P.O. Box 6457-Fairleigh Station St. Joseph, MO 64506-0457
Emetine HCl	Eli Lilly and Company Lilly Research Laboratories Lilly Corporation Center Indianapolis, IN 46285
Enrofloxacin (Baytril®)	Miles Agriculture Division Animal Health Products 12707 W. 63rd Street Shawnee Mission, KS 66216-1846
Fenbendazole (Panacur®)	Hoechst-Roussel Agri-Vet Co. Somerville, NJ 08876
Flunixin meglumine (Banamine®)	Schering-Plough Animal Health 1095 Morris Avenue Union, NJ 07083-1982
Forceps (10-in., tissue)	See suppliers of chemicals and general labware listed below.
Formaldehyde (37% solution)	See suppliers of chemicals and general labware listed below.
Frog Brittle®	Nasco; see suppliers listed below for address.
Furazolidone (Furoxone®)	Roberts Pharmaceutical Corporation Meridian Center III 6 Industrial Way West Eatontown, NJ 07724
Furazolidone (Furox® Aerosol Powder)	Solvay Animal Health, Inc. 1201 Northland Drive Mendota Heights, MN 55120-1149
Furosemide (Lasix®)	Hoechst-Roussel Agri-Vet Co. Somerville, NJ 08876
Gentafair® (Gentamicin opthalmic)	Pharmafair, Inc. Hauppauge, NY 11788
Gentamicin sulfate (Gentocin®)	Schering-Plough Animal Health 1095 Morris Avenue Union, NJ 07083-1982
Gentocin®-Durafilm®	Schering-Plough Animal Health 1095 Morris Avenue Union, NJ 07083-1982
Glycerine	See suppliers of chemicals and general labware listed below; also available at pharmacies.
Granulex®	Dow B. Hickam, Inc. P.O. Box 2006 Sugar Land, TX 77487-2006
Hay (e.g., alfalfa, timothy)	Feed and seed stores.

Product	Manufacturer/Available*
Humidifier (fine mist)	Durocraft Corporation 490 Boston Post Road Sudbury, MA 01776-9102; also available at discount merchandise stores.
Hydrogen peroxide	Grocery markets and pharmacies; also see suppliers of chemicals and general labware listed below.
Incubator (poultry chick)	Several suppliers including Alabama Poultry Supply Co., Inc. 1403 3rd Avenue, SE Culman, AL 35056
Infrared bulb	Several suppliers including hardware stores.
Ivermectin (Ivomec®)	Merck AgVet Division of Merck & Company, Inc. P.O. Box 2000 Rahway, NJ 07065
Kanamycin sulfate (Kantrim®)	Fort Dodge Laboratories, Inc. 800 Fifth St., NW Fort Dodge, IA 50501
Kaopectate®	Pharmacies.
Kelp tablets	Health Food Stores.
K.Y.® Jelly (Johnson & Johnson)	Pharmacies.
Lactated Ringer's solution	Several pharmaceutical supply houses including Durvet, Inc. P.O. Box 279 24010 Highway 40 Eastbound Blue Springs, MO 64015
Levamisole HCl (Tramisol®)	American Cyanamid Co. One Cyanamid Plaza Wayne, NJ 07470
Levamisole phosphate (Ripercol®)	American Cyanamid Co. One Cyanamid Plaza Wayne, NJ 07470
Lincomycin HCl (Lincocin®)	The Upjohn Company Animal Health Division 7000 Portage Road Kalamazoo, MI 49001
Mafenide acetate (Sulfamylon® cream)	Dow B. Hickam, Inc. P.O. Box 2006 Sugar Land, TX 77487-2006
Malachite green	Kordon Hayward, CA 94545; also available at many pet stores.
Mealworms	Several suppliers including Georgia Mealies P.O. Box 1854 Tifton, GA 31793-1854
Mebendazole (Telmin®)	Pitman-Moore, Inc. 421 E. Hawley Street Mundelein, IL 60060
Mesh (polyethylene plastic)	Several suppliers including InterNet Incorporated 2730 Nevada Avenue, No. Minneapolis, MN 55427
Metronidazole (Flagyl®)	G.D. Searle and Co. Box 5110 Chicago, IL 60680
Miconazole nitrate cream (2%) (Monistat®-Derm	Ortho Pharmaceutical Corporation Dermatological Division Route 202, P.O. Box 300 Raritan, NJ 08869-0602
Needle (teasing)	See suppliers of chemical and general labware listed below.
Niclosamide (Niclocide®)	Miles Inc., Pharmaceutical Division 400 Morgan Lane West Haven, CT 06516
Nitrofurazone (Furacin® cream)	Roberts Pharmaceutical Corporation Meridian Center III 6 Industrial Way West Eatontown, NJ 07724
Nutrical®	Evsco Pharmaceutical Corporation P.O. Box 209, Harding Highway Buena, NJ 08310
Oat bran	Supermarkets.

Product	Manufacturer/Available*
Oxytetracycline (Liquamycin®)	Pfizer, Inc. North American Animal Health Division 1107 S. State Rt. 291 Lee's Summit, MO 64081-2998
Panalog® cream & ointment (Nystatin-Neomycin sulfate-Thiostrepton-Triamcinolone-acetonide)	Solvay Animal Health, Inc. 1201 Northland Drive Mendota Heights, MN 55120-1149
Paromomycin®	Park-Davis Division of Warner-Lambert Co. 201 Tabor Rd. Morris Plains, NJ 07950
Peat moss	Plant nurseries.
Petri dishes	See suppliers of chemicals and general labware listed below.
Piperacillan (Pipracil®)	Lederle Laboratories Division of American Cyanamid Co. One Cyanamid Plaza Wayne, NJ 07470
Polymyxin B-Bacitracin (Polysporin® ointment)	Burroughs Wellcome Co. 3030 Cornwallis Road Research Triangle Park, NC 27709
Poly-Vi-Sol®	Supermarkets.
Potassium permanganate	Spectrum Chemical Mfg. Corp.; see suppliers listed below for address.
Poultry water dispenser	Feed and seed stores.
Povidone iodine solution (Betadine®)	The Purdue Frederick Company 100 Connecticut Avenue Norwalk, CT 06850-3590
Praziquantel (Droncit®)	Miles Agricultural Division Animal Health Products 12707 W. 63rd Street Shawnee Mission, KS 66216-1846
Pyrantel pamoate (Nemex®)	Pfizer, Inc. North American Animal Health Division 1107 S. State Rt. 291 Lee's Summit, MO 64081-2998
Pyrantel pamoate (Strongid-T®)	Pfizer, Inc. North American Animal Health Division 1107 S. State Rt. 291 Lee's Summit, MO 64081-2998
Roccal®-D	Winthrop Veterinary Sterling Animal Health Products Division of Sterling Drug, Inc. 90 Park Ave. New York, NY 10016
Saline (physiological)	See suppliers of chemicals and general labware listed below
Salt (iodized)	Grocery markets.
Scalpel	See suppliers of chemical and general labware listed below.
Scissors (dissecting)	See suppliers of chemical and general labware listed below.
Snake hook	Fuhrman Diversified, Inc. 905 South 8th Street La Porte, TX 77571
Sodium biphosphate	Roxane Laboratories, Inc. 1809 Wilson Road Columbus, OH 43228
Sodium iodide	Several pharmaceutical supply houses including Pro Labs, LTD. 6221 N. K Highway St. Joseph, MO 64505
Spatula (rubber)	Supermarkets.
Sphagnum moss	Plant nurseries.
Stock tanks (cattle)	Several suppliers including feed and seed stores.
Straight pins	Several suppliers including fabric/sewing supply stores.
Streptomycin sulfate	Several pharmaceutical supply houses including Pitman-Moore, Inc. 421 E. Hawley Street Mundelein, IL 60060
Sulfadimethoxine (Albon®)	Roche Chemical Division of Hoffman-LaRoche, Inc. Nutley, NJ 07110
Sulfadimethoxine (Bactrovet®)	Pitman-Moore, Inc. 421 E. Hawley Street Mundelein, IL 60060
Sulfamethazine	Several pharmaceutical supply houses including American Cyanamid Co. One Cyanamid Plaza Wayne, NJ 07470

Product	Manufacturer/Available*
Surgical masks	Several suppliers including veterinary clinics.
Tetracycline	Several pharmaceutical supply houses including Med-Tech, Inc. P.O. Box 338 Elwood, KS 66024
Thiabendazole (Equizole®)	Merck Ag Vet Division of Merck & Company, Inc. P.O. Box 2000 Rahway, NJ 07065
Thiabendazole (Mintezol®)	Sharp and Dohme Divsion of Merck and Company, Inc. West Point, PA 19486
Thiabendazole (Thibenzole®)	Merck AgVet Division of Merck & Company, Inc. P.O. Box 2000 Rahway, NJ 07065
Thiamin HCl Injection	Several pharmaceutical supply general including Elkins-Sinn, Inc. 2 Esterbrook Lane Cherry Hill, NJ 08003-4099
Thiamin HCl Tablets	Several pharmaceutical supply houses including Kenwood Laboratories, Division of Bradley Pharmaceuticals, Inc. 383 Route 46 West Fairfield, NJ 07004-2402
Ticarcillin (Ticar®)	SmithKline Beecham Animal Health 812 Springdale Drive Exton, PA 19341
Tobramycin (Nebcin®)	Eli Lilly and Company Lilly Research Laboratories Lilly Corporation Center Indianapolis, IN 46285
Tolnaftate cream (Tinavet®)	Schering-Plough Animal Health 1095 Morris Avenue P.O. Box 3182 Union, NJ 07083-1982
Trichlorphon (Neguvon®)	Miles Agriculture Division Animal Health Products 12707 W. 63rd Street Shawnee Mission, KS 66216-1846
Trimethoprim-sulfadiazine (DiTrim®)	Diamond Laboratories, Inc. 2538 SE 43rd St. Des Moines, IA 50317
Trimethoprim-sulfadiazine (Tribrissen®)	Jensen-Salsbery Laboratories Division of Burroughs Wellcome Co. P.O. Box 167 Kansas City, MO 64141
Trimethoprim-sulfamethoxazole (Bactrim™)	Roche Chemical Division Hoffmann-LaRoche, Inc. 340 Kingsland St. Nutley, NJ 07110
Tripelennamine (Re-Covr®)	Solvay Animal Health Inc. 1201 Northland Drive Mendota Heights, MN 55120-1149
Triple Antibiotic Ointment (Bacitracin, Neomycin sulfate, Polymixin B sulfate)	Several pharmaceutical supply houses including Legere Pharmaceuticals 7326 E. Evans Road Scottsdale, AZ 85260
Tubes (transparent, plastic)	See suppliers of chemicals and general labware listed below.
Tylosin (Tylan®)	Elanco Products Company Lilly Corporation Center Indianapolis, IN 46285
Utility lamps (clamp-on)	Several suppliers including supermarkets and hardware stores.
Vionate®	United Pharmacal Co., Inc. 3705 Pear Street, Box 969 St. Joseph, MO 64502
Vitamin B-1 (Thiamine)	Several pharmaceutical supply houses including Sanofi Animal Health, Inc. 7101 College Boulevard Overland Park, KS 66210
Vitamin B-12	Several pharmaceutical supply houses including Sanofi Animal Health, Inc. 7101 College Boulevard Overland Park, KS 66210

Reptile Keeper's Handbook

Product	Manufacturer/Available*
Vitamin C (Sodium Ascorbate)	Several pharmaceutical supply houses including Med-Tech, Inc. P.O. Box 338 Elwood, KS 66024
Vitamin E	Several pharmaceutical supply houses including Med-Tech, Inc. P.O. Box 338 Elwood, KS 66024
Vitamin K-1 (Konakion®)	Phoenix Pharmaceuticals, Inc. 4621 Easton Road P.O. Box 6457-Fairleigh Station St. Joseph, MO 64506-0457
Wax Moth larvae	Several suppliers including Nasco; see suppliers listed below for address.
Wheat bran	Supermarkets.

The mention of the products listed in the text and their availability, does not imply endorsement by the author. Products and distributors are listed to assist the reader. The list is not meant to be exhaustive; numerous other suppliers exist with equally good products.

Suppliers

Aldrich, 1001 West Saint Paul Ave., Milwaukee, WI 53233

Baxter Scientific, 1430 Waukegan Rd., McGraw Park, IL 60085

BioQuip Products, 17803 LaSalle Ave., Gardena, CA 90248

Carolina Biological Supply Co., 2700 York Rd., Burlington, NC 27215

Cole-Parmer Co., 7425 North Oak Park Ave., Chicago, IL 60648

Edmund Scientific, 101 E. Gloucester Pike, Barrington, NJ 08007

EMD Labs, 4901 W. LeMoyne St., Chicago, IL 60651

Fisher Scientific, 711 Forbes Ave., Pittsburgh, PA 15219

Frey Scientific, 905 Hickory Lane, P.O. Box 8101, Mansfield, OH 44901

Hardwood Products Co., Guilford, ME 04443

J.T. Baker, Inc., Phillipsburg, NJ 08865

Markson Sciences, 10201 S. 51st St., Phoenix, AZ 85044

Medical Supply Corporation of New Jersey, Inc., 1900 Adams Ave., Toms River, NJ 08753

Midwest Scientific, 228 Meramec Station Rd., P.O. Box 458, Valley Park, MO 63088

Nasco, 901 Janesville Ave., Fort Atkinson, WI 53538

Nebraska Scientific, 3823 Leavenworth St., Omaha, NE 68105

PGC Scientifics, P.O. Box 7277, Gaithersburg, MD 20898

Research Products International, 410 N. Business Center Dr., Mt. Prospect, IL 60056

Sargent-Welch, 7400 North Linder Ave., P.O. Box 1026, Skokie, IL 60077

Sigma Chemical Co., P.O. Box 14508, St. Louis, MO 63178

Southern Biological Supply, P.O. Box 368, McKenzie, TN 38201

Spectrum Chemical Mfg. Corp., 14422 South San Pedro St., Gardena, CA 90248

Thomas Scientific, Vine Street at Third, P.O. Box 779, Philadelphia, PA 19105

VWR Scientific, P.O. Box 1002, 600C Corporate Court, So. Plainfield, NJ 07080

Wards Natural Science, 5100 West Henrietta Rd., P.O. Box 92912, Rochester, NY 14692

Appendix XIV

Measurement Conversion Factors

When you know—	Multiply by—	To find—
Volume		
Milliliters (ml)	0.03	fluid ounces (fl oz)
Liters (L)	2.1	pints (p)
Liters (L)	1.06	quarts (qt)
Liters (L)	0.26	U.S. gallons (gal)
Liters (L)	0.22	imperial gallons (gal)
Cubic centimeters (cc)	16.387	cubic inches (cu in)
Cubic meters (m^3)	35	cubic feet (cu ft)
Cubic meters (m^3)	1.3	cubic yards (cu yd)
Teaspoons (tsp)	5	milliliters (ml)
Tablespoons (tbsp)	15	milliliters (ml)
Fluid ounces (fl oz)	30	milliliters (ml)
Cups (c)	0.24	liters (L)
Pints (pt)	0.47	liters (L)
Quarts (qt)	0.95	liters (L)
U.S. gallons (gal)	3.8	liters (L)
U.S. gallons (gal)	231	cubic inches (cu in)
Imperial gallons (gal)	4.5	liters (L)
Imperial gallons (gal)	277.42	cubic inches (cu in)
Cubic inches (cu in)	0.061	cubic centimeters (cc)
Cubic feet (cu ft)	0.028	cubic meters (m^3)
Cubic yards (cu yd)	0.76	cubic meters (m^3)
Temperature:		
Celsius (°C)	multiply by 1.8, add 32	Fahrenheit (°F)
Fahrenheit (°F)	subtract 32, multiply by 0.555	Celsius (°C)

Glossary

aberrant. Deviating from normal form, structure or course.

acanthocephalan. Any intestinal worm of the phylum Acanthocephala having a proboscis bearing rows of thornlike hooks and lacking a digestive tract.

acetylcholine. An alkaloid normally found in the body which is important in the transmission of nerve impulses; is also extracted from ergot for use in medicine.

adipose (adipoce, adj.). Fat.

ad libitum As one wishes or pleases.

adrenal gland. An endocrine gland located immediately above the kidney which consists of a medulla that produces epinephrine and norepinephrine, and a cortex that produces many steroidal hormones.

aerobic (adj.). Living or active only in the presence of oxygen.

agar. An agent used as a semisolid medium for growing bacteria and other microorganisms.

algae (pl.). A group of one-celled, colonial plants containing chlorophyll and other pigments (esp. red and brown), and having no true root, stem, or leaf; algae are found in water and damp places and include seaweeds and pond scum.

alimentary tract. The passage in the body that extends from the mouth, passing through the esophagus, stomach, and intestines to the anus, and through which food passes and in which it is digested.

alkaline. Of, like, or having the properties of alkali; containing alkali.

anthelmintic. A medicine that kills or ejects intestinal worms.

antibiotic. A substance that inhibits or destroys the growth of bacteria and other microorganisms.

antibody. Any substance (protein) produced in the body, having the capacity to create immunity to an antigen.

antiemetic. A substance that prevents nausea or vomiting.

antigen. Any substance (e.g., enzyme, toxin) eliciting an immunologic response.

antimuscarinic (adj.). Any substance that inhibits the action of muscarine; a poisonous alkaloid obtained from certain mushrooms such as *Amanita muscaria*.

antioxidant. Any substance that prevents or delays oxidation.

antiseptic. Preventing infection; any substance preventing the growth of microorganisms.

anus. The opening at the lower end of the gastrointestinal tract.

aorta. The large vessel distributing blood to every part of the body through its branches.

aortic arches. In mammals, of the six pairs of embryonic vascular arches, the left fourth arch becomes part of the systemic circulatory system, and the sixth pair incorporates in the pulmonary circulation.

apposition. Putting side by side.

arboreal. Living in trees.

arbutin. A toxic glycoside found in plants in the family Ericaceae.

arecoline. A liquid alkaloid from the seeds of the nut palm, *Areca catechu;* used in veterinary medicine as a parasiticide.

aril. An additional cover that forms on certain seeds after fertilization.

arroyo. Stream or dry gulley.

arteriole. Small artery.

arthritis (arthritic, adj.). Inflammation of a joint or joints.

arthropod. Any animal in the phylum Arthropoda (e.g., crustaceans, insects, myriopods, arachnids, etc.).

ascaridid. A roundworm in the order Ascaridida (Phylum Nematoda)

ascomycetous (adj.). Any type of fungi which reproduce through spores that have developed in saclike structures called asci (e.g., mildews, yeasts, gill fungi).

asphyxia, asphyxiation. Suffocation.

Aspidogastrea. A taxonomic category denoting a subclass of flukes.

aspirate (aspiration, n.). The act of sucking up, in, or withdrawing fluids and/or gases from a body cavity (e.g., lungs, thorax, peritoneum, urinary bladder, etc.).

atrophy. The physiological or pathological reduction in size of a cell, tissue, organ, or region of the body.

atropine. A belladonna alkaloid found in plants in the family Solanaceae, and is used in medicine to diminish secretions, dilate the pupil of the eye, and to relieve muscle spasms.

autoinfection. Infection by an organism within the body.

autolysis. The destruction of cells by enzymes within them which occurs after death or by some diseases.

avidin. A protein in raw egg white that inactivates biotin, a vitamin B.

axilla (axillae, pl.). The armpit.

bacteria (bacterium, sing.). Minute, single-celled plants in which the principal forms are round, rod-like, or spiral.

bacteriophage. A virus infecting bacteria resulting in its destruction.

barbituric acid. Malonylurea, the parent compound of the barbiturates.

basal. Pertaining to the most fundamental, basic, lowest or least, or deepest level.

belladonna alkaloids. A group of "antimuscarinic" alkaloids (e.g., atropine, scopolamine, homatropine) found in plants in the family Solanaceae.

belladonnin. A belladonna alkaloid found in plants in the family Solanaceae.

benzalkonium chloride. A white or yellowish white powder, or in gelatinous pieces, that are soluble in water and used as a surface disinfectant which is germicidal for many pathogenic, nonsporulating bacteria and fungi.

b.i.d. *bis in die;* two times a day.

bifurcate (adj.). Forked; divided into, or the site of, two parts or branches.

bilaterial. Pertaining to two sides.

biopsy (biopsies, pl.). Removal of tissue from a living body for diagnosis.

blood serum. The clear fluid of blood after it clots.

boid. Any snake in the family Boidae (boas and pythons).

brackish. Slightly salty (e.g., water in marshes near seas).

bronchial (adj.). Of, pertaining to, or involving the bronchi or their branches.

bronchopneumonia. An inflammatory condition of the lungs, in which air passages are filled by exudate or other fluids.

bryonidin. A toxic glycoside found in the plant genus *Bryonia.*

bryonin. A toxic glycoside found in the plant genus *Bryonia.*

buccal (adj.). Mouth cavity.

caecilian. Legless amphibian resembling a worm.

caecum, cecum. A pouch that is the beginning of the large intestine.

caesarean section. A surgical procedure to deliver an infant by cutting through the abdominal and uterine walls of the mother.

calcareous (adj.). Of, like, or containing calcium.

calcification. The deposition of calcium salts in body tissues.

calcium carbonate. A white powder or colorless, crystalline compound found primarily in limestone, marble, and chalk as calcite, aragonite, etc. It is also found in bones, teeth, shells, and plant ash.

calculi (pl.). Any abnormal stony deposit formed in the body (e.g., kidney, gallbladder).

caliche. Crusted calcium carbonate formed on certain soils in dry regions.

canker. An ulcerlike sore, especially in the mouth.

cannibalism (cannibalistic, adj.). Eating one's own kind.

capillaria. A roundworm in the family Capillariidae (Phylum Nematoda).

capillary. A minute blood vessel connecting arterioles with venules.

carapace. The upper shell of a turtle (and other animals with horny, protective coverings).

carbamate. Salt of carbamic acid (aminoformic acid).

carbohydrate. An organic compound comprising the starches, sugars, celluloses, and dextrins.

carbon tetrachloride. A colorless, nonflammable liquid used as a parasiticide and solvent for fats.

cardiac muscle. The muscle of the heart, characterized by striated muscle fibers and intercalated discs.

cardiovascular (adj.). Pertaining to the heart and blood vessels as a unified body system.

carnivore (carnivorous, adj.). Any animal feeding primarily on flesh.

carotenoid, carotinoid. Any of several red and yellow plant and animal pigments related to and including carotene.

carotid artery. One of two great arteries, contained on each side of the neck, which convey the blood from the aorta to the head.

carotine. Any of three red or orange-colored isomeric hydrocarbons found in carrots and certain other vegetables; are changed into vitamin A in the body.

carrion. Decaying flesh of a dead body which may serve as food for scavenging animals.

caseous (adj.). Cheesy; of or like cheese.

cataract. Opacity of the crystalline lens or capsule of the eye.

cathartic (adj.). Purgative; in medicine, a substance used to stimulate evacuation of the bowels.

catheter. A rigid or flexible tube used to pass fluids into or out of a body cavity, passage or vessel.

cation. A positively charged atom.

caudomedial (adj.). Located toward the tail and in the middle of the body.

cecum, caecum. A pouch that is the beginning of the large intestine.

cellulitis. Inflammation of connective tissue.

cellulose. The primary substance composing cell walls (or fibers) of all plant tissues.

cement substance. The substance that holds together the endothelial cells of the *tunica intima* of blood vessels.

centimeter (cm). One one-hundreth of a meter (1/100 m) and is equal to approximately 2/5 inch.

cervical (adj.). Of the neck.

chaparral. A thicket of shrubs, thorny bushes, etc.

cheleritrine. A toxic alkaloid of plants such as *Chelidonum* spp. and *Sanguinaria* sp.

chelidonine. A toxic alkaloid of the plant *Chelidonium majus*.

chemotherapy. The treatment or prevention of disease with the use of drugs.

chitin (chitinous, adj.). The structural material of animals mainly in the phylum Arthropoda; exoskeleton

cholinergic (adj.) Of, or pertaining to the mimicry or actual chemical activity characteristic of acetylcholine.

chromosome. The heredity-carrying factors of genes that are present in a constant number in each species.

chrysalid, chrysalis. The form of a butterfly that is between the larval and adult stages, also called pupa, cocoon.

cicutoxin. A powerful nervous system stimulant found in plants of the genus *Cicuta*.

cilia (cilium, sing.). Hairlike cytoplasmic processes of cells, comprised of microtubules, that serve in locomotion or in the movement of substances.

ciliate. A single-celled organism that locomotes by cilia, belonging to the phylum Ciliophora.

clitoris. A small and sensitive erectile organ of the female which corresponds to the penis of the male.

cloaca. A common chamber for the passage of feces, urine, and reproductive material.

cloacitis. Inflammation of the cloaca.

cm. An abbreviation for centimeter. One one-hundredth of a meter (1/100 m) and is equal to approximately 2/5 inch.

coccidia (coccidium, sing.). A group of single-celled parasites belonging to the phylum Apicomplexa.

coccidiosis. Infection caused by protozoa in the suborders Adeleorina and Eimeriorina.

codeine. An alkaloid constituent of opium used in medicine to relieve pain and coughing.

coelenterate. Mainly a marine invertebrate that includes the hydroid, jellyfish, sea anemone, and coral.

coelomic cavity. The cavity of most higher multicellular animals in which the visceral organs are suspended.

colchicine. An alkaloid from the plant genus *Colchicum* used in the treatment of gout.

colitis. Inflammation of the colon.

collagen. A fibrous protein found in connective tissue, bone, and cartilage.

colon. Large intestine.

colubrid. Any snake in the family Colubridae (typical snakes).

commensal. An organism (parasite) living in or on another organism (host) without causing harm.

concave. Hollow and curved like the inside half of a hollow ball.

conduction. The transmission of heat (and electricity, etc.) by the passage of energy from particle to particle.

condyle. A rounded process at the end of a bone occurring in joints (e.g., femur, humerus, mandible).

cone. Flask-shaped cells in the retina of the vertebrate eye which is sensitive to bright light and color.

congenital. Existing before or at birth.

coniceine. Either of two isomeric toxic alkaloids found in the plant genus *Conium*.

conidrine. A toxic alkaloid found in the plant genus *Conium*.

conifer (coniferous, adj.). A tree or shrub that bears cones (e.g., pine, spruce, fir, cedar, etc.).

coniine. A toxic alkaloid found in the plant genus *Conium*.

conjunctivitis. Inflammation of the mucous membrane lining the inner surface of the eyelids, called the conjunctiva.

connective tissue. Any tissue of the body that supports the essential part of an organ or other tissues.

conspecific. Belonging to the same species.

contaminant. Any substance that pollutes, infects, corrupts, or makes impure.

contractility. Having the power to contract; producing contraction.

convallamarin. A toxic glycoside found in the plant genus *Convallaria*.

convallarin. A toxic glycoside found in the plant genus *Convallaria*.

convection. A transference of heat caused by the differences in density of air due to temperature; the upward movement of warm, light air.

convex. Curving outward like the outer half surface of a ball.

convulsant. Any substance that causes seizures.

copepod. Any salt or freshwater crustaceans of the subclass Copepoda.

coprophageous. Eating feces.

coprozoic (adj.). Living in feces.

copulation (copulate, v.). The act of sexual intercourse; coitus.

cornea. The transparent tissue which forms the outer surface of the eyeball; the covering of the iris and pupil.

cortex. The outer portion of an organ situated just beneath the capsule.

coumarin. A toxic glycoside once used to conceal odors, and as a food flavoring.

cranial (adj.). Of, or pertaining to the skull.

crepuscular (adj.). Active at dawn and dusk.

crotalid. Any member of the rattlesnake family Crotalidae.

crustacean. An aquatic arthropod that includes the shrimp, crab, barnacle, and lobster.

culture. The growth of microorganisms on artificial media.

curettage. The process of cleaning or scraping tissues from body surfaces.

cutaneous (adj.). Of, belonging to, or involving the skin.

cyanogenetic (adj.). Capable of producing hydrocyanic acid or cyanide.

Cyclophyllidea. A taxonomic category denoting an order of tapeworms.

cyst. A structural form in the life cycle of certain parasites in which they form a protective wall; a saclike structure in the body when abnormal is filled with fluid or diseased matter.

cytisine. A nicotine-like alkaloid capable of producing paralysis.

cytotoxic (adj.). Any chemical agent that kills cells.

debridement (debride, v.). To cut away tissue; the cutting away of dead or contaminated tissue from a wound to prevent infection; chemical agents may be used to achieve similar results.

decapitation (decapitate, v.). Removal of the head.

deciduous. The falling off or shedding at maturity, certain stage of growth or season (e.g., leaves, antlers, teeth, skin).

decongestant. A medication used to relieve congestion, as in nasal passages.

definitive host. A host in which sexual maturation of a parasite occurs.

dehydrate. To remove water as in the body.

delphinine. A toxic alkaloid, found in the plant genus *Delphinium,* affecting the cardiovascular system.

dentine. Hard, dense, calcareous tissue which forms the body of a tooth underneath the enamel surface.

dermatitis. Inflammation of the skin.

dermis. The skin.

dewlap. A loose fold of skin hanging from the throat of certain animals.

Digenea. A taxonomic category denoting a subclass of flukes.

digenetic (adj.). Pertaining to flukes in the subclass Digenea.

digitalin. A toxic glycoside found in the seeds of the plant *Digitalis purpurea.*

digitalis. A toxic, cardioactive glycoside found in the plant *Digitalis purpurea* and similar plants.

digitoxin. A toxic, cardioactive glycoside found in the plant *Digitalis purpurea.*

dihydroxyphenylalanine (dopa). The precursor of dopamine and an intermediate product in the biosynthesis of norepinephrine, epinephrine, and melanin. In medicine, used in parkinsonism and manganese poisoning.

disarticulation. Separation at a joint.

disinfectant. Any substance used to destroy pathogens.

diuretic. A substance that increases the flow of urine.

diurnal. Active in the daytime.

dorsal. Pertaining to the back part of a body.

dorsoventral. Extending in a direction from the dorsal surface to the ventral surface.

duct. A small enclosed tube conducting fluid.

duodenum. The first section of small intestine just after the stomach.

dysecdysis. Unable to slough off outer epidermis.

dyspnea. Labored breathing.

dystocia. Difficult labor.

ecdysis. Sloughing off outer epidermis.

ectoparasite. An organism that lives on another organism (host).

ectotherm (ectothermic, adj.) (= poikilothermic, cold blooded). An organism that regulates its body temperature by means of outside sources.

edema. Excessive accumulation of fluid in cells, tissues or cavities of the body resulting in swelling.

elapid. Any member of the snake family Elapidae (e.g., cobra, krait, coral snake).

electrocardiograph. An instrument used to make a tracing showing the changes in electric potential produced by the contractions of the heart.

electrolyte. In medicine, a solution placed into the body for the purpose of rehydration.

ellipsoid. Spindle-shaped, ovoid.

emaciation. Being abnormally lean; a wasted condition.

embryo. Constituents of a fertilized ovum from which an offspring develops.

embryogenesis. The development of the embryo.

embryonated. Containing an embryo.

embryonic (adj.). Pertaining to an embryo.

embryophore. Bearing an embryo.

encephalitis. Inflammation of the brain.

encephalomyelitis. Inflammation of the brain and spinal cord.

encyst. To form a cyst.

endocrine gland. A gland which produces secretions that are introduced directly into the bloodstream and carried to other parts of the body, and whose functions regulate or control (e.g., thyroid, adrenal, and pituitary glands).

endogenous. Originating from within; internally.

endoparasite. An organism that lives in another organism (host).

endoscope. An instrument used to examine the interior of a body cavity.

endoscopy. Pertaining to visual examination of the interior of a body cavity with an endoscope.

endothelial cells. Thin, flat cells forming the lining of the heart, blood and lymph vessels, and serous cavities of the body, and referred to as the endothelium.

endothelium. The epithelium lining of internal cavities of the body.

endotoxin. A toxic substance found in certain disease-producing bacteria, and which is liberated by the disintegration of the bacterial cell.

Enoplida. A taxonomic category denoting an order of nematodes.

enteric. Intestinal.

enteritis. Inflammation of the intestinal tract.

enteroepithelial. Pertaining to the intestinal epithelium.

enucleation. The removal of an organ (e.g., eye) or a tumor in its entirety.

envenomate. To inject venom as from a venomous snake.

enzyme (enzymatic, adj.). A catalytic protein formed by living cells, having a specific action in bringing about a chemical change (e.g., using water and other materials in a cell to make sugar).

ephedrine. An alkaloid extracted from certain plants and used in medicine to relieve nasal congestion, asthma, and to constrict blood vessels.

epidemic dropsy. A disease, epidemic among natives of India, thought to be related to the ingestion of mustard-oil, characterized by fever, diarrhea, skin rash, and edema.

epidermis. The outermost portion of the skin composed of a dead, horny layer and a living, cellular part.

epididymus. Oval-shaped structure attached to the posterior upper portion of each testis, primarily serving as excretory ducts.

epinephrine. A hormone, secreted by the medulla of the adrenal gland, that stimulates the heart.

epithelium. Tissue composed of contiguous cells lining the internal and external body surfaces.

ergot. The dried sclerotium of *Claviceps purpurea*, a fungus that develops on rye plants. Certain ergot alkaloids are used to constrict blood vessels and smooth muscle tissue; the alkaloid ergotamine is used in the treatment of migraine headaches.

erythrocyte. Red blood cell.

esophagus. The musculomembranous passage extending from the pharynx to the stomach.

estivate. The act of becoming dormant to survive hot dry conditions.

estuary. Part of the seacoast over which the tide ebbs and flows; the wide mouth of a river where the tide meets the current.

etiology (etiological, adj.). The scientific study of the causes of disease.

eucalypt (adj.). Pertaining to the Australian evergreen trees of the Myrtle family, valued for their timber, gum, and oil.

euphorbin. The toxic principle of the plant genus *Euphorbia*, used in veterinary medicine as a purgative and vesicant.

euthanize (euthanasia, n.). To kill painlessly; painless death.

eutrophication. Deficient in oxygen, but rich in organisms.

evobioside. A toxic, cardioactive glycoside found in the plant genus *Euonymus*.

evomonoside. A toxic, cardioactive glycoside found in the plant genus *Euonymus*.

evonoside. A toxic, cardioactive glycoside found in the plant genus *Euonymus*.

excreta. Waste matter eliminated (excreted) from the body, especially sweat and urine.

excyst. To escape from a cyst.

exogenous. Originating from without; externally.

exostoses. Abnormal bony growth on the surface of a bone or tooth.

extracellular. Outside of cells.

extrahepatic (adj.). Outside of, or not connected with the liver.

exudate. Any substance discharged through pores, incisions, etc.

fatty acid. Any saturated or unsaturated, monobasic organic acid occurring naturally in the form of glycerol esters in fats and oils.

febrile. Pertaining to fever.

fecal flotation. A concentration technique whereby a small amount of feces are mixed with a solution having a greater specific gravity than the organisms being searched for. The organisms float to the top of the solution.

fecal sedimentation. A concentration technique whereby a small amount of feces are mixed with a solution having a lesser specific gravity than the organisms being searched for. The organisms settle to the bottom of the solution.

fecal smear. A technique for searching for organisms

in feces whereby a small portion of fecal matter is smeared on a glass slide, then mixed with saline solution, using a wooden applicator. A cover-slip is placed over the specimen and is examined with a microscope.

feces. The excretions of the bowels.

femoral pore. One of many small openings on the thigh of some male lizards.

fibropapilloma. Fibroadenoma; a benign tumor containing both fibrous and glandular elements.

fibrosis. Abnormal increase in fibrous connective tissue.

filarial (adj.). Pertaining to parasitic nematodes in the superfamily Filarioidea; adults live in the vertebrate host's circulatory or lymphatic systems, the connective tissues, or serous cavities; larval forms (microfilariae) are found in the bloodstream or lymph spaces.

filial. Generations following the original parents (e.g., first generation is referred to as F-1); offspring.

flagella (flagellum, sing.). Whiplike, filamentous cytoplasmic processes that contain microtubules, and are used for locomotion by certain protozoa.

flagellate. A single-celled organism possessing a slender, whiplike process for locomotion, and belonging to the subphylum Mastigophora.

flora. The entire plant life of any geographic area.

foci (pl.). In medicine, parts of the body where infections are localized.

fossorial. Burrowing.

fungus (fungi, pl.). A parasite that feeds on living organisms or dead organic material; includes mold, mildew, rust, smut, and the mushroom.

furocoumarin. A toxic substance found in the plant genus *Ruta*.

galantamine. A toxic alkaloid found in the plant genus *Galanthus*.

gallbladder. A hollow, pear-shaped organ of the body for storage and concentration of bile.

gallery forest. A forest along a river bank, and not dependent upon the climate but on the water table.

gamont. An undifferentiated/immature sex cell (gamete).

gangrene. Necrosis of a part of the body when the blood supply is obstructed by injury, disease, etc.

gastric (adj.). Of, or pertaining to the stomach.

gastritis. Inflammation of the stomach.

gastroenteritis. Inflammation of the stomach and intestines.

gastrointestinal (adj.). Pertaining to the stomach and intestines.

genital pore. An external opening to the male and/or female reproductive structures.

genus. The principal taxonomic subdivision of a family.

gingiva (gingival, adj.). The mucous membranes and underlying soft tissue surrounding a tooth; the gums.

globoid. Shaped like a globe (spherical).

glycoalkaloid. In chemistry, any compound of glucose, glycerin or glycine bonded with an alkaloid; a toxic substance found in plants in the family Solanaceae.

glycoside. Any of a group of sugar derivatives that yield a sugar and other substances when hydrolyzed (e.g., cyanogenetic glycosides, such as amygdalin, & give off cyanide under action with certain enzymes; saponins such as githasin generate soapy foam when mixed with water, and still other glycosides such as aesculin reduce the ability of blood to clot).

goiter. Enlargement of the thyroid gland.

goitrogenic (adj.). Producing goiter; iodine-deficient; the administration of drugs of the sulfonamides or thiourea group.

gonad. An ovary or testis.

gout. A disease characterized by an excess of uric acid in the blood and deposits of uric acid salts in various tissues, especially the viscera and joints.

Gram negative. Pertaining to microorganisms that appear pink microscopically after the Gram's stain process is completed.

granulation. Formation into granules such as new capillaries on the surface of a wound.

granuloma (granulomatous, adj.). A small nodule or granule.

gravid. Pregnant.

ground substance (= matrix, interstitial substance). The materials (e.g., fluids, semifluid solids) filling the spaces between cells and fibers in connective tissues, cartilage, and bone.

gular (adj.). Of, or pertaining to the throat.

hallucinogen. Any substance which produces perceptions of sights and sounds, etc., that are not actually present.

hammock. A raised piece of land with fertile soil where hardwood trees grow.

Harderian gland. A gland situated at the inner junction of the eyelids (inner canthus) in vertebrates, but especially those having a well-developed nictitating membrane.

heath, heathland. Wasteland which may be covered with low-growing shrubs.

helleborein. A toxic glycoside found in the plant genus *Helleborus*, and used in medicine as a purgative.

helleborin. A toxic glycoside found in the plant genus *Helleborus*, and used in medicine as a purgative.

helminth. Refers to worms of the platyhelminthes, nematoda, or annelida.

hematocrit. The portion of blood cells to the volume of blood.

hematological (adj.). Referring to the blood, its nature, functions, and diseases.

hematophagous. Feeding on blood; sanguinivorous; sanguivorous.

hemicellulose. A carbohydrate which is extracted from wood or corn fiber; similar to cellulose but less complex.

hemipenis (hemipenes, pl.). Either one of the paired copulatory organs situated laterally in a cavity at the base of the tail of snakes and lizards.

hemoglobin. The respiratory pigment of red blood cells.

hemorrhagic (adj.) Heavy bleeding.

hepatic (adj.), Pertaining to the liver.

hepatic veno-occlusive disease. Also known as Budd-Chiari syndrome; occlusion of the hepatic veins due to idiopathic thrombosis, tumor, or other causes, resulting in hepatosplenomegaly, jaundice, ascites, and portal hypertension.

hepatogenic (adj.). Originating in or produced by the liver.

hepatomegaly. Enlargement of the liver.

hepatotoxic (adj.). Any substance that is injurious or lethal to liver cells.

herbivore (herbivorous, adj.). Any animal feeding primarily on plant material.

herpesvirus. Any of several acute, inflammatory viral diseases characterized by the eruption of small blisters on the skin and mucous membranes.

herpetologist. One who studies reptiles and amphibians.

heteroxenous. Living within more than one host during a parasite's life cycle.

hexacanth embryo. Pertaining to the six-hooked Eucestoda larva (oncosphere) within an egg.

hibernaculum. An artificial or natural place where certain animals spend the winter in a dormant condition.

histocyte. A large phagocytic cell (macrophage) of loose connective tissue.

histologically (adv.). To study or examine microscopically the tissue structure of an organism.

histopathology. The study of microscopically visible changes in diseased tissue.

homeothermic (adj.). The ability of an organism to maintain itself at a constant temperature.

homogenize. To make uniform in texture, mixture, etc. by breaking down and blending the particles.

hopper. Herpetoculturist's slang describing a particular-sized mouse based upon its hyperactivity; fully furred juvenile at the "jumping" stage of its life.

homoxenous. Living within only one host during a parasite's life cycle.

hormone. Any chemical substance produced by an organ or cells of an organ, and is carried by the bloodstream or other body fluids to cells for a specific regulatory effect.

host. An organism that supports the life of another organism.

humic soil. Soil containing dark material which consists of decaying organic matter.

hydration. Fluid replacement.

hydrolysis. Any chemical reaction with water.

hydroponic (adj.). The science of growing plants in solutions or moist, inert material containing the necessary minerals, rather than in soil.

hydroquinone. A substance found in certain plants (e.g., *Xanthium*), and used in medicine and photography as an antioxidant (e.g., skin depigmentation; developer); also secreted by adult mealworms, *Tenebrio molitor,* and is potentially lethal when larvae taken from media containing adults is fed to insectivorous animals.

hydroscopic (adj.). Having the capacity to absorb or take up fluids from bodily tissues.

hygienic (adj.). Sanitary.

hyoscyamine. A very toxic alkaloid found in plants in the family Solanaceae and used in medicine as a sedative and antispasmodic.

hyperactivity. Excessive or abnormal activity.

hyperplasia. An abnormal increase in the number of cells composing a tissue or organ.

hyperthermia. The treatment of disease by inducing fever.

hyperthyroidism. A disorder resulting from excessive thyroid hormone.

hypertonic (adj.). Excessive, or above normal in tone or tension, especially muscles; having an osmotic pressure greater than that of physiologic salt solution or of any other solution taken as a standard.

hypoallergenic (adj.). Having a low tendency to induce an allergic reaction.

hypochromic (adj.). A lack of color; incomplete saturation of the red blood cells with hemoglobin.

hypoglycemia (hypoglycemic, adj.). An abnormally low concentration of sugar in the blood.

hypotensive (adj.). Abnormally low blood pressure.

hypothermia. Subnormal body temperature.

hypothyroidism. A disorder resulting from insufficiency of thyroid hormones.

hypovitaminosis. A condition resulting in a lack of one or more essential vitamins in the diet.

hypoxia (hypoxic, adj.). An abnormal condition resulting from oxygen deficiency.

IM. Intramuscular.

immobilize. To prevent the movement of; to keep in place.

immunology (immunologically, adv.). The study of the immune system.

immunosuppressive (adj.). The action of inactivating

a specific antibody by various agents to permit the acceptance of a foreign substance by an organism, as in a transplanted organ.

inanition. A state of starvation.

inbreeding. Reproduction of the same or closely related genetic material.

inclusion body. A minute foreign particle within a cell (e.g., a virus).

indigenous. Naturally of, or belonging to a region or country; innate; inherent; inborn.

indole. A substance obtained from plants, intestinal putrefaction and other sources; responsible, in part, for the odor of feces; used in perfumery as a reagent.

inflammation. The body's reaction to injury characterized clinically by heat, swelling, redness, and pain.

innocuous. Harmless.

inorganic (adj.). Not organic (e.g., not of animal or vegetable matter).

insectivorous (adj.). Feeding on insects.

integument. The skin.

intercalated disc. Transverse thickening at the abutting surface of cardiac muscle cells.

intercellular cement substance. A substance that holds epithelial cells together.

intercostal (adj.). Between the ribs.

intermediate host. An organism that harbors the asexual or intermediate phases of a parasite.

intracellular (adj.). Within cells.

intraerythrocytic. Within erythrocytes.

intramuscular (IM). Within, or into muscle.

intraperitoneal (IP). Within, or into the coelom or abdominal cavity.

intravenous (IV). Within, or into the veins.

intromission. Insertion; the act of putting the penis into the vagina.

intussusception. Telescoping, slipping, prolapsing, or passage of one part of the intestine into another.

invertebrate. An animal possessing no spinal column.

in vitro. Artificially maintained, as in a culture dish or test tube.

ion. An atom or group of atoms capable of conducting electricity.

IP. Intraperitoneal.

iridine. An irritating resinous substance found in the plant genus *Iris* producing digestive disorders when consumed; also causes dermatitis.

isoquinoline. A toxic alkaloid found in the plant genus *Argemone*, and used in medicine to synthesize antimalarials and other drugs.

IV. Intravenous.

Jacobson's organ. A sensory structure located in the roof of the mouth in reptiles which is used for smell and taste.

jasciamine. A belladonna alkaloid.

kelp. Any of various large, coarse, brown seaweeds of the brown algae, the ashes of which iodine is obtained.

keratitis. Inflammation of the cornea.

Kg. An abbreviation for kilogram. One thousand grams (1,000 g) or 2.2 pounds.

kidney. One of a pair of glandular organs of the body producing urine; the kidney filters out waste products from the bloodstream.

kilogram (Kg). One thousand grams (1,000 g) or 2.2 pounds.

lacrimation. Secretion of tears.

lamina propria. Connective tissue of the mucosa.

lantodene. A toxin found in the plant *Lantana camara* causing gastrointestinal irritation, diarrhea, and circulatory system failure.

large intestine. The lower portion of the gastrointestinal tract extending from the small intestine to the anus, and consisting of the cecum, colon, and rectum.

larva (larvae pl.). The free-living immature form of any animal that changes structurally when it becomes an adult.

lateral. Away from the midline of the body; on the side.

lavage. The irrigation or washing out of an organ.

lethargy. Pathologic drowsiness.

leukocyte. White blood cell.

life cycle. Stages through which an organism passes, generation after generation.

lignin. A substance deposited in the cell walls of plants which is a modification of cellulose.

ligustrin. A toxic glycoside found in the plant *Ligustrum vulgare* causing vomiting and diarrhea if consumed.

littoral. The region along the coast (e.g., seashore).

liver. The largest organ in the vertebrate body, located in the upper anterior part of the abdomen, and functions in the metabolism of carbohydrates, fats and proteins, and contains a substance necessary for the production of red blood cells.

loam. A rich soil composed of clay, sand, and some organic matter.

lobulated (adj.). Lobe-shaped; lobe-like.

longitudinal (adj.). Lengthwise.

LSD. Abbreviation for lysergic acid diethylamide.

lumen. The space inside of a tube (e.g., inside the intestine).

lycorine. A toxic alkaloid found in the plant genus *Galanthus*.

lymph gland. Lymph node; tissue in which interstitial fluid is filtered.

macrophage. A highly phagocytic, mononuclear cell which participates in the process of inflammation.

malnutrition. Poor nourishment resulting from improper diet.

mammillated. Nipple-like projections.

mandibular (adj.). Of, or pertaining to the mandible (lower jaw).

mandragorin. A toxin of the plant *Mandragora officinarum* combining hyoscyamine and scopolamine; when consumed it causes loss of feeling and insensitivity to pain, followed by sedation coma and death; in medicine, it was used as an anesthetic.

medial (adj.). Toward the midline of the body.

medulla. The central portions of certain organs (e.g., adrenal glands).

melena. The discharge of feces colored black by altered blood.

meningoencephalitis. Combined inflammation of the membranes covering the brain (meninges), the brain and the spinal cord.

meront. Asexual stage of some protozoa that undergoes the formation of merozoites by a series of divisions of a nucleus (or nuclei) followed by a division of the cytoplasm, resulting in a number of parts equal to the original number of nuclei.

mesa. A small, high plateau with steep sides.

mesonephros. The adult kidney of fishes and amphibians.

mesophytic (adj.). Pertaining to plants that have adapted to grow under moderate conditions of water.

metabolism (metabolic, adj.). The process of assimilating food into complex elements which are then disassimilated into simple ones to produce energy.

metacercaria (metacercarial, adj.). The stage of development between juvenile (cercaria) and adult of most digenetic trematodes; usually encysted and quiescent.

metanephric (adj.). Pertaining to the permanent kidney of reptiles, birds, and mammals which develops from the excretory organ lying behind the mesonephros in an embryo. In higher vertebrates the mesonephros develops into the epididymis and vas deferens.

meter. A unit of length in the metric system equal to 39.37 inches.

mg. An abbreviation for milligram. One one-thousandth of a gram (1/1000 g).

microbial (adj.). Pertaining to microorganisms, especially bacteria.

microfilaria (microfilariae, pl.). First-stage juvenile of any filariid nematode that is viviparous, and is usually found in the blood or tissue fluids of the definitive host.

microflora. Flora of a small area; in medicine, the microorganisms of the intestine.

micron (u). One one-thousandth of a millimeter (1/1000 mm).

microorganism. A microscopic organism being plant or animal (e.g., bacterium, protozoan, virus, etc.).

Microspora. A taxonomic category denoting a phylum of intracellular parasites which form unicellular spores.

milligram (mg). One one-thousandth of a gram (1/1000 g).

milliliter (ml). One one-thousandth of a liter (1/1000 L), and is equal to one cubic centimeter (1 cc).

mint. Any of the aromatic plants of the mint family (esp. *Mentha*) whose leaves are used for flavoring and in medicine.

ml. An abbreviation for milliliter. One one-thousandth of a liter (1/1000 L), and is equal to one cubic centimeter (1 cc).

mollusk. An aquatic invertebrate animal of the phylum Mollusca (e.g., chiton, oyster, clam, mussel, snail, slug, squid, octopus, etc.).

monocyte. A phagocytic white blood cell with a single, ovoid or kidney-shaped nucleus; the blood-borne stage of a macrophage.

Monogenea. A taxonomic category denoting a class of hermaphroditic flukes.

monogenetic (adj.). Pertaining to animals without alternating asexual and sexual generations.

monotypic (adj.). Having only one type (e.g., a genus consisting of only one species, the feeding of only one food type, etc.).

monsoon forest. A forest situated geographically where winds flow constantly between land and adjacent water, or where winds shift direction seasonally.

montane forest. High-altitude forest in a mountain region.

morphine. An alkaloid constituent of opium.

morphology. The scientific study of form and structure.

mucosa (mucosal, adj.). Mucous membrane; the membrane lining body cavities that come in contact with air.

mustard-oil. A volatile oil (primarily allylisothiocyanate) which causes severe redness of the skin and blisters.

mycobacterial (adj.). Infection, etc., caused by rod-shaped, aerobic, Gram-positive bacteria of the family Mycobacteriaceae.

mycotic dermatitis. Inflammation of the skin due to a fungus infection.

myiasis. Infection by fly larvae (maggots).

myocardial (adj.). Pertaining to the muscular substance of the heart.

myoglobin. The respiratory pigment of muscle fibers, differing from blood hemoglobin in that it has a higher affinity for oxygen and a lower affinity for carbon dioxide.

Myxozoa. A taxonomic category denoting a phylum of intracellular parasites which form multicellular spores.

nanometer (nm).   A unit of length equal to one billionth of a meter.

narcotine.   An alkaloid used in medicine as an agent to relieve coughing (also known as noscapine).

nares.   Nasal passages; the nostrils.

necropsy.   Examination of a dead animal; postmortem examination.

necrosis.   The death of tissue.

necrotizing dermatitis.   Inflammation of the skin resulting in the death of the tissue.

neonate (neonatal, adj.).   A newly born infant.

neoplasm.   A tumor or aberrant new growth of abnormal cells or tissues.

neotropic, neotropical (adj.).   Of the zoogeographical region that includes South America, West Indies, Central America, and tropical Mexico.

nephritis.   An acute or chronic disease of the kidneys characterized by inflammation, degeneration, fibrosis, etc.

nephrotoxic (adj.).   A toxic substance that destroys the cells of the kidneys.

nerioside.   A cardiac glycoside found in the plant *Nerium oleander* producing a wide variety of symptoms including nausea, bloody diarrhea, irregular heartbeat, and paralysis of the muscles which control breathing.

neuromuscular blocking agents.   Drugs that interrupt transmission of nerve impulses at the skeletal neuromuscular junction, at autonomic ganglia, and other important sites; used as adjuvants to anesthesia, especially to facilitate tracheal intubation.

neurotoxic.   Harmful to nerve tissue.

nicotine.   A poisonous, water-soluble alkaloid found in tobacco leaves; used in an aqueous solution of its sulfate as an insecticide.

nictitating membrane.   Thin, transparent conjunctival tissue in certain vertebrates (e.g., birds, reptiles) called the third eyelid which serves to protect the eyeball without obscuring vision.

nitrate.   A salt or ester of nitric acid.

nm.   An abbreviation for nanometer. A unit of length equal to one billionth of a meter.

nocturnal (adj.).   Active at night.

nodule.   A small node.

nonpathogenic (adj.). Not causing disease.

norepinephrine.   A hormone secreted by the medulla of the adrenal gland, and is related to epinephrine; used medically to constrict blood vessels and to stop bleeding.

nucleic acid.   Any of a group of complex organic acids found in nuclei and cytoplasm, which on complete hydrolysis yields pyrimidine and purine bases, a pentose sugar, and phosphoric acid.

nymph.   Pentastomida: the stage of development between larvae in a mammalian intermediate host and adult in a reptilian definitive host; larvae in a mammalian intermediate host encapsulate and nymphs form; reptile eats mammal and nymphs develop into adults in the reptile.

obligatory (adj.).   Required; necessary.

occipital (adj.).   Pertaining to the bone (occipital bone) that forms the posterior part of the skull.

occlude.   To prevent the passage of.

ocotillo.   A desert shrub, native to the southwestern United States and Mexico, with thorny branches and scarlet flowers (*Fouquieria splendens*); in Mexico, ocotillo is used in making charcoal.

ocular (adj.).   Of, or pertaining to the eye.

oenanthetoxin.   A substance found in the plant genus *Oenanthe* causing convulsions.

oleandrin.   A cardiac glycoside causing a wide variety of symptoms including nausea, bloody diarrhea, irregular heartbeat, and paralysis of the muscles that control breathing.

oleandroside.   A cardiac glycoside causing a wide variety of symptoms including nausea, bloody diarrhea, irregular heartbeat, and paralysis of the muscles that control breathing.

olfaction.   The sense of smell.

omnivore (omnivorous, adj.).   Any animal feeding on both plant and animal matter.

onchosphere.   A larva within a tapeworm egg.

oncomiracidium (onchomiracidia, pl.).   Ciliated larva of a monogenetic trematode.

oocyst.   Cyst stage of apicomplexans containing sporozoites, resulting from sporogony.

opalinid.   Any member of the order Opalinida.

operculum (opercular, adj.).   A lid or covering.

ophthalnologic disease.   Also called panophthalmitis; inflammation of all of the tissues of the eyeball.

opisthotonic spasm.   Describes a condition in which the head (and lower limbs of animals other than snakes) is bent backwards while the body is arched forward.

opium.   An addicting narcotic prepared from the juice of unripe seed capsules of the opium poppy (*Papaver somniferum*), and used in medicine to relieve pain and produce sleep.

opportunistic.   Referring to any organism which is incapable of inducing disease in a healthy host, but is able to produce infections in a less resistant or injured host.

organic (adj.).   Derived from or pertaining to living organisms.

organophosphate.   Any organic compound containing phosphorus (e.g., as the insecticide, malathion).

oropharyngeal cellulitis.   A diffuse inflammation of the subcutaneous tissue of the oral pharynx.

oropharynx.   Oral pharynx.

osmotic (adj.).   Pertaining to the passage of a solvent through a membrane from a dilute solution into a more concentrated one.

osteoderm. A bony deposit in the form of a plate or scale found in the dermal layers of the skin.

osteoid. Bone-like; young hyalin bone matrix in which calcium salts are deposited.

osteomalacia. A bone disease characterized by a softening due to a deficiency of calcium.

osteomyelitis. Infection of bone marrow or bone structure, usually caused by a bacterium (e.g., *Staphylococcus*) that produces pus.

ova (ovum, sing.). Eggs.

ovicidal (adj.). Lethal to ova (e.g., eggs of parasites).

oviduct. A tube through which ova pass from an ovary to the uterus or to the outside.

oviparous (oviparously, adj.). Producing eggs which hatch after leaving the body of the female.

ovipositor. An organ of many female insects for depositing eggs in a suitable place (often a host).

oxalate. A salt or ester of oxalic acid.

oxalic acid. A poisonous substance in plants; prepared synthetically for use in dyeing and bleaching.

oxalosis. Overproduction of oxalic acid and deposition of calcium oxalate in body tissues characterized clinically by renal calculi, nephrocalcinosis, and renal insufficiency.

oxidation. The process by which electrons are removed from atoms or ions.

oxyurid. Any member of the nematode order Oxyurida; pinworms.

Oxyurida. A taxonomic category denoting an order of nematodes.

paddock. An enclosed piece of land such as a small field.

palpate. To examine by touching.

palpebra (palpebral, adj.). Having to do with the eyelids.

pancreas. An elongated gland located behind the stomach secreting a clear, alkaline juice into the small intestine, where its constituent enzymes break down food passed from the stomach.

panophthalmitis. Inflammation of all of the tissues of the eyeball.

papaverine. An alkaloid toxin found in certain plants.

paramyxovirus. Also known as OPMV, ophidian paramyxovirus infection has been isolated in a wide variety of reptilian and mammalian cell types; clinical signs of illness are variable from going unnoticed altogether, to loss of appetite, muscle tone, or equilibrium, and in one epizootic, a snake underwent violent convulsions.

parasite. Any organism that lives in or on another organism (host) to obtain some advantage, but contributes nothing useful in return.

parasiticide. A substance or agent used to destroy parasites.

parasitologist. "Quaint person who seeks truth in strange places; he sits on one stool while staring at another" (Schmidt and Roberts, 1985).

parasitology. The study of parasites.

paratenic host. A host in which a parasite survives without undergoing further development; a transport host.

parathyroid gland. A gland that secretes a hormone important in the control of the calcium/phosphorus balance of the body.

parenteral. Brought into the body in a way other than the digestive tract (e.g., via injection).

parietal eye. A sensory structure capable of light reception which may serve as a temperature detector.

parthenogenesis (parthenogenetic, adj.). Reproduction by the development of an unfertilized egg, seed, or spore.

pathogen (pathogenic, adj.). An organism producing or capable of producing disease.

pectin. A water-soluble carbohydrate obtained from certain ripe fruits, which yields a gel that is the basis of jams and jellies.

pelagic. Of, the ocean surface or open sea.

pentastome. Any member of the phylum Pentastomida; tongue worms.

periocular (adj.). Surrounding the eye.

peristalsis. Rhythmic, wavelike motion of the digestive tract resulting in the movement of its contents.

peritoneum. The serous membrane lining the peritoneal cavity.

peritonitis. Inflammation of the serous membrane lining the interior of the abdominal cavity.

petechial (adj.). Referring to the minute rounded spot(s) of hemorrhage on body surfaces such as skin, mucous, and serous membranes, or on the cross-sectioned surface of an organ.

Petri dish. A shallow dish with cover used for culturing microorganisms.

phagocyte (phagocytic, adj.). Any white blood cell that ingests other cells, microorganisms, etc. in the blood and other tissues.

pharynx. A musculomembranous cavity located behind the nasal cavities, mouth, and larynx, and becoming continuous with the esophagus.

phenolic (adj.). Refers to the white crystalline compound produced from coal tar or by hydrolysis of chlorobenzene.

phenylalanine. An amino acid.

photomicrograph. A photograph of a minute object, requiring the use of a microscope.

photoperiod. The number of daylight hours best suited to an organism for proper growth and maturation.

photosensitive (adj.). Reacting or sensitive to radiant energy.

photosensitization. Being photosensitive.

phylogenetically (adj.). Pertaining to the evolution of a species.

phylum. A primary taxonomic division of the animal or vegetable kingdoms.

physiological (adj.). Characteristic of, or aiding normal functioning.

phytobezoar. A ball of vegetable fiber sometimes found in the stomach.

pinky (pinkies, pl). Herpetoculturist's slang describing a newly born mouse which is furless, exposing its pink skin.

piperidine. A liquid base used as a reagent.

piscivore (piscivorous, adj.). Any animal feeding primarily on fish.

pituitary gland (= hypophysis). A small endocrine gland, attached to the brain by a stalk, which secretes hormones that regulate body growth, metabolism, and the activity of other endocrine glands.

plasma. The fluid part of blood.

plastron. The under shell of a chelonian.

plerocercoid. The second larval stage in the intermediate host of certain cestodes.

poikilotherm (poikilothermic, adj.). Ectotherm; an animal that is "coldblooded" such as a reptile.

polysaccharide. Any of a group of complex carbohydrates (e.g., starch) that decompose by hydrolysis into a large numbers of single saccharide units.

polyunsaturated fatty acid (PUFA). Fats containing more than one molecular double or triple bond.

portal-renal system. See renal-portal system.

posterior (posteriorly, adj.). Situated behind or to the back of a part.

posteroventral. In most animals, behind and under the body.

postmortem. After death.

povidone iodine. A water-soluble antiseptic used topically for the prevention of cutaneous infections susceptible to iodine (betadine).

primary host. First or main host.

proboscis. An elongated structure located at the anterior end of an organism.

progeny. Children; descendants; offspring.

proglottid. Any of the segments of a tapeworm's body; each segment has both male and female reproductive organs.

prolapse. The falling down of an organ.

prophylaxis. The prevention or protection against disease.

prosector. An individual who is skilled at dissection and prepares subjects for anatomical demonstration.

Proteocephalidea. A taxonomic category denoting an order of tapeworms.

proteolytic (adj.). The breaking down of proteins to form more simple substances.

protoanemonin. A toxin found in certain plants (e.g., *Actaea* spp., *Anemon* spp.) which affects the gastrointestinal tract; also causes dermatitis.

protopine. An alkaloid of certain plants, containing anodyne and hypnotic properties.

protozoa. Unicellular eukaryotes in the Kingdom Protista.

Pseudophyllidea. A taxonomic category denoting an order of tapeworms.

pseudopodia (pseudopodium, sing.). Temporary protrusions of an ameboid cell that aids in locomotion and feeding.

pupa (pupae, pl.). An insect in the stage of development between the larval and adult forms.

purgative. A substance used to stimulate evacuation of the bowels (a cathartic).

purse-string suture. A running stitch placed in a circle and pulled together to close an opening.

purulent. Consisting of, containing, or forming pus.

putrid. Decomposed; rotten and foul-smelling.

pyridine. A nicotine-like substance that has been used as an antiseptic and germicide.

pyrrolizidine. An alkaloid toxin found in certain plants.

quarantine. The act of isolating individuals, for purposes of examination, for the duration of the incubation period of most diseases for which they may have been exposed.

quaternary ammonium. Any compound that is a derivative of an ammonium ion in which the four hydrogen atoms have been replaced by organic radicals.

quinolizidine. An alkaloid toxin found in the seeds of certain plants.

radiation. The process in which energy in the forms of light, heat, etc. is sent out through space from atoms and molecules as they undergo internal change.

radiograph (v.), (radiographically, adj.). To make a photograph on a sensitive film by projection of roentgen rays through a part of the body.

raphe. A seam or ridge.

raphide. A needle-shaped crystal, usually of calcium oxalate, found in plant cells.

refluxing. Flowing back.

regurgitation. The return of food from the stomach.

renal perfusion. The passage of fluids (esp. blood) through the vessels of the kidneys.

renal-portal system. Refers to the anatomical variation of reptiles whereby blood leaving the tail and pelvic limbs of these animals passes through the kidneys before returning to the heart.

reservoir host. An animal that provides a parasite with a suitable environment, and while doing so, serves as a source of infection for other animals.

residual yolk. The yolk that remains in the body

cavity of certain reptiles just after hatching; provides nourishment to the neonate for approximately 5–10 days, after which it is used up and the animal must begin hunting for food.

resin. Any of various organic substances exuded from certain plants and trees; used in varnishes, lacquers, and as modifiers in synthetic plastics.

resinoid. A complex substance which has some of the properties of a resin.

retention enema. An enema in which the liquid is held within the rectum, in order to soften the feces, or to deliver medication.

retina. In part, an expansion of the optic nerve fibers which are sensitive to light; the image formed by the lens of the eye on the retina is carried to the brain by the optic nerve.

rhabditid. Any nematode of the order Rhabditida.

Rhabditida. A taxonomic category denoting an order of nematodes.

Ringer's solution. A physiologic salt solution.

rostral (adj.). Pertaining to, or resembling a beak or projection.

saline. A salt solution. Physiological saline contains 0.9 grams of sodium chloride to 100 ml of water.

salmonellosis. Infection of an organism in the genus *Salmonella* (e.g., septicemia, gastroenteritis, food poisoning).

saponin. A glycoside widely distributed in nature and used as a detergent; because saponins alter the permeability of cell walls, they are toxic.

saurian. Reptile in the order Sauria; lizard.

savanna. A grassland with or without scattered trees.

SC. (SQ). Subcutaneous.

scansorial. Climbing in bushes, shrubs, and other relatively low-growing vegetation; capable of climbing, but not arboreal.

sclerophyll forest. Forest of evergreen trees which have tough, leathery leaves (e.g., holly or pine).

scolex. Head of a tapeworm.

scopolamine. A belladonna alkaloid found in plants in the family Solanaceae, and is used in medicine as a sedative, hypnotic, and with morphine to relieve pain.

scute. Scale; any external bony or horny plate.

selenium. A gray, nonmetallic chemical element of the sulfur group.

self-limiting. A disease that is limited by its own characteristics, rather than outside influence.

sensitivity test. A procedure which measures the degree of change or responsiveness of a pathogen to a particular antibiotic.

septicemia (septicemic, adj.). A disease spread throughout the body via the bloodstream by pathogenic microorganisms and their toxic products.

serous (adj.). Thin and watery-like serum; containing serum.

serum. Any watery animal fluid including the clear yellowish fluid which separates from blood

sex chromosome. A sex-determining chromosome in the egg and sperm cells of most animals and some plants.

sexual dimorphism. The two sexes having distinctly different structural forms; denotes observable sexual differences.

sibling. Brother; sister; litter mate.

s.i.d. *Signa in die.* One time daily.

small intestine. The narrow, convoluted upper part of the gastrointestinal tract extending from the stomach to the large intestine.

sodium chloride. A common salt, comprising over 90% of inorganic constituents of blood serum.

sodium citrate. A crystalline compound used primarily as an anticoagulant.

solanin. A glycosidic alkaloid found in various plants of the nightshade family causing a variety of symptoms including nausea, dizziness and convulsions.

solute. The dissolved substance in a solution.

somatic. Pertaining to the framework of the body, but not to the viscera.

spargana (sparganum, sing.). Cestode plerocercoids of unknown identity.

species. A taxonomic group of individuals similar in morphology and physiology.

spermacidal. Anything which kills sperm cells (e.g., chemicals, high temperatures).

sphagnum. An absorbent, spongelike moss found in bogs.

spherical. Ball or globe-shaped.

spigeline. A toxin affecting the nervous system, found in the plant *Spigelia* spp.

spinifex desert. Refers to any desert in Australia growing a particular grass with pointed leaves and bristly seed heads (e.g., grasses in the genus *Spinifex*).

spirurid. Any nematode of the order Spirurida.

Spirurida. A taxonomic category denoting an order of nematodes.

spleen. The vascular, lymphatic organ of the body which functions to modify the structure of blood.

splenomegaly. Enlargement of the spleen.

spore. Reproductive cell of certain lower organisms.

sporocyst. A structure from which sporozoites are produced; the saclike larval stage of some flukes from which cercariae sometimes develop (asexual stage of reproduction).

sporozoite. The infective form of a protozoan (phylum Apicomplexa) that undergoes asexual reproduction in a host.

sporulation (sporulate, v.). Formation of sporocysts and sporozoites.

spurious. Not true or genuine.

sputum. Saliva, mucus, etc. which is spit out of the mouth.

steatitis. Inflammation of adipose tissue.

steppe. Usually refers to a great plain with few trees in primarily southeast Europe and Asia.

steroidal (adj.). Pertaining to any group of compounds which characteristically have the carbon-atom ring structure of sterols.

sterol. Any of a group of solid cyclic, unsaturated alcohols found in plant and animal tissues (e.g., cholesterol).

stomach. A saclike organ of vertebrates into which food passes for storage during the early stages of digestion.

stomatitis. Inflammation of the mouth.

striated border. A modified cytoplasmic layer on the intestinal epithelium in which perpendicular striations are microscopically observed.

striated muscle. Muscle tissue consisting of cross-striated fibers (skeletal muscle).

strobila. Cestode body.

strongylid. Any nematode of the order Strongylida.

Strongylida. A taxonomic category denoting an order of nematodes.

strychnine. A poisonous alkaloid found in certain plants which is used in medicine as a nervous system stimulant.

subcaudal. A scale lying on the ventral side of the tail in reptiles.

subclass. The taxonomic category below a class and above an order.

subcutaneous (SC, SQ). Under the skin.

subcutis. The superficial areolar tissue layers (fascia) under the skin.

suborder. A taxonomic category below an order and above a family.

subphylum. A taxomonic category below a phylum and above a class.

subspectacular (adj.). Referring to the area just beneath the fixed, transparent watchglass-like covering (spectacle; eye cap) of the eye in snakes and some lizards.

substrate. In herpetology, material placed on a cage bottom (e.g., newspaper, gravel, mulch, etc.).

surface membrane. Outer membrane of a cell.

symbiont (symbiotic, adj.). Any organism involved in a mutualistic relationship.

symmetrical. Exhibiting corresponding characteristics on opposite sides of a plane.

symphysis. The line of junction and fusion of certain bones such as the mandibles and pubic bones.

talus (adj.). A slope that may contain a pile of rock fragments at the base.

tannin. Tannic acid.

taxine. An alkaloid found in the plant *Taxus spp.* which depresses function of the heart.

tepid. Moderately warm.

terrestrial (adj.). Living on the ground.

tetrachloroethylene. Carbon tetrachloride.

tetrahydro-cannabinol. A resinous mixture contained in the plant *Cannabis sativa* which produces hallucinogenic effects when taken into the body; overdoses lead to depression and coma.

therapeutic (adj.). Serving to cure or to heal; a curative.

thermoregulation (thermoregulate, v.). Reptiles: regulation of body temperature by the voluntary movement between warm and cool places.

thiaminase. An enzyme present in raw fish (and in certain bacteria) which causes the cleavage of thiamine rendering it unavailable to the body.

thoracic (adj.). Pertaining to the thorax.

thorax. The part of the body between the neck and abdomen; the chest.

thymus. A ductless organ located in the upper thorax of vertebrates.

thyroid gland. A ductless gland secreting the hormone thyroxin, which regulates body growth and metabolism.

torpid. A state of being dormant or inactive.

toxalbumin. A poisonous protein obtained from certain plants and bacterial cultures.

toxicology. The study of poisons, their effects and antidotes.

transport host. Host in which a parasite survives without undergoing further development; also known as a paratenic host.

trichlorfon. A chemical used in veterinary medicine as an anthelmintic, animal insecticide, and fly bait.

trigonelline. A toxic alkaloid found in the plant genus *Mirabilis*.

Trypanorhyncha. A taxonomic category denoting an order of cestodes.

trypanosome. Any flagellate protozoan of the genus *Trypanosoma* that lives in the blood of vertebrates and is usually transmitted by the bite of an insect.

tumor. A swelling on some part of the body, especially a mass of new tissue growth independent of its surrounding structures, having no physiological function.

tunicate. Any of a subphylum, Tunicata, of solitary or colonial sea chordates, having a saclike body enclosed by a thick cellulose tunic.

tympanitic colic. Abdominal pain due to the accumulation of gas in the intestine.

tympanum. The middle ear.

tyrosine. An amino acid formed by the decomposition of proteins (e.g., as in the decomposition of cheese).

ulcer (ulcerate, v.). An open sore on the skin or mucous membrane which often discharges pus.

ultimobranchial body. Also called lateral thyroid; considered to be a rudimentary fifth pharyngeal pouch, or a lateral thyroid primordium and fourth pouch derivative.

um. An abbreviation for micrometer (micron). One one-thousandth of a millimeter (1/1000 mm).

umbilical scar. A mark on the plastron of a hatchling turtle at the attachment site of the yolk sac.

urate. A salt of uric acid.

urechitoxin. A cardiac glycoside found in certain plants (e.g., *Urechites* spp.).

uric acid. A product of protein metabolism which is present in the blood and urine.

varanid. Any member of the lizard family Varanidae.

vas deferens. The portion of the excretory duct system of the testes which runs from the epididymal duct to the ejaculatory duct.

vector. An organism or agent that transfers infective microorganisms from one host to another.

vent. The external opening of the cloaca

ventral. Pertaining to the belly.

vermiculite. Alteration of mica, producing hydrous silicate minerals which occur in tiny, leafy scales that expand greatly when heated.

vermin (verminous, adj.). Any animal regarded as objectionable by humans (e.g., flies, roaches, lice, rats, etc.).

vertebral column. Spinal column; backbone.

vertebrate. An animal possessing a spinal column.

vertical transmission. The transmission of a trait, disease, etc. from parent to offspring across the placenta.

vestigial (adj.). Refering to a remnant of something formerly present or more fully developed.

virus. A vast group of minute infectious structures relying totally on living cells for reproduction and metabolism.

viscera (viscus, sing.). Organs enclosed within one of the four great body cavities (cranium, thorax, abdomen, or pelvis), but especially the abdomen.

viscid (adj.). Adhesive; glutinous.

viscous (adj.). Glutinous; sticky; semifluid; having high viscosity.

vitellogenesis. Development of the yolk part of an egg in the ovary

viviparous. Bearing live young.

volatile oil. Also called essential oil; an oil that gives a distinctive odor, flavor, etc. to a plant, flower or fruit.

xantotoxin. A toxic substance found in the plant genus *Ruta*.

yeast. Single-celled ascomycetous fungi.

References

Adkins, M. 1983. Chelonian nutrition. *Reprinted in:* Anim. Keep. For., 10(9):274–275.

Allen, M. E. 1984. A review of the composition of live prey in zoo animals. Am. Assoc. Zoo Veterinarians, Abstracts of Papers of the Annual Meeting, Louisville, KY.

Almandarz, E. 1978. Husbandry. *In: Zoo and Wild Animal Medicine,* Fowler, M. E. (Ed.). W.B. Saunders Company, Philadelphia, PA. pp. 117–122.

Alperin, J. B., Hutchinson, H. T., and Levin, W. C. 1966. Studies of folic acid requirements in mcgaloblastic anemia of pregnancy. Arch. Internal Med., 117:681–688.

Althausen, T. L. 1949. Hormones and vitamin factors in intestinal absorption. Gastroenterology, 12:467–480.

Anderson, R. C. 1978. Keys to genera of the superfamily Metastrongyloidea. *In: CIH Keys to the Nematode Parasites of Vertebrates,* Anderson, R. C., Chaubaud, A. G., and Willmott, S. (Eds.), No. 5. Commonwealth Agricultural Bureaux, Farnham Royal, Bucks. pp. 1–40.

Anderson, R. C. and Bain, O. 1976. Keys to genera of the order Spirurida, Part 3. Diplotriaenoidea, Aproctoidea and Filarioidea. *In: CIH Keys to the Nematode Parasites of Vertebrates,* Anderson, R. C., Chaubaud, A. G., and Willmott, S. (Eds.), No. 3. Commonwealth Agricultural Bureaux, Farnham Royal, Bucks. pp. 59–116.

Appleby, E. C. and Siller, W. G. 1960. Some cases of gout in reptiles. J. Path. Bact., 80:427–430.

Ashley, B. D. and Burchfield, P. M. 1966. Maintaining a snake colony for venom collection. U.S. Army Medical Research Laboratory Report, 696:1–27.

Axelrod, A. E. 1971. Immune processes in vitamin deficiency states. Am. J. Clin. Nutr., 24:265.

Baker, E. M. 1967. Vitamin C requirements in stress. Am. J. Clin. Nutr., 20:583–590.

Baker, M. R. 1987. *Synopsis of the Nematoda Parasitic in Amphibians and Reptiles.* Occasional Papers in Biology, No. 11, Memorial University of Newfoundland, St. John's Newfoundland.

Barbour, T. 1932. About iguanas. Copeia, 1932:97.

Barnard, S. M. 1983. A review of some fecal pseudoparasites of reptiles. J. Zoo Anim. Med., 14:79–88.

Barnard, S. M. 1984. Reptile care: Relating to the inquiring novice; Housing (design and construction). Anim. Keep. For., 11(9):268–269.

Barnard, S. M. 1985a. Reptile care: Relating to the inquiring novice; Environment (lighting). Anim. Keep. For., 12(1):12–13.

Barnard, S. M. 1985b. Reptile care: Relating to the inquiring novice; Commonly encountered disorders. Anim. Keep. For., 12(9):284–285.

Barnard, S. M. 1986a. An annotated outline of commonly occurring reptilian parasites. Acta Zoologica et Antverpiensia, 79:39–72.

Barnard, S. M. 1986b. Color atlas of reptilian parasites, Part IV. Pseudoparasites. Compend. Contin. Educ. Pract. Vet., 8:365–369.

Barnard, S. M. 1986c. Feeding captive insectivorous bats: Maintenance of food colonies. Anim. Keep. For., 13(13):81–87.

Barnard, S. M. 1990. Snakebite first aid down under or elapids vs. vipers. Anim. Keep. For., 17(4):138–140.

Barnard, S. M. and Upton, S. J. 1994. *A Veterinary Guide to the Parasites of Reptiles:* Protozoa, Vol. I. Krieger Publishing Company, Malabar, FL.

Bellairs, A. 1970. *The Life of Reptiles.* Universe Books, New York, NY.

Bellairs, A. d'A. 1981. Congenital and developmental diseases. *In: Diseases of the Reptilia,* Cooper, J. E. and Jackson, O. F. (Eds.). Academic Press, New York, NY. pp. 469–485.

Bernstein, J. J. 1972. A clinical view of some reptilian medical problems. J. Zoo Anim. Med., 3:3–7.

Bird, D. M. and Ho, S. K. 1976. Nutritive values of whole animal diets for captive birds of prey. Raptor Research, 10(2):45.

Branch, B. 1988. *Field Guide to the Snakes and Other Reptiles of Southern Africa.* Ralph Curtis Publishing, Sanibel Island, FL.

Breen, J. F. 1974. *Encyclopedia of Reptiles.* T.F.H. Publications, Inc., Neptune, NJ.

Brownstein, D. G., Standberg, J. D., Montali, R. J., Bush, M., and Fortner, J. 1977. *Cryptosporidium* in snakes with hypertrophic gastritis. Vet. Pathol., 14:606–617.

Bull, J. J. and Vogt, R. C. 1979. Temperature-dependent sex determination in turtles. Science, 206:1186–1188.

Burchfield, P. M. 1982. Husbandry of reptiles. *In: Zoological Park and Aquarium Fundamentals,* Sausman, K. (Ed.). Am. Assoc. Zool. Parks & Aquariums, Wheeling, WV. pp. 265–282.

Burke, T. J., Rosenberg, D., and Smith, A. R. 1978. Infectious stomatitis—a perspective: Study of normal flora and report of an unusual case. Am. Assoc. Zoo Veterinarians Annual Proc.:190–196.

Burquez, A., Flores-Villela, O., and Hernandez, A. 1986. Herbivory in a small iguanid lizard, *Sceloporus torquatus torquatus.* J. Herpetol., 20(2):262–264.

Bush, M. 1974. Reptilian medicine. Am. Assoc. Zoo Veterinarians, Annual Proc.:68–78.

Bush, M., Custer, R., Smeller, J., and Charache, P. 1980. Recommendations for antibiotic therapy in reptiles. *In: Reproductive Biology and Diseases of Captive Reptiles,* Murphy, J. B. and Collins, J. T. (Eds.). SSAR Contributions to Herpetology, No. 1. pp. 223–226

Bush, M., Smeller, J. M., Charache, P., and Arthur, R. 1978. Biologic half-life of gentamicin in gopher snakes. Am. J. Vet. Res., 39(1):171–173.

Bustard, H. R. 1969. Tail abnormalities resulting from high temperature egg incubation. Brit. J. Herpetol., 4:121–123.

Bustard, H. R. 1980. Captive breeding of crocodiles. *In: The Care and Breeding of Captive Reptiles,* Townson, S., Millichamp, N. J., Lucas, D. G. D., and Millwood, A. J. (Eds.). The Brit. Herp. Soc., London. pp. 1–20.

Campbell, J. A. and Lamar, W. W. 1989. *The Venomous Reptiles of Latin America.* Comstock Publishing Associates. Ithaca, New York.

Campden-Main, S. M. 1970. *A Field Guide to the Snakes of South Vietnam.* Smithsonian Institution, Washington, D.C.

Canning, E. U. 1981. *Encephalitozoon lacertae* n. sp., a microsporidian parasite of the lizard *Podarcis muralis. In: Parasitological Topics. A Presentation Volume of P.C.C. Garnham, F.R.S. on the Occasion of His 80th Birthday,* Canning, E. U. (Ed.). Society of Protozoologists, Lawrence, KS. pp. 57–64.

Canning, E. U. and Landau, I. 1971. A microsporidian infection of *Lacerta muralis.* Trans. Royal Soc. Trop. Med. Hyg., 65:431.

Carr, A. 1952. *Handbook of Turtles.* Cornell University Press, Ithaca, NY.

Chabaud, A. G. 1974. General introduction: Keys to subclasses, orders and superfamilies. *In: CIH Keys to the Nematode Parasites of Vertebrates,* No. 1, Anderson, R. C., Chabaud, A. G., and Willmott, S. (Eds.). Commonwealth Agricultural Bureaux International, Wallingford, Oxon. pp. 1–17

Chabaud, A. G. 1975a. Keys to genera of the order Spirurida, Part, 1, Camallanoidea, Dracunculoidea, Gnathostomatoidea, Physalopteroidea, Rictularioidea and Thelazioidea, No. 3, Anderson, R. C., Chabaud, A. G., and Willmott, S. (Eds.). Commonwealth Agricultural Bureaux, Farnham Royal, Bucks. pp. 1–27.

Chabaud, A. G. 1975b. Keys to genera of the order Spirurida, Part, 2, Spiruroidea, Habronematoidea and Acuaroidea, No. 3, Anderson, R. C., Chabaud, A. G., and Willmott, S. (Eds.). Commonwealth Agricultural Bureaux, Farnham Royal, Bucks. pp. 29–58.

Chabaud, A. G. 1978. Keys to genera of the superfamilies Cosmocercoidea, Seuratoidea, Heterakoidea and Subuluroidea, No. 6, Anderson, R. C., Chabaud, A. G., and Willmott, S. (Eds.). Commonwealth Agricultural Bureaux, Farnham Royal, Bucks. pp. 1–71.

Chatterjee, G. C. 1967. Effects of ascorbic acid deficiency in animals. *In: The Vitamins,* 2nd Ed., Vol. I., Sebrell, W. H., Jr. and Harris, R. E. (Eds.). Academic Press, New York, NY. pp. 407–457.

Chatterjee, I. B. 1970. Biosynthesis of L-ascorbate in animals. *In: Methods in Enzymology,* Vol. 18, Part A., McCormic, D. B. and Wright, L. D. (Eds.) Academic Press, New York, NY. pp. 28–34.

Chatterjee, I. B. 1973. Vitamin C synthesis in animals: Evolutionary trend. Sci. and Cultr., 39(5):210–212.

Cheng, T. C. 1964. *The Biology of Animal Parasites.* W.B. Saunders Company, Philadelphia, PA.

Cheng, T. C. 1973. *General Parasitology,* 1st Ed. Academic Press, New York, NY.

Choy, B. K., Balazs, G. H., and Daily, M. 1989. New therapy for marine turtles parasitized by the piscicolid leech *Ozobranchus branchiatus.* Herp. Review, 20:89–90.

Clarke, G. K. and Marx, T. I. 1960. Heart rates of unanesthetized snakes by electrocardiography. Copeia, 1960:236–238.

Cochran, D. M. 1941. *Herpetology of Hispaniola.* U.S. National Museum Bull. No. 177, U.S. Gov't. Print. Office, Washington, D.C.

Cogger, H. G. 1975. *Reptiles and Amphibians of Australia.* A.H. & A.W. Reed, Sydney, NSW.

Cogger, H. G., Cameron, E. E., and Cogger, H. M. 1983. *Zoological Catalogue of Australia: Amphibia and Reptilia,* Vol. I. Australian Gov't Printing Service, Canberra, NSW.

Collins, P. W. P. 1980. The captive breeding of Mediterranean tortoises in Britain. *In: The Care and Breeding of Captive Reptiles,* Townson, S., Millichamp, N. J., Lucas, D. G. D., and Millwood, A. J. (Eds.). The Brit. Herp. Soc., London. pp. 21–36.

Conant, R. 1975. *A Field Guide to Reptiles and Amphibians of Eastern and Central North America.* Houghton Mifflin Company, Boston, MA.

Cooper, J. E. 1971. Disease in East African snakes associated with *Kalicephalus* worms (Nematoda: Diaphanocephalidae). Vec. Rec., 89:385–388.

Cooper, J. E. 1981. Bacteria. *In: Diseases of the Reptilia,* Cooper, J. E. and Jackson, O. F. (Eds.). Academic Press, New York, NY. pp. 165–191.

Cooper, J. E. 1984. Physical influences. *In: Diseases of Amphibians and Reptiles,* Hoff, G. L., Frye, F. L., and Jacobson, E. R. (Eds.). Plenum Press, New York, NY. pp. 607–624.

Cooper, J. E. and Jackson, O. F. 1981. *Diseases of the Reptilia,* Academic Press, New York, NY.

Cooper, J. E., Klempau, A. E., and Zapata, A. G. 1985. Reptilian immunity. *In: Biology of the Reptilia,* Vol. 14, Gans, C., Billett, F. S., and Maderson, P. F. A. (Eds.). Wiley and Sons, NY. pp. 599–678.

Cooper, J. E., Ewbank, R., Platt, D., and Warick, C. 1989. *Euthanasia of Amphibians and Reptiles: Report of a Joint UFAW/WSPA Working Party,* London. Universities Federation for Animal Welfare and World Society for the Protection of Animals.

Cosgrove, G. E., Deakins, D. E., and Self, J. T. 1984. Pentastomiasis. *In: Diseases of Amphibians and Reptiles,* Hoff, G. L., Frye, F. L., and Jacobson, E. R. (Eds.). Plenum Press, New York, NY. pp. 205–211.

Costanzo, J. P. 1985. The bioenergetics of hibernation in the eastern garter snake *Thamnophis sirtalis sirtalis.* Physiol. Zool., 58:682–692.

Cowan, D. F. 1968. Diseases of captive reptiles. J. Am. Vet. Med. Assoc., 153:848–859.

Cowan, D. F. 1980. Adaptation, maladaptation and disease. *In: Reproductive Biology and Diseases of Captive Reptiles,* Murphy, J. B. and Collins, J. T. (Eds.). SSAR Contributions to Herpetology, No. 1. pp. 191–196.

Cowles, R. B. and Phelan, R. L. 1958. Olfaction in rattlesnakes. Copeia, 1958:77–83.

Cruickshank, L. Personal Communication, Boynton Beach, FL.

Daniel, J. C. 1983. *The Book of Indian Reptiles.* Bombay Natural History Society, Bombay.

Dawbin, W. H. and Batham, E. J. 1969. Notes on keeping tuatara in captivity. New Zealand Dept. of Internal Affairs, The Wildlife Service. Wellington, New Zealand.

Dawes, B. 1946. *The Trematoda.* Cambridge University Press, Cambridge, MA.

Deakins, D. E. 1973. Diagnosis and treatment of parasites of amphibia and reptiles. Am. Assoc. Zoo Veterinarians Annual Proc.:37–46.

Deoras, P. J. 1978. *Snakes of India.* National Book Trust, India, New Delhi.

Dillehay, D. L., Boosinger, T. R., and Mackenzie, S. 1986. Gastric cryptosporidiosis in a chameleon. J. Am. Vet. Med. Assoc., 189:1139–1140.

Dixon, J. R. and Soini, P. 1986. *The Reptiles of the Upper Amazon Basin, Iquitos Region, Peru.* Milwaukee Public Museum, Milwaukee, WS.

Donaldson, M., Heynemen, D., Dempster, R., and Garcia, L. 1975. Epizootic of fatal amebiasis among exhibited snakes: Epidemiologic, pathologic and chemotherapeutic considerations. Am. J. Vet. Res., 36:807–817.

Doyle, R. E. and Moreland, A. F. 1968. Diseases of turtles. Lab. Anim. Digest, 4:3–6.

Duellman, W. E. (Ed.). 1979. *The South American Herpetofauna: Its Origin, Evolution and Dispersal.* Museum of Natural History, The University of Kansas, Lawrence, KS.

Dupouy, J. and Kechemir, N. 1973. Bull. Soc. Hist. Nat. Afr. Nord Alger., 64:47–98.

Dutky, S. R., Thompson, J. V., and Cantwell, G. E. 1962. A technique for mass rearing the greater wax moth (Lepidoptera: Galleriidae). Ent. Soc. Washington, 64(1):56–58.

Ehmann, H. 1980. The natural history and conservation of the bronzeback (*Ophidiocephalus taeniatus* Luca and Frost) (Lacertilia, Pygopodidae). *In: Proceedings of the Melbourne Herpetological Symposium,* Banks, C. B. and Martin, A. A. (Eds.). The Royal Melbourne Zoological Gardens, Melbourne, Victoria. pp. 7–13.

Elkan, E. 1974. Host-feeding patterns of Florida mosquitoes, IV. Deinocerites. J. Med. Ent., 11:105–107.

Evans, E. E. and Cowles, R. B. 1959. Effect of temperature on antibody synthesis in the reptile, *Dipsosaurus dorsalis.* Proc. Soc. Exp. Biol. Med., 110:482–483.

Evans, H. E. 1978. Reptiles: Introduction and anatomy. *In: Zoo and Wild Animal Medicine,* Fowler, M. E. (Ed.) W.B. Saunders Company, Philadelphia, PA. pp. 91–113.

Evans, R. H. 1994. "Ask the D.V.M."—Reduce your reptile infection risk. Wildl. Rehab. Today, 6(2);39–40.

Fain, A. 1962. Les acariens mesostigmatiques ectoparasites des serpents (Entonyssidae: Mesostigmata). Bull. Inst. Roy. Sci. Nat. Belg., 37:1–135.

Fain, A. 1966. Pentastomida of snakes: Their parasitological role in man and animals. Mem. Inst. Butanta. Sim. Int., 33:167–174.

Fantham, H. B. and Porter, A. 1954. The endoparasites of certain South African snakes, together with some remarks on their structure and effects on their hosts. Proc. Zool. Soc. Lond., 120:599–647.

Farnsworth, R. J., Brannian, R. E., Fletcher, K. C., and Klassen, S. 1986. A vitamin E-selenium responsive condition in a green iguana. J. Zoo Anim. Med., 17:42–45.

Feeley, J. C. and Treger, M. D. 1969. Penetration of turtle eggs by *Salmonella braenderup*. Public Health Rep., 84:156–158.

Fiennes, R. N. T-W. 1959. Report of the society's pathologist for the year 1957. Proc. Zool. Soc. Lond., 132:129–146.

Fitch, H. S., Henderson, R. W., and Hillis, D. M. 1982. Exploitation of iguanas in Central America. *In: Iguanas of the World: Their Behavior, Ecology, and Conservation,* Burghardt, G. M. and Rand, A. S. (Eds.). Noyes Publications, Park Ridge, NJ. pp. 397–441.

Fletcher, K. C. 1979. Clinical use of mafenide acetate in reptiles. Am. Assoc. Zoo Veterinarians Annual Proc.:27–32

Flynn, R. J. 1973. *Parasites of Laboratory Animals.* Iowa State University Press, IA.

Fowler, K. Personal Communication, Atlanta, GA.

Fowler, M. E. 1986. Metabolic bone disease. *In: Zoo and Wild Animal Medicine,* Fowler, M. E. (Ed.), 2nd Ed. W.B. Saunders Company, Philadelphia, PA. pp. 69–90.

Frank, W. 1981a. Endoparasites. *In: Diseases of the Reptilia,* Vol.1, Cooper, J. E. and Jackson, O. F. (Eds.). Academic Press, New York, NY. pp. 291–358.

Frank, W. 1981b. Ectoparasites. *In: Diseases of the Reptilia,* Vol.1, Cooper, J. E. and Jackson, O. F. (Eds.). Academic Press, New York, NY. pp. 359–383.

Frank, W. 1984. Non-hemoparasitic protozoans. *In: Diseases of Amphibians and Reptiles,* Hoff, G. L., Frye, F. L., and Jacobson, E. R. (Eds.). Plenum Press, New York, NY. pp. 269–384.

Freiberg, M. 1982. *Snakes of South America.* T.F.H. Publications, Inc., Neptune, NJ.

Frye, F. L. 1973. *Husbandry, Medicine and Surgery in Captive Reptiles.* Veterinary Medicine Publishing Company, Edwardsville, KS.

Frye, F. L. 1981a. *Biomedical and Surgical Aspects of Captive Reptile Husbandry* Veterinary Medicine Publishing Company, Edwardsville, KS.

Frye, F. L. 1981b. Traumatic and physical diseases. *In: Diseases of the Reptilia,* Cooper, J. E. and Jackson,

O. F. (Eds.). Academic Press, New York, NY. pp. 387–407.

Frye, F. L. 1984. Euthanasia, necropsy technique and comparative histology of reptiles. *In: Diseases of Amphibians and Reptiles,* Hoff, G. L., Frye, F. L. and Jacobson, E. R. (Eds.). Plenum Press, NY. pp. 703–735.

Frye, F. L. 1986. Feeding and nutritional disease. *In: Zoo and Wild Animal Medicine,* Fowler, M. E. (Ed.), 2nd Ed. W.B. Saunders Company, Philadelphia, PA. pp. 139–151.

Frye, F. L. 1991a. *Biomedical and Surgical Aspects of Captive Reptile Husbandry.* Krieger Publishing Company, Malabar, FL.

Frye, F. L. 1991b. *A Practical Guide for Feeding Captive Reptiles.* Krieger Publishing Company, Malabar, FL.

Frye, F. L. and Dutra, F. R. 1974. Hypothyroidism in turtles and tortoises. VM/SAC, 69:990–993.

Funk, R. S. 1988. Herp Health Hints and Husbandry: Parasiticide dosages for captive amphibians and reptiles. Bull. Chicago Herp. Soc., 23(2):30.

Gardiner, C. H., Fayer, R., and Dubey, J. P. 1988. *An Atlas of Protozoan Parasites of Animal Tissues.* U.S. Dept. Agriculture Handbook No. 651, Washington, D.C.

Gavaud, J. 1983. Obligatory hibernation for completion of vitellogenesis in the lizard *Lacerta vivipara.* J. Exp. Zool., 225:397–405.

Gharpurey, K. G. 1962. *Snakes of India and Pakistan.* G.R. Bhatkal, Bombay.

Gillingham, J. C. and Carpenter, C. C. 1978. Snake hibernation: Construction of and observations on a man-made hibernaculum (Reptilia, Serpentes). J. Herpetol., 12:495–498.

Glenn, J. L., Straight, R., and Snyder, C. C. 1973. Vermiplex®, an anthelmintic agent for snakes. J. Zoo Anim. Med., 4:3–7.

Godshalk, C. P., MacCoy, D. M., Patterson, J. S. and McKiernan, B. S. 1986. Gastric hypertrophy associated with cryptosporidiosis in a snake. J. Am. Vet. Med. Assoc., 189:1126–1128.

Goin, C. J., Goin, O. B., and Zug, G. R. 1978. *Introduction to Herpetology.* W.H. Greeman and Company, San Francisco, CA.

Goris, R. C. 1971. The hibernation of captive snakes. Snake, 3:65–69.

Graham-Jones, O. 1961. Notes on the common tortoise. IV. Some clinical conditions affecting the North African tortoise («Greek») tortoise *Testudo graeca.* Vet. Rec., 73:317–321.

Gray, C. W., Davis, J., and McCarten, W. G. 1966. Treatment of *Pseudomonas* infections in the snake and lizard collection at Washington Zoo. Int. Zoo Yrbk., 6:278.

Greenberg, N. 1976. Observations of social feeding in lizards. Herpetologica, 32(3):349–352.

Greenberg, N. 1978. Ethological consideration in the experimental study of lizard behavior. *In: Behavior and Neurology of Lizards,* Greenberg, N. and MacLean, P. D. (Eds.). Institute of Mental Health, Rockville, MD. pp. 203–204.

Greer, A. E. 1989. *The Biology and Evolution of Australian Lizards.* Surrey Beatty and Sons Pty Ltd., Chipping Norton, NSW.

Greer, G. C. Personal Communication, Marietta, GA.

Gregory, P. T. 1987. Snake hibernation: Attempting to mimic natural conditions. Am. Assoc. Zool. Parks and Aquariums Annual Proc.:442–452.

Grenard, S. 1991. *Handbook of Alligators and Crocodiles.* Krieger Publishing Company, Malabar, FL.

Grier, J. W., Bjerke, M. S., and Nolan, L. K. 1993. Snakes and the *Salmonella* situation. Bull. Chicago Herp. Soc., 28(3):53–59.

Guyer, C. and Savage, J. M. 1986. Cladistic relationships among anoles (Sauria: Iguanidae). Systematic Zool., 35(4):509–531.

Grzimek, B. 1975. *Grzimek's Animal Life Encyclopedia,* Vol. 6. Van Nostrand Reinhold Company, New York, NY.

Habermann, R. T. and Williams, F. P., Jr. 1958. The identification and control of helminths in laboratory animals. J. Natl. Cancer Institute, 20:979–1009.

Harvey, S. C. 1975. Antiseptics and disinfectants; Fungicides; Ectoparasiticides. *In: The Pharmacological Basis of Therapeutics,* Goodman, L. S. and Gilman, A. (Eds.), 5th Ed. Macmillan Publishing Company, Inc., New York, NY. pp. 987–1017.

Harwood, P. D. 1932. The helminths parasitic in the amphibia and reptiles of Houston, Texas, and vicinity. Proceedings U.S. National Museum, 81:1–66.

Hazen, T. A., Aho, J. M., Murphy, T. M., Esch, G. W., and Schmidt, G. D. 1978. The parasite fauna of the American alligator (*Alligator mississippiensis*) in South Carolina. J. Wildl. Dis., 14:435–439.

Heatwole, H. 1987. *Sea Snakes.* The New South Wales University Press, Kensington, NSW.

Henderson, R. W. and Binder, M. H. 1980. The ecology and behavior of vine snakes (*Ahaetulla, Oxybelis, Thelotornis, Uromacer*): A review. Milwaukee Public Museum, No. 37, Milwaukee, WI.

Herman, D. W. and George, G. A. 1986. Research, husbandry and propagation of the bog turtle, *Clemmys muhlenbergi* (Schoepff) at the Atlanta Zoo. *In: Proc. 9th Int. Herp. Symp. Captive Propagation and Husbandry,* McKeown, S., Caporaso, F., and Peterson, K. (Eds.). pp. 125–135.

Heuschele, W. P., Oosterhuis, J., Janssen, D., Robinson, P. T., Ensley, P. K., Meier, J. E., Olson, T., Anderson, M. P., and Benirschke, K. 1986. Cryptosporidial infections in captive wild animals. J. Wildl. Dis., 22:493–496.

Heywood, R. 1968. *Aeromonas* infection in snakes. Cornell Vet., 58:236–241.

Hirth, H. F. 1966. Weight changes and mortality of three species of snakes during hibernation. Herpetologica, 22:8–12.

Hoffman, G. L. 1967. *Parasites of North American Freshwater Fishes.* University of California Press, Berkeley, CA.

Holt, P. E. 1981. Drugs and dosages. *In: Diseases of the Reptilia,* Vol. 2, Cooper, J. E. and Jackson, O. F. (Eds.). Academic Press, New York NY. pp. 551–584.

Holt, P. E., Brown, A., and Brown, B. 1978. A case of *Strongyloides* infection in a speckled king snake. Vet. Rec., 102:404–405.

Huff, T. A. 1980. Captive propagation of the subfamily Boinae with emphasis on the genus *Epicrates. In: Reproductive Biology and Diseases of Captive Reptiles,* Murphy, J. B. and Collins, J. T. (Eds.). SSAR Contributions to Herpetology, No. 1. pp. 125–134.

Hughs, B. O. and Wood-Gush, D. G. M. 1973. An increase in activity of domestic fowls produced by nutritional deficiency. Anim. Behav., 21:10–17.

Hyman, L. H. 1951. *The Invertebrates: Acanthocephala, Aschelminthes, Entoprocta,* Vol. 3. McGraw-Hill Book Company, Inc., New York, NY.

Isemonger, R. M. 1962. *Snakes of Africa.* Thomas Nelson and Sons, New York, NY.

Iverson, J. P. 1980. Colic modifications of iguanine lizards. J. Morphol., 163:79–93.

Iverson, J. P. 1982. Adaptations to herbivory in iguanine lizards. *In: Iguanas of the World: Their Behavior, Ecology,* and *Conservation.* Burghardt, G. M. and Rand, A. S. (Eds.). Noyes Publications, Park Ridge, NJ. pp. 60–76.

Iverson, J. P. 1985. Checklist of the turtles of the world. SSAR Herp. Cir. No. 14.

Jackson, O. F. 1974. Reptiles and the general practitioner. Vet. Rec., 95:11–13.

Jackson, O. F. 1982. Chelonian diets. Testudo, 2(1):17–21.

Jackson, O. F. and Cooper, J. E. 1981. Nutritional diseases. *In: Diseases of the Reptiles,* Vol. 2., Cooper, J. E. and Jackson, O. F. (Eds.). Academic Press, New York, NY. pp. 409–428.

Jacobson, E. P. Personal Communication, Gainesville, FL.

Jacobson, E. R. 1976. Use of Ripercol®-L for the

treatment of lungworms in snakes. J. Zoo Anim. Med., 7(2):14–15.

Jacobson, E. R. 1977. Histology, endocrinology, and husbandry of ecdysis in snakes: A review. VM/SAC, 72:275–280.

Jacobson, E. R. 1978. Diseases of the respiratory system in reptiles. Vet. Med. Small Anim., J. Am. Vet. Med. Assoc., 183:1192–1194.

Jacobson, E. R. 1981. Diseases of reptiles, Part I. Noninfectious diseases. Compend. Contin. Educ. Pract. Vet., 3(2):122–126.

Joanen, T. and McNease, L. 1979. Culture of the American alligator. Int. Zoo Yrbk., 19:61–66.

Johnson, C. A. 1969. A redescription of *Mixidium chelonarum* Johnson, 1969 (Cnidospora: Myxidiidae) from various North American turtles. J. Protozool., 16:700–702.

Kaplan, H. M. 1957. Septicemic, cutaneous ulcerative disease of turtles. Proc. Anim. Care Panel, 7:273–277.

Karsen, S. J., Wai-neng Lau, M., and Bogadek, A. 1986. *Hong Kong Amphibians and Reptiles*. Urban Council, Hong Kong.

Kauffeld, C. F. 1953. Methods of feeding captive snakes. Herpetologica, 9:129–131.

Keymer, I. F. 1981. Protozoa. *In: Diseases of Reptilia*, Cooper, J. E. and Jackson, O. F. (Eds.). Academic Press, New York, NY. pp. 233–290.

Khalaf, K. T. 1959. *Reptiles of Iraq With Some Notes on Amphibians*. Ar-Rabitta Press, Baghdad.

Kiel, J. L. 1975. A review of parasites in snakes. The Southwestern Veterinarian, 28:209–220.

Kiel, J. L. and Schmidt, G. D. 1984. Mature Acanthocephalan infection of king cobras. Avian/Exotic Practice, 1:26–30.

Kingsbury, J. M. 1964. *Poisonous Plants of the United States and Canada*. Prentice-Hall, Inc., Englewood Cliffs, NJ.

Kluger, M. J. 1978. *Fever: Its Biology, Evolution and Function*. Princeton University Press, NJ.

Kuntz, R. E. no date. *Snakes of Taiwan*. U.S. Naval Medical Research Unit No. 2, Taipei, Taiwan.

Lampe, K. F. and McCann, M. A. 1985. *American Medical Association Handbook of Poisonous and Injurious Plants*. Am. Med. Assoc., Chicago, IL.

Lang, J. W. 1987. Crocodilian behaviour: Implications for management. *In: Wildlife Management: Crocodiles and Alligators*, Webb, J. W., Manolis, S. C., and Whitehead, P. J. (Eds.). Surrey Beatty and Sons Pty Limited, Chipping Norton, NSW. pp. 301–317.

Langham, R. F., Zydeck, F. A., and Bennett, L. R. 1971. Steatitis in a captive Marcy garter snake. J. Am. Vet. Med., 159:640–641.

Laszlo, J. 1973. Practical sex recognition of snakes by method of probing with Furmont reptile probes. Circular, Fuhrman Diversified, Inc., La Porte, TX.

Laszlo, J. 1979. Notes on reproductive patterns of reptiles in relation to captive breeding. Int. Zoo Yrbk., 19:22–27.

Lavier, G. 1927. *Protoopalina nyanza* n. sp., opaline parasite d'un reptile. C.R. Soc. Biol. Paris, 97:1709–1710.

Lawler, H. E. Personal Communication, Tucson, AZ.

Lawrence, K. 1983. Treatment of parasitic infestations in reptiles. Brit. Herp. Soc. Bull., No. 8.

Lee, J. C. 1980. An ecogeographic analysis of the herpetofauna of the Yucatan Peninsula. University of Kansas Misc. Pub. No. 67. Lawrence, KS.

Leutscher, A. 1961. *Vivarium Life*. Cleaver-Hume Press Limited, London.

Lichtenfels, J. R. 1980a. Keys to genera of the superfamily Strongyloidea. *In: CIH Keys to the Nematode Parasites of* Vertebrates, Anderson, R. C., Chabaud, A. G., and Willmott, S. (Eds.), No. 7. Commonwealth Agricultural Bureaux, Farnham Royal, Bucks. pp. 1–41.

Lichtenfels, J. R. 1980b. Keys to genera of the superfamilies Ancylostomatoidea and Diaphanocephaloidea. *In: CIH Keys to the Nematode Parasites of* Vertebrates, Anderson, R. C., Chabaud, A. G., and Willmott, S. (Eds.), No. 7. Commonwealth Agricultural Bureaux, Farnham Royal, Bucks. pp. 1–26.

Lint, K. C. 1961. Insect diets for animals. Int. Zoo Yrbk, 3:104.

Liu, S. K. and King, F. W. 1971. Microsporidiosis in the tuatara. J. Am. Vet. Med. Assoc., 159:1578–1582.

Loveridge, A. 1946. *Reptiles of the Pacific World*. Macmillan Company, New York, NY.

Marais, J. 1992. *A Complete Guide to the Snakes of Southern Africa*. Krieger Publishing Company, Malabar, FL.

Marcus, L. C. 1981. *Veterinary Biology and Medicine of Captive Amphibians and Reptiles*. Lea & Febiger, Philadelphia, PA.

Mattison, C. 1982. *The Care of Reptiles and Amphibians in Captivity*. Sterling Publishing Company, Inc., New York, NY.

Mattison, C. 1986. *Snakes of the World*. Facts on File Publications, New York, NY.

Mayhew, W. W. 1963. Observations on captive *Amphibolorus pictus* an Australian agamid lizard. Herpetologica, 20:95–113.

Meek, R. 1978. Reptilian hibernation: A study of a mixed collection of temperate forms hibernating under identical conditions. Herptile, 3:28–36.

Meerovitch, E. 1961. Infectivity and pathogenicity of polyxenic and monoxenic *Entamoeba invadens* to snakes kept at normal and high temperatures and the natural history of reptile amoebiasis. J. Parasitol., 47:791–794.

Meggitt, F. J. 1933. On some tapeworms from the bull

snake (*Pituophis sayi*) with remarks on the species of the genus *Oochoristica* (Cestoda). J. Parasitol., 20:181–189.

Mehrtens, J. M. 1984. *Turtles.* T.F.H. Publications, Inc., Neptune, NJ.

Mehrtens, J. M. 1987. *Living Snakes of the World in Color.* Sterling Publishing Company, Inc., New York, NY.

Mengden, G. A., Platz, C. G., Hubbard, R., and Quinn, H. 1980. Semen collection, freezing and artificial insemination in snakes. *In: Reproductive Biology and Diseases of Captive Reptiles,* Murphy, J. B. and Collins, J. T. (Eds.). SSAR Contributions to Herpetology, No. 1. pp. 71–78.

Meylan, P. A. 1987. The phylogenetic relationships of soft-shelled turtles (Family Trionychidae). American Museum of Natural History, New York, NY.

Mirtschin, P. J. and Ormerod, S. 1990. Indications for the treatment of cryptosporidiosis in snakes. Australian Herp. News, 5:3.

Mitchell, L. G. 1977. Myxosporida. *In: Parasitic Protozoa,* Kreier, J. P. (Ed.), Vol. IV. Academic Press, New York, NY. pp. 115–154.

Morris, M. A. 1986. Anesthesia of snakes (*Pituophis melanoleucus* and *Python regius*) fed ether-killed rats. Herp. Rev., 17(4):88.

Muenscher, W. C. 1970. *Poisonous Plants of the United States.* The Macmillan Company, New York.

Murphy, J. B. 1973. The use of macrolide antibiotic tylosin in the treatment of reptilian respiratory infections. Brit. J. Herp., 4:317–321.

Murphy, J. B. and Collins, J. T. 1983. *A Review of The Diseases and Treatments of Captive Turtles.* AMS Publishing, Lawrence, KS.

Naulleau, G. 1975. Cycle d'activite de *Vipera aspis* (L.) et choix entre des conditions climatiques naturelles et artificielles. Vie Milieu, 25C:119–136.

NAVMED, P-5099 1965. *Poisonous Snakes of the World.* Dept. of the Navy Bureau of Medicine and Surgery, U.S. Gov't. Printing Ofc., Washington, D.C.

Newman, D. 1987. *Tuatara.* John McIndoe Limited, Dunedin, NZ.

Nigrelli, R. F. and Maraventano, L. W. 1944. Pericarditis in *Xenopus laevis* caused by *Diplostomulum xenopi* sp. nov., a larval strigeid. J. Parasitol., 30:184–1909.

Nigrelli, R. F. and Smith, G. M. 1943. The occurrence of leeches, *Ozobranchus branchiatus* (Menzies), on fibro-epithelial tumors of marine turtles, *Chelonia myda* (Linnaeus). Zoologica, 28:107–108.

Noble, E. R. and Noble, G. A. 1964. *Parasitology,* 2nd Ed. Lea & Febiger, Philadelphia, PA.

Norton, T. M. and Jacobson, E. R. 1989. Cyclic changes in cryptosporidial infection in a San Diego

Mountain kingsnake, *Lampropeltis zonata pulchra.* Proc. 3rd Int. Coll. Path. Reptiles and Amphibians, 51:52.

Obst, F. J., Richter, K., and Jacob, U. 1988. *The Completely Illustrated Atlas of Reptiles and Amphibians for the Terrarium.* T.F.H. Publications, Inc., Neptune City, NJ.

Page, L. A. 1966. Diseases and infections of snakes: A review. Bull. Wildl. Dis. Assoc., 2:111–126.

Peters, J. A. and Donoso-Barros, R. 1970. *Catalog of the Neotropical Squamata: Snakes,* Part I, with new material by P. E. Vanzolini. Smithsonian Institution Press, Washington, D.C.

Peters, J. A. and Orejas-Miranda, B. 1986. *Catalog of the Neotropical Squamata: Lizards and Amphisbaenians,* Part II, with new material by P. E. Vanzolini. Smithsonian Institution Press, Washington, D.C.

Petter, A. J., and Quentin, J-C. 1976. Keys to genera Oxyuroidea. *In: CIH Keys to the Nematode Parasites of Vertebrates,* Anderson, R. C., Chabaud, A. G., and Willmott, S. (Eds.), No. 4. Commonwealth Agricultural Bureaux, Farnham Royal, Bucks. pp. 1–30.

Pinney, R. 1981. *The Snake Book: Habitat, Collecting, Care and Feeding.* Doubleday & Co., Inc., Garden City, NY.

Pitman, C. R. S. 1974. *A Guide to the Snakes of Uganda.* Wheldon & Wesley, Ltd., Great Britain.

Pope, C. H. 1935. *The Reptiles of China.* American Museum of Natural History, New York, NY.

Pritchard, C. H. 1979. *Encyclopedia of Turtles.* T.F.H. Publications, Inc., Neptune, NJ.

Radcliffe, C. W. and Chiszar, D. 1983. Clear plastic hiding boxes as a husbandry device for nervous snakes. Herp. Review, 14(1):18.

Rand, A. S., Dugan, B., Monteza, H., and Vianda, B. 1990. The diet of generalized folivore: *Iguana iguana* in Panama. J. Herpetol., 24:211–214.

Reichenback-Klinke, H. H. 1977. *Krankheiten Der Reptilien.* G. Fischer Verlag, New York, NY.

Reichenbach-Klinke, H. H. and Elkan, E. 1965. *The Principal Diseases of Lower Vertebrates.* Academic Press, New York, NY.

Report of the AVMA Panel on Euthanasia. 1993. J. Am. Vet. Med. Assoc., 202:229–249.

Ritchie, B. W., Personal Communication, Athens, GA.

Robb, J. 1986. *New Zealand Amphibians and Reptiles.* Ralph Curtis Books, Sanibel, FL.

de Rooij, N. 1917. *Reptiles of the Indo-Australian Archipelago,* Vol. II. E.J. Brill Ltd., Holland.

Rosenberg, J. M. 1989. Review and critique of a proposed field treatment for pit viper bites. Notes from Noah, 17(2):15–20.

Ross, R. A. Personal Communication, Stanford, CA.

Ross, R. A. 1980. The breeding of pythons (subfamily

Pythoninae) in captivity. *In: Reproductive Biology and Diseases of Captive Reptiles,* Murphy, J. B. and Collins, J. T. (Eds.). SSAR Contributions to Herpetology, No. 1. pp. 135–139.

Ross, R. A. and Marzec, G. 1984. *The Bacterial Diseases of Reptiles: Their Epidemiology, Control, Diagnosis and Treatment.* Institute for Herpetological Research, Stanford, CA.

Ross, R. A. and Marzec, G. 1990. *The Reproductive Husbandry of Pythons and Boas.* The Institute for Herpetological Research, Stanford, CA.

Rosskopf, W. J., Jr. 1977–78. Medical information and case histories on turtles and tortoises. The Tortuga Gazette, California Turtle & Tortoise Club, 6:39–44.

Rost, D. R. and Young, M. C. 1984. Diagnosing white-muscle disease.. VM/SAC, 80:1286–1287.

Rothman, N. and Rothman, B. 1960. Course and cure of respiratory infection in snakes. Philadelphia Herp. Soc. Bull., 8:19–23.

Ruhr, L. P. 1986. Ornamental toxic plants. *In: Current Veterinary Therapy IX: Small Animal Practice.* W.B. Saunders Company, Philadelphia, PA. pp. 216–220.

Schell, S. C. 1970. *The Trematodes.* Wm. C. Brown, Company, Dubuque, IA.

Schmidt, G. D. 1970. *How to Know the Tapeworms.* Wm. C. Brown, Company, Dubuque, IA.

Schmidt, G. D. and Roberts, L. S. 1985. *Foundations of Parasitology.* Times Mirror/Mosby College Publishing, St. Louis, MO.

Schmidt, K. P. 1928. *Scientific Survey of Porto Rico and Virgin Islands.* New York Academy of Science, New York, NY.

Schmidt, K. P. and Inger, R. F. 1957. *Living Reptiles of the World.* Doubleday & Co., Inc., Garden City, NY.

Schwartz, A. and Henderson, R. W. 1985. *A Guide to the Identification of the Amphibians and Reptiles of the West Indies Exclusive of Hispaniola.* Milwaukee Public Museum, Milwaukee, WI.

Schweinfurth, W. 1970. Perorale Behandlung der Amoebiasis bei Sclangen. Salamandra, 6:44–45.

Self, T. J. and Kuntz, R. E. 1967. Host-parasite relations in some Pentastomida. Exp. Parasitol., 24:63–119.

Shine, R. 1986. Natural history of two monotypic snake genera of southwestern Australia, *Elapognathes* and *Rhinoplocephalus* (Elapidae). J. Herpetol., 20(3):436–439.

Siebeling, R. J., Neal, P. M., and Granberry, D. 1975. Evaluation of methods for the isolation of *Salmonella* and *Arizona* organisms from pet turtles treated with antimicrobial agents. Appl. Microbiol., 29:240–245.

Skrjabin, K. I. and Spasskii, A. A. 1951. *Essentials of*

Cestodology, Vol. 5: *Proteocephalata in Fish, Amphibians,* and *Reptiles* (English translation from Russian by Freze, V. I., 1969). Available from U.S. Dept. of Commerce.

Smith, H. M. 1946. *Handbook of Lizards.* Comstock Publishing Association, Ithaca, NY.

Smith, M. A. 1935. *Fauna of British India,* Vol. II. Ralph Curtis Books, Sanibel, FL.

Soifer, F. 1978. Parasitic diseases of reptiles. *In: Zoo and Wild Animal Medicine,* Fowler, M. E. (Ed.). Philadelphia, PA. pp. 138–143.

Soulsby, E. J. L. 1968. *Helminth, Arthropods, and Protozoa of Domestic Animals* (Moennig). Lea & Febiger, Philadelphia, PA.

Stebbins, R. C. 1966. *A Field Guide to Western Reptiles and Amphibians.* Houghton Mifflin Company, Boston, MA.

Streiff, R. R. and Little, A. B. 1967. Folic acid deficiency in pregnancy. N. Eng. J. Med., 276:776–779.

Stone, A. 1930. The bionomics of some Tabanidae (Diptera). Ann. Entom. Soc. Am., 23:262–304.

Stuart, M. D. 1978. Ova of intestinal nematodes from Louisiana snakes. M.S. Thesis, Northeast Louisiana University, Monroe, LA.

Sun, L. 1985. Pionus Breeders' Association Newsletter, Riverdale, CA.

Sutherland, S. K. 1988. First aid for snakebite in Australia with notes on first aid for bites and stings by other animals. Commonwealth Serum Laboratories, Parkerville, Western Australia.

Sutherland, S. K. and Coulter, A. R. 1981. Early management of bites by the eastern diamondback rattlesnake (*Crotalus adamanteus*): Studies in monkeys (*Macaca fascicularis*). Am. J. Trop. Med. Hyg., 30(2):497–500.

Switak, K. H. 1984. *The Life of Desert Reptiles and Amphibians.* Karl H. Switak, San Francisco, CA.

Tanaka, S. 1986. Thermal ecology of the forest-dwelling agamid lizard, *Japalura polygonata ishigakiensis.* J. Herpetol., 20(3):333–340.

Taylor, E. H. 1963. *The Lizards of Thailand.* University of Kansas Science Bull. No. 14, Vol. XLIV.

Telford, S. R. Jr. 1971. Parasitic diseases of reptiles. J. Am. Vet. Med. Assoc., 159:1644–1652.

Toft, J. D. II and Schmidt, R. E. 1975. Pseudophyllidean tapeworms in green tree pythons (*Chondropython viridis*). J. Zoo Anim. Med., 6:25–26.

Tremper, R. L. 1983. A note on the use of black light fluorescent tubes for reptiles. The Tortuga Gazette, California Turtle & Tortoise Club. 19(2):4–5.

Troyer, K. 1982. Transfer of fermentative microbes between generations in a hervivorous lizard. Science, 216:540–542.

Troyer, K. 1984a. Behavioral acquisition of the hindgut

fermentation system by hatching *Iguana iguana*. Behav. Ecol. Sociobiol., 14:189–193.

Troyer, K. 1984b. Structure and function of the digestive tract for herbivory in a neotropical lizard, *Iguana iguana*. Physiol. Zool., 56(1):1–8.

Trutnau, L. 1986. *Nonvenomous Snakes*. Barron's Educational Series, Inc., Woodbury, NJ.

Tryon, B. W. 1980. Observations on reproduction in the west African crocodile with a description of parental behavior. *In: Reproductive Biology and Diseases of Captive Reptiles,* Murphy, J. B. and Collins, J. T. (Eds.). SSAR Contributions to Herpetology, No. 1. pp. 115–117.

Tryon, B. W. 1985. Snake hibernation and breeding: In and out of the zoo. *In: Reptiles: Breeding, Behaviour and Veterinary Aspects,* Townson, S. and Lawrence, K. (Eds.). Brit. Herp. Soc., London. pp. 19 31.

Tweedie, M. W. 1983. *The Snakes of Malaya*. Singapore National Printers (Pte) Ltd., Singapore.

United States Department of Agriculture Handbook No. 8. (See Watt and Merill, 1975 below).

Upton, S. J. 1990. *Cryptosporidium* spp. in lower vertebrates. *In: Cryptosporidiosis of Man and Animals,* Dubey, J. P., Speer, C. A., and Fayer, R. (Eds.). CRC Press, Boca Raton, FL. pp. 149–156.

Upton, S. J. and Barnard, S. M. 1987. Two new species of coccidia (Apicomplexa: Eimeriidae) from Madagascar gekkonids. J. Protozool., 34:452–454.

Vagvolgyi, A. and Halpern, M. 1983. Courtship behavior in garter snakes: Effects of artificial hibernation. Can. J. Zool., 61:1171–1174.

Van Cleave, H. J. 1948. Expanding horizons in the recognition of a phylum. J. Parasitol., 34:1–20.

Van Devender, R. W. 1982. Growth and ecology of spiny-tailed and green iguanas in Costa Rica, with comments on the evolution of herbivory and large body size. *In: Iguanas of the World: Their Behavior, Ecology, and Conservation,* Burghardt, G. M. and Rand, A. S. (Eds.). Noyes Publications, Park Ridge, NJ. pp. 162–183.

Vitale, J. J. 1976. *Vitamins*. The Upjohn Co., Kalamazoo, MI.

Vogel, Z. 1964. *Reptiles and Amphibians: Their Care and Behavior*. Viking Press, New York, NY.

Vosburgh, K. M., Brady, P. S., and Ullrey, D. E. 1982. Ascorbic acid requirements of garter snakes: Plains (*Thamnophis radix*) and eastern (*T. sirtalis sirtalis*). J. Zoo Anim. Med., 13:38–42.

Wagner, 1980. Gecko husbandry and reproduction. *In: Reproductive Biology and Diseases of Captive Reptiles,* Murphy, J. B. and Collins, J. T. (Eds.). SSAR Contributions to Herpetology, No. 1. pp. 115–117.

Wallach, J. D. 1966. Hypervitaminosis D in green iguanas. J. Am. Vet. Med. Assoc., 149:912–914.

Wallach, J. D. 1969. Medical care of reptiles. J. Am. Vet. Med. Assoc., 155:1017–1034.

Wallach, J. D. 1971. Environmental and nutritional diseases of captive reptiles. J. Am. Vet. Med. Assoc., 159:1632–1643.

Wallach, J. D. 1976. The pathogenesis and etiology of ulcerative shell disease in turtles. Aquatic Mammals, 4:1–4.

Wallach, J. D. 1977. Ulcerative shell disease in turtles: Identification, prophylaxia and treatment. Int. Zoo Yrbk., 17:170–171.

Wallach, J. D. 1978. Feeding and nutritional diseases. *In: Zoo and Wild Animal Medicine,* Fowler, M. E. (Ed.). W.B. Saunders Company, Philadelphia, PA. pp. 123–128.

Wallach, J. D. and Hoessle, C. 1967. Visceral gout in captive reptiles. J. Am. Vet. Med. Assoc., 151:897–899

Wallach, J. D. and Hoessle, C. 1968. Steatitis in captive crocodilians. J. Am. Vet. Med. Assoc., 153:845–847.

Wallach, J. D., Hoessle, C., and Bennett, J. 1967. Hypoglycemic shock in captive alligators. J. Am. Vet. Med. Assoc., 151:893–896.

Walshaw, S. O. 1983. Reptilian management and medical care. Anim. Health Tech., 4(3):147–155.

Walton, A. C. 1964. The parasites of amphibia. Wildl. Dis., 40 (microcard and microfiche).

Wardle, R. A. and McLeod, J. A. 1952. *The Zoology of Tapeworms*. University of Minnesota Press, Minneapolis, MN.

Wardle, R. A., McLeod, J. A., and Radinovsky, S. 1974. Advances in the zoology of tapeworms, 1950–1970. (A revision of Wardle, R. A.. and McLeod, J. A., 1952). University of Minnesota Press, Minneapolis, MN.

Watt, B. K. and Merrill, A. L. 1975. *Composition of Foods*. Handbook No. 8, United States Dept. of Agriculture, Washington, D.C.

Weber, A. 1973. Uber einen Behandlungsversuch bei latent mit Salmonellen infizierten SchildKroten. Kleintier-Praxis, 18:48–50.

Weigel, J. 1988. *Care of Australian Reptiles in Captivity*. Reptile Keepers Association, Gosford, NSW.

Welch, K. R. G. 1982. *Herpetology of Africa*. Krieger Publishing Company Malabar, FL.

Welch, K. R. G. 1983. *Herpetology of Europe and Southwest Asia*. Krieger Publishing Company, Malabar, FL.

Welch, K. R. G. 1988. *Snakes of the Orient; A Checklist*. Krieger Publishing Company, Malabar, FL.

Whitaker, R. 1978. *Common Indian Snakes: A Field Guide*. Macmillan India Limited, Delhi.

Widmer, E. A. 1966. Helminth parasites of the prairie rattlesnake, *Crotalus viridis* Rafinesque, 1818, in

Weld County, Colorado with studies on the life history of *Oochoristica osheroffi* Meggitt, 1934 (Cyclophyllidea: Anoplocephalidea). Diss. Abstr., 26:5612.

Wilhoft, D. C. 1958. The effect of temperature on thyroid histology and survival in the lizard, *Sceloporus occidentalis*. Copeia, 1958:265–276.

Will, R. 1975. Die Entstehungsursachen (Atiologie) der Lebererkrankungen bei reptilien. Zbl. Vet. Med. B., 22:626–634.

Wilson, L. D. and Meyer, J. R. 1985. *The Snakes of Honduras*. Milwaukee Public Museum, Milwaukee, WI.

Woodward, L. 1985. *Poisonous Plants: Color Field Guide*. Hippocrene Books, Inc., New York, N.Y.

Wright, A. H. and Wright, A. A. 1957. *Handbook of Snakes of the United States and Canada,* Vols. I & II. Comstock Publishing Association, Ithaca, NY.

Yamaguti, S. 1958. *Systema Helminthum: Trematodes,* Vol. I. Interscience Publishers, Inc. New York, NY.

Yamaguti, S. 1959. *Systema Helminthum: Cestodes,* Vol. II. Interscience Publishers, Inc. New York, NY.

Yamaguti, S. 1961. *Systema Helminthum: Nematodes,* Vol. III. Interscience Publishers, Inc. New York, NY.

Yamaguti, S. 1963. *Systema Helminthum:* Acantho-cephala, Vol. V. Interscience Publishers, Inc. New York, NY.

York, W. 1974. Treatment of anorexia in an anaconda. J. Zoo Anim. Med., 5:11–12.

York, W. and Maplestone, P. A. 1926. *The Nematode Parasites of Vertebrates*. Blakiston, Philadelphia, PA.

Yntema, C. L. 1976. Effects of incubation temperatures on sexual differentiation in the turtle, *Chelydra serpentina*. J. Morphol., 150(2):453–461.

Yunker, C. E. 1956. Studies on the snake mite, *Ophionyssus natricis,* in nature. Science, 124:979–980.

Zappalorti, R. T. 1976. *The Amateur Zoologist's Guide to Turtles and Crocodilians*. Stackpole Books, Harrisburg, PA.

Zimmermann, E. 1986. *Breeding Terrarium Animals*. T.F.H. Publications, Inc., Neptune, NJ.

Zwart, P. 1963. Studies on renal pathology in reptiles. Thesis, University of Utrecht.

Zwart, P. 1972. Ziekten van reptilien I: Ectoparasieten, huidaandoeningen. Lacerta, 30:41–48.

Zwart, P. 1977. Reptiles in veterinary praxis. Paper presented at 6th World Congress, WSAVA, Amsterdam.

Zwart, P. and Jansen, J. 1969. Treatment of lungworms in snakes with tetramisole. Vet. Rec., 84:374.

Index